18-6-75

MUSIC NOTATION

A MANUAL OF MODERN PRACTICE

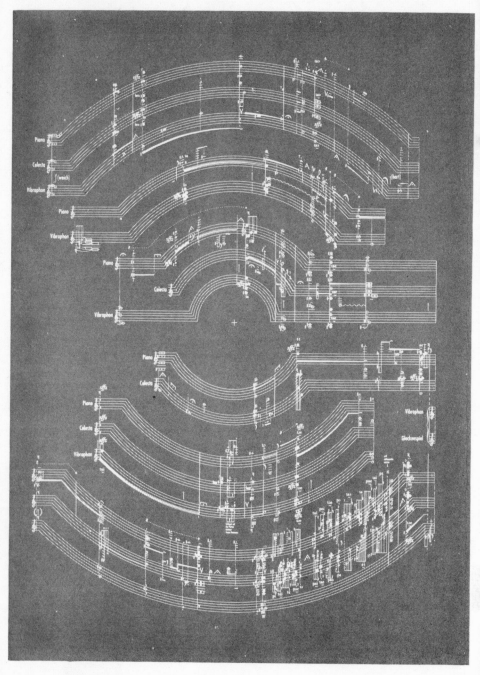

KARLHEINZ STOCKHAUSEN: From *Nr. 11, Refrain* (1961)

MUSIC NOTATION

A Manual of Modern Practice

by

GARDNER READ

Composer-in-Residence and Professor
of Composition, Boston University

LONDON
VICTOR GOLLANCZ LTD
1974

ISBN 0 575 01758 9

ACKNOWLEDGMENTS

No TEXTBOOK SEEMS EVER TO BE WRITTEN WITHOUT the combined thoughts and concrete efforts of family, friends, and professional acquaintances of the author. **MUSIC NOTATION** is no exception to this truism, and I should be remiss not to pay tribute here to the minds and hands that helped shape this book.

First and foremost, my deepest gratitude to my wife, whose critical eye caught many an error both of commission and of omission, and whose devoted labor was responsible for the many drafts which preceded the final manuscript. To Herbert Fromm, John Hasson, Kent Kennan, and Kurt Stone my grateful thanks for essential suggestions, for invaluable text criticism, and for the checking of foreign terminology. To them, and to the editorial staff of Allyn and Bacon as well, my appreciation for the keen interest evinced in the destiny of this manual of modern notational practices.

Gardner Read

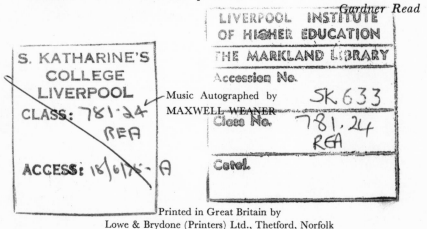

Music Autographed by MAXWELL WEANER

Printed in Great Britain by
Lowe & Brydone (Printers) Ltd., Thetford, Norfolk

INTRODUCTION

As a teacher of composition and instrumenta-
tion I have had thrust into my hands each week during the past 25
years countless reasonable facsimiles of the following manuscript:

In this notational nightmare the musical amateur stands revealed—
his creative emptiness further burdened by misplaced stems, mis-
aligned chord members, strayed accidentals, and missing marks of
expression. The performer does not live who would not prefer to read
the precisely notated, clear, and accurate version below.

In **MUSIC NOTATION** I propose to offer a tool to make effective and accurate notation more accessible. The widespread lack of knowledge concerning this vital element of music—which properly ought to precede the formal study of harmony, counterpoint, form, and orchestration—is not wholly the result of laziness or indifference on the part of musicians. Performers, conductors, composers, theory students—all must have access to up-to-date notational information, concisely presented against a minimum historic background, and with ample opportunity to put basic principles into practice.

Part I of this manual, then, is a brief historical survey of the evolution of music notation. In Part II each single element—staves, systems, clefs, notes, rests, expression markings—is presented first in traditional practice, then in modern usage, with occasional suggested reforms. Each chapter is followed by selective notation exercises, involving both traditional and modern practices. Part III—on idiomatic notation—treats the unique problems of notating for voices and individual instruments. Part IV contains explicit directions for the actual writing process in music manuscript, reading of proofs, and the preparation of full and condensed scores and of instrumental parts.

Because today's musician, like his contemporaries in every creative field, is inevitably a citizen of the world, almost every chapter adds to his imperative notational tools a minimum basic terminology in French, German, and Italian. With this vocabulary he increases his viability in the world of western music. All music from the time of Bach and Handel to the present has drawn heavily upon Italian as an international idiom, but Mahler and Schönberg are inaccessible without German terminology, and Debussy and Ravel without French.

The complete book is designed to function on many levels. The beginning student or nonprofessional musician with a limited background may first cover only the material on traditional practice in Chapters 1 through 16. When he has mastered the basic elements of notation, he may round out his knowledge by studying the sections on modern practice. Hence Parts I and II may be considered as supplying basic information on music essentials.

Advanced students and professional musicians may go directly to the Modern Innovations section of each chapter in Part II, bypassing the more elementary material on traditional usage. Here they will find information not generally available even in the most comprehensive theory textbooks, such as the Table of Unequal Note-Groups found on pages 194–211. Parts III and IV can serve as a day-by-day reference source for the most advanced music students, performers, composers, orchestrators, arrangers, and teachers of music theory. Many sections, in fact, are included especially to serve the performer *reading* difficult music, rather than the notator or composer *writing*. The wider the range of music performed by his orchestra or band, chorus or chamber group, the more will the performer need to consult a notational guide of near-universal compass.

No author, of course, can adequately encompass all potential problems in the elusive art of music—which exists in time rather than in space, yet is tied to a space-bound vocabulary of symbols created for the ear but accessible only through the eye. The composer will always be ahead of his *written* expression; he speaks today in a panchromatic, atonal, or microtonal style that merits something far more flexible than a five-line staff, three clef-signs, five accidentals, and two kinds of note-heads—all geared to diatonic music in a seven-note scale. Yet the practicing musician of the twentieth century exercises a craft indispensably based on the existing system as practiced by the most reputable publishers the world over. We cannot condone his ignorance thereof any more than we would excuse—out of pity for a shiftless self-education—any misspellings or mangled syntax from a professional novelist. In automatic command of this basic technique, the composer or performer should be able to solve the notational problems inherent in any new idea with a modicum of logic and common sense.

To master the proper written language of his chosen profession is the minimum obligation of the aspiring musician to his art. **MUSIC NOTATION** is dedicated to that mastery.

Gardner Read

CONTENTS

MUSIC ACKNOWLEDGMENTS

Frontispiece—Karlheinz Stockhausen: from *Nr. 11, Refrain* (1961)
  Copyright 1961 by Universal Edition, A.G. Used by permission of the origi-
  nal copyright owner and Theodore Presser Co., Bryn Mawr, Pa., agents.
Neumes—Plate XIX, in Coussemaker: from *Histoire de l'Harmonie au Moyen
  Age*   2
EXAMPLE 1 - 8—Elliott Carter: from *String Quartet No. 1* (1951)   31
  © Copyright 1956 by Associated Music Publishers, Inc. Used by permission.
EXAMPLE 2 - 7—Igor Stravinsky: from *Movements for Piano and Orchestra*
  (1959)   40
  Copyright 1960 by Hawkes & Son (London) Ltd. Reprinted by permission
  of Boosey & Hawkes Inc.
EXAMPLE 5 - 21—Earle Brown: from *Hodograph I* (1959)   72
  Copyright 1961 by Associated Music Publishers, Inc. Used by permission.
EXAMPLE 14 - 14—Bo Nilsson: from *Frequenzen* (1959)   257
  Copyright 1963 by Universal Editions, A. G. Used by permission of Theo-
  dore Presser Co., Bryn Mawr, Pa., agents.
EXAMPLE 15 - 4—Arnold Schönberg: from *Five Piano Pieces*, Op. 23
  (1923)   263
  Copyright © 1923–1951 by Wilhelm Hansen, Copenhagen. By permission
  of the publishers.
EXAMPLE 17 - 3—Gardner Read: from *A Mountain Song* (1963)   289
  Copyright 1964 by J. Fischer & Bro., Glen Rock, N. J. Used by permission.
EXAMPLE 17 - 5—Gardner Read: from *Though I Speak With the Tongues of
  Men* (1960)   292
  Copyright 1965 by Abingdon Press, Nashville. Used by permission.
EXAMPLE 17 - 7—Paul Hindemith: from *When Lilacs Last in the Dooryard
  Bloom'd* (1946)   294
  Copyright 1948 by Schott & Co., Ltd. of London. Used by permission of

MUSIC NOTATION

A MANUAL OF MODERN PRACTICE

PART I

Brief History of Music Notation

O Iudei uerbum dei qui negatis hominem Uestro legis teste regis
auditur p[er] ordinem Et uos gentes non credentes peperisse uirginem
Uestre gentis documentis pellite caliginem Isrt.
Isrt. ur lens inque de xpo nostri firme[n]t[ur] Dux deiuda non
tollitur donec adht qnuotour Saluare dei uerbum expecta
bant gentes mecum Moyses Legis lator huc ppinq
et de xpo pme digna K[?] Dabit deus uobis uatem huic ut m
aurem date Q ui non audit hunc audientem ex pellitur Sua
gento Isaias Isaias uerum quisquis uenta tem cur

THAT "MUSIC IS THE INTERNATIONAL LANGUAGE OF mankind" is a myth perpetuated, I regret to say, by countless writers on music. If music were indeed an international language, we of the western world would be equally moved by the musical speech of the Chinese peasant, of the African bushman, or by the *gagaku* music of the ancient Japanese court. In their turn the Himalayan mountaineer, the Arab camel driver, and the Eskimo seal hunter would respond like Bostonians to a Bach fugue or the latest jazz.

We know, however, that the music of the native African and of the Japanese court is alien and frequently incomprehensible to our ears. No less strange to Oriental and African audiences must be the sophisticated and formalized music of western civilizations. It is not the *language* (sound) of music, then, that is international, any more than one spoken word-language is universal.

But the *written symbols* of western musical notation are universally understood wherever western culture has developed, though the musical ideas may have originated in Yugoslavia, Argentina, Sweden, or the United States—among composers whose verbal expression may be mutually incomprehensible. How these symbols evolved to this impressive status we can consider only so far as their history is fundamental to understanding modern notational practices. It is to be hoped that any student with serious pretensions toward a musical career will be so fascinated that he will consider this brief survey only an introduction, for many aspects of early musical style are best assimilated through study of the music in its original notation.

In concentrating on the *enduring* musical symbols of the western world we must eliminate many eras of experiment and discard, including much impressive music. Primitive societies have no written systems at all, but pass on their songs and dances by rote from one generation to another. When changes are made in the process of aural transference, they are almost imperceptibly absorbed into the endless chain. Music of the East, on the other hand, has developed its independent systems of notation without influencing notational development in the West. In the western world—which will be our point of concentration —the genealogy of modern notation, now some 300 years old, reaches back almost 3000 years to the *letter notation* of ancient Greece.

3

LETTER NOTATION

Musicologists have deduced from their research that the pre-Christian Greeks had at least four different systems of music notation, all derived from the letters of the alphabet. To see how this early music was written, we may compare an alphabetical version with the modern two-octave scale from **A** in the bass clef to a′ in the treble clef (refer to page 44 for a chart of the register symbols).

EXAMPLE A

In addition to their normal upright form—used to designate the basic tones—the letters might assume an altered position to indicate that the pitch was to be made higher or lower, for the same end that we now employ sharps or flats. For this reason, the performer might see versions like the following:

Reversed: h = ᖷ E = Ǝ K = ꓘ

Turned sidewise: H = I F = ш T = ⊢

When certain letters did not lend themselves to reversal (H = H) or to being placed sidewise (N = Z), the letters themselves had to be altered into new signs. The duration of the notes involved was sometimes indicated by a sign in conjunction with the letter, showing how many counts (or beats) the note was to receive:

—— = 2 beats ⌊—— = 3 beats ⌊__⌋ = 4 beats ⌊_⊥_⌋ = 5 beats

In such a system a melody might be notated with the following sequence of letters and metrical signs:

EXAMPLE B

We are told that around the middle of the fourth century A.D. the alphabetical systems contained well over 1600 different signs, symbols, and letter-forms. To complicate matters still further, the Greeks employed one system for the notation of vocal music (the Ionic alphabet) and a completely different system for instrumental music (Phoenician letters and related signs). Whatever one may say regarding the complexities or inadequacies of our present system, one basic and uniform set of symbols does serve for all media.

In sixth-century Italy the monk-scholar Boethius devised a personal adaptation of the alphabetical systems. The "Boethian system" (more famous as a theory than as a practice) designated the fifteen notes of a two-octave span by using the first fifteen letters of the Latin-Greek alphabet.

EXAMPLE C

Employing this scheme of notation we might notate another improvised melody in the following manner:

EXAMPLE D

Many other systems of letter-signs were tried out during the Middle Ages (eighth to fourteenth centuries). But the most significant new development in music notation was the use of *neumes* (from the Greek *neuma,* meaning a "sign" or "nod"), which gradually replaced alphabet letters in the plainchants of the Christian church. (See the example on page 2.)

NEUMES

In their earliest form the neumes derived, simply enough, from the two basic signs of Greek prosody: the *acutus* (╱) for a rising inflection of the voice, and the *gravis* (╲) for a falling inflection. Various combinations of the *acutus* and the *gravis* resulted in such inherently descriptive symbols as these:

∧ = a rising inflection followed by a descending one
∨ = a falling inflection followed by an ascending one
∿ = rise—fall—rise
〜∧ = fall—rise—fall

Interestingly enough, some of the prosodic signs are still valid in modern Romance languages. French, for instance, has its *accent aigu* (′) as in *prélude,* and its *accent grave* (ˋ) as in *première,* as well as the *accent circonflexe* (∧) as in *tête.*

Yet—pictorial though they were—the neumes could not indicate exactly *how high* the melodic rise should be, or *how low* the fall; whether the interval was as small as the modern half- or whole-step, or as large as our third or fourth. True, the distance at which the neumes were placed above the plainchant words could roughly indicate a melodic interval. But they certainly had no capacity to describe any more subtle time-value than the spoken length of the Latin syllables over which they were written. Had notation persevered in this system—so restricted in its control of either pitches or time-values—our complicated modern masterpieces could never have been written.

Still, as the Gregorian chant developed during the Middle Ages, neumic notation underwent significant changes and modifications. With more efficient quill pens replacing their primitive reed pens, the monks who so laboriously copied out the manuscripts could inscribe neume-shapes more freely varied. Some signs acquired a "head" (the *virga,* for instance); others were even more radically altered (the *torculus* and the *porrectus,* for example—see the Table of Neumes, page 8).

During this transitional period for the neume-system, the *acutus* (╱) came to be known as the *virga* (Latin for "rod"), though it retained its former slanting character. The other basic sign, the *gravis* (╲), however, was replaced occasionally by a small curved line (◡) but more frequently by a heavy dot (•), and in this form was called by its Latin name, *punctum.* These neumic modifications may be considered as pivotal between the older forms—which were clearly related to the Greek grammatical signs—and the first tentative development of modern note-shapes in the sixteenth and seventeenth centuries. Especially fascinating for their graphic character and descriptive names are some of these neume-forms, shown below:

Podatus (sometimes *Pes*) literally "foot" ◡   ; low to high

Clivis—a "bend"   ⌒   ; high to low

Scandicus—"climb"   •╱   ; 3 ascending tones

Climacus—"ladder" /·.   ; 3 descending tones ♪♪♪

Torculus—"twist" ∫   ; low—high—low ♪♪♪

Porrectus—"stretch" ⋏   ; high—low—high ♪♪♪

At this same time the neumes came to be classified according to the manner in which they functioned. Used for *melodic notation only* were the *normal* neumes—both *simple* neumes (such signs as the *virga* and the *punctum* for single notes, and others for two- and three-note groups) and *compound* neumes (various amalgams or variations of simple neumes, used for four- and five-note groups). In addition to the "normal" neumes there was a second category: neumes indicating *ways of performance* or interpretation. These, however, were so complicated as to make them the exclusive province of the advanced musicologist, rather than material for the modern notator. The sole attribute we must note is that even these "performance" neumes had nothing to do with rhythmic indication, which was a much later development.

After this pivotal period—and between the ninth and the thirteenth centuries—the neumes were further modified into squarish shapes that more closely resemble our modern notes than do any previous symbols, though still without any implication of time-values. This evolution was primarily the result of their being placed on or between staff lines, a development we shall follow on later pages, but once again the single-note neumes were the basis for all the changes made to larger combinations. The original *virga* (/) came to be written as a squared note-form (¶), while the *punctum* (•) was altered to the shape of a square dot (■). The genesis of all the other squared neume-symbols—simple and compound—is evident in the Table of Neumes on page 8.

In their squared-note forms, known as *Gothic*, two or more notes could be joined to form a single group called a *ligature*. These square notes and ligatures may still be seen in the editions of Gregorian chant used by the Solesmes monks of France, and in the various Vatican editions—including the *Liber Usualis* ("Book of Use") of the Catholic church (see Examples I and N).

By now it should be quite clear that the whole system of neumes, despite changes and improvements, had many limitations, particularly in the teaching of music. Useful solely as a *reminder* to the singers, refreshing their memory of a general rise and fall originally learned by rote, the neumes provided only the over-all contour of the plainsong melodic line—not an exact map by which a novice might approach an unknown musical territory.

EXAMPLE E. TABLE OF NEUMES

Neume Names	9th to 10th Centuries	11th to 13 Centuries	In Modern Notation
Virga			
Punctum			
Podatus (Pes)			
Clivis			
Scandicus			
Climacus			
Torculus			
Porrectus			
Scandicus flexus			
Porrectus flexus			
Torculus resupinus			
Pes subpunctis			

To achieve a notational system worthy of permanence it was necessary to find a method of indicating the *exact pitch,* at least in relation to preceding and succeeding melodic tones. Furthermore, it was
essential to denote the *precise duration* of all the tones, so that their
length need not always duplicate the spoken syllabic length. These two
problems were solved with varying degrees of immediate success by
the invention of *staff lines* and the codification of *rhythmic modes.*

STAFF LINES

Taking the solution of the two problems in chronological order, we
discover an isolated prophet of the modern *staff* in the anonymous
author of *Musica Enchiriadis* ("Handbook of Music"), a ninth-century
theoretical tract giving examples of early polyphonic music, especially
of *parallel organum.* (Parallel organum was the practice of duplicating a liturgical melody, given to the tenor voice, at a fixed interval—
either a perfect fourth or a perfect fifth—below the original line.)
This innovator abandoned the neume-signs and placed the syllables
of the text in the spaces of a six-line staff. At the margin of the page,
the spaces between the lines were labeled as whole steps (marked **T,**
for *tonus*) or half steps (marked **S** for *semitonium*). The position of the
words or syllables in the appropriate spaces indicated the relative
pitches of the melody.

EXAMPLE F

If for some obscure musicological reason we should wish to notate
America, the Beautiful by this system, we would begin the first phrase
thus:

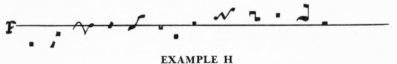

The music notation at the top of the page shows a syllabic staff-like arrangement:

```
of
b' ─────────────────────────────────
   T                              waves
a' ─────────────────────────────────
 , T  O Beau -    for  spa -        ber        grain
g' ─────────────────────────────────
   T                         am -
f' ─────────────────────────────────
   S         ti - ful           For
e' ─────────────────────────────────
   T              cious  skies,
d' ─────────────────────────────────
```

EXAMPLE G

It should be noted that the rhythmic duration of the separate pitches could not be expressed by this system any better than by neumes; hence our well-known melody is here notated in arbitrary and equal whole-note values.

How astounding it is that this device of using horizontal lines, so closely allied to our modern system of staff notation, should have created no permanent following in the century after its appearance, so that the "invention" of a single pitch-line in the tenth century seemed a completely new idea in music notation! Staves of five and six lines did not reappear until well into the twelfth century, almost 400 years after their bow in the *Musica Enchiriadis.*

The first enduring progress toward the establishment of a definite pitch—a central point to which all melodic intervals could be related—came with the drawing of a *single horizontal line* above the words of the Latin plainchant text. This line represented a *fixed pitch,* and the position of the neumes in relation to the line indicated their degrees of high and low. This tenth-century invention, its author unknown to us, marks the true beginning of modern staff notation.

EXAMPLE H

The single line, usually colored red in the early parchments, stood for the pitch of f below c'. No doubt it was chosen as the midway point in most plainsong melodies, as well as middle ground between tenor- and bass-voice registers (only male voices were permitted to sing the early Gregorian chants). Somewhat later the line was actually prefaced by the Latin letter f : F———— . Now the neumes could be placed on, below, or above this red line, thus giving a far more accurate indication of their pitch relationships than had been possible before. (See Example H.)

It was not long before a *second horiozntal line* was drawn above the existing f-line, further establishing consecutive interval relationships in the plainchant melody. This added line was colored either yellow or green, and represented the pitch of c′, a fifth higher than the f-line: **₵**——————— or **₵**——————

Both the pitches represented by these two horizontal lines, it is interesting to note, have natural half-steps below them (b below c′, and e below f). The choice of f- and c′-lines, therefore, may also have been designed to draw attention to these half-step intervals, an important consideration in distinguishing between the various modal scales in use at the time.

Since two lines representing fixed pitches proved of inestimable value to the singers of plainchant, it was only a matter of time before a *third line* was added to clarify still further the matter of pitch reference. This third line, colored black, was placed midway between the f- and c′-lines, representing the pitch of a. Thus each pair of lines indicated the distance of a third.

By the twelfth century a *fourth line,* again drawn in black, had been added. Sometimes the interval of a third so designated was placed above the c′-line (which made it e′), and sometimes below the f-line (making it d), the choice depending on the over-all range of the plainsong melody. This systemization was largely the work of the celebrated monk-scholar, Guido d'Arezzo, whose invaluable contribution to notational evolution will be detailed later (see pages 17–21). It is this four-line staff, combined with square-note neumes and ligatures, that— as previously noted—is still used in Roman Catholic liturgical music.

Some manuscripts of the early thirteenth century had all four lines drawn in black. From the fourteenth century on, however, most plainsong manuscripts had the four lines colored red. It might be wondered why these early staves should have four lines, rather than five, six, or more. The reason is that the plainchant melody rarely exceeded an octave in range; the notes, therefore, could be accommodated completely on four lines and three spaces. As the range of music increased, so did the size of the staff. Instrumental music, which required a greater range than vocal music, later on frequently used a staff varying from six to as many as fifteen lines.

But whether employing a two-line staff, a four-line staff, or even one of five or six lines (a somewhat later development) the process of neumic notation was basically the same. The neumes were placed

in relation to the lines and the intervening spaces, just as our note-
heads today are displayed on lines or in spaces. It must not be
imagined, however, that the process of adding lines one by one above
the plainchant text was either rapid or systematic. As with all evolutionary processes, the development of measured-interval notation
(termed *diastematic*) was leisurely—even erratic. So scanty was communication between such widely separated countries as Italy and the
Netherlands that each might be struggling simultaneously with the
identical innovation, or pursuing quite different theses. Thus handi-
capped, the process of groping toward a completely satisfactory system
of linear notation covered many centuries.

RHYTHMIC NOTATION

In the foregoing exposition of staff development we have observed that
the adoption of parallel horizontal lines drawn above the plainchant
text helped to establish the indication of successive *pitch relationships*.
But this was only half of the problem confronting the theorists and
musicians of the Middle Ages. The other crucial unknown was how to
represent the *duration* of the tone—through the neumes or the later
squared-note forms, or by some other method. This problem became
acute once music expanded into two or more voices singing independent parts. Two voices could coordinate with reasonable accuracy, but
more than two required a stricter method of time control.

True, there were rhythmic implications in the symbols of the liturgical manuscripts of this early period, but music historians are not in
total agreement as to their interpretation, and document their diver-
gent views by impressive research. Their arguments center on the
question of whether the actual performances were measured strictly
(employing what we would call *mensural rhythm*) or were free (in the
sense that there was no regularly recurring stress).

We may briefly illustrate these areas of contention by comparing the
following transcriptions of a portion of a Gregorian plainchant—the
Antiphon *Asperges Me*. The melody is first given in Gregorian notation, as it appears today in sources such as the *Liber Usualis*. Then
follows a "free" rhythmic translation (without regular recurring
stresses), as advocated and practiced by the Solesmes monks. Next is a
mensural transcription (with an established pulsation creating recurring patterns). This is followed by a different kind of mensuralism
known as the "neume beat"—a version rather like a combination of
the two previous interpretations.

A - spér - ges — me, Dó - - mi - ne, — hyssó - po —

EXAMPLE I

No reader of this Brief History will expect all such scholarly disputations as those above to be resolved by the quick action of one professorial pencil. Such arguments are in themselves proof that the neume system of notation was not perfectly clear. But it should still be possible to get a fairly coherent view of the process by which musical symbols came to indicate both pitch and duration.

One thirteenth-century system has been given the confusing title of *rhythmic modes.* In practice, these modes were actually very simple groupings of long and short time-values in three-part measure, repeated as a complete unit a number of times in much the same way that a certain grouping of syllables is repeated over and over in a line of poetry. For this reason, the rhythmic modes are often made graphic by comparing them with poetic symbols as well as with modern note-values.

Mode I—	▰ ▪	long-short	— ⏑	or	♩♪
Mode II—	▪ ▰	short-long	⏑ —	or	♪♩
Mode III—	▰ ▪ ▪	long-short-short	— ⏑ ⏑	or	♩.♪♩
Mode IV—	▪ ▪ ▰	short-short-long	⏑ ⏑ —	or	♪♩♩.
Mode V—	▰ ▰ ▰	long-long-long	— — —	or	♩.♩.♩.
Mode VI—	▪ ▪ ▪	short-short-short	⏑ ⏑ ⏑	or	♫

Though these patterns were clear, and fairly flexible in use, their evident limitations reduced their possibility for continuing development. During the same period, however, the neume-forms began to assume an individual rhythmic significance that has slowly evolved into the modern note-forms.

As a first step, by the mid-thirteenth century, the two forms of the single-note neumes—the *virga* (¶) and the *punctum* (■)—became the symbols for long and short time-duration, respectively. In its rhythmic form the *virga* was called the *longa*, or "long" (literally, a "long note"), while the *punctum* was called *brevis*, or *breve* (Latin for "short"). By the end of the century another symbol, called the *semi-breve*, had come into use. Its shape (◆) obviously derived from the square *breve*, and logically enough its duration was half that of the *breve*.

From this point, the evolution of the note-forms of *musica mensura-bilis* (measured music) can be more plainly followed in the graphic presentation of the Table of Note-Shapes. It traces the transition from the Greek prosodic accents to neumes; from neumes to the various mensural forms (time-indicating symbols) that formed the basis for the rhythmic "modes," and from mensural neumes to approximate modern notation.

As shown in the Table of Note-Shapes, there were by the end of the fourteenth century five note-symbols in use for rhythm: the *maxima*, or *duplex long* (equal to two *longs*), the *long*, the *breve*, the *semibreve*, and a new value called the *minim* ("least"). The sign for this new value was the same as for the *semibreve*, but with a stem attached. By the following century it became apparent that the *minim* was not the "least" note-value, as the *semiminima*, the *fusa*, and the *semifusa* had been added at the short end of the rhythmic scale.

Unfortunately, the mathematical relationship of the note scheme shown above was historically not so precise as the table may indicate. In the table each succeeding note has exactly *half* the value of the note-symbol that precedes it in the scale of values: the *semifusa* is half the value of the *fusa*; the *fusa* half the value of the *semiminima*. And this was true in the fourteenth century—but only in *duple* (two-part) *meter*. As we shall describe in more detail on page 156, the entire system of mensural notation was at first devised exclusively for triple (three-count) meter—known then as "perfect" meter. Hence in the earliest period each note was *one-third* as long as the note-symbol that preceded it in the scale. In this three-part scheme a *long* (¶) was equal to three *breves* (■ ■ ■), so that when duple meter was first notated there was extreme confusion on the proper method for distinguishing note-values in the two meters. One method employed was "coloration," in which the notes in two-count meter were written open (or "white") and the notes in three-count meter were written in red, and later in

EXAMPLE J. TABLE OF NOTE-SHAPES

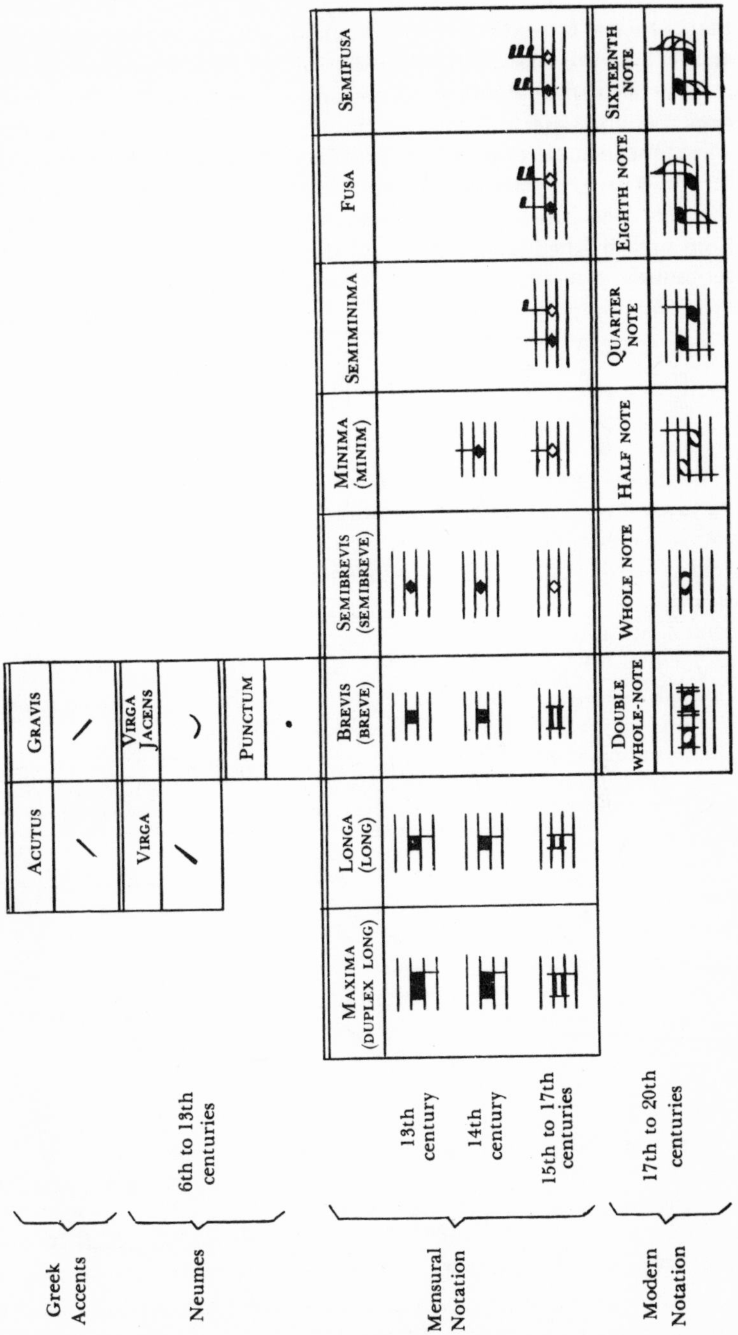

black. By the fifteenth century black and white note-heads were standard—a practice that has extended to present-day notation.

That we can at this historic distance make such a Table of Notes
does not, of course, indicate that the notation of this period was in any
way stabilized. Certain Italian and French composers of the late fourteenth century invented a great many other note-shapes that—since
they did not appear in other manuscripts of the period—must have
been used by them alone. A few of these symbols, shown below, make
interesting comparison with the more standard forms given in the
foregoing table.

EXAMPLE K

Differences in interpretation, as well as in actual note-shapes, reflect
the unsystematized state of mensural notation in this period. So dis-
parate were the interpretations of identical note-patterns that in the
field of secular music there developed an identifiable "French manner"
of interpretation and an "Italian manner." Then, further to compound
confusion, a fourteenth-century French musician might on occasion
perform in the "Italian manner" and an Italian performer in the
"French manner." The following example shows some characteristic
variants in performances of basic mensural signs:

14TH CENTURY NOTATION	"FRENCH" MANNER OF INTERPRETATION	"ITALIAN" MANNER OF INTERPRETATION
♦ ◆	♪⌣♫	♩ ♫
◆ ◆ ◆	♫ ♪	♫♫
♦ ◆ ◆	♪ ♫	♫ ♫
◆ ◆ ◆ ◆	♫ ♫	♫♫

EXAMPLE L

While all the previous phases of indicating the pitch and duration of musical *sound* were feeling their way, there was developing simultaneously a mensural notation to care for the pauses—or moments of *silence*—that are of equal importance with sound. In the early neume-notation such pauses, which had no exact value, were indicated by short slashes at the top of the line or lines being used, as seen below. In mensural notation, rests were sometimes shown by vertical lines drawn through the staff. The number of beats involved determined the length of the vertical line: a rest of one beat would cover one space; that of two beats would occupy two spaces, and so on.

13TH CENTURY   14TH CENTURY

EXAMPLE M

As the vertical line came to assume other duties, it became necessary to search for more distinctive rest-symbols at a later historic period. These modern symbols will be fully discussed in Chapter 7.

SCALE SYLLABLES

Although it is only indirectly related to the twin problems of pitch and rhythm notation, the development of *scale syllables* merits our attention here, being contemporaneous with the systematizing of staff lines and clef signs. All three accomplishments are often attributed to a scholarly Italian monk of the eleventh century, Guido d'Arezzo, though modern research has verified incontestably only his invention of the syllable system of reading music. But if not the actual originator of staff lines and clef signs, Guido was largely responsible for establishing their use in notated music.

The origin of Guido's concept of scale syllables—*ut, re, mi, fa, sol, la* —has been recounted many times. Faced with the eternal tedium of teaching liturgical melodies by rote, this monk—by accident or design —made the crucial discovery that six successive lines in the Sapphic hymn to St. John the Baptist begin on six successive rising pitch-degrees.

Guido's pedagogical mind seems at once to have transformed discovery to opportunity, for he was inspired to name each ascending scale-step by the first syllable found beneath it in the hymn. Using these short syllables, easily learned even by young students, he was able to transform his teaching, and that of the centuries to come. For this syllable method of identifying scale-degrees became the foundation of our modern nomenclature, given here in the forms in which they are written and sung. (See top of page 19.)

EXAMPLE N

It will be noticed, of course, that there is a discrepancy between Guido's scale of six tones and our modern major-minor scales of seven notes. The missing note and syllable is *si*, the seventh degree of any major scale.

SCALE SYLLABLES IN C MAJOR

English and Italian		French		German	
Written:	Sung:	Written:	Sung:	Written:	Sung:
C c	do	C c	ut	C c	do
D d	re	D d	ré	D d	re
E e	mi	E e	mi	E e	mi
F f	fa	F f	fa	F f	fa
G g	sol	G g	sol	G g	sol
A a	la	A a	la	A a	la
B b	si (ti)	B b	si	H h	si

ut   re   mi   fa   sol   la   si
(do)   (ti)

EXAMPLE O

The syllable *si* is thought to be derived from the initial letters of *Sancte Iohannes,* Latin form of "St. John." The seventh scale-degree, however, was not so named until several centuries after Guido's six-note scale was established. Modern practice—as shown above—has changed the *si* to *ti,* and in English, German, and Italian the *ut* has been altered to *do.*

THE HEXACHORDS

The six successive notes of Guido's scale were known as a *hexachord* (from the Greek *hexa,* meaning "six," and *chordé,* meaning "string" or "note"). This hexachord was a fixed pattern of intervals: two whole-steps (c to d, d to e), a half-step (e to f), and two whole-steps (f to g, g to a). (See Example P, Nos. 2 and 5.)

When a different register was needed, to accommodate higher or lower voices, the hexachord was moved up or down so as to begin on a different tone. It was found that when the hexachord was moved down or up to begin on **G** or **g** the same relationship of scale-degrees prevailed. (See Example P, Nos. 1, 4, and 7.) But when the hexachord was moved up to begin on **f,** the fourth degree above **f** (**b**) had to be lowered by a half step so as to conform to the original pattern of intervals (Example P, Nos. 3 and 6).

To distinguish between this lowered form of **b** and the natural form found in the hexachord starting on **g,** two forms of the letter were employed. The lowered form was a rounded letter **b** (*b rotundum;* in

Latin ♭). The natural form was a square-shaped b (*b quadrum:* ♮).
It was the practice to call the round ♭ "soft" (in Latin, *molle*) and the
squared ♮ "hard" (in Latin, *durum*). Thus it came about that the
hexachord on **g** (which used the natural or square ♮) was a "hard"
hexachord, while that beginning on **f** (which employed the rounded
or soft ♭) was a "soft" hexachord. The original hexachord on **c** was
termed "natural" as it did not contain the tone **b** in either
form.

EXAMPLE P. TABLE OF THE HEXACHORDAL SYSTEM

In order to cover the entire vocal compass in use during the eleventh century (from **G** to **e''**), certain of the hexachords were moved up or down by an octave. The "hard" hexachord could be moved down to begin on **G**, as well as up an octave to commence on **g'**. The "soft" hexachord beginning on **f** could only be moved higher, as an octave below its original pitch was considered too low for vocal comfort. For the same reason, the "natural" hexachord on **c** could only be placed an octave higher. Thus the fifth, sixth, and seventh hexachords were merely duplications of the second, third, and fourth hexachords in a higher range, and the fourth duplicated the first at a higher octave. It will be noted in the preceding table of the hexachordal system that the first note of the lowest hexachord is marked with the sign: **Γ** instead of the syllable *ut*. This is the Greek *gamma,* or letter **G**, which was the lowest tone of the first hexachord and hence designated the beginning of the "gamut" of tones that followed. *Gamut,* meaning "scale" or "range," derives from the combination of *gamma* with *ut*—the syllable sung on the lowest tone of the hexachord.

TABLATURE NOTATION

Our brief survey of the history of music notation would not be complete without a description of the *tablature notation* employed for keyboard instruments and for the lute during the sixteenth century. Briefly, tablature notation made use of letters or numbers instead of neumes or squared notes. Furthermore, the numbers, letters, or combinations of both were placed on a staff-like diagram that literally represented the strings, the frets, or the keys of the instrument. The basic principle of lute tablature, for example, was that its six strings were represented by six horizontal lines—the lowest line indicating the lowest string in Spanish notation, and the highest string in Italian notation. The numbers referred to the frets on the fingerboard: 0 was the open string, 1 the first fret (a half step higher), 2 the second fret (two half-steps higher), and so on—the frets making it simple for the player to place his fingers accurately. In one system the rhythm was indicated by notes placed over the six-line "staff"; in another system, flagged stems set just above the fret numbers showed the rhythmic scheme.

Tablature notation was, however, basically unsatisfactory because it had no graphic relation to the *intervals* played, but showed only the location of the *fingers* on key, fret, or string. What is more, the system varied widely from instrument to instrument. Lute tablature and organ tablature were utterly unlike, and even the system used

French tuning

Italian tuning

EXAMPLE Q.   LUTE TABLATURE

by Italian lutenists differed from that of the French or the Spanish performers—as shown in the example on page 22.

So it was that some kind of universal system of notation had to be designed, adaptable to all instruments and voices. *Five-line staff notation* with modern note-forms was the ultimate answer, but this was not standardized until well into the seventeenth century. Even then the process of refinement continued another full century, during which the system added all the necessary signs for interpretation: accents, slurs, dynamic and tempo markings.

EARLY MUSIC PRINTING

Our modern *orthochronic notation* (see page 64) dates roughly from the beginning of the sixteenth century. This was the period in which the square open (or "white") notes and the square black (or "colored") notes came to be written in a rounded form. This consolidation may be considered a fairly direct consequence of music printing, established soon after letter printing was invented. In 1455 the Gutenberg Bible was published, and around 1480 the first musical works were issued, using essentially the same printing procedures. Initially this method combined two processes—the staff lines being printed first in red, and then the note-heads and text in black. In following this plan the music printers were merely imitating the practices of the monastic manuscripts, in which the lines were drawn in red and the neumes (or note-ligatures) in black.

An important side-effect of the invention of music printing was to slow down the evolutionary process of notation. Just as letter-shapes became standardized by the invention of book printing, so did the shape of musical notes, clef signs, and accidentals become more settled when music printing supplanted hand copying. Whether this was a desirable outcome is a moot point. No one can prove incontrovertibly that the state of music notation in the sixteenth and seventeenth centuries represented the highest possible development, nor would one contend today that there is no room for improvement in the historic system.

Certainly, however, staff notation as it has evolved since the advent of printing has this advantage: it combines in one simultaneous process the graphic representation of pitch distinction and of time duration. Furthermore, it fulfills many basic requirements for a visual system of communication. The symbols used are characteristic of their subject—even suggestive of the musical sounds they represent. In addi-

tion, these symbols are clear and concise; they are distinct to the eye
(a note, a rest, and an accent cannot be confused one with the other)
and they are relatively easy to write and to print. Finally—and of
utmost importance—the total number of symbols required in music
notation is comparatively small, an aspect of notation that is of inestimable help to the memory.

Admittedly compressed, and necessarily incomplete, the preceding
Brief History has been meant to serve only as an introductory chronicle
of the elements of notation that relate to present practice. Some further
developments will be recounted in the appropriate chapters of Part II.
For those who wish to fill in completely the impressive background of
this historical evolution, however, the books listed in the Bibliography
will prove rewarding sources.

Even from this truncated survey, it is surely evident that music
notation, like any other written language, did not appear as the invention of one man, nor even of a dozen—geniuses though they may have
been. It flowered from the combined and protracted efforts of hundreds
of musicians, all hoping to express by written symbols the essence of
their musical ideas. Improvement in those symbols came about because
it was necessary, not because one or two individuals decided arbitrarily
on a change and imposed the innovation on others. The resultant
notation is, after all, a kind of alphabet, shaped by a general con-
sensus of opinion to serve as a general expressive technique.

For musical *thought*—creation—and its visual realization—*notation*
—are completely interdependent. By itself notation is not music; it is
only the vehicle by which the composer indicates his ideas and wishes
to the performer. Notation, therefore, is not the end but the significant
means to the end. As the written language by which the composer communicates with an audience through a performer, it is a study in
human relationship as well—to be judged by the effectiveness with
which it communicates what to do, when to do it, and how to do it.

A musical score, then, is rather like an instruction manual—comparable perhaps to a playwright's script awaiting its actors or to an
architect's blueprint awaiting a builder. A score can truly come to
life only through the performer; its message can be translated only
when symbols on the printed page are adequate for intelligent trans-
formation into living musical reality. To the end that the tools of all
notators may be more adequate, we now proceed to survey the basic
elements of written music—to define, illustrate, discuss, and practice
the various factors that comprise music notation.

PART II

The Elements
of Notation

1

Staves

Music notation is the visual manifestation of the interrelated properties of musical sound—pitch, intensity, time, timbre, and pace. Symbols indicating the choice of tones, their duration, and their manner of performance form the written language we call music notation (Fr. *notation* or *sémeiographie;* Ger. *Notenschrift* or *Notation;* It. *notazione* or *semeiografia*).

THE STAFF

The *staff* (Fr. *portée,* pl. *portées;* Ger. *Liniensystem,* pl. *Liniensysteme* or *Notensystem,* pl. *Notensysteme;* It. *sistema,* pl. *sistemi* or *rigo,* pl. *righi*) is the most basic of all the music symbols, for it serves as the locale for almost all the other signs used in music notation. Note elements (note-heads, stems, flags, and beams) must be positioned on a staff; accidentals, rests, barlines, and time signatures must also be accommodated by its lines and spaces. Even accents, dynamics, and phrase marks are placed in relation to the notes they affect, and so are dependent on the staff for proper notation.

The modern staff is an arrangement of five parallel lines, together with the spaces between them; all are called *staff degrees.* We number the lines (Fr. *ligne,* pl. *lignes;* Ger. *Linie,* pl. *Linien;* It. *linea,* pl. *linee*) from the lowest to the highest. In the same way, the spaces (Fr. *espace,* pl. *espaces;* Ger. *Zwischenraum,* pl. *Zwischenräume;* It. *spazio,* pl. *spazi*) are counted upward.

EXAMPLE 1 - 1

The terms "line above" the staff or "line below" the staff refer to the first extra (or *ledger,* frequently spelled *leger*) line added above or below the regular staff lines. The terms "space above" or "space below" refer to the corresponding spaces immediately above or below the staff.

EXAMPLE 1 - 2

First used in the early thirteenth century for vocal polyphonic music, the five-line staff did not become standard for all music until the mid-seventeenth century. As we recounted in the historic survey, a staff consisting of four lines was widely used from the eleventh to the thir-teenth centuries, and indeed still exists in the Gregorian plainsong notation of the Roman Catholic Church. (See Example I.) Some key-board music of the sixteenth and seventeenth centuries employed staves of as many as fifteen lines. But such large staves were unwieldy, and were gradually replaced by the present five-line staff. In this settled form it was probably consolidated from the two accepted forms of the four-line staff in use during the early period of neumic notation. (See pages 9–12.)

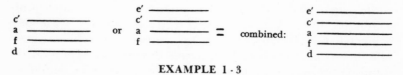

EXAMPLE 1 - 3

The so-called "Great Staff" of eleven lines is actually a combination of staves bearing the three clefs in common use during the rise of staff notation. It carries the **F** (or bass) clef joined to the **G** (or treble) clef, with **c'** (the **C,** or alto-tenor clef) on a common line between them. (See page 40 for the Table of Register Symbols used throughout this book.) But this was never a staff used in actual music notation, and may be considered a theoretical staff only. Today we separate the treble and bass staves by more space, and **c'** appears as a note added both below the treble and above the bass on a single ledger line.

The visual advantages of the modern arrangement should be im-mediately obvious: the eye takes in a staff of five lines more easily than one of eleven. At the same time, the separate identities of the two staves are given a visual emphasis.

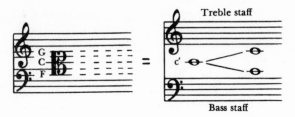

EXAMPLE 1 - 4

Modern staff notation is eminently successful in showing the perpendicular distance between tones: that is, in demonstrating *pitch*
relationships. It is far less graphic in outlining relations of time or
duration; less suited to *horizontal* than to *vertical* significance. If we
see two notes on a staff, we know immediately when one is higher than
the other, and by how many scale degrees. Our reaction to the interval
distance would be the same, regardless of the relative horizontal position of either note in the measure.

EXAMPLE 1 - 5 *

On the other hand, horizontal relationships on a staff are sometimes
more difficult to grasp because different written note-values (a whole
note and a 32nd note, for instance) both occupy the same *written space.*

EXAMPLE 1 - 6

To distinguish between the two notes in relative length or shortness
we need to cope with three elements: the shape or color of the note-
head (whether open 𝅗𝅥 or closed 𝅘𝅥); the stem or lack of stem (𝅝 or 𝅘𝅥
or 𝅘𝅥); the presence or absence of a flag joined to the stem (𝅘𝅥𝅮 or 𝅘𝅥𝅯
or 𝅘𝅥𝅰). These three notational elements will be taken up in detail in
subsequent chapters.
Sometimes, of course, staff notation can be misleading even with

---

* In many examples throughout this book, clef and/or meter signs are omitted
when the notational principle involved does not depend upon a specific clef or a
time signature to make its point.

respect to pitch relationships. Ordinarily, the position of a note on the
staff, whether on a line or in a space, serves to give a visual image of
that pitch. Thus in the example on the left, below, f' is notated below
g' because the pitch of f' is lower than that of g'. But if we now notate
f' double sharp followed by g' flat, we will not *hear* the same relationship our eyes *see*. The f' double sharp of the center example is the
same as g' natural in tempered tuning (shown in the example on the
right), and g' flat is the enharmonic spelling of (the same as) f' sharp.
Thus the written pitch-relationships in the center example are literally reversed, the lower written note sounding a higher pitch than the
note written in a higher position!

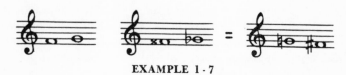

EXAMPLE 1 - 7

Like all exceptions, these visual complications do not controvert the
general rule.

Composers today customarily make use of the same five-line staff
that western music adopted almost universally in the seventeenth
century—except where it is abandoned completely for the graphs used
in electronic music and in experimental systems of notation. But notation during the past century has added at least one new *function* of the
staff: to show by the use of supplementary staves placed above the
normal staff (or appended as a footnote) some additional material or
editorial corrections and suggestions, or to give *ossia* (alternative)
passages.

In piano reductions of full orchestra or operatic scores, supplementary staves showing additional material are quite common. The tran-
scriber includes for the two hands as much as they can play, but
important elements of the score must frequently be left out because
the pianist's ten fingers cannot encompass every detail. Therefore this
additional and highly important material has to be given on a small
supplementary staff—linked to the main staff by dotted barlines—to
round out the picture of the full orchestral score.

In the instrumental parts for chamber music, supplementary staves
("cue" lines) are also used to show what other instruments are doing.
This is especially important when rhythmic complexity, tempo coordination, or difficult entrances create performance hazards. In a sonata
for two instruments, for example, the piano part might be indicated
on a small staff superimposed in the other instrumental part where a
momentary musical complexity makes it advisable.

Chamber-music scores also frequently rely on "cue" lines to make performance problems clearer to the score-reader as well as to the performers, such as the following example:

EXAMPLE 1 - 8. Elliott Carter: From *String Quartet No. 1*

Somewhat different is the function of the auxiliary staff in modern editions of Baroque or Classical music, where we frequently find suggested alternates or corrections of the printed ornaments and embellishments given in supplementary staves, either directly above the passage or in a footnote.

EXAMPLE 1 - 9. Franz Joseph Haydn: From *Sonata in C major*

Traditionally, too, fingering variants, different distribution of the notes between the hands, or dynamic modifications may be given on a supplementary staff.

As for *ossia* passages, these are technically simplified versions of difficult sections. The word itself is the Italian term for "or"; hence it means one plays *either* the original version of the music *or* the alternate given on the small auxiliary staff. The works of Liszt are full of such *ossia* passages, and other examples may be found in almost any virtuoso solo or concerto work. Hardly innovations in a drastic sense, they provide by simple means a more flexible function for the staff.

EXAMPLE 1-10. Frédéric Chopin: From *Waltz in A-flat major*

EXAMPLE 1-11. Franz Liszt: From *Hungarian Rhapsody No. 2*

MODERN INNOVATIONS

Over the years many proposals have been made either to rearrange the
existing staff-lines, to increase their number, or to reduce them to a
single-line staff. Walter Steffens, for example, proposed an arrangement of the present five lines to parallel the visual appearance of the
keyboard with its black and white keys. To obviate the use of accidentals (see Chapter 9) each note of the twelve-note octave was placed
on successive lines and spaces, as shown on the opposite page.

Another proposed system, called "Klavarskribo" by its inventor, C.
Pot, is also based on five lines, but these are arranged *vertically* rather
than horizontally. Visually the system somewhat resembles sixteenth-
century lute tablature. Because pitches are represented in a horizontal
manner, durations are shown vertically—just the opposite of our
traditional system. (See Example 1-13.)

Yet another recently formulated system, named "Equiton" by the inventor Rodney Fawcett, reduces the staff to a single line. Primarily
designed, as was "Klavarskribo," to avoid all accidental signs, this system uses a single C-line per octave span; the note-heads are placed on

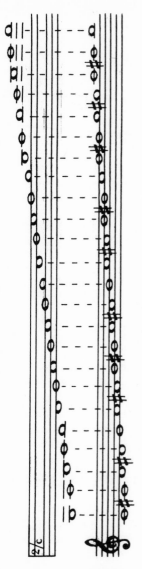

EXAMPLE 1-12

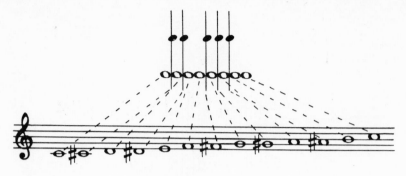

EXAMPLE 1 - 13

graded levels above or below this line, somewhat in the manner of the neume notation of earlier centuries. Chromatic distinctions are designated by alternating white and black note-heads:

EXAMPLE 1 - 14

All of these attempts to "modernize" the staff are commendable; not all, however, are equally effective, and some—such as "Klavarskribo" —require a complete reorientation of one's normal habits of reading notation. For that reason these new systems are not likely to gain worldwide advocacy, at least in the immediate future.

NOTATION EXERCISES

1. Write an example of two pitches demonstrating that one of the two may be written lower, yet sound higher than one written above it.
2. Copy out the first nine measures, second movement, of the violin part of Beethoven's *Sonata No. 5, in F major,* Op. 24; on a single staff above make a "cue" line from the piano part.
3. Copy out the first phrase (note-heads only) of Chopin's *A major Prelude for Piano* in "Klavarskribo" and in "Equiton."

2
Braces and Systems

Wʜᴇɴ ᴀ ɴᴏᴛᴀᴛᴏʀ ꜱᴇʟᴇᴄᴛꜱ *BRACKETS* ᴏʀ *BRACES* ᴛᴏ impose an organized pattern upon his staves, he has begun his progress toward a clear expression—the fundamental aim of his entire undertaking. He will choose braces (sometimes called *curved brackets;* they are shaped something like an archer's bow) when he wishes to unite two or more staves into the entity we shall later in this chapter discuss as a "system." He will choose brackets, on the other hand, to group essentially independent or diverse elements.

BRACES AND BRACKETS

The *brace* { (Fr. *accolade*, pl. *accolades;* Ger. *Klammer*, pl. *Klammern;* It. *accolada,* pl. *accolade*) is most frequently used to connect such elements as the two or more staves of a keyboard or harp composition. In this capacity it will be found not only in piano scores but also in music for celesta, harpsichord, and organ. Note in the examples below

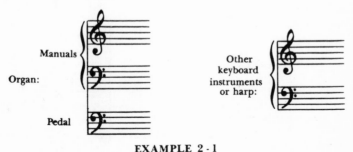

EXAMPLE 2-1

35

that the staves are further joined by a single vertical line following the
brace sign.

The *bracket* [most commonly functions, in contradistinction to
the brace, to connect such basically individual lines as the four staves
of a string quartet score or the several staves of a choral work. Again,
a single vertical line joins all the staves; the bracket itself is somewhat
thicker than the brace, with thin curved ends extending above and
below the outer staves.

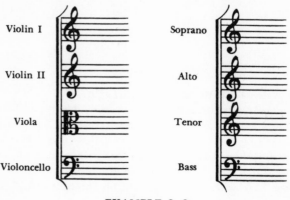

EXAMPLE 2 - 2

It is customary to use the bracket rather than the bow-shaped brace
to group two or more staves bearing quite separate or individual parts,
whether vocal or instrumental. A duet for oboe and clarinet, for instance, would have the two staves connected by a bracket rather than
by a brace, as the two instruments are of different families. Likewise,
a trio for three violins would be linked in a score by a bracket (despite
belonging to the same instrumental family) because of the individual
character of their parts.

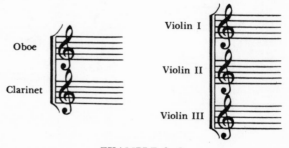

EXAMPLE 2 - 3

Small braces are further used *between* staves (for keyboard instruments or for two or more related instruments) to indicate that dynamics or technical directions apply to both staves. This practice is very useful in full scores, where the repetition of such markings for every single staff would be time-consuming for the notator and fussy in appearance. (See also Example 2-7.)

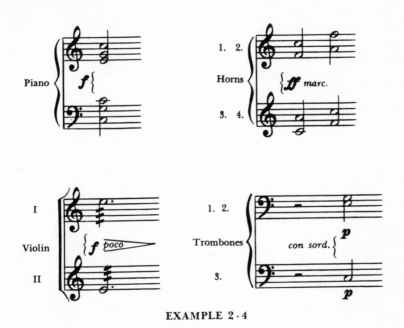

EXAMPLE 2-4

In its longest, most extended form the bracket is used to set off the four principal sections of a full orchestral score: woodwinds, brasses, percussion, and strings. (See Example 26-1.)

SYSTEMS

A *system* (Fr. *système,* pl. *systèmes;* Ger. *System,* pl. *Systeme;* It. *sistema,* pl. *sistemi*) is a group of staves, with their individual clef-signs, designed to be read simultaneously rather than one by one. This intent is made clear to the reader or performer by the use of the curved brace or straight bracket, followed by a single vertical line, at the left of the group. In its simplest form a system is the combination of two staves, treble and bass, used by keyboard instruments. (See Example 2-1.) This two-staff system for notation was first used in the fifteenth

century for harpsichord and organ music, and became well established
shortly thereafter. The staves, however, were not universally in the
five-line form; at one time there was even a staff of fifteen lines: six
lines for the left hand, eight for the right hand, with a linking ledger-
line.

The three staves required for organ music, two for the manuals
and one for the pedals, are also a system. Note in Example 2-1 that,
although the continuous vertical line at the left joins the three staves,
the brace encloses only the two for the manuals.

In its most extended form a system would be the entire page of an
orchestra or band score, comprising some 20 to 30 separate staves, each
for a different instrument. (Again, see Example 26-1.) Publishers vary
in their methods of bracketing or bracing these large systems. Some
editions enclose the entire system with a single large bracket at the left,
using smaller outside braces to mark the two or more staves of similar
or related instruments. Other publishing firms favor the use of brackets
to enclose each principal choir of the orchestra, with or without additional braces before the staves of instrumental families (compare Examples 23-1, 26-1, 26-2, and 26-5). Universally, however, the staves of
keyboard instruments (piano, celesta, harpsichord, and organ) and of
the harp are joined with a brace, in both orchestral scores and solo
works.

Universally, too, publishers must utilize available space to best advantage. Hence most pages of published piano, vocal, choral, or chamber music will contain a number of systems, or joined groups of staves.
Even orchestral scores are frequently printed with several systems to
the page when the scoring is light and staves may be momentarily
omitted for those instruments not playing. (See Example 26-3.)

When two or more systems are included on a page of orchestral
music, or of ensemble music requiring more than two staves together,
it is customary to separate each pair of systems with two broad dashes
(slanted slightly from left to right) placed at the left-hand margin of
the page. Similar dashes may also be placed at the right-hand margin,
although it is not so common to find them there. In any case, the
separation symbol is a distinct help to the eye in score-reading, and
assists toward the accuracy and facility that mark the accomplished
notator. (See Example 26-3.)

MODERN INNOVATIONS

Many recent avant-garde scores display left-hand margin brackets
minus their usual terminal jogs; these are placed—somewhat arbi-

trarily, it would seem—either before the staff (or staves) in question, or *following* the clef sign, as shown below:

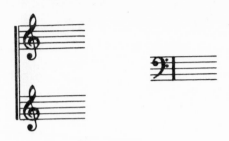

EXAMPLE 2 - 5

Other contemporary publications for keyboard instruments have used the brace in the following unorthodox positions:

EXAMPLE 2 - 6

The perceptive reader has no doubt already noticed Stravinsky's recent habit (see Example 2-7) of employing the straight bracket rather than the usual curved brace before the joined staves of piano and of harp, a practice now followed by many European avant-gardists.

In printed music through the mid-twentieth century it has been the custom to make each system complete as far as staff lines were concerned. Even if an instrument should not play on any given system, its staff would be written out—with or without rest signs, but otherwise intact. A recent innovation in the printing of such systems is to omit the actual staff-lines for all measures in which an instrument or voice is silent. This is done even if an instrument remains *tacet* ("silent") for only a single measure or two. At the other extreme, if a part has only a single measure to play on any given page, only that particular measure is printed, the remainder of the line being left blank. A page from Igor Stravinsky's *Movements for Piano and Orchestra* illustrates vividly the visual aspect of such incomplete systems. (See page 40.)

EXAMPLE 2-7. Igor Stravinsky: From *Movements for Piano and Orchestra* (1959)

Minor variations of this device of printing incomplete systems are shown below. In each, the solid or dotted horizontal lines that link together the full staves in each part fill the space in which the instrument or voice momentarily rests.

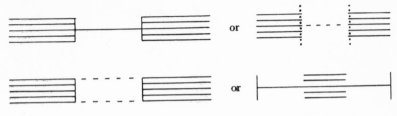

EXAMPLE 2·8

NOTATION EXERCISES

1. Place the proper brace or bracket before the following instrumental and vocal staves:

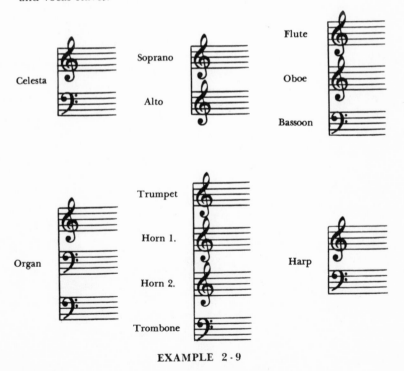

EXAMPLE 2·9

2. Rewrite the lower system on page 2 of Beethoven's *Symphony No. 3,* *"Eroica"* (Kalmus Ed.) in the manner of a modern incomplete system.

3

Ledger Lines and Octave Signs

As CHAPTER 1 POINTED OUT, THE PRIMARY FUNCTION of the staff is to demonstrate pitch distinctions. These differences are made graphic by the position of notes on the lines or in the spaces of the staff: higher for higher pitches, lower for lower pitches. But when required pitches are so high or so low as to move off the five lines and four spaces of the staff, auxiliary symbols must be used to show these extensions in relation to the normal staff compass. These additional symbols are *ledger lines* and *octave signs*.

LEDGER (LEGER) LINES

Ledger lines (Fr. *lignes supplémentaires;* Ger. *Hilfslinien;* It. *lineette*) are short horizontal lines just longer than a note-head, drawn above or below the staff. They are spaced at the same vertical distance apart, one from the other, as the staff lines themselves. In effect, then, ledger lines are supplementary lines that literally expand the staff vertically, and one might think of them as portions of additional staves. (See Example 3-5, for instance.)

As a matter of fact, when ledger lines were first used—in Italian organ music of the early sixteenth century—they were drawn as complete staff-lines superimposed on the existing staff. This practice no doubt accounted for the ungainly staves of 13, 14, and 15 lines commonly found in instrumental notation from the thirteenth to the sixteenth centuries. Today ledger lines are drawn short, and are added only where the notes go too high or too low for inclusion on the staff itself.

If we are to discuss the full range of the staves plus their ledger lines, we must use standard symbols to indicate the exact octave for each

43

pitch-letter. The Table of Register Symbols (below) shows several of the systems currently used.

EXAMPLE 3 - 1.   TABLE OF REGISTER SYMBOLS

SUB (SUB-CONTRA OR 32-FOOT) OCTAVE	CONTRA (16-FOOT) OCTAVE	GREAT (8-FOOT) OCTAVE
A_2 — B_2 (AAA — BBB) * (A_0 — B_0)	C_1 — B_1 (CC — BB) (C_1 — B_1)	C — B (C_2 — B_2)

SMALL (4-FOOT) OCTAVE	ONE-LINE (2-FOOT) OCTAVE	TWO-LINE (1-FOOT) OCTAVE
c — b (C_3 — B_3)	c^1 — b^1 (c' — b') (C_4 — B_4)	c^2 — b^2 (c" — b") (C_5 — B_5)

THREE-LINE OCTAVE	FOUR-LINE OCTAVE	FIVE-LINE OCTAVE
c^3 — b^3 (c''' — b''') (C_6 — B_6)	c^4 — b^4 (c'''' — b'''') (C_7 — B_7)	c^5 — (c''''' —) (C_8 —)

* Recommended and used by the Acoustical Society of America.

OCTAVE SIGNS

Quite obviously, the continued use of many added lines and spaces can create unnecessary reading hazards; it is tiring to the eye, and tired eyes read inaccurately. For this reason it is often desirable, instead of using ledger lines, either to change clef (see Chapter 4) or to employ one of the standard octave (Fr. *octave;* Ger. *Oktave;* It. *ottava*) signs. These include the following:

1. *8ᵛᵃ* (or *8*)—abbreviation of the Italian *all' ottava,* meaning "at the octave." The sign (used with treble clef only) is placed *over* the staff, and is followed by a broken or dotted line ending with one or two downstrokes to indicate the conclusion of the passage.

EXAMPLE 3 - 2 *

Formerly, this sign was written as *8ᵃ alta,* but the word *alta,* meaning "high," is no longer necessary.

2. *8ᵛᵃ bassa* (or *8ᵃ b.* or *8*) (It. *ottava bassa*)—abbreviation of "at the octave below." The sign (used with the bass clef only) is normally placed *beneath* the staff, again followed by a broken line, concluded with an upstroke. (The word *loco,* sometimes found after an *8ᵛᵃ* or *8ᵛᵃ bassa* passage, means "at place," or at the written pitch. In other words, it cancels the *8ᵛᵃ* sign, although the termination of the dotted or broken line normally achieves the same result.)

EXAMPLE 3 - 3

Actually, the full term *8ᵛᵃ bassa* is necessary only on rare occasions when for reasons of space the sign must be placed *over* the staff. Otherwise, it is sufficient merely to use *8ᵛᵃ* (or *8*) beneath the staff, with the required dotted lines and upstroke.

---

* The fact that nearly all the examples created for this manual are notated in **C** major has no significance other than that of simplicity.

3. *15ᵐᵃ* (or *15*) (It. *quindicesima*)—abbreviation for "at the fifteenth," or two octaves higher than written. Note that the figure is *15* and *not 16*. Even professional musicians sometimes forget that the eighth tone of the first octave is duplicated as the first tone of the octave above, so that twice *8* in this case is *15*! (See Example 3-4.)

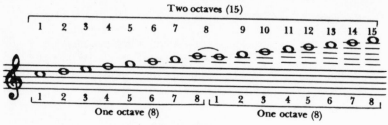

EXAMPLE 3 - 4

Although there is no good reason why the sign *15ᵐᵃ bassa* would not be used for the double octave below the bass staff, its use is so rare as to be virtually nonexistent. The test for all octave signs, as for other musical symbols, must be: "Would this sign make the music easier to read? Easier to understand?" Mentally, the notator must envision just such a comparison as is demonstrated in the following two versions of the same passage:

EXAMPLE 3 - 5

It is evident that, correctly used, octave signs are invaluable in notating and reading music, and save space on the page. Incorrect practices, however, must be studiously avoided. The *8ᵛᵃ bassa* sign should never be used beneath treble, alto, or tenor staves. If the passage should require either excessive ledger lines (center, below) or the theoretical use of the *8ᵃ b.* sign (right, below), it should be written using a lower clef. Needless to say, the *correct* clef must be chosen for the instrument involved (see pages 54–56).

EXAMPLE 3 - 6

Likewise, the *8va* sign should not be used above the bass, tenor, or alto staves. Unless it is written for an instrument that normally requires either alto or tenor clef, a passage such as that shown below at the right or—theoretically—as given on the next line, should be notated using treble clef (left).

EXAMPLE 3 - 7

4. *Coll' 8va* (or *coll' 8*)—abbreviation of the Italian *coll'ottava*, meaning "with the octave"—has a different function from that of the symbols discussed in 1. and 2. Instead of changing the position of the written notes, it signifies that the written notes are to be played *in octaves*. In other words, it is a shorthand system of writing a melodic line that is either doubled at the octave above (usually found in the treble staff) or below (normally found in the bass staff). For visual distinction between this and the other octave signs, an unbroken line or a series of longer broken lines, ending in a vertical jog, is used after the *coll' 8* sign and runs to the end of the passage.

With the addition of these simple devices—the ledger lines and the various octave signs—the staff remains the focus of musical notation, but the aperture has been widened for a broader expression.

EXAMPLE 3 - 8

MODERN INNOVATIONS

Contemporary notation has added nothing new either to the conception or to the use of ledger lines, but such lines are common—even excessive—in works by today's composers. This occurs especially in the technique of *fragmentation* (the literal scattering of notes played by a single instrument from high to low to high, and so on) so prevalent in contemporary musical expression. With this technique, single isolated notes are written very low in an instrumental compass, followed immediately by a very high note. Obviously, one cannot continually change clefs for these widely contrasted pitches, so the use of many ledger lines (or *8va* signs) is a necessity.

EXAMPLE 3 - 9

Nor are there radically new conceptions of the function of octave signs, although some composers (and music editors) have devised slightly different forms of notating the *8va* symbol. A few of these variants are given below:

15ma

15 = = = = = ‖   or   2 Okt.   or   4 ......

EXAMPLE 3 · 10

Other than these simple and obvious developments, no significant changes have been made in the traditional functions and symbols of octave transposition.

NOTATION EXERCISES

1. Rewrite the following example using ledger lines instead of the *8ᵛᵃ* sign:

EXAMPLE 3 · 11

2. Rewrite the following example using the *15ᵐᵃ* sign instead of the present ledger lines:

EXAMPLE 3 · 12

3. Rewrite the following example using ledger lines instead of the *8 bassa* sign:

EXAMPLE 3 · 13

4. Notate the following example correctly:

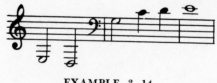

EXAMPLE 3 - 14

5. Write an original example for violin using the modern forms of *8va* and *15ma*.

4
Clefs

T HE TERM *CLEF* IS DERIVED, LOGICALLY ENOUGH, FROM
the Latin word *clavis*, meaning "key" (Fr. *clef*, pl. *clefs*; Ger. *Schlüssel*,
pl. *Schlüssel*; It. *la chiave*, pl. *le chiavi*). Early theorists and musicians
observed that the clef sign literally unlocked the secret of the staff, for
without a guidepost to specific pitch—which a clef sign represents—
the staff itself is meaningless.

As we pointed out in the Brief History, the earliest form of a clef
sign was the Latin letter **F**, which preceded a single horizontal line
drawn above the plainchant text in the early manuscripts. The neume
signs (see page 8) were placed below, on, or above this line in order
to show an approximate pitch relationship to that of the horizontal
line, in this case the tone f (*fa*). (See Example H.)

When a second line was later drawn above the text over the **F**-line,
the letter **C** was affixed upon it, representing the pitch of **c′** (*ut* or
do). Still later, other lines were added, including one marked with the
letter **G** (*sol*). Thus the three clef-signs in common use today had
their origins in pitch letters.

Nor was it by accident that the pitches of **f**, **c′**, and **g′** were chosen
as the early clef-forms. Between them they indicated the starting points
of the three kinds of hexachord established by Guido: the natural (on
c), the soft (on f), and the hard (on g). (See page 20.)

The **F** clef became the bass clef because of its lower register; the
C clef, with its middle-register position, became either tenor or alto
clef; and the **G** clef became the soprano or treble clef. Of these three
clefs, only the C-clef is movable in modern usage; that is, the sign
itself may be moved up or down the staff so as to place **c′** (middle C)
on either the third line (alto clef) or the fourth line (tenor clef).

In the past, the C-clef was moved to two additional positions: with
c′ centered on the second staff line (creating the mezzo-soprano clef),
and on the bottom line (soprano clef). Both of these clefs were widely

EXAMPLE 4·1. TABLE OF CLEF DEVELOPMENT

used in Baroque music (such as that of Handel and Bach), but have since become obsolete. Likewise, the so-called "French violin" clef, which placed g′ of the treble clef on the bottom rather than the second staff line, is no longer in use. Nor is the baritone clef found in modern notation; this placed the f of the bass clef on the middle line (rather than on the fourth). The Table of Clefs (Example 4-2) shows all of

EXAMPLE 4-2. TABLE OF CLEFS

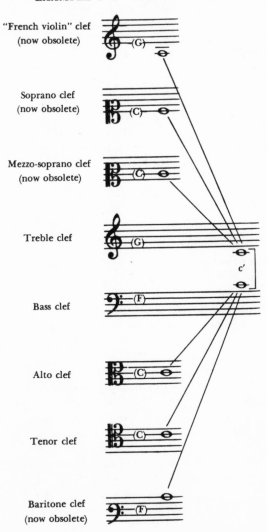

the clefs referred to, and their relation in pitch to the now standard bass and treble clefs.

THE F (OR *BASS*) CLEF

The modern bass-clef (Fr. *clef de fa;* Ger. *F-Schlüssel;* It. *chiave di basso)* sign looks somewhat like a reversed letter **C**, followed by two dots: **𝄢** . (In many older English publications the bass-clef sign was printed in this form: **𝄢** .) Notice that the two dots (originally a part of the Gothic letter **F**—see Example 4-1) are on either side of the fourth line, which is **f**. This serves to focus the eye on the f-line, which gives the clef its name.

As the name implies, the bass clef is used for all voices and instruments of essentially a bass register. These include both bass and baritone voices, either solo or choral; the left-hand (or lower) staff for all keyboard instruments (piano, organ, celesta, harpsichord, harmonium); the pedal part for the organ; and such orchestra instruments as the bass clarinet using the so-called "German system" (see page 341), contrabass clarinet, bassoon, contrabassoon, horns (when used extremely low), trombones, baritone (euphonium), tuba, timpani, 'cellos and double basses.

THE C (*ALTO* OR *TENOR*) CLEF

In modern usage the C-clef (Fr. *clef d'ut;* Ger. *C-Schlüssel;* It. *chiave di tenore*) retains only two of its historic positions. As the alto clef, it carries **c′** on the *third* staff line. As the tenor clef, it has **c′** on the *fourth* line (see Example 4-1). Simple though it appears, the C-clef is the most difficult of all clef-signs to notate perfectly. Complete instructions for all the clefs, with the acceptable variant forms, are supplied in Chapter 25.

The following instruments use the alto clef in modern notation: English horn (mainly in Russian publications); trombones (in music of the early Romantic period—Beethoven, Schubert, Mendelssohn, and so on), and violas. It should be pointed out that none of these instruments uses the alto clef exclusively; only the viola employs it with consistent regularity.

No vocal parts are today notated in either alto or tenor clefs. And only those instruments that in effect combine bass and treble ranges in their over-all compass are notated using the tenor clef. Bassoon, tenor trombone, 'cello, and double bass from time to time employ tenor clef; none of them uses it exclusively.

THE G (OR *TREBLE*) CLEF

The treble-clef (Fr. *clef de sol;* Ger. *G-Schlüssel;* It. *chiave di violino*) sign evolved from an ornamental Latin letter **G** (see Example 4-1). It is the largest of all the clef signs, beginning as it does considerably below the staff and extending above it. Though not so complicated to write as the alto-tenor clef symbols, it does require precision of calligraphy.

All instruments and voices of high range customarily employ the treble clef. These include coloratura or lyric soprano, mezzo-soprano, and alto voices; the right-hand staff part for all keyboard instruments; and such band and orchestra instruments as piccolo, flute, alto flute, oboe, English horn, clarinet, bass clarinet using the so-called "French system" (see page 341), saxophone, horn, trumpet, glockenspiel, xylophone, marimba, vibraphone, antique cymbals, chimes, violin, occasionally viola and 'cello, and the double basses when written extremely high.

HYBRID CLEF-SIGNS

Some published choral music has solved the problem of tenor-voice notation by using the **G**-clef with a joined **8** *beneath* it; by a double clef-sign; or by a variant treble and **C**-clef combined.

EXAMPLE 4-3

There is much to recommend the substitution of the treble-tenor clef-sign for the two forms of the **C**-clef now in use in instrumental music—the alto and the tenor. For one thing, the visual placement of **c′** is almost identical on all three staves.

EXAMPLE 4-4

There is also much to be said for the idea of a bass-clef sign with
a joined **8** *above* it (far left, below). It would be extremely useful for
rather high bass parts that ordinarily would not move into another
clef (bass or baritone voices, tuba, and the like). By the same token, the
bass-clef sign with the joined **8** *below* it (left center) would—if generally adopted—be a useful clef symbol for *8va bassa* transposing instruments (contrabassoon and double basses). Continuing the principle,
the treble clef with the joined **8** *above* (right center) might then be
used for the consistently transposing *8va* instruments (piccolo and
xylophone),* while the treble clef with the joined **15** *above* (far right)
would be a logical clef for the glockenspiel, which habitually transposes
two octaves higher than written. At the present time, however, none of
these hybrid clef-signs is in common use, and none should be written
by the notator without an accompanying explanatory note.

EXAMPLE 4 - 5

PRACTICAL APPLICATIONS

As with every other aspect of notation, the choice of clefs must be
determined by two factors: "Does this make the composer's intention
clear?" and "Will this ensure the best performance possible from the
singers or instrumentalists?" For a ready answer in each notation situation, the notator must first know without question the overlapping
ranges of the four clefs in modern use. These are shown in chart form
in Example 4-6.

So far, the decision is simple. When, however, notes run either higher
or lower than the staff, the notator must choose to employ a new clef,
extensive ledger lines, or one of the octave signs. Here no simple rule
can be offered, for much depends on the basic good sense of the copyist.
But a number of practical suggestions and cautions can be offered for
use until practical experience supersedes them.

1. Extended passages that lie so high above or so low below a staff
as to require constant use of ledger lines (review Chapter 3) should
signal a change of clef. The new clef will be determined by the instru-

---

* This clef-sign is to be found in some modern editions of music for soprano recorder.

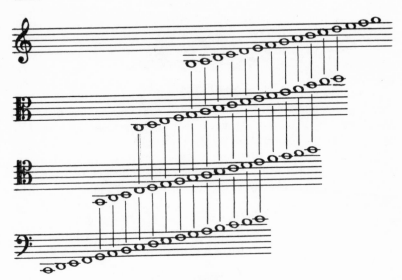

EXAMPLE 4 - 6

ment being written for; a keyboard instrument, for example, would use only treble and bass clefs. When writing for piano, then, if notes below the treble staff go so low as to require many ledger lines, the passage should be notated using the bass clef; if written above the bass staff so as to require many added lines, the treble clef should be used instead. To take an orchestral instrument as a further example— if a passage for the bassoon, normally notated in the bass clef, should go consistently above the staff, the tenor clef should then be employed —not the treble clef, as the bassoonist never uses that clef.

2. On the other hand, the notator should avoid a constant change of clef signs. If a few ledger-lines, or the brief use of one of the octave signs, will suffice, it is better to use them than to change excessively the clef being normally employed. Nothing is more annoying to a performer than an unreasonable change of clef. An irritated performer is a careless or indifferent performer; in either case, the music-making suffers and the composer is done a disservice.

correct notation

unnecessary clef change

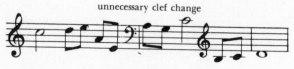

EXAMPLE 4-7

3. In employing the various octave-signs, the rules detailed in Chapter 3 must be kept in mind. One does not use an *8va* sign *over* the bass clef, nor an *8va bassa* sign *beneath* the treble clef.

4. When a change of clef is indicated for any instrument, and the change is to take place at the *beginning* of the following measure, the new sign should be placed *before* the barline (see Examples 4-7, 4-10, 26-15, and 26-19).

5. If the change of clef follows a *unit rest* (a half rest in $\frac{2}{2}$; a quarter rest in $\frac{4}{4}$ or $\frac{2}{4}$; an eighth rest in $\frac{6}{8}$, and so on), the new clef-sign is put just before the next note rather than before the preceding barline.

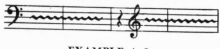

EXAMPLE 4-8

6. Should the change of clef become necessary within the measure, the new sign is placed *before* the note it affects (example below) unless by so doing the rhythmic division of the measure becomes obscure (left-hand example on the bottom line). It is better in this second example to place the new clef-sign before the unit rests (eighth and sixteenth) rather than immediately before the following note, as this plan shows the metrical division of the measure more clearly (right-hand example on the bottom line).

EXAMPLE 4-9

7. It will be observed that the changing clef-signs are normally written slightly *smaller* than those put at the beginning of each staff line.

8. As a reminder, the sign is sometimes put in parentheses (⟨),
especially when it is to be used by an instrument that does not regularly read in that particular clef.

9. It is also customary to indicate the change of clef at the very end
of a staff if the new clef is to take effect at the beginning of the next
staff (as in Example 4-14).

Once he is master of the flexible resources of his clefs, the notator
or composer may employ them as he considers most practical and most
expedient.

MODERN INNOVATIONS

Although strictly speaking it is not a twentieth-century innovation, we
must mention here the simultaneous use of *two* clef-signs on one staff.
This occurs mainly in keyboard compositions when it is necessary to
show the prolongation of notes on one staff and a new tone (or chord)
following in the same hand, but at an extreme level. To notate this
otherwise would mean either an excessive number of ledger lines, or
the necessity of a third staff (example at the left). Held sonorities in
the left hand, notated in the treble clef, are sometimes followed by
very low notes in the bass clef; these also require the use of two clef-
signs on one staff. Such an instance may be found in Debussy's *La
Danse de Puck* from the *Préludes pour Piano* (example at the right):

EXAMPLE 4-10

Modern composers have frequently used the existing clefs in unorthodox ways. This practice is most clearly illustrated in the orchestral
scores of the twelve-tonalists (Arnold Schönberg and many of his fol-
lowers), where all the instrumental parts are written at concert pitch
(non-transposed). To obviate the use of more than two clef-signs (treble

and bass), instruments that normally might use the tenor clef for high parts are now written on the treble staff (the bassoon, tenor trombone, and 'cello). Also, instruments that normally use the treble clef but frequently go well below it in sounding pitch (clarinet, English horn, horn, and trumpet, for example) are frequently written in non-transposing scores on the bass staff.

Some contemporary composers (or their publishers, at least) omit clef signs altogether for instruments that customarily use but one clef. In the *Zeitmasse* for winds by Karlheinz Stockhausen, to cite one example, the flute, oboe, English horn, and clarinet parts are written in the score without any clef-signs at all, as these instruments by tradition use only the treble clef. The bassoon part, however, has bass or treble clef shown in Stockhausen's score, but only at those places where the clef changes; otherwise the sign is omitted, the previous clef continuing until a change is indicated.

The omission of clef signs is a common practice in the instrumental parts of jazz and other popular music (see Chapter 24). As many jazz players read only one clef, it is not thought necessary to put a clef sign at the beginning of each line. This practice has sometimes been extended to include arrangements for high school and semiprofessional orchestras and bands, but it is not endorsed by professional musicians. There is perhaps a certain amount of justification for omitting clef signs in individual parts, but a full score should present them even when they are obvious. There are already enough hazards in the reading of complicated contemporary scores, without the added confusion caused by omitted clef-signs.

A more legitimate and logical short cut in clef usage is shown in all the more recent printed scores of Igor Stravinsky. When one particular clef-sign is used for adjacent staves, the sign is placed in the customary manner on the uppermost staff, and a vertical line is then drawn to the bottom of the lowest staff to employ the identical clef-sign. (See Example 2-7.)

The standard clef-signs have frequently been placed in unorthodox positions by avant-garde composers; a few of these are shown below:

EXAMPLE 4-11

Note in the last two examples above that the dots have been omitted in the bass-clef symbol and that the customary jog at the bottom of the treble-clef sign is missing.

Modern variations on the alto-tenor clef symbol are illustrated in Example 4-12, together with two entirely new indications for treble and bass clefs. In all fairness, one must admit that these have considerable eye appeal and are simple to draw. Furthermore, they can be used for alto-tenor clef positions as well. Modern notation can surely benefit from the adoption of such concise, logical, and unequivocal symbols.

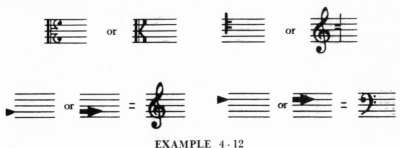

EXAMPLE 4-12

NOTATION EXERCISES

1. Notate the following examples in the proper clefs for the indicated instruments and voice:

Trombone

Viola

Flute

Tenor

The — first — No - ël the — an - gel did say,

EXAMPLE 4-13

2. Rewrite the following passage for bassoon, with a minimum of clef changes, using the correct clef:

EXAMPLE 4 - 14

5
Note-heads and Stems

PROPERLY WRITTEN, A MUSICAL *NOTE* (FROM THE
Latin *nota*, meaning "sign" or "mark") indicates without question
two aspects of a musical sound. It is first a symbol indicating—by its
position on the staff and by the clef used—a definite *pitch* to be played
or sung. And second, it establishes—by the exact appearance of its three
integral parts—the relative time *duration* of this musical sound.

NOTES

Individual note-symbols (Fr. *note,* pl. *notes;* Ger. *Note,* pl. *Noten;* It.
nota, pl. *note*) must be unequivocal combinations of three elements:
1. The *note-head.* This is somewhat oval in shape, and is either open
   (or "white"—*o*) or closed ("black"— *●*).
2. The *stem.* This is the thin vertical line joined to the side of the
   note-head (white or black). When the stem is to go *down,* it is placed
   on the *left* side of the note-head— *♩ ♩* . When the stem is to go *up,*
   it is put on the *right* side of the note-head—*♩ ♩* .*
3. The *flag* (also called a *hook, tail,* or *pennant*). This is a curved
   stroke joined to the end of the stem, and always goes to the *right*
   of the stem— *♪ ♪* —never to the left. This note-element will be
   fully treated in Chapter 6.
   When the note-symbol is complete—black or white; with a stem or
without; carrying a certain number of flags or no flags at all—the
entity represents a fixed, though relative, time-span. This time-value
is measured by musicians as a certain number of beats or fractions of

---

* It is not considered correct to reverse these positions, even though one sees this
practice in old manuscripts (those of J. S. Bach, for example) and in some modern
scores—notably the early holograph scores of Igor Stravinsky.

the beat. The orderly succession of these time-values in a definite mathematical relationship gives our notation the designation of *ortho-chronic* (from the Greek *ortho,* meaning "correct," and *chronos,* meaning "time").

This established and regular relation between the various written notes is illustrated by the accompanying Table of Notes. In this table the longest time-value is the double whole-note, though this value appears very rarely in ordinary practice. Beginning with the double whole-note, each succeeding note-value represents exactly one-half the preceding value, and twice that of the next lower note-value.

As tables are included in this manual only with the aim of becoming the automatic resource of the notator and the performer, a quick visual organization of the Table of Notes may be used to assist memorization. These general observations might be made:

1. That outside of the fairly obsolete double whole-note, there are only two *open* note-heads: the *whole* note and the *half* note.
2. That these two forms are easily distinguished: the whole note by the *absence* of a stem; the half note by the *presence* of a stem.
3. That the filled-in, or black, note-form can represent some six different values, depending upon the number of *flags* employed.
4. That the black note-head is never used without a stem.
5. That a stem without any flags represents one of two different note-values: the half note ♩ and the quarter note ♩.

STEMS

For *stem direction,* the general rules are simple. When the note-head is *above* the center line of the staff, the stem (Fr. *queue,* pl. *queues;* Ger. *Hals,* pl. *Hälse;* It. *asta,* pl. *aste,* or *gamba,* pl. *gambe*) goes *down* (example at the left, below). When the note is *below* the middle line of the staff, the stem goes *up* (center example). When the note is centered on the staff (on the third line), the stem *may* go in either direction, although it is the more common practice to draw it *down* (example at the right).

EXAMPLE 5-1

Proper *stem length* is proportional: that is, it is measured in terms of the note-position on the staff. Generally the stem length is one octave (eight staff degrees), which means that the end of the stem touches the

EXAMPLE 5 - 2. TABLE OF NOTES

Note symbol	Terminology				
	AMERICAN	BRITISH	FRENCH	GERMAN	ITALIAN
	Double whole-note	Breve	Double-ronde	Doppelganze **or** Doppelganzenote	Breve
	Whole note	Semibreve	Ronde	Ganze **or** Ganzenote	Semibreve
	Half note	Minim	Blanche	Halbe **or** Halbenote	Minima **or** Bianca
	Quarter note	Crochet	Noire	Viertel **or** Viertelnote	Semiminima **or** Nera
	Eighth note	Quaver	Croche	Achtel **or** Achtelnote	Croma
	Sixteenth note	Semiquaver	Double-croche	Sechzehntel **or** Sechzehntelnote	Semicroma
	Thirty-second note	Demisemiquaver	Quadruple-croche	Zweiunddreissigstel **or** Zweiunddreissigstelnote	Biscroma
	Sixty-fourth note	Hemidemisemiquaver	Octuple-croche	Vierundsechzigstel **or** Vierundsechzigstelnote	Semibiscroma
	One hundred and twenty-eighth note	Semihemidemisemiquaver	Cent-vingt-huitième (note)	Hundert und achtundzwanzigstel **or** Hundert und achtundzwanzigstelnote	Cento-ventottavo (nota)

line or space an octave higher or lower than its note-head. This principle is not literally observed when the end of the stem is extended
above the second added space over the staff (for upward stems) or below the second added space under the staff (for downward stems) as
shown below. Such stems are usually somewhat shortened (second line
of music).

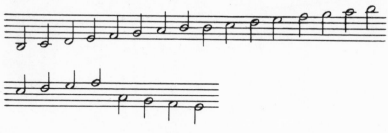

EXAMPLE 5 - 3

For all note-heads that lie higher than the second added space above
the staff, a downward stem-end touches the middle staff line (left, below); likewise, for all note-heads positioned lower than the second
added space below the staff, upward stems are similarly drawn to the
middle line (right, below).

EXAMPLE 5 - 4

Careful comparison of the two examples below will demonstrate the
greater clarity of this unorthodox notational practice. If the stems here
were proportional throughout, they would become somewhat lost
among ledger lines, especially if flags were joined to the stems. The
addition of beams (see Chapter 6) would further obscure the ledger
lines.

EXAMPLE 5 - 5

If one or two flags (see also pages 79–80) are joined to the stem, the length of the stem remains the same as for half notes and quarter notes. Three flags (for the 32nd note) require an even longer stem. Generally speaking, for each additional flag beyond the eighth-note or sixteenth-note forms, the stem is lengthened by two staff degrees.

EXAMPLE 5 - 6

TRADITIONAL PRACTICES

Choice of note-size and stem-length, matters of placement on the staff— all are strictly regulated for the sake of clarity, and not as devious tortures. In order that the notator and the performer may be familiar with the situations most frequently recurring, they are described below under headings designed to make them readily accessible.

1. **Trills**   Separate stems are required when out of a structure of two or more notes only one note is trilled (example at the left, below). If one should write a single stem connecting both notes, it would indicate that both notes are to be trilled (right, below). (See also material on trills, pages 232–234.)

EXAMPLE 5 - 7

2. **Ossia Passages**   Alternate, or *ossia*, notes (refer to page 31) in instrumental parts, in sonatas for chamber ensemble, or in vocal and choral music are always written in small notes, whether on a supplementary staff or on the normal staff. Frequently they are also enclosed in parentheses.

EXAMPLE 5 - 8

3. **Double-stemmed Unisons**   In contrapuntal music two different voices often come together on a unison note, a fact that the
notator must make clear by a very exact indication. If the time-value
of a unison note is the same in both voices, a single note-head with
stems up and down usually suffices.

EXAMPLE 5 - 9

A double stem on a single note-head may be used when the rhythmic
distinction of either stem is quite clear, as in the first example, below.
But separate note-heads with stems up and down are absolutely essential when the basic unit for counting is different, as in the second and
third lines of music.

EXAMPLE 5 - 10

When two separate note-heads are required for a unison, it is important to differentiate the voices clearly. The note having its stem *up*
(almost invariably the upper voice) is positioned first, to the left, while
the note with a *downward* stem (lower voice, usually) goes to the right

—as shown in the previous two lower examples. The validity of this principle is especially apparent when the down-stemmed note is dotted (left-hand example below). When, however, the upward-stemmed note is dotted, it is positioned to the right so that the dot will not be obscured (right, below).

and

not

EXAMPLE 5 · 11

A unison note sometimes consists of a stemmed note and an unstemmed one (as a quarter note or a half note next to a whole note). It is better to put the stemmed note to the right, so that its stem does not touch the whole note.

and

not

EXAMPLE 5 · 12

4. Intervals, Chords   Intervals (involving two note-heads) or chords (three or more note-heads) may use a single stem to join all the notes as a unit provided they are of equal value. The direction of the stem has to be determined by the general position of the chord or interval on the staff. If most of the notes lie at the *top* of the staff, the stem will ordinarily go *down* (far left, below). If the chord is positioned on the *bottom* part of the staff, the stem usually goes *up* (left center). When chord notes are both high and low on the staff, the direction of the stem has to be determined by the *available room* above or below the staff (right center and far right). Common sense should determine which direction is best for visual clarity.

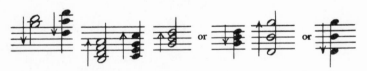

EXAMPLE 5 · 13

Even when the rhythmic values are equal, *two stems* rather than one may be required to outline a voice-leading. Note-heads and stems are then arranged as shown in Example 5-14.

Two stems are also required on a chord if it serves two *different rhythmic functions,* such as the sustained quarter-notes and the alter-

EXAMPLE 5-14

nating eighth-note pattern seen in the left-hand example below. This
pattern can also be correctly notated as shown at the right.

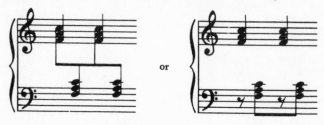

or

EXAMPLE 5-15

When an inner note of a static chord moves to another pitch—that
is, when its time-value is different from that of the other chord members—the note should be placed *outside* of the rest of the chord, with
its stem going in the opposite direction (left, below). If, however, the
moving voice begins with a dotted note, this must always be placed
to the right of the chord proper (center, below); otherwise the dot will
interfere with the chord notes. It most certainly cannot be put at the
other side of the chord stem!

EXAMPLE 5-16

The necessity for clear placement of stems in such chords or intervals
is illustrated in Example 5-17. From the notation at the left, one
is not sure whether the upper two notes are held (as interpreted
by the center illustration) or whether only the highest note is to be sustained as a quarter note (the interpretation shown at the right). Either

EXAMPLE 5-17

of the latter two notations is perfectly clear in meaning, while the left-hand notation is not.

The interval of a *second* (the two notes on adjacent scale-steps) should be written with the stem *between* the note-heads (Example 5-18). The higher pitch is always placed to the *right*, never to the left, regardless of stem direction. When, however, *separate stems* must be used for seconds, they are usually aligned vertically; the higher note is then placed to the left (example at the right, below).

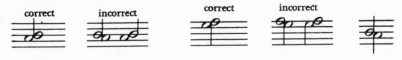

EXAMPLE 5 - 18

Likewise, chords consisting of notes of equal duration and containing tones a second apart should be written with the stem centered between the component note-heads of this interval. Observe that the "adjacent" tone (which creates the interval of the second) is placed to the *right* of the chord when the stem is *upward,* and to the *left* of the chord when the stem goes *down* (left and center examples). If the chord consists of unstemmed notes—whole notes or dotted whole-notes—the note placement is exactly the same as though a stem were being used (example at the right).

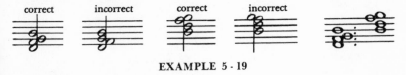

EXAMPLE 5 - 19

With intervals or chords that contain seconds, the rule for vertical alignment is the same whether the two structures are on one staff or divided between two or more. The note-heads that determine stem direction are aligned perpendicularly from top to bottom (as shown below on two staves).

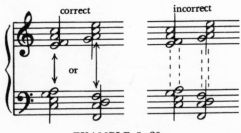

EXAMPLE 5 - 20

MODERN INNOVATIONS

1. Note Shapes   Throughout musical history, unorthodox note-shapes have frequently appeared as the notational code of one composer, and this is no less true in our own century (refer to Example K). A case in point is the "time-notation" of the American avant-gardist Earle Brown. To show the duration of individual notes this composer elongates the note-heads (minus stems) instead of using the standard shapes traditionally placed. For example:

EXAMPLE 5 - 21. Earle Brown: From *Hodograph I* (1959)

Berio, on the other hand, usually employs conventional note-heads with stems for his own brand of "time notation," but places them at linear distances from note to note proportionate to their "distances" in time. (See Example 27-1.) Though both systems have a logic quite independent of the conventional note-symbols, reading such music necessitates a complete re-education of the eye.

2. Stemming Without Note-heads   Among the interesting variants of stemming in modern music notation is the use of a stem, with or without flags and beams, not attached to any note-head. This device is used by some composers for spoken words in a choral composition or for the *Sprechstimme* effect.

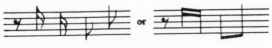

EXAMPLE 5-22

Small stems, appropriately flagged or beamed but again not attached to note-heads, have been used by Béla Bartók and certain other composers to mark off pulsations in an extended *glissando*. The stems, therefore, are used to show the beats of the measure and have no precise pitch significance.

EXAMPLE 5-23

3. Stemming Altered Unisons   One of the most intriguing modern stemming problems relates to *altered unisons*: a single note that is to be played simultaneously in two forms—as a natural and a flat (**G** natural and **G** flat, for instance); or as a natural and a sharp (**C** natural and **C** sharp). Two problems are actually present: where to place the accidentals (see Chapter 9), and where to put the stem(s). The first problem is solved by putting the correct accidental before each of the written note-heads. The stemming question is answered in a variety of ways. One solution is to begin the stems on the normally correct side of the note-head; that is, to the left if the stem goes *down*, and to the right if the stem goes *up*. Then both stems are bent inward to join a common perpendicular stem, up or down (example at the left, below). Another way of notating altered unisons is to write the two notes with normal stems—one up, one down—with a *bracket* placed over or under the two notes to show that they are to be played simultaneously (center, below). Still another method is to write a double note-head with single stem and two accidental signs (right, below).

EXAMPLE 5-24

When more than the two notes of an altered unison are involved in a chord structure or cluster, a single stem joins the notes that do *not* comprise the altered unison. Note that, in the examples shown at the left below, the central common stem has to be considerably lengthened so as to accommodate the bent stem joining it.

When three or more notes are present in the context of an altered unison, and one of these pitches is somewhat removed from the unison, the following notational variant is used: the common stem joins the highest and lowest notes of the structure, and the stem of the inner note is bent to join the common stem just above the lowest written note (examples at the right).

EXAMPLE 5 - 25

Another variation of this modern stemming problem occurs when the two lowest members of the chord are the altered unison notes. In the instance below it would be too crowded to bend the f♮′ stem to join the common stem in the middle; therefore, it is bent upward from the bottom of a normal perpendicular stem to join the lower end of the stem linking f♯′ and d″.

EXAMPLE 5 - 26

For an altered unison combined with an adjacent scale-step, a straight stem goes up or down from the middle note, the other two stems being bent to join it as in the examples given below. Note that the altered unison shown below is separated by the lowest *sounding* note; this is done to show the three different pitches more clearly.

EXAMPLE 5 - 27

4. Clusters   In keyboard chords or sonorities that are cluster-like in formation—meaning they contain many tones a second apart—the component notes should be arranged by lines and spaces. That is to say, all the notes occupying *spaces* are vertically aligned together, and all those on *lines* are likewise vertically aligned. This principle holds good regardless of the number of notes in the sonority—whether three, four, five, or more.

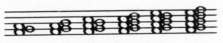

EXAMPLE 5 - 28

In densely constructed clusters containing too many notes to write individually, only the top and bottom pitches are written, with a thick vertical bar drawn from one note-center to the other. If the outer limits of the cluster formation exceed a single staff, two staves may be employed, and the thick bar used to join the note-heads on each separate staff. (See Examples 18-33 and 18-34.)

SUGGESTED PRACTICES

Though modern orthochronic notation varies the stems and flags added to the note-heads to indicate their relative time-values, the note-heads themselves are uniformly of one shape. If the other elements may vary, we may well ask why the note-shape itself may not occasionally be altered to serve a useful function.

Proposals for changing the existing note-shapes are periodically advanced by eccentrics and serious musicians alike. One such proposal, made in 1919 by the Russian Nicolas Obouhov, suggested that all accidentals could be eliminated by notating sharped notes (or their enharmonic equivalents) as X's rather than standard oval notes preceded by a sharp sign.

EXAMPLE 5 - 29

Rhythmic values were to be indicated as follows:

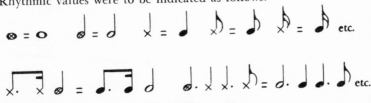

EXAMPLE 5 - 30

Other than in compositions by Obouhov himself and two brief piano pieces by Arthur Honegger, this proposed system has made no noticeable impact on the current development of notation.

The triangular-shaped note is used by some orchestral composers for—of all instruments—the triangle! A cross, or ✗ , is also used by many orchestrators as notation for certain percussion instruments of indefinite pitch, such as cymbals or drums (see pages 365 and 367). And the diamond-shaped note has long been used in string notation to designate a harmonic (see page 385). Other than the diamond notes for string harmonics, however, these odd note-shapes have had only sporadic use.

Yet there is a sensible historic precedent for shaped notes in the hymns, spirituals, and fuguing tunes of the southern United States; and in the *fasola* (fa-sol-la) system of solmization (singing with scale-syllables) much used in both England and the United States during the seventeenth and eighteenth centuries. Around 1802 a vocal instruction book was put out by one William Little, who utilized the following note-forms for a seven-note scale:

fa   sol   la   fa   sol   la   mi   fa

EXAMPLE 5-31

Even today Mr. Little's four note-shapes may be found in such hymn-tune collections as *The Sacred Harp,* first published around 1850. But their function is to indicate not time-values but only a position in the scale.

Why not, I propose, overcome ingrained habit when it hampers us? Why not utilize the advantages of shaped notes in modern music by employing them in the metric and rhythmic sense, as Henry Cowell suggested in his admirable *New Musical Resources?* This proposal, I realize, cannot be given weighty consideration until the aspirant notator has completed the material on notating meters (Chapter 10), but it does concern note-heads and so is presented here as a preview —to be returned to at a later and more learned hour. Here, then, is the essence of the scheme:

Because we have no single symbols in notation that express rhythmic units other than one (the whole note) and its divisions (the half note, quarter note, eighth note, and so on), Cowell suggested the employment of new note-shapes to express three, five, seven, and higher values that cannot now be notated by means of a single sign. The chart on the opposite page shows the proposed note-shapes and their values.

In spite of the logic and conciseness of Cowell's proposal, it has made no more impact on modern notation than Obouhov's suggestion, previously discussed.

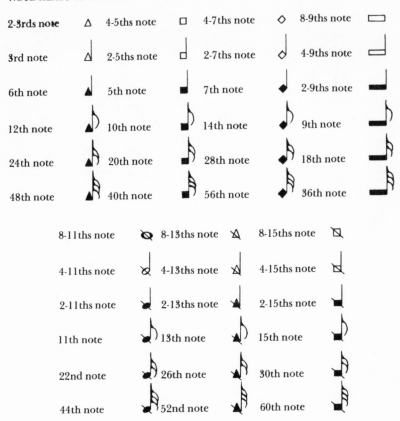

EXAMPLE 5 - 32

NOTATION EXERCISES

1. Add stems to the following note-heads according to the principles of stem direction:

EXAMPLE 5 - 33

2. In the following example change the direction of the stems wherever required. Place each stem on the proper side of the note-head, and lengthen or shorten it to the correct proportion.

EXAMPLE 5 - 34

3. Arrange the following sequences of four notes into vertical chords, and place a stem on each chord:

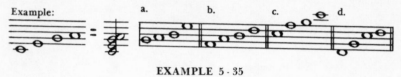

EXAMPLE 5 - 35

4. Write an original example for an instrument or voice of your choice, using some of the shaped notes given in Example 5-32.

6

Flags and Beams

In CHAPTER 5 WE BECAME FAMILIAR WITH THE SHAPE
and color of note-heads and with the manipulation of note-stems. We
must now consider the remaining elements that indicate the time-value
of a note: the separate *flags*, and the *beaming* that substitutes for individual flags in groups of small-value notes.

FLAGS

In modern notation *flags* (Fr. *crochet*, pl. *crochets*; Ger. *Fähnchen*, pl.
Fähnchen; It. *coda uncinata*, pl. *code uncinate*), or *tails*, are employed
to indicate the relative time-values of the notes with black note-heads
from the eighth note to the 128th note. The pattern of our orthochronic
notation is very exact: each succeeding note has *half* the time-value of
its predecessor in the scheme. The employment of flags is equally
precise. The eighth note has half the time-value of a quarter note, and
carries one flag on the right of its stem. The sixteenth note has half
the time-value of an eighth note, and carries two flags. Each successive
fractional note-value requires one additional flag, so that the 128th
note displays five flags. (See the Table of Notes on page 65.)

The earliest form of the flag—dating from the fifteenth to the seventeenth centuries, as illustrated in the chart of mensural notation on
page 15—was a short, slanted line added to the top of the stem: ♪ .
The flag of the modern eighth-note is made as a thin curved line that
flares from slightly below the top of an upward stem to just opposite
the middle of the note-head (left-hand note in the example below).
When a dot follows the note-head, the end of the curved line is often
shortened so as not to conflict with the dot (center note in the example).
On a downward stem the curved line, which here goes up, barely
touches the bottom of the note-head (right-hand note below).

EXAMPLE 6-1

For each additional flag beyond two, the stem is extended by two staff degrees, and the new flag is drawn parallel to the previous one(s), with the additional curved line joining the curved line of the first flag. As previously stated, flags always go to the *right* of the stem, regardless of whether the stem goes up or down (see page 63).

The 64th note and the 128th note are somewhat uncommon in to-day's music, doubtless because they are clumsy to notate. Besides, the eye does not quickly take in four or five flags, or their equivalent in beaming.

On the other hand, both 16ths and 32nds are quite common both as small note-values and as beats in a measure. Signatures of $\frac{9}{16}$, $\frac{12}{16}$, or of $\frac{3}{32}$, $\frac{8}{32}$, and so on may be found in much contemporary music (see Chapter 10). But to find 64th and 128th notes copiously employed one must go back to such nineteenth-century works as the piano and chamber music of Beethoven. See, for instance, the opening pages of the *Sonata Pathétique* for piano. Other works of Beethoven illustrating the use of 128th notes include: *Piano Sonata in c minor,* Op. 10, No. 1 (*Molto adagio*); *Piano Sonata in E-flat major,* Op. 27, No. 1 (*Adagio*); *Violin Sonata,* Op. 47, "*Kreutzer*" (fourth variation of the *Andante*); *Violin Sonata,* Op. 30, No. 2 (*Adagio*).

BEAMS

Beams (Fr. *barre,* pl. *barres;* Ger. *Balken,* pl. *Balken;* It. *barra,* pl. *barre*), first introduced into music notation in the early eighteenth century, are compound flags used to connect notes in note-groups. The number of beams (sometimes called *ligatures*) always equals the number of flags appropriate for each note. Groups of eighth notes, for example, require one beam; of sixteenth notes, two beams; of 32nd notes, three beams; of 64th notes, four beams; and of 128th notes, five beams. Although minor variations in size occur even in published music, beams are normally the thickness of half a staff space. Eighth- and sixteenth-note beams may be accommodated on the usual stem length of one octave; for each additional beam the stem is extended one staff degree. This principle applies also to notes on ledger lines above or below the staff; if these stems touch the center staff-line, they must be lengthened, too, for three or more attached beams.

Beams are obviously serviceable: they visually demonstrate the metrical and rhythmic divisions within the measure (and, as we shall see later in the chapter, also indicate note-groupings in opposition to the normal patterns of the measure). No comment is necessary to point out the superior clarity of the beamed example below as opposed to the contrasting dense forest of individual flags outlining the same pattern.

EXAMPLE 6-2

The visual advantages of beaming can be further illustrated by a comparison of the following two versions of a compound two-beat meter (see material on meters, Chapter 10).

EXAMPLE 6-3

In the example at the left above, no beams are required—the meter being $\frac{6}{4}$, with the quarter note as the counting unit. However, it is not immediately obvious to the eye what the pulsation actually is: it could be either 3 plus 3 (normal for a six-count measure—left, below) or 2 plus 2 plus 2 (normal for a three-count measure—right). Only the use of accents or phrase-marks (as shown below) would indicate the division desired by the composer.

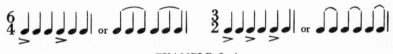

EXAMPLE 6-4

When, however, the same pattern is beamed—as in the $\frac{6}{8}$ version paired with the first $\frac{6}{4}$ version (Example 6-3)—the beams immediately show the *natural division* of the measure, so that accents or phrasing are not necessary in the metric sense, and can be reserved to indicate expressive qualities in the music.

If different note-values are brought into the measure groups, the use of beaming for clarity is even more firmly dictated. The unbeamed pattern of the example on the first line below might signify either $\frac{6}{4}$ (compound duple time) or $\frac{3}{2}$ (syncopation in triple time). But if we should change the notation to correctly beamed and flagged $\frac{6}{8}$ or $\frac{3}{4}$, it would be immediately evident what basic pulse was required (examples on the second line).

EXAMPLE 6 - 5

Still, the aspirant notator must not be misled into considering beaming a medicine for all ills. It is more accurate to employ simple flagging rather than beams when beams would confuse the subdivision of the measure rather than make it more clear. A simple syncopated figure, for instance, is often better notated with flags rather than by beaming two adjacent eighth-notes, for such beaming disguises the normal measure division between the second and third beats.

EXAMPLE 6 - 6

In the section that follows, we shall discuss under appropriate headings some flagging and beaming problems frequently met, and outline the logic underlying at least one satisfactory solution for each problem.

TRADITIONAL PRACTICES

1. **Primary Beams**   Beams are most usefully considered in two categories: primary and secondary. *Primary beams* are those that link an entire note-group; in other words, the primary beam is an unbroken one. *Secondary beams* are those that are interrupted or else are partially broken.

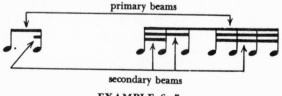

EXAMPLE 6 - 7

Note-stems should always extend to the primary beam, going through all secondary beams, as shown in the example at the left, below. A few foreign editions (French, mainly) print beams as shown at the right, but the overwhelming bulk of printed music employs the method first illustrated.

correct   incorrect

EXAMPLE 6 - 8

Primary beams must always make clear the *inner divisions* of the meter. If the notator must choose between flagging and beaming, it will be on this basis. In the example at the left below, for instance, the use of flagged notes (which might be indicated because of the staccato dots) makes the passage appear as a possible $\frac{6}{8}$. Beamed as in the example at the right, it is clearly in $\frac{3}{4}$.

ambiguous   clear

EXAMPLE 6 - 9

If there are dotted notes (see Chapter 8) that obscure the normal division of the measure (example at the left, below) it may be better to substitute a tied note for the dot and thus extend the beam (example at the right).

unclear   clear

EXAMPLE 6 - 10

The normal division to be observed in a $\frac{6}{8}$ measure—♫ ♫—must be kept in mind when the value of a quarter note is substituted for two eighth-notes. The example at the left below correctly indicates the two groups of three by tieing two eighth-notes, so that the beaming may show a group of three. The example in the center would incorrectly indicate a $\frac{3}{4}$ measure, and would be justified only if a pronounced three-against-two rhythm were demanded (see Chapter 11). When, however, there is simultaneous use of compound duple and simple triple time—as in the first movement of Brahms's *Symphony No. 2 in D major,* at letter **B**—a patently $\frac{6}{8}$ beaming is frequently encountered in $\frac{3}{4}$ measure.

2. Secondary Beams   For secondary beams, as for primary beams, the fundamental rule is that they must always be broken in

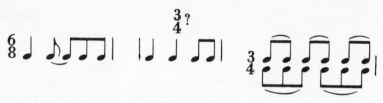

EXAMPLE 6 - 11

such a way as to indicate correctly the *measure rhythm*. For this reason, the example at the left below is obviously more accurate than the one at the right.

EXAMPLE 6 - 12

The general procedure for achieving this clarity is to break the secondary beams according to the smaller units of the beat. If the beat is a quarter note (as in $\frac{2}{4}$, $\frac{3}{4}$, $\frac{4}{4}$, $\frac{5}{4}$, and so on), the units would be *two* eighth-notes per beat (beaming shown at the left, below). If the beat is a dotted quarter (in $\frac{12}{8}$, $\frac{9}{8}$, $\frac{6}{8}$, $\frac{3}{8}$), then the units within each beat would be equal to *three* eighth-notes (example at the right). Observe again that the stems go through the secondary beams; it is not considered correct to notate otherwise.

EXAMPLE 6 - 13

3. **Broken Beams**   All secondary beams are by definition broken in some way, but here we shall consider especially those broken beams illustrating some general principle. First, *mixed rhythmic values* have to be expressed by breaking one or more secondary beams. When the flagged notes at the left below are combined under a beam (center example below), it must be noted that the broken beam is always placed *inside* the group, never outside it!

EXAMPLE 6 - 14

When such broken beams are used within groups of three, four, or more notes, the broken beam points in the direction of the note of which it is a fraction (left-hand examples on next page). The principle is more apparent if we think of the first figure notated as on the second line of Example 6-15.

EXAMPLE 6-15

Broken beaming is not simply a convenient grouping of notes within the meter. It is also useful to point out the *end of a phrase* or the *beginning* of a new one. For this reason, the example at the left below —though not so academic as the one at the right—is actually preferable for its clarity. Broken beams are also helpful in calling attention to a *sudden change* of accent or dynamics (second line, below).

EXAMPLE 6-16

One might call such a momentary evasion of beaming principles "psychological beaming"; the evasion, in other words, is justified by increased reading facility and musical comprehension. In the example below, the normal pattern of six sixteenth-notes to the half-measure in $\frac{6}{8}$ is broken into three groups of two in order to dramatize the special inner accents.

EXAMPLE 6-17

If this type of broken beaming occurs between the two staves of keyboard music, or in any other music notated on two staves, the beaming pattern is usually as shown in Example 6-18. Here the interrupted secondary beams are positioned *below* the primary beam rather than above it. There is, however, no hard and fast rule governing this practice; therefore, secondary beams placed above the primary beam may sometimes be found in similar notational situations.

EXAMPLE 6 · 18

Even *primary beams* sometimes have to be broken for practical considerations—because there is insufficient space above or below the staff for writing the note-group (example at the left). Here, as we see, it would require too much space over the treble staff to put the primary beam above; nor should it be placed below, on account of the medium position of the chord on the staff. Moving the *8va* sign to the left and then dropping the chord into the ledger-line basement is likewise an awkward notation.

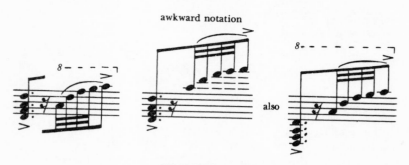

EXAMPLE 6 · 19

The only practical solution, then, in terms of space and proper use of the *8va* sign, is to break the primary beam as shown in Example 6-19, at the left.

By now it is surely evident that the notator must approach his decisions with a flexible mind. In order that he may be flexible within the bounds of acceptable practice, we offer a Table of Beaming Patterns citing representative examples (by no means complete) of normal beaming patterns in the various common meters. (Example 6-20.)

EXAMPLE 6 - 20. TABLE OF BEAMING PATTERNS

4. **Beaming Placement**   The problem of placing flags and
beams above or below the staff is solved by the same general principles
that govern stem direction. If the majority of stems (marked in Example 6-21 with asterisks) normally go *up* in the group to be beamed,
then all the stems will go *up* and the beams will be placed *above* the
notes (example at the left). If, on the other hand, most of the notes
require a *downward* stem (if most of the note-heads lie above the staff
center), then the stems of all the notes must be written *down* and the
beams placed *below* the note-heads (right-hand example).

EXAMPLE 6 - 21

The *direction* of all beams, whether confined to one staff or divided
between two or more, should more or less parallel the main body of
notes they connect. For the best visual effect the beams should, moreover, follow the *over-all contour* of the note-group, although there will
be instances where space limitations will dictate otherwise. The eye
must be the final judge, for the correct solution is the one that produces
the clearest and neatest visual result (see Example 6-21).

For this reason, when beaming a figure that begins and ends at the
same pitch level, the beam should be horizontal, and not slanted in the
direction of the majority of the notes (examples on the top line). Short
groups of alternating notes should also be beamed on the level instead
of slanting from first to last (second line, below).

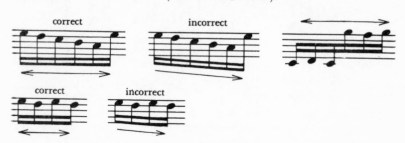

EXAMPLE 6 - 22

5. **Exceptional Beaming**   Exceptional forms of beaming are
sometimes necessary when there are very high and very low notes in a
group to be beamed on one staff. When this problem occurs, it is

proper to place the beams *midway* between the note-groups, slanting in the general direction of one group of the note-heads. (See the right-hand illustration in the first line of Example 6-22 for an exception to this rule.)

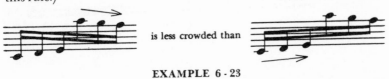

EXAMPLE 6 - 23

The beaming shown in Example 6-23 is especially suitable for pointillistic music, in which notes constantly alternate between high and low. Even if the high and low notes are relatively static, it is best to slant the beams slightly for easier readability (left, below). The only alternative to this procedure would be to write the necessary beams *entirely* over or under the note-groups, which can often be exceedingly clumsy and space-consuming.

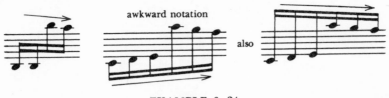

EXAMPLE 6 - 24

Even short groups containing only two or three notes can be beamed midway between the notes if the space between the staves is crowded.

EXAMPLE 6 - 25

An expert notator quickly learns that many notational situations are in a sense exceptional, and salts his notational principles with a generous pinch of common sense. When, for instance, he encounters a *very large group* of notes of unequal number in relation to beat or measure, he beams them together. (See Example 6-26.)

When *grace notes* (single, or in groups) must be combined with normal beaming, he makes the picture clear by drawing the grace-note stems, flags, and beams in the direction opposite that of the regular notes, if it is logical or possible to do so, as in Example 6-27.

EXAMPLE 6·26. Frédéric Chopin: From *Impromptu,* Op. 29

EXAMPLE 6·27

And if beams are required on groups of *altered unisons* (see page 73), he will be able to devise some clear indication such as the following:

EXAMPLE 6·28

MODERN INNOVATIONS

Among the many beaming practices transformed in twentieth-century notation the foremost is *beaming over barlines*. A primary cause for this phenomenon is the prevalence of syncopated rhythms, for consistent syncopation employing beamed notes is more logical and more graphic when the beaming is carried across the existing barlines.

EXAMPLE 6·29

Beaming over barlines also makes especially intelligible *ostinato*-like figures of equal metric length (although not necessarily of equal note-values) displaced in reference to normal recurrence of the beat. A version beamed over the barlines (example on the first line below) is easier to comprehend than one notated in a more traditional fashion (example on the bottom line).

more clear

less clear

EXAMPLE 6 - 30

Sometimes a lengthy section, or even an entire movement of a work, will be notated with the beaming carried consistently over the barlines. Such an example may be found in Serge Prokofiev's *Classical Symphony,* the *Larghetto* movement, in which one section is beamed as follows:

EXAMPLE 6 - 31

A consistent practitioner of such beaming habits, Igor Stravinsky in his early *Etude in F♯ major* for piano employed this same device for all but the last five measures. And in his *Chant du rossignol* (at No. 23), for another instance, he used the following pattern for a three-note *ostinato:*

EXAMPLE 6 - 32

This type of beaming is essential when several metrical arrangements within a basic time-signature are used. In Aram Khachaturian's *Piano Concerto,* for example, the composer notated a $\frac{3}{8}$ pattern in a basic $\frac{2}{4}$ meter by a consistent beaming of the groups of three (last movement, measure 304 and following).

EXAMPLE 6 - 33

Irregular beaming over barlines is valid also when *rhythmic imitation* is involved between two or more voices or instrumental parts. The following pattern of irregular beaming was used by Arnold Schönberg in his *Variations for Orchestra* (see measures 72–73) to show clearly the exact rhythmic imitation between two instrumental lines:

EXAMPLE 6-34

A similar kind of irregular beaming is illustrated in Béla Bartók's *String Quartet No. 3*. At one point in the coda (after No. 9) Bartók beamed two voices as follows:

EXAMPLE 6-35

In the example above it will be noticed that the lower beam is not carried over the barline as one might expect. Possibly this was to clarify the distinction between the moving lower voices and the stationary upper part.

Sometimes a single beaming over the barlines may extend for several measures. This exceptional practice may be justified if the single long beam makes a rhythmic pattern more clear.

EXAMPLE 6-36

Beaming over the barlines frequently occurs at the end of a line or system, the interrupted beams continuing into the first measure of the next line or system. The practice in such cases is to continue the beams *beyond* the final note of the upper line, and to begin the next beams just *before* the first note of the lower line. In Example 6-37 the beams are shown as extended *to* the right-hand barline and *from* the left-hand barline. If the rhythmic pattern should compel the termination of a secondary beam, then only the primary beam would be extended in both measures.

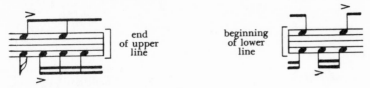

end
of upper
line

beginning
of lower
line

EXAMPLE 6 - 37

Another modern beaming innovation involves the *inclusion of rests* at the beginning or at the end of a beamed figure. When such rest-symbols are a part of the beamed group, the beams are extended over or under the rests in the following ways:

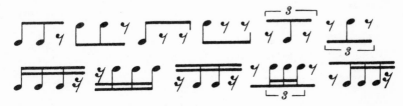

EXAMPLE 6 - 38

The practices above approximate the visual effect of all the notes being present within a beamed group. Once the eye has become accustomed to the sight of the extended beams, the sense and logic of such a practice will be apparent.

Sound practical sense has furthered the career of another innovation—the short, incomplete beams rather than flags for separate notes, used by many contemporary composers:

EXAMPLE 6 - 39

This practice has much to recommend it, as short beams are easier to read and draw than the traditional flags. If such a notation should in time become standard, it would be a reform to which no one could seriously object.

On the other hand, certain composers anxious to maintain an *avant-garde* status have invented notational devices that appear to have little justification beyond sheer novelty. Pierre Boulez, for example, in his *Le Marteau sans maître* combines flags and beams (left, below) instead of using four beamed sixteenth-notes (right).

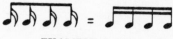

EXAMPLE 6 - 40

Except to initiates, the justification for this device is obscure; the new presentation seems to employ an unfamiliar symbol for one quite adequate *and* familiar. According to Erhard Karkoschka the device signifies that each note in the group is to be played in an independent, especially stressed manner. This may be true, yet Boulez himself nowhere offers an explanation as to what he really means and furthermore is inconsistent in the application of his invention. Modern notation needs amplification in its symbols, but the new forms must help, not hinder, the writing and reading of music.

A current beaming device that *does* make good visual sense is one found in many avant-garde works: *accelerandos* (left, below) and *ritardandos* (right, below) are expressed by beams that fan in or out—a highly graphic representation of rhythmic flexibility.

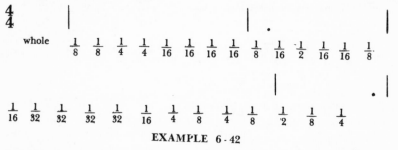

EXAMPLE 6 - 41

NOTATION EXERCISES

1. Write the proper note-heads for the note pattern indicated below; draw stems, and place flags on each as needed. Note the dots indicated in measures 3 and 5:

EXAMPLE 6 - 42

2. In the following example change the beaming direction as required:

EXAMPLE   6 - 43

3. In the example below, all note-heads represent eighth notes. Add stems; beam the groups according to the accents and slurs, and carry the beams over the rests in the modern manner:

EXAMPLE 6-44

4. Employing sixteenth-note *beams* rather than flags, notate a sequence of four altered unisons.

7

Rests and Pauses

As MUSIC CONSISTS OF MEASURED SILENCE NO LESS than of sound, it was necessary to invent symbols to indicate the exact duration of such moments of rest (Fr. *soupir,* pl. *soupirs;* Ger. *Pause,* pl. *Pausen;* It. *pausa,* pl. *pause*). Each note-value, therefore, has its corresponding rest-sign.

EXAMPLE 7 - 1

RESTS

The written position of a rest between two barlines—like the position of a note—is determined by its location in the meter. In other words, a rest always occupies the same position in a measure that an equivalent note-value would fill—with one important exception that will be cited in the paragraph following Example 7-2.

Observe in Example 7-2 that the half rest is lined up directly under the *first* eighth-note of the four-note unit it equals. The quarter rest, too, is placed directly above the first eighth-note of the equivalent fourth count. The only exception to the rule of rest placement is the

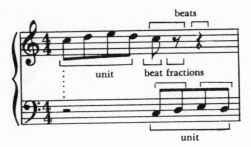

EXAMPLE 7 - 2

whole rest, which is always *centered* in the measure, whereas the whole note would of course occupy the written position of the first beat of the measure.

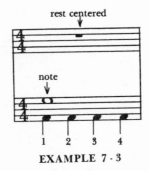

EXAMPLE 7 - 3

The Whole Rest   The whole rest is a solid, oblong symbol the length of a note-head, placed just beneath the fourth line of the staff, regardless of the clef used. It is incorrect to place it elsewhere (beneath the third line, for instance) unless two voices or instruments share a common staff. When this happens, the whole rest is usually written beneath the *top* line for the upper part, and beneath the *bottom* line for the lower part. (See page 344 for further explanation.)

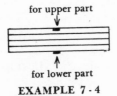

EXAMPLE 7 - 4

Although the whole rest literally signifies only the value of a whole note (or of two half-notes combined), it now commonly serves as the symbol for any completely silent measure, regardless of the meter or time-signature (see Chapter 10). Formerly, it served for all measure values except $\frac{4}{2}$, this rest being indicated by a sign borrowed from the *breve* symbol of thirteenth- and fourteenth-century music (see page 15). But today the whole rest stands for any empty measure—for all meters from a theoretical $\frac{8}{2}$ to a $\frac{3}{16}$. For a $\frac{2}{16}$ ($\frac{1}{8}$) or smaller silent bar, an actual eighth (or smaller) rest would be used.

Conversely, as the whole rest is now used almost solely to represent an *entire* measure of rest, it must not ordinarily be employed for *less* than a measure. An exception to this rule could possibly occur in a $\frac{4}{2}$ or $\frac{8}{4}$ meter, where half of the measure length could be expressed by using a whole rest rather than two half-rests: $\frac{4}{2}$ ▬ ♩ ♩ . Conceivably, too, a whole rest could be used to express part of a measure in $\frac{3}{1}$ or $\frac{2}{1}$ meter, the 1 standing for the whole note as the beat, though such meters are quite rare.

EXAMPLE 7 - 5

With the above exceptions, a whole rest must not be used to indicate a fractional portion of a measure. This is particularly true in triple meters: $\frac{3}{2}$ or $\frac{6}{4}$. If two beats of a $\frac{3}{2}$ measure are to be silent, we must write two half-rests, rather than a whole rest. In compound triple meter ($\frac{6}{4}$) we notate the rests equivalent to four quarter-notes as a dotted half-rest and a quarter rest, to indicate the natural division of the measure after the third quarter-note value.

EXAMPLE 7 - 6

The Half Rest   The half rest (so called because it has one-half the time-value of the whole rest) is an oblong mark of the same length as the whole rest, located *on* the third staff line. Again, it is incorrect to place this rest symbol on any other line unless two voices or instrumental parts share the staff. In this case, the half rest goes above the *top* line for the upper part, and above the *bottom* line for the lower part. (See page 368 for further discussion of this problem.)

Restrictions similar to those applied to the whole rest in triple meter also apply to the half rest. Although the half rest is equal to two quar-

EXAMPLE 7-7

ter-rests combined, it cannot always substitute for them. It is correct to write ³₄ 𝄽 𝄽 ♩ but not ▬ ♩ ; or ³₄ ♩ 𝄽 𝄽 but not ♩ ▬ . In other words, the half rest should be used to express two quarter-note values only when the measure is capable of being divided into two equal halves: ²₂ or ⁴₄ or ⁸₈.

EXAMPLE 7-8

The principle of equal division of a duple measure is all-important, for it means that we cannot notate the following pattern in a simple duple meter: ²₂ or ⁴₄ ♩ ▬ ♩ . We must notate this pattern as: ♩ 𝄽 𝄽 ♩ , in spite of the fact that a syncopation, using notes instead of rests, would correctly be written ♩ ♩ ♩ .

The Quarter Rest   Of all the rest symbols, the quarter rest is probably the most difficult to write or draw accurately. Hence a simplified form is sometimes found in music manuscripts, although it is not to be recommended. Another variant form appears in many older English editions, where the quarter rest is simply a reversed printing of the conventional eighth-rest: 𝄽 . This sign is actually the same as the "shorthand version," minus its bottom "hook."

In its authoritative printed version the quarter rest may be examined in Example 7-1. Note that the sign is centered on the staff, with the top "tail" ending in the fourth space and the bottom "hook" resting in the first space.

As in the case of the whole and half rests, when two parts share a common staff, the quarter rest goes somewhat *above* the staff center for the upper part, and just *below* it for the lower part. The actual distance must depend on individual circumstances, especially on the amount of space available at the moment. When rules cannot operate normally, the eye—and common sense—must determine the most logical placement of all the rest signs. (See Example 7-9.)

In actual practice we have already discovered that the *choice* of rests depends only in part on the number of beats of rest; the notator must always consider the *normal division* of beats in the measure. For this sound reason, a quarter-rest sign cannot take the place of two eighth-

EXAMPLE 7 - 9

rests when by so doing it would obscure the normal organization of the measure. The correct notation at the left below cannot be properly written as demonstrated in the center. Though the second version is mathematically correct, only the first version clearly indicates the correct division of the measure. On the other hand, a consistently used syncopated rhythmic pattern—as shown at the right—is entirely correct in that notated form. (See the discussion of compound time-signatures in Chapter 10, and Example 10-15.)

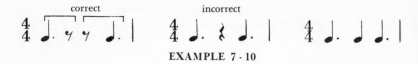

EXAMPLE 7 - 10

In compound meters (see Chapter 10) the quarter rest is more informative than two eighth-rests because it indicates the unit of time at once. Thus in $\frac{6}{8}$ measure the left-hand notation below is more accurate than that directly following, because the latter version is ambiguous. We do not know from the two adjacent eighth-rests, taken out of context, which of the two readings on the bottom line is the correct interpretation of the pulse of the measure:

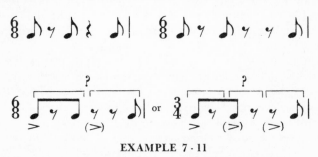

EXAMPLE 7 - 11

To give a further example, if we read the left-hand sequence of rests and notes below, we cannot immediately know whether the beat is triple $\left(\frac{3}{4}\right)$ or compound duple $\left(\frac{6}{8}\right)$. If the group is in triple time, the two eighth-notes should be beamed so as to show the proper beat unit (as in the center example). If the pattern is in compound duple time, the last quarter-rest ought to be notated as two eighth-rests (as shown in the example at the right).

EXAMPLE 7 - 12

Again, standing by itself the following notation would be ambiguous: 𝄾 𝄿 ♪♪. This notation could be either $\frac{3}{4}$ or $\frac{6}{8}$ depending on the inner accent, as shown below. To avoid any ambiguity, $\frac{6}{8}$ measure should be used here and the quarter rest should be dotted, thus clearly indicating the required measure division.

EXAMPLE 7 - 13

The Eighth Rest   The eighth rest, with half the value of the quarter rest, is written as a slanting stem with a single hook. Note in Example 7-1 that the stem rests on the *second staff line* and that the hook, ending in a thick dot, occupies the *third space*.

In some older music one sometimes finds the eighth rest written backward (identical with the English quarter-rest described in the previous section). Because these two signs are so easily confused, the archaic English form of the quarter rest has by now become obsolete.

The Sixteenth Rest   Equal to half the value of the eighth rest, the 16th rest adds another hook to the slanting stem. As this second hook occupies the second staff space, the stem must be extended to touch the bottom line. (See Example 7-1.)

The Thirty-second Rest   Half the value of the 16th rest, the 32nd rest consists of three hooks and a further extended stem. The three hooks now occupy the second, third, and fourth spaces, with the stem resting on the bottom line. This is a more logical arrangement than the form, found in some editions, with the stem extended below the staff; the sign is best contained where possible within the limits of the staff. (See Example 7-1.)

The Sixty-fourth Rest   Though equal to just half the value
of the 32nd rest, the 64th rest is an elaborate structure with its four
hooks. Each hook must occupy one of the four staff spaces, and the
slanting stem must accordingly be extended the distance of one space
below the staff. (See Example 7-1.)

The One Hundred Twenty-eighth Rest   Although it is very
rare indeed, there *is* a 128th rest, equal to half the value of the 64th
rest. It carries five hooks, the fifth one placed below the staff in the
first added space, with the stem proportionately extended beneath it.

   The Table of Rests on page 103, with the names of the rests in four
principal languages, should be consulted as a parallel to the Table of
Notes on page 65.

Dotted Rests   With the possible exception of the 128th
rest, all the rests may be dotted exactly as notes are dotted to increase
their temporal length. A full treatment of this phase of rest usage
is found on pages 119 and 120. Because of their peculiar written form,
however, rests cannot be beamed as note-groups are beamed; but they
can be included in beamed units, placed on the staff so as to occupy
approximately the space that the corresponding note-heads would fill
(examples on the top line). In the case of exceptional beaming—when
the note stems and beams reverse their normal position—the rests
should be positioned with the note-group of which they are a part
(examples on the bottom line).

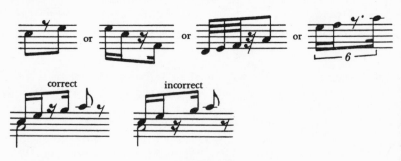

EXAMPLE 7 - 14

Multiple Rests   Although a full score must of necessity include every silent measure, each usually filled in with a whole-rest
sign, individual parts often use shorthand symbols to indicate the long
rests. These symbols, evolved to conserve time and space, are shown
in the Table of Multiple Rests on page 104.

EXAMPLE 7 · 15. TABLE OF RESTS

Rest symbol	Terminology				
	AMERICAN	BRITISH	FRENCH	GERMAN	ITALIAN
	Double whole-rest	Breve rest	Double-pause	Doppelganze Pause	Pausa di breve
	Whole rest	Semibreve rest	Pause	Ganze Pause	Pausa di semibreve
	Half rest	Minim rest	Demi-pause	Halbe Pause	Pausa di minima
	Quarter rest	Crochet rest	Soupir	Viertelpause	Pausa di semiminima
	Eighth rest	Quaver rest	Demi-soupir	Achtelpause	Pausa di croma
	Sixteenth rest	Semiquaver rest	Quart de soupir	Sechzehntelpause	Pausa di semicroma
	Thirty-second rest	Demisemiquaver rest	Huitième de soupir	Zweiunddreissigstelpause	Pausa di biscroma
	Sixty-fourth rest	Hemidemisemiquaver rest	Seizième de soupir	Vierundsechzigstelpause	Pausa di semibiscroma
	One hundred and twenty-eighth rest	Semihemidemisemiquaver rest	Trente et deuxième de soupir	Hundert und achtundzwanzigstelpause	Pausa di centoventottavo

EXAMPLE 7 · 16.   TABLE OF MULTIPLE RESTS

1 measure		whole rest under fourth line
2 measures		double whole-rest in third space
3 measures		two-measure rest plus whole rest
4 measures		two double whole-rests joined as one in second and third spaces
5 measures		four-measure rest plus whole rest
6 measures		four-measure rest plus two-measure rest
7 measures		four-measure rest plus two-measure rest plus whole rest
8 measures		two four-measure rests
9 measures and longer		thick horizontal bar on third line with vertical ends plus large numeral above or below staff

The symbol for a two-measure rest was logically borrowed from the medieval sign for two whole-notes—the *brevis* (or *breve*). (See page 15.) For measures of rest from three to eight, the signs are extensions and combinations of the double whole-rest and single whole-rest symbols.

Although this system is logical and accurate, it is a bit "fussy." The practice now is to employ, from the two-measure rest on, a single heavy bar, either horizontal or slantwise on the staff. This is terminated by short vertical bars, with the figure indicating the number of measures of rest centered above or below the staff. Note that the bar, when horizontal, is placed normally on the center line (left, below). When a slanting line is used, one end rests on the second line, the other on the fourth line. The bar is always slanted upward from left to right, whether with or without short perpendicular "ends" (right, below).

EXAMPLE 7 - 17

PAUSES

Written rests, of whatever duration, are always given a time-value: that is, the rest symbols merely substitute for a written note-value. But there is one type of rest that has no specific time-value, and that is the *pauses* (Fr. *pauses*; Ger. *Luftpausen*; It. *pause*). Pauses are indicated in various ways: ❜ or // or ⁀// .

The comma indicates a very brief pause, equivalent to taking a short breath. This sign is sometimes preferable to a very small rest, for it ensures that the note it follows will not be cut too short, but will receive full value.

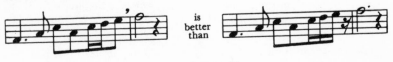

EXAMPLE 7 - 18

The two small slanting lines—always placed through the *top space* of the staff—are used at the end of long phrases or sections, where a desired pause is not adapted to an actual written rest.

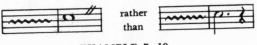

EXAMPLE 7 - 19

Placing a *fermata* sign (see section below) above the slanting symbol prolongs the pause. It is generally used following a long note-value, which thereby maintains its full duration.

FERMATAS

Fermatas (⌒) or holds (Fr. *pauses;* Ger. *Fermaten;* It. *fermate* or *pause*)—first used in polyphonic music of the sixteenth century—are signs for indicating a prolonged sound or silence of indefinite time-value. The exact length of a fermata depends in large measure on the general tempo and emotional character of the music. In a quick tempo the fermata tends to be relatively brief; in a moderate to slow tempo the pause would be correspondingly longer. The important point is that all normal pulsation stops during the fermata.

Placed over a single barline or over a pause sign (left, below) the fermata means that all sound should stop briefly before the music resumes in the following measure. Unless otherwise indicated by a *ritardando* or similar direction, the previous tempo is resumed following the fermata. When placed over a double bar, the fermata signifies the end of a section, movement, or an entire work. It is usually not necessary over a final double-bar, as the double bar in itself fulfills the same function. Only if the final measure should end on the last part of the concluding beat would the fermata over the double bar be justified (right, below).

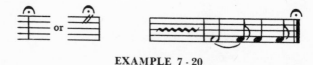

EXAMPLE 7 - 20

Fermatas are sometimes accompanied by the terms *lunga*, meaning "long," or *poco*, meaning "little" or short. Over a silent measure the fermata sign means a prolonged pause for all voices or instruments. The same effect is sometimes indicated as **G.P.** (from the German *Grosse Pause*, or "long pause") or as **L.P.** (abbreviation for the Italian *lunga pausa*).

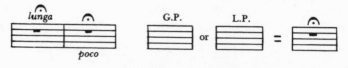

EXAMPLE 7 - 21

The fermata sign should always be placed over the *exact beat* of the measure that is to be prolonged. This is especially important when a number of voices or parts are involved, each concluding its phrase on a different portion of the measure. In the following example at the left it is the fourth beat *only* that is held for all parts, so that putting a fermata on other beats in other parts is both inaccurate and clumsy. Note that the fermata sign is inverted when placed beneath a note or rest. If, however, all voices or parts terminate together on the beat to be prolonged, only one fermata sign is necessary over each staff, regardless of the number of notes or the number of staves in use (second line, below).

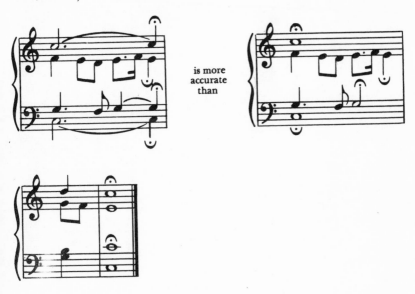

is more
accurate
than

EXAMPLE 7 - 22

When there is a "pick-up" note immediately following a fermata, it is better to put the hold-sign over the first half (or fraction) of the beat, tied from a previous note, than to write the held value as a dotted note.

is more
accurate
than

EXAMPLE 7 - 23

The terms *fermata* and *tenuto* are sometimes equated in meaning by amateurs. These are not identical terms, even though *tenuto* implies a prolonged note. (We find the first use of the term in the vocal music of the ninth century. It was abbreviated as **b.t.** in plainsong manuscripts, standing for the Latin *bene tene*, "hold well.") In modern practice, *tenuto* is more a matter of stress than of stopping, with notes or chords sustained for their full value. It is generally indicated by the dash, the historic sign for a pressure accent (see Chapter 15).

MODERN INNOVATIONS

Oddly enough, the most significant contribution of contemporary notation in the field of rests is the omission of rest-signs altogether in *tacet* measures. Today a blank measure is one that is silent—a practice especially time-saving in the preparation of full orchestral and band scores. A modification of this practice is to fill in with the whole-rest sign the silent measures of only those instruments or voices that do play or sing on the page in question. If the part is *tacet* for the entire page, no rests are put in the blank measures.

Certain modern composers have also devised ingenious alterations of the fermata sign to signify degrees of pause (first examples shown below), and of holds (lower examples).

Short pause   Medium pause   Long pause

Short hold   Medium hold   Long hold

EXAMPLE 7 - 24

Squared fermata symbols accompanied by figures have been used by other contemporary composers to designate pauses or holds of specified time-duration. In the following, for example, the pause is to last six seconds; the note thereafter is to be held for five seconds.

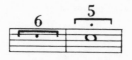

EXAMPLE 7 - 25

Innovations such as these fermata symbols are clear and precise as to their meaning. When new notational signs of comparable clarity become available, the composer or notator should not hesitate to abandon the ambiguous symbols of the past for something better.

NOTATION EXERCISES

1. In the following example re-notate all the rests, placing them in the proper positions and changing their values where necessary:

EXAMPLE 7 - 26

2. At the end of each measure below place the appropriate pause-sign to correspond to the punctuation mark indicated:

(comma)	(semicolon)	(period, as end of a sentence)	(period, as end of a paragraph)

EXAMPLE 7 - 27

3. Using the modern forms of the *pause* shown in Example 7-24, notate an original melody for flute.

8

Ties and Dots

MUSIC NOTATION SINCE THE SEVENTEENTH CENTURY
has regularly employed two signs that prolong the time-value of a
written note into the following beat (or beats, or fraction of a beat).
These signs are the *tie* and the augmentation *dot*.

TIES

Ties (Fr. *liaison*, pl. *liaisons;* Ger. *Bindung*, pl. *Bindungen;* It. *legatura*,
pl. *legature*) are a notational device used to show the *prolongation* of a
note into succeeding beats, as opposed to the *repetition* of a note.
Before the consolidation of our standard practices there appeared
for a time the curious experiment of prolonging a note by making it
literally "straddle" the barline. This occurred in triple meter when a
white note was to be tied across the barline to another white note.
Instead of the now accepted notation, the idea of a tie was expressed
by combining the value of the two notes and placing the single note
directly on the barline.

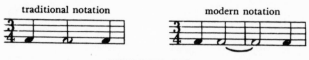

traditional notation   modern notation

EXAMPLE 8-1

Happily, this notational device is now extinct. Our modern tie-mark,
first systematically used in the early sixteenth century, is a curved line
that connects the two successive note-heads indicating, together, the
total time-value desired. Though the tie-mark and the slur (see page
266) appear identical, the tie almost touches the note-head center
(example to the left), while the slur of necessity is set somewhat above
or below the note-head, especially when accompanied by accent markings (see Chapter 15).

EXAMPLE 8 - 2

If stems get in the way of the normal ending of the tie-sign, it then barely touches the side of the note-head, as shown in Examples 8-5, 8-6, and 8-7.

What is more, ties are normally employed to join the time-value of two notes of *identical pitch,* while slurs have a totally different function. When the tied notes do not appear identical, it is because the tie is being used to show a change of pitch spelling. Such ties are called "enharmonic," and occur when for harmonic or tonal reasons the second of the tied notes must be respelled according to its scale function in a new harmony or key.

EXAMPLE 8 - 3

TRADITIONAL PRACTICES

When the tied notes have their stems going *up,* the tie-mark loops *below* the note-heads; when the two stems go *down,* the tie is curved *above* the note-heads. In other words, the tie always loops in the direction opposite that of the stem (see Example 8-2).

When unstemmed notes are tied, the tie-marks are looped as though the notes were stemmed. This means that all notes positioned *below* the third staff line (thus requiring upward stems) will have their ties looped *below;* all notes *above* the second staff space (normally requiring downward stems) will have the tie-marks curved *up.*

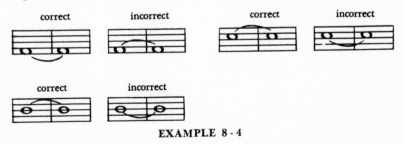

EXAMPLE 8 - 4

In any chord or interval the uppermost note has its tie curved *above;* the lowest note has it curved *below.* The inner notes have their ties curved according to their location on the staff: those lying high have their ties looped above, and those on the lower part of the staff have their ties looped below. All four-note structures have the two upper ties looped above, and the two lower ones curved below.

EXAMPLE 8 - 5

In a five-voice structure the middle note has its tie looped according to its relative position on the staff. In the left-hand example below, the middle note lies below the staff center; hence its tie is looped downward. In the center example, the middle note is above the center line and so has its tie looped upward. If, however, the center note of a five-note chord lies to the left of the main body of notes, its tie must loop so as to avoid conflicting with the note-head just above, as shown at the right.

EXAMPLE 8 - 6

When two notational principles are in direct conflict, one of them must be bypassed. In the two following examples of a tied chord, both versions containing adjacent notes, the notation at the left observes the correct placing of the upper note of the second (to the right when the stem goes up) but of necessity loops the c″ tie *below* rather than above

EXAMPLE 8 - 7

(as it ought to be). The added **d″** above prevents the tie from looping upward. In the version at the right, the tie-mark is correctly positioned but the adjacent note is not. Thus either notation is not entirely correct, but current practice favors the example at the left.

It is frequently necessary to carry a tie-sign through various note stems. In the left-hand example below, the lower tied note has its slur carried through the stems of the off-beat intervals. To loop the tie excessively below in order to avoid the chord stems would be both awkward and ambiguous. If beams are present on the stems through which a tie-sign must go, the stems are lengthened in order to place the beam(s) well out of the way (right, below).

EXAMPLE 8 - 8

When dotted notes (see pages 113–119) are tied, the main problem is to place the tie-sign so that it does not interfere with the dot. Since the dot must always be in the appropriate space next to the note-head, the tie-sign must be slightly raised or lowered so as to clear the dot. This is difficult to do in chords where notes are closely spaced, for there can sometimes be very little room to insert the tie between the vertical dots.

EXAMPLE 8 - 9

Other special situations related to combining dots and tie-signs will be discussed later in this chapter.

THE SINGLE AUGMENTATION DOT

In the long history of notation the single *dot* (Latin, *punctum;* Fr. *point,* pl. *points;* Ger. *Punkt,* pl. *Punkte;* It. *punto,* pl. *punti*) has had a checkered career. In the sixteenth century a dot placed beneath the note signified either a sharp or a flat. It has also been used to represent a pause or rest—either as a textual division or with the function of a modern barline. In the second capacity, the dot was eventually replaced by a vertical line drawn through the staff; as an accidental, it was superseded by the actual sharp and flat signs placed before the note (see Chapter 9).

Ever since music notation became standardized in the seventeenth century, however, the dot following a note-head has had a single function: it *increases by one-half* the length of the note it follows. The augmentation dot is, in fact, the equivalent of tieing one note to another note of one-half its time value. Placed after a half note, therefore, a dot increases the note's over-all length to the equivalent of three quarter-notes, or a half note tied to a quarter note.

EXAMPLE 8 - 10

The Table of Dotted Notes shows the value of all dotted notes in terms of their metrical equivalents.

EXAMPLE 8 - 11.   TABLE OF DOTTED NOTES

Dotted note	𝅝·	𝅗𝅥·	♩·	♪.	♪.	♪.	♬.
Beat value	𝅝 𝅗𝅥	𝅗𝅥 ♩	♩ ♪	♪ ♪	♪ ♪	♪ ♪	♪ ♪

The dot itself is always placed to the direct *right* of the note-head, never to the left. Furthermore, it is always placed in the center of a *space,* regardless of whether the note is on a line or in a space. For all dotted notes requiring flags, the dot goes in the space *above* and *beyond* the tail of the flag. The general rule governing dotted notes placed on lines is that the dot is placed in the *space above* rather than below (example at the left, top line). The same procedure is followed for dotted note-heads on ledger lines (right, top line). An important exception to this rule occurs when the interval of a second places one note-head on a line and one in a space. If the lower of the two notes is on a line, its dot(s) must go in the space *beneath* it, rather than above, as illustrated on the second line, below. (See also Example 18-24.) The inflexible rule is: Never put two independent augmentation dots in the same staff space. Note, then, that in the final chords shown, *all* of the augmentation dots of the "lined" notes are set *down* a space.

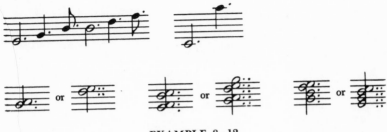

EXAMPLE 8 - 12

In addition, when two dotted notes that are somewhat adjacent on the staff require separate stems, the lower note being on a line, its dot(s) must also be placed in the space below (see also Example 15-4).

and not

EXAMPLE 8 - 13

So useful is the single dot in notating the metrical patterns of syncopation that the syncopated note-group has been given its own designation: *inverted* (or *reverse*) *dotting*. This by no means indicates that the dot itself is put in front of the note it affects; it only means that the *second note* within a unit of time (or beat fraction) is lengthened by the dot, rather than the first note.

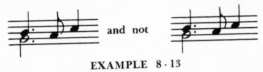

instead of

EXAMPLE 8 - 14

This is the conventional order of syncopation, in which the accented portion of the beat is shorter than the unaccented part. The dot is simpler and actually clearer to the eye than the use of ties. The smaller the unit of time, the more desirable is the dot as substitute for the written tie showing displacement of the beat.

instead of

instead of

EXAMPLE 8 - 15

Even the highly conventional syncopation of an eighth note followed by a dotted quarter is better notated in that manner than with the clumsy equivalent using a tied note.

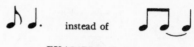

EXAMPLE 8-16

THE DOUBLE AUGMENTATION DOT

First used in the late fifteenth century, the double dot signifies an increase of three-fourths in the note duration. In other words, just as the single dot increases the *note length* by one-half, so the second dot increases the time-value of the *first dot* by one-half. This principle is made graphic by the following diagram:

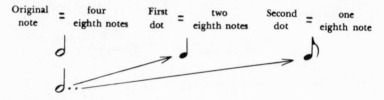

EXAMPLE 8-17

On this basis, the Table of Double-Dotted Notes displays the equivalent small-note value for all useful double-dotted notes.

EXAMPLE 8-18. TABLE OF DOUBLE-DOTTED NOTES

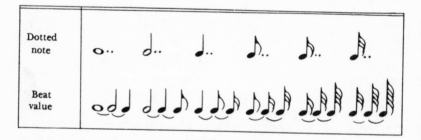

THE TRIPLE AUGMENTATION DOT

Seldom is the triple augmentation dot employed, notators preferring to express the equivalent time-value by the use of ties. If used, however, the three dots following a note increase its length by seven-eighths. The third dot has half the value of the second dot; the second, half the value of the first; and the first dot, half the time-value of the note itself. Again, we may diagram the principle as shown in Example 8-19. It is on this basis that the Table of Triple-Dotted Notes demonstrates the value of all practical triple-dotted notes.

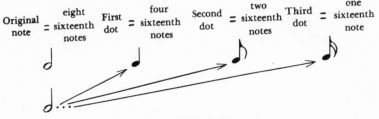

EXAMPLE 8-19

EXAMPLE 8-20. TABLE OF TRIPLE-DOTTED NOTES

Dotted note	𝅝···	𝅗𝅥···	𝅘𝅥···	𝅘𝅥𝅮···	𝅘𝅥𝅯···
Beat value	𝅝· 𝅘𝅥·	𝅗𝅥· 𝅘𝅥𝅮·	𝅘𝅥· 𝅘𝅥𝅯·	𝅘𝅥𝅮· 𝅘𝅥𝅰·	𝅘𝅥𝅯· 𝅘𝅥𝅱·

By comparing the above three tables of dotted notes it will be seen that with each addition of a dot the available number of note values decreases. Single-dotted notes include 64th notes; double-dotted notes go to 32nd notes, while triple-dotted notes take in only 16ths. Smaller dotted values are not possible, as in each category a value so rare as to be nearly non-existent—the 256th note—would be required. The only example of this note-value known to the author is found in the *4 Movements for Piano and Orchestra* by the Polish avant-gardist Boguslav Schäffer.

TRADITIONAL PRACTICES

Single, double, and triple dots should be used only when the combined time-value of note and dot(s) lies *within* a measure—in other words, always between two barlines. Historically, this regulation was not always in effect; hence the curious practice—widely prevalent in the sixteenth and seventeenth centuries—of placing an augmentation dot outside of the measure to which it belongs. Ranging from Renaissance madrigals to the keyboard works of Johannes Brahms, one often finds such a notation as the one at the left below. This practice has long since become obsolete, and today one would notate this example as seen at the right.

older notation   modern notation

EXAMPLE 8-21

In modern notation of a $\frac{4}{4}$ measure we can write ♩.. ♪ because both the half note and its dots, followed by the single eighth-note, properly fill out the measure. But we cannot write ♩ ♩.. because in this case the second dot actually lies outside the compass of the measure—beyond the barline. This pattern would have to be notated as a note tied into the following measure. In a $\frac{3}{4}$ meter we may write ♩. , which fills the entire measure, but we cannot write ♩ ♩. for the obvious reason that the dot represents a note tied into a succeeding measure.

correct dotting   incorrect dotting   notate as

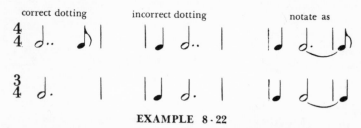

EXAMPLE 8-22

With the exception of the half note, notes that fall on a weak (unaccented) beat of a duple meter (such as $\frac{4}{4}$) should *never* be dotted. The left-hand example below is correct. The center example is not acceptable in that the dotted note is on a weak beat. The right-hand example is the correct notation of the same rhythmic pattern because it clearly indicates the natural division of the measure into two parts.

incorrect   correct

EXAMPLE 8-23

In modern practice, however, a *consistent* syncopated figure notated as $\frac{4}{4}$ ♩ ♩. ♩. | ♩ ♩. ♩. | would be entirely correct. (See section on compound meters, pages 168–170.)

A curious dotting practice, often referred to as "Bach dotting" because of its prevalence in Bach's autograph scores (left, below), is now almost universally notated as shown at the right:

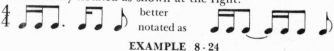

better
notated as

EXAMPLE 8-24

Dots—which are, after all, a shorthand way of writing ties—are always preferable to ties when their meaning is absolutely clear. For example, it is quite possible, and perfectly correct, to write the note-pattern at the left below, but it is more cumbersome than writing the equivalent and graphic version at the right.

EXAMPLE 8 - 25

Both versions clearly show the two-part pulsation, but the second version is simpler to write and easier to read. Thus dots—by minimizing the number of notes necessary—facilitate the writing and reading of music.

DOTTED RESTS

Augmentation dots may be used in conjunction with a rest in the same way they are used for the notes themselves. Just as one can write a dotted quarter-note as the equivalent of a quarter note tied to an eighth, so can he dot a quarter rest to mean the same as a quarter rest "tied to" an eighth rest.

EXAMPLE 8 - 26

The single, double, and triple dots following a whole-rest symbol (or after the half, quarter, eighth, and 16th rests) are always placed in the *third* staff space, if the rest itself is in its normal position. (See Table of Dotted Rests.) If the rest is placed elsewhere, on or off the staff, the dot is put in the same relative position: opposite the highest hook of the rest. For the 32nd, 64th, and 128th rests, all of which require more staff space, the dot is placed opposite the highest hook of the rest, wherever it may be located.

EXAMPLE 8 - 27

It should be pointed out again that it is impossible to tie rests; only notes can be tied. As silence, expressed by a rest, is "non-sound," there is no logic to the tieing of rest-symbols; one can only indicate such an extension of silence by a dotted rest, or by a combination of rests.

The Table of Dotted Rests displays these valuable notation resources and their equivalent in undotted rests.

EXAMPLE 8-28. TABLE OF DOTTED RESTS

DOTS AND TIES COMBINED

Dots and ties have to be used together when there is no single symbol for indicating what the two of them together represent. For instance, a full measure can be shown by a single symbol in a $\frac{9}{8}$ meter (see Chapter 10) only by tieing a dotted half-note to a dotted quarter: ♩. ♩. ; or in $\frac{9}{4}$ only by tieing a dotted whole-note to a dotted half-note: ○. ♩. . No single notation shows these time-lengths.

In many instances dots and ties must also be combined to show the proper rhythmic division of the measure. The following is probably an extreme example, but serves to illustrate the point:

EXAMPLE 8 - 29

The first version above is the correct one because it clearly indicates the division of the measure into four beats. The inverted dotted note (see page 115) must be tied over to the third beat in order to show the inner division between the second and third quarters of the measure. The second notated version has the right number of quarter notes (subdivided though they may be) but gives no indication of the pulsation. And though this right-hand version expresses the consecutive values of the notes, and with one note-symbol less than the first version, it obviously is awkward to read and confusing to comprehend. This comparison, then, underscores the importance of visual clarity added to correctness—a prime requisite of effective musical notation.

MODERN INNOVATIONS

Just as the contemporary composer has tampered with clefs, octave signs, note-heads, and beams—so he has left his mark on the principles of dots and ties. Some composers (notably Béla Bartók) have side-stepped the principle of combining dots and ties for syncopation when the displacement of the notes is relatively uncomplicated. In the example at the left below we see a rather mild form of syncopation traditionally written with both dot and tie. We now sometimes find the figure notated as seen in the second example, which is fairly clear to the eye, especially when the basic beat is stated in another voice or part, as in the third and fourth instances.

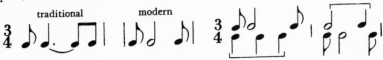

EXAMPLE 8 - 30

When the syncopation is more complex, however, and especially when an ambiguous beaming would have to be used, it is certainly better to revert to the more traditional and academic form of notation.

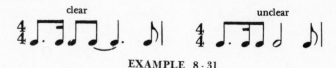

EXAMPLE 8-31

In modern notation one frequently encounters single tones, intervals, or whole chords *tied over many barlines.* In such cases the notes themselves may be omitted after the first measure, and short ties put at the appropriate level directly over, under, or through each succeeding barline. This is a perfectly legitimate shorthand notation that saves time in copying and printing. The final notes of such an extended tie must be written out; otherwise the end of the tie is not perfectly clear (top line, below).

When the tied-through measures are very wide, owing to a great many notes in other parts in each measure, the tied notes may be written out but the ties themselves interrupted (lower line, below).

EXAMPLE 8-32

Another altered tradition—the *tie-sign left incomplete,* and not joining the head of any other note—is frequently used to indicate a pronounced *vibrato* in string instruments playing *pizzicato* (see Chapter 23). The incomplete tie-mark is also used to indicate that a long note is to be held its maximum length, and not released too soon.

EXAMPLE 8-33

The most unusual contribution to the modern conception of ties is that of the *broken tie.* This is used between notes of the same pitch that are articulated in some way—as in a tremolo, a trill, flutter-tongue (in woodwind or brass instruments)—or as ties between harmonics in string instruments.

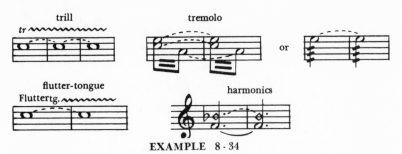

EXAMPLE 8-34

The broken form of the tie has a psychological impact: the affected notes cannot be *literally* tied (except for the sustained string harmonics), yet the tie-sign indicates that no accenting or obvious pulsation is desired. In the case of the tied harmonics (see also Chapter 23) a normal unbroken tie connects the notes firmly stopped by the player's first finger; the diamond note—representing the place on the string where the player lightly touches his fourth finger—is connected to the following note with a broken tie, as this is not a pitch that actually sounds.

In our traditional system of notation, augmentation dots express only the ratio of 1:2. Other relationships (1:3, 1:4, etc.) can only be written as combinations of dotted and/or tied notes. A recent proposal by the American composer Emmanuel Ghent suggests that the lengthening of a note by one-fourth might be expressed by placing a small *cross* after the note-head:

EXAMPLE 8-35

As a related device, this writer would like to suggest a small **x** after the note-head to express the ratio of 1:3, as shown below:

EXAMPLE 8-36

All of the innovations just discussed may be considered acceptable. They fill practical needs and are immediately accessible—requiring of performers no extended initiation ceremonies.

NOTATION EXERCISES

1. Re-notate the following, expressing the tied notes as dotted notes wherever feasible:

EXAMPLE 8-37

2. Correctly notate the following, expressing the dotted notes as tied notes where necessary to show the beats of the measure:

EXAMPLE 8-38

3. In the various chord structures below, place tie-signs in the correct positions:

EXAMPLE 8-39

4. Illustrate *double-* and *triple-dotting* by an original melody written for violin.

5. Compose and notate an original passage for 'cello illustrating various uses of the *broken tie-sign*.

9

Accidentals and Key Signatures

THEORETICALLY SPEAKING, ANY NOTATED PITCH (OR scale degree) can exist in five different forms: it has its original form as an unaltered note on a line or in a space; it can be lowered or doubly lowered; it can also be raised or doubly raised.

EXAMPLE 9-1

ACCIDENTALS

Practically speaking, no one scale degree is ever subjected to *all* five variants of itself. But any tone can be both lowered or raised; and some may be doubly lowered or raised. To achieve these simple alterations, signs must be placed before the note to designate changes in sounding pitch. These signs are called *accidentals* (Fr. *accidents*; Ger. *Vorzeichen*; It. *accidenti*), and are five in number:

1. The *natural*—♮
2. The *flat*—♭
3. The *sharp*—♯
4. The *double flat*—♭♭
5. The *double sharp*—×

The general principles governing the use of accidentals (independent of key signatures) are as follows:

1. To lower a *natural* scale-degree, use a *flat*.
2. To lower a *flatted* degree, use a *double flat*.
3. To raise a *double flat*, use a *natural* followed by a *single flat*.*
4. To raise a *flatted* degree, use a *natural*.

* See page 128 for modern practice.

5. To raise a *natural* degree, use a *sharp*.
6. To raise a *sharped* degree, use a *double sharp*.
7. To lower a *double sharp*, use a *natural* followed by a *single sharp*.*
8. To lower a *sharped* degree, use a *natural*.

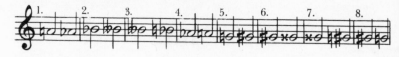

EXAMPLE 9 - 2

Although there are double flats and double sharps, there is no such thing as a double natural. Triple flats and sharps are likewise meaningless, as they would only duplicate the single flat or sharp of the next adjacent note.

EXAMPLE 9 - 3

THE FLAT

Considering the accidental signs as they appeared chronologically, we begin with the flat (Fr. *bémol;* Ger. *Be;* It. *bemolle*). Its derivation is simple: it is literally the rounded small letter **b** (*b rotundum*) found in Guido's "soft" hexachord on **f** (see page 21). Originally applied only to the pitch **b**, the flat sign had to be used with other notes when the **f**-hexachord was transposed. As the rounded **b** meant the lowered form of the pitch **b**, it was logical to continue to use the sign when other notes, too, were to be lowered—**e** to e♭, **a** to a♭, and so on.

In modern practice, the shape of the flat is somewhat more slanted upward than the ordinary small letter **b**. When the flat is placed on a *line,* the top of the stem extends to the second line above. When the symbol is notated in a *space,* the stem extends to the center of the second space above.

EXAMPLE 9 - 4

---

* See page 129 for modern practice.

THE NATURAL

The sign for the natural (Fr. *bécarre;* Ger. *Auflösungszeichen;* It. *bequadro*) looks very much like its original derivation— the square ♮ (*b durum*) found in Guido's "hard" hexachord (see page 21). This sign represented the raised form of the pitch b, and hence was a logical symbol for all pitches to be raised from a lowered form. By adding a short tail to the square ♮, and slightly slanting the horizontal strokes, we get our natural sign, in fairly common use by the seventeenth century.

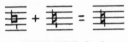

EXAMPLE 9 - 5

When some German scholars of the sixteenth century were attempting to decipher the old plainsong manuscripts, they mistook the square ♮ for a small, squarish h. As a result of this error, the pitch b-natural (the "hard" b of the hexachord on g) was called H in the German language, and it is so called even to this day. In German the note B♭ —the soft, or round b of the f-hexachord—is called B.

The two "tails" of the natural sign are not extended quite as far on the staff as the stem of the flat. When the sign is on a line, the upper tail of the natural extends only to the *next higher* space, the lower tail to the *next lower* space. If the sign is in a space, the tails go respectively to the *adjacent lines* above and below. Note that the vertical strokes are thin lines, and that the horizontal strokes are thicker dashes, slightly slanted upward.

EXAMPLE 9 - 6

THE SHARP

In its earliest period the sharp symbol (Fr. *dièse;* Ger. *Kreuz;* It. *diesis*) was written in a variety of ways, beginning with what looks like a carelessly notated natural sign, and continuing with modified forms of the St. Andrew's cross (in fact, it was at first called a *crux*—Latin for "cross" —before being termed a "sharp"). Now it more closely resembles an elaborated natural-sign, for by slightly extending both the vertical lines and the horizontal dashes of the natural we get in essence the modern sharp-sign.

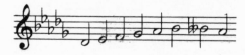

EXAMPLE 9-7

THE DOUBLE FLAT

The double flat (Fr. *double bémol;* Ger. *Doppel-Be;* It. *doppio be-molle*) is merely two flat-signs placed together. It did not come into use until the beginning of tonal (rather than modal) harmony—the period of J. S. Bach. Some sign was necessary to indicate the lowered form of the sixth scale-degree in keys of five, six, and seven flats.

EXAMPLE 9-8

To cancel the double flat and restore the original single flat, it was formerly required—as cited in the rules on page 125—to write a natural sign plus the single flat: ♮♭. Today the tendency is to use merely the single flat-sign without the natural. It may be less academic, but its meaning is perfectly clear, and it is simpler to write.

EXAMPLE 9-9

THE DOUBLE SHARP

The double sharp (Fr. *double dièse;* Ger. *Doppelkreuz;* It. *doppio diesis*) was first used in Bach's *The Well-tempered Clavier* (1744), concurrently with the double-flat sign. The harmonic demands of the new chromaticism made the invention imperative, for a new sign had to be used for the leading tone (seventh scale-degree) in the keys of **g♯** minor and **d♯** minor.

In its earliest form the double sharp consisted simply of two sharp-signs—♯♯. The modern double-sharp is a more literal adoption of the cross symbol—✗. Resembling an elaborate small letter **x**, it has four heavy "feet." These feet rest against the lines above and below them when the symbol stands in a space, and are centered in the space above

EXAMPLE 9 - 10

and below a staff line that carries the sign. (See Examples 9-2 and 9-3, among others.) To cancel a double sharp, one now merely writes a single sharp-sign.

TRADITIONAL PRACTICES FOR ACCIDENTALS

A definite code governing the use of accidentals is stringently observed by any notator who does not wish to cause confusion among his performers. First of all, he must observe the limited extent to which his symbols are effective.

1. **Extent**   When an accidental not included in a key signature precedes any note, it affects the pitch it precedes—and *no other*—for that *one measure only*. In the example at the left below, which carries a key signature of three sharps, the natural sign before the c″ affects only that pitch, not c′ nor c‴. If these other c-pitches are to be natural also, it is necessary to use a natural sign before them.

EXAMPLE 9 - 11

If, as in the example at the left, above, the natural sign should be omitted before c′ and c‴, they would be correctly interpreted as sharped notes because of the key signature. In conservative tonal music this omission might be merely a careless error on the copyist's part. But in music of a highly chromatic or atonal character it might be quite correct to have a c♮ in one voice and c♯ in two others. Compare the following three examples, illustrative of three periods and styles, for the use of these so-called "cross relation" notes.

Our concern is not the musical "rightness" or "wrongness" of the two forms of a pitch used together, but simply their notation. In such

EXAMPLE 9 - 12

a case as this the proper accidental signs must be used before each pitch to avoid any ambiguity.

2. **Use as "Reminder"**   Such an accidental as the ♯ enclosed in parentheses in Example 9-11—though not strictly required—is important as a reminder to the performer. On occasion the accidental-as-reminder is placed not before, but over, the note in question, with or without enclosure in parentheses. This is the usual practice when the note, though affected by a key signature, has been altered just previously by an accidental.

EXAMPLE 9 - 13

The accidental-as-reminder functions significantly when a note affected by an accidental is tied across a barline. In such cases the accidental remains in full effect until the conclusion of the tie, regardless of its length. It does not affect a repetition of the same pitch following the tied note. Alert performers will, of course, remember that barlines have intervened, and that the accidental does not affect the repetition of the same pitch following the tied note. But because the player's eye—seeing another note on the same line or space—might mislead him into repeating the accidental, it is wise to put in any desired natural sign, in parentheses, as a gentle reminder.

EXAMPLE 9 - 14

It is not necessary to repeat the accidental before a *tied* note (as in the example at the left, below). The tie itself serves to prolong the effect of the accidental. The one exception to this general rule occurs when the note or notes affected by an accidental and tied over the barline come at the end of a system or at the bottom of the page. It is helpful to the performer if the accidental is repeated before the tied note(s), on the following system or page. If the repetition gets in the way of the tie-sign, the curved slur may be placed somewhat higher or lower than usual to avoid running into the accidental.

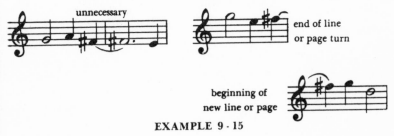

EXAMPLE 9 - 15

In scholarly editions of old music, accidentals in parentheses over the notes are not reminders but editorial emendations. Such accidentals were not found in the original manuscript or early editions, but have been supplied in modern editions as a result of research or of theorizing.

3. Necessary Repetitions   Sometimes it is necessary to repeat an accidental even within the measure. For instance, in writing contrapuntal music consisting of two or more individual parts, all notated on one staff, one must be careful to repeat an accidental sign originally placed before a note in one voice, should another voice move to the same pitch.

This precaution is doubly necessary if the several contrapuntal voices are performed by different instruments. Were the example below to be

EXAMPLE 9 - 16

played by two oboes in an orchestra, for instance, each would have his separate copy from which to play. Should the accidentals be omitted before the c″ on beat 2, and before b′ on beat 4, a careless copyist would invariably omit them in the second oboe part. The result in actual performance can well be imagined. Valuable rehearsal time would have to be expended in correcting a needless error, and the performers' opinion of the composer-notator would hardly be enhanced by the incident.

Accidentals must also be repeated in a measure if any of the octave signs is used over or under a note affected by an accidental. In the left-hand example below, the sharp before the g″ must be repeated for the g‴, even though the same written pitch is used. The reverse also holds true: if an octave sign is canceled, a pitch repetition must again have the required accidental written before it.

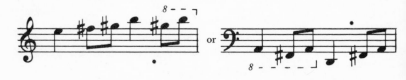

EXAMPLE 9 - 17

The zenith of repeated accidentals is reached in music that is *atonal* or *dodecaphonic* (twelve-tone), where it is often the practice to place an accidental before every note, even when the same pitch is imme-

EXAMPLE 9 - 18

diately repeated. Sometimes only sharps or flats are given, the absence
of any accidental meaning that the note is natural. In such cases, the
natural sign would be used only to cancel a sharp or flat just used.

4. **Alignment**   Fairly consistent principles govern the vertical
alignment of accidentals placed before the separate notes of intervals
(two notes) and of three-note chord structures. In intervals from the second up to the sixth, the accidental governing the upper note is put
closer to the note-head, while that affecting the lower pitch is put diagonally to the left (1. to 5. below). All intervals wider than a sixth (seventh, octave, ninth, and up) have their respective accidentals aligned
perpendicularly (6. to 9. below). The same procedures are followed for
any *two* accidentals affecting these same intervals in a chord structure, regardless of the total number of notes in the chord (10. to 18.).

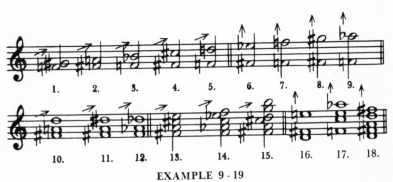

EXAMPLE 9 - 19

When the upper accidental in the interval of a sixth is a flat, some
music engravers and autographers align this flat with the accidental
beneath it. This occasional exception may be justified, in that the flat
sign has no lower "extremities" and consequently does not interfere
with another accidental aligned beneath it.

EXAMPLE 9 - 20

When *three* accidentals are required, the alignment process is generally as follows: if the outer notes of the chord do not exceed the
interval of the sixth, the highest accidental is placed closest to the
note-head, the lowest accidental diagonally to the left, and the central

accidental at the far left (1. and 2. below). If the top and bottom notes are farther apart than a sixth, the highest and lowest accidentals are aligned (3. and 4. below). Whenever the interval of the second is present in a chord structure that requires three accidentals, the alignment is usually as shown in 5. to 8. below. If one of the accidentals can be aligned over or under a projecting note-head without interference, it is so placed (6. and 8.).

EXAMPLE 9 - 21

There can be no inflexible rules for accidental placement in structures that require *four* or more accidental signs. One can only say that usually the highest and lowest accidentals are aligned whenever possible, and the center accidentals arranged diagonally from highest to lowest (first two chords below). The examples below illustrate the more common solutions to the problem of placing multiple accidentals.

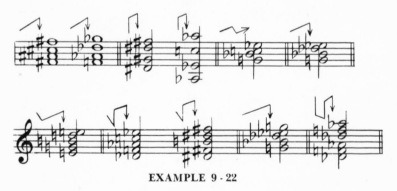

EXAMPLE 9 - 22

A final word of caution in placing accidentals: the signs are always placed before an *entire structure,* whether of two notes or a theoretical dozen. This practice must be observed even when the note-heads

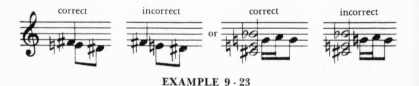

EXAMPLE 9 - 23

are set apart from each other, and up- and down-stems employed. To put the accidentals immediately in front of each note-head would displace the vertical alignment and make the reading awkward.

KEY SIGNATURES

Key signatures (Fr. *signes des accidentals;* Ger. *Vorzeichen;* It. *segni di chiave*) are carefully regulated groups of accidentals placed at the beginning of each staff, directly after the clef sign. For the performer they function principally as a convenient indication that certain pitches are to be raised or lowered throughout the music to come—unless canceled. Unlike the use of accidentals within a measure, which affect only the individual pitch they precede, those of a key signature affect the pitches to which they refer in *all* octaves and all measures and as long as there is no change of signature. In a signature of two sharps, for example, every **F** and **C** available to the performer would be sharped. What this key signature would imply for bassoon, for soprano voice, and for piano is shown below.

EXAMPLE 9 - 24

The additive process that creates the key signatures should already be familiar to the notator well-grounded in theory. A diagram of the historic "circle of fifths" may be consulted in any comprehensive theory text, such as Hindemith's *Elementary Training for Musicians* (page 147).

Beginning with **C** major (or **a** minor), requiring no sharps or flats and hence no signature, one progresses in the "circle" to **G** major (or **e** minor) a fifth *higher,* and adds one sharp to the signature; or to **F** major (or **d** minor) a fifth *lower,* adding one flat to the signature. A fifth higher than **G** major is **D** major, which takes a signature of two sharps; a fifth lower than **F** major is **B♭** major, requiring two flats. By using the same process we traverse the entire circle of key fifths, ending with seven sharps on one side and seven flats on the other—one accidental for each note of the seven-note scale.

From the order in which sharps or flats are added as we progress in the key circle we derive the order of sharps and flats in the key signatures. In early music history, however, the key signature did not always include all the accidentals necessary for a given key. Much eighteenth-century music omitted from the key signature the final sharp or flat, this being written into the music as an accidental. Handel's *Harmonious Blacksmith* in **E**, for example, has a signature of only three instead of four sharps, and a number of Bach's cantatas have solo arias in which the flat signatures contain one flat less than the tonality requires. At the other extreme, some music of the period employed a kind of duplicate key-signature, in which a sharp or flat would appear twice.

EXAMPLE 9 - 25

Today, however, the conventional signature displays all the altered pitches for the key, and is a direct indication of the keynote (tonic) as well. For convenience and ready reference, the complete Table of Key Signatures shows accepted modern practices for the placement of the accidentals on the four standard clefs: treble, alto, tenor, and bass.

TRADITIONAL PRACTICES FOR KEY SIGNATURES

The position of key-signature accidentals on the staff is determined largely by visual logic: the general principle involved is to keep all the accidentals on the staff, and closely grouped for reading ease. In the alternate choices illustrated in Example 9-27 it is usually evident that clarity and neatness have been the deciding factors.

EXAMPLE 9 - 26. TABLE OF KEY SIGNATURES

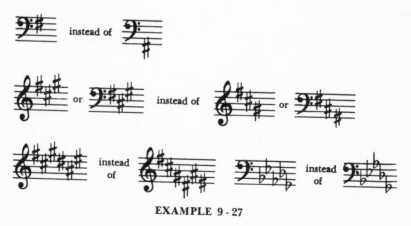

EXAMPLE 9 - 27

A *change* in key signature, even in orthodox and tonal music, now reflects a somewhat relaxed modern practice. Traditionally, a new signature was given after a double bar consisting of two thin vertical lines, and was preceded by natural signs canceling the previous signature.

EXAMPLE 9 - 28

Formerly, should the key change occur at the end of a line or system, the canceled accidentals and the new signature would appear both at the end of this line (following a double bar as above) and at the beginning of the line or system following (without cancellations). Notice (below) that the staff is left open following the new signature on the first system, no final barline being necessary.

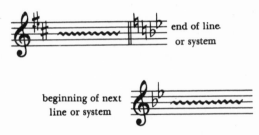

EXAMPLE 9 - 29

Today, however, the use of excess accidental signs in a change of signature is considered pedantic and unnecessary. Instead of indicating the cancellation of *every* previous accidental before giving the new signature (as in Example 9-29), the notator now usually allows the double bar to serve as automatic cancellation of all previous accidentals.

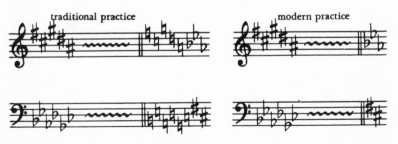

EXAMPLE 9 - 30

The sole exceptions to this newer and less cluttered practice would be: in changing from a major key to its parallel minor (having the same keynote); from a minor tonality to its parallel major; or from any tonality to **C** major or **a** minor (with no accidentals). In going from **E** major (four sharps) to **e** minor (one sharp), for instance, reading accuracy is enhanced by including the naturals that cancel the previous sharps. Or in going from **c** minor (three flats) to **C** major (no accidentals) the presence of the three natural signs helps both the reading and the comprehension of the shift in tonality. Without the canceling accidentals the key changes might in these instances be overlooked or misinterpreted.

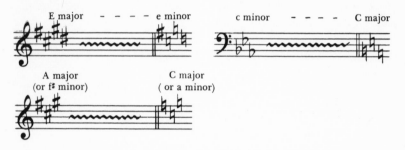

EXAMPLE 9 - 31

As coda to our survey of key-signature practices, we insert a warning regarding the need for *double* flats or *double* sharps. Writing only one flat does not constitute a double flat, even though the key signature may already call for a flat on that same staff-degree. One must actually write the double-flat sign where it is needed, no matter how many single flats appear in the signature. And, in the same way, we must notate a double sharp where it is needed, no matter how many sharps appear in the signature.

EXAMPLE 9 - 32

MODERN INNOVATIONS

Abandonment of Signatures   Modern music has contributed
to notation several significant modifications of the traditional system
of key signatures. Foremost is the abandonment of *all* key signatures
in music that is essentially atonal, non-tonal, or frequently changes its
key center. Key signatures have no validity in music that avoids traditional tonalities, for they exist because of the wish to *establish* a
tonality. Of what use is a key signature when nearly every note of every
measure requires a cancellation of that signature? If key signatures are
absent from all but a minute percentage of the serious music being
written today, it is simply because this music does not move within
the traditional framework—keys, harmonies, and chord progressions—
that brought key signatures into being.

Unorthodox Key Signatures   Not all contemporary music,
however, consistently avoids the use of signatures. Often the composer
will merely alter the traditional placement or make-up of a key signature when he considers that this change makes musical sense. The signature of one sharp (for **G** major or for its relative minor, **e**) might conceivably be placed in the first space of the treble clef rather than on
the top line when only the lower **f♯** occurs in the music (left, below).
As a matter of fact, Béla Bartók observed this practice in several pieces
of his *Mikrokosmos* (Nos. 8, 15, 47, 76, 82, and 93).

   In the same way, a signature of one flat (**B♭**) might be placed in the
space above the bass staff rather than on the second line, if musical
logic permitted (center example). The second flat in any flat signature
(**E♭**) could also be placed unconventionally in treble, alto, or tenor
clef should the other pitch level on that staff never be used in the music
(examples at the right).

EXAMPLE 9 - 33

   Mention has already been made of Bartók's placement of the **F♯**
in a one-sharp signature on the bottom space of the treble clef. In the
six volumes of the *Mikrokosmos* the composer frequently positioned
his conventional one, two, three, or four sharps in non-conventional
locations on the staff.

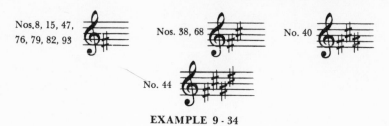

EXAMPLE 9 - 34

As long as the displacement of the accidentals in any key signature does not move them completely off the staff, any unconventional arrangement might be justified were only those particular altered pitches to be sounded. Although it is difficult to imagine a work calling for only the sharped notes illustrated at the left, below, the four-sharp key-signature might possibly serve. The flat signature in the viola clef (right-hand example) might also be possible, if improbable!

EXAMPLE 9 - 35

In addition to his unorthodox *placement* of accidentals, Bartók (and many other composers as well) also created *new signatures* of sharps or flats in combinations unsanctioned by proper sequence in the circle of fifths.

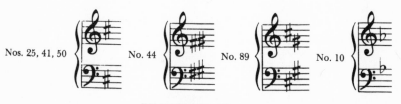

EXAMPLE 9 - 36

Similar possibilities for unusual flat signatures are indicated below:

EXAMPLE 9 - 37

Mixed Signatures   Though the examples above consistently use one type of accidental—sharps or flats—the *Mikrokosmos* also exhibits mixed signatures with flats and sharps together. Below we have a single flat in the right hand (and an E♭ instead of a B♭, at that) against two sharps in the left hand—unconventionally placed and in non-traditional sequence!

No. 99

EXAMPLE 9 - 38

A further extension of the mixed-signature principle would be the simultaneous combination of sharps and flats on both the staves of a keyboard work, or in each of the two parts of an instrumental or vocal duo. Far from being a random experiment, the signature below is tonally valid for a combination of two modal scales—the Lydian and the Mixolydian—both commencing on **C**.*

Mixolydian (lowered 7th)

Lydian (raised 4th)

EXAMPLE 9 - 39

A few other possibilities for such mixed signatures are given below:

---

* The Lydian mode is the white-note scale beginning on **F** (having no **B♭**); the Mixolydian mode is the white-note scale starting on **G** (having no **F♯**).

EXAMPLE 9 - 40

Another variant of the mixed signatures uses a signature in one hand of a keyboard piece (or one instrument of an ensemble) and no signature at all in the other hand or instrument.

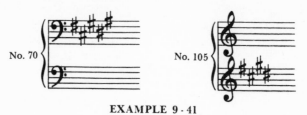

EXAMPLE 9 - 41

Both of the above examples from Bartók's *Mikrokosmos* actually illustrate *polytonality* (two or more keys used simultaneously), as indicated by poly-signatures. Other applications of this principle in keyboard music are seen in the *Mikrokosmos* No. 44, for two pianos (left, below) and in Serge Prokofiev's *Sarcasmes,* No. 3 (at the right).

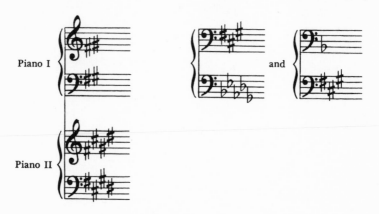

EXAMPLE 9 - 42

As polytonality is a fairly common device in contemporary literature, the enterprising musician will also find numerous illustrations of poly-signatures in orchestral and chamber music. In Leonard Bernstein's *Serenade for Solo Violin, String Orchestra, Harp and Percussion,* for instance, the solo violin is notated in two flats, while the solo 'cello staff bears a signature of two sharps. At the beginning of the third

movement of Arthur Honegger's *Symphony No. 2 for String Orchestra*
the first violins have a written signature of six sharps, but the balance
of the orchestra has a "neutral" signature: no sharps or flats. In terms
of notation, however, polytonality is more often expressed by the
use of measure accidentals than by actual poly-signatures.

Quarter-Tones   Contemporary composers have done considerable experimenting with microtonal music, based on the division of
the octave into quarter-tones rather than the conventional half-steps.
In our usual diatonic or chromatic music, based on 12 equal half-steps
to the octave, we recognize a half-step between the notes F♮ and F♯,
and between G♭ and G♮. In our tempered tuning there is no aural
difference between F♯ and G♭, yet a stringed instrument (or a specially
constructed instrument such as the quarter-tone piano, the Theremin,
or the *ondes Martenot*) can make an actual microtonal distinction. To
notate this difference it was necessary to invent symbols to indicate
microtones. The necessity is even more acute now that the woodwind
and brass instruments are required by avant-garde composers to produce various microtonal intervals (see Example 20-21).

Rather than create an entirely new set of symbols for the 24 quarter-
tones of the octave, most of the composers using these microtones have

EXAMPLE 9 - 43. TABLE OF QUARTER-TONE SYMBOLS

♯	♯	♯	♭	=	sharped note to be played a quarter-tone high
♯	♯	♯	ᴅ	=	sharped note to be played a quarter-tone low
♩	♭	♭	♭	=	flatted note to be played a quarter-tone high
♭	♭	♭	ᴅ	=	flatted note to be played a quarter-tone low
♮	╱	↑	♭	=	natural note to be played a quarter-tone high
♩	╲	↓	ᴅ	=	natural note to be played a quarter-tone low

continued to employ traditional flats and sharps, but with modified forms and new auxiliary signs placed before conventional note-heads. A few of these are shown in the Table of Quarter-Tone Symbols.

As a practical illustration, the following example shows a segment of the octave scale written in quarter-tones.

EXAMPLE 9 - 44

Alban Berg in his *Chamber Concerto for Violin, Piano, and 13 Winds* utilized still another ingenious form of quarter-tone notation. As the German term for quarter-tones is *Zwischentöne* (literally, "between-tones"), Berg placed a large letter **Z** on the stem of each note to be so played: **ƒ** or **ƶ**

Should quarter-tone music become more generally adopted, a stabilized notation will doubtless follow.

NOTATION EXERCISES

1. Write all the flat key-signatures on: the treble staff; the tenor staff.
2. Write all the sharp signatures on: the alto staff; the bass staff.
3. Write in all the accidentals called for in the series of intervals and chords below:

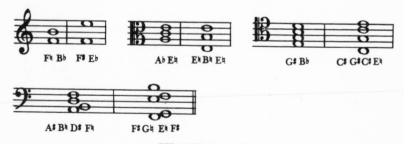

F♮ B♭   F♯ E♭   A♭ E♮   E♮ B♮ E♮   G♯ B♭   C♯ G♯C♯ E♮

A♯ B♮ D♯ F♮   F♯ G♮ E♮ F♯

EXAMPLE 9 - 45

4. Correct the erroneous placement of accidentals before all the intervals and chord structures below:

EXAMPLE 9 - 46

5. Using one or the other system of quarter-tone notation, write in the necessary indications for quarter-tones where marked with an asterisk (*) in the example below:

EXAMPLE 9 - 47

10

Meter and
Time Signatures

TIME, METER, TEMPO, RHYTHM—MUSICIANS OFTEN
use these terms imprecisely. But the four expressions are not synonymous, and only two are interchangeable. The analogous terms are
time and *meter,* for both refer to the pattern of musical pulsations.
Hence we may accurately say that a piece of music is in *triple meter,*
or in $\frac{3}{4}$ (or $\frac{3}{2}$, or $\frac{3}{8}$) *time.* "$\frac{4}{4}$ *time*" is also *quadruple meter,* and *quintuple meter* is one designation for $\frac{5}{4}$ or $\frac{5}{8}$ *time,* for time signatures are
merely convenient indications of a meter already inherent in the music
itself.

Though *tempo* and *rhythm* catalogue other elements of time, we shall
deal with them in later chapters and be concerned here only with
meter—and therefore with its analogue, time.

METER

Meter (Fr. *mètre;* Ger. *Takt* or *Metrum;* It. *metro*) is—traditionally
speaking—a recurring pattern of stress, and an established arrangement
of strong and weak pulsations. These pulsations are also known as
beats. Thus in $\frac{3}{4}$ meter, for example, there are recurring groups of
three quarter-notes (three beats)—the first with a primary stress, the
second and third with less stress.

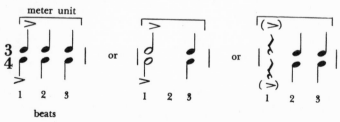

EXAMPLE 10 - 1

148

In $\frac{5}{8}$ meter there are recurring groups of five eighth-notes (five beats); of these, the first usually receives the primary stress.

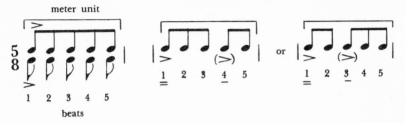

EXAMPLE 10 - 2

The *measure* (Fr. *mesure*, pl. *mesures;* Ger. *Takt, pl. Takte;* It. *misura*, pl. *misure*) is a single, complete pattern of the recurring beats, framed by barlines (see Chapter 11) and arranged so that the first beat is normally the strongest pulsation. Measures of short duration have one primary stress; those of longer duration have two or more.

EXAMPLE 10 - 3

TIME SIGNATURES

As the time-measurement of sound relationships, meter is inextricably related to time signatures (Fr. *signes de valeur;* Ger. *Taktvorzeichnung* or *Taktvorzeichen;* It. *segni di tempo*). A *time signature* is the vertical arrangement of two figures placed on the staff following the clef sign and any key signature. Though the upper figure is commonly termed the *numerator* and the lower figure, the *denominator,* a time signature is not to be regarded as a fraction. Hence the two figures properly should not be separated by the short horizontal line that distinguishes a numerical fraction, although a few contemporary scores do follow that unorthodox practice. When placed on the staff (the normal position), the numerator occupies the two top spaces, the denominator the two bottom spaces. Other positions are illustrated in the Modern Innovations section of this chapter and in Example 26-5.

In simple time the numerator indicates the *number of beats* within each measure that follows the signature; in compound time, the number of inner pulsations. The denominator, on the other hand, in simple time indicates the *unit of time*, or note-value, that receives one beat (for compound time, refer to the discussion just below). If the half note, therefore, is to be the unit of simple time, it is expressed by the figure 2 in the denominator; if a quarter note, by the figure 4; if an eighth note, by the figure 8, and so on.

PERFECT AND IMPERFECT TIME

From the time signature the performer also knows immediately whether he is reading *perfect* or *imperfect* time, for the numerator will indicate whether the measure can be divided into equal halves or thirds. If the numerator is exactly divisible by two or three, we have *perfect time.* Duple or quadruple time can be divided exactly into halves, triple time into thirds; therefore these are perfect time. *Imperfect time* includes all meters not equally divisible by two or three; quintuple and septuple meters, for instance, are called imperfect because five and seven cannot be divided equally into either halves or thirds.

Perfect time (both duple and triple) is further classified as *simple* and *compound.* In simple time each beat of the measure is subdivided only in units of two or its multiples. For example: $\frac{4}{4}$ measure is *perfect* time because the number of beats (four) is exactly divisible by *two.* It is *simple* time because a quarter note receives one beat, and any subdivision will be at the ratio of two eighth-notes to a beat; four sixteenth-notes to a beat, and so on—all divisible by two.

In *compound time* the beats of the measure are subdivided not by two but by *three.* For example: $\frac{12}{8}$ is *perfect* time, because the measure can be divided into exact halves; but it is also *compound* quadruple time because it is performed with four beats per measure, each beat being subdivided into three eighth-notes (or their equivalent).

Because we have no single figure-symbol that indicates the true denominator in compound time, common practice is to use the note-values of simple time: quarter notes, eighth notes, sixteenth notes, and so on. In actuality, the denominator is a unit made by combining *three* such values, expressed in notation by a dotted note: *i.e.,* $\frac{6}{8} = ♩. ♩. .$

The Table of Time Signatures gives all the time signatures possible under each heading—perfect and imperfect. Some are fairly common in practice, some very rare.

Two familiar time-signatures do not appear in the Table. One is the sign used to represent $\frac{4}{4}$ (simple quadruple) time and erroneously

EXAMPLE 10-4. TABLE OF TIME SIGNATURES

	PERFECT METER	
	Simple (units divisible by 2)	Compound (units divisible by 3)
Duple Time	2/1	6/2
	2/2	6/4
	2/4	6/8
	2/8	6/16
	2/16	6/32
Triple Time	3/1	9/2
	3/2	9/4
	3/4	9/8
	3/8	9/16
	3/16	9/32
Quadruple (double duple) Time	4/2	12/4
	4/4	12/8
	4/8	12/16
	4/16	12/32

EXAMPLE 10-4 (continued)

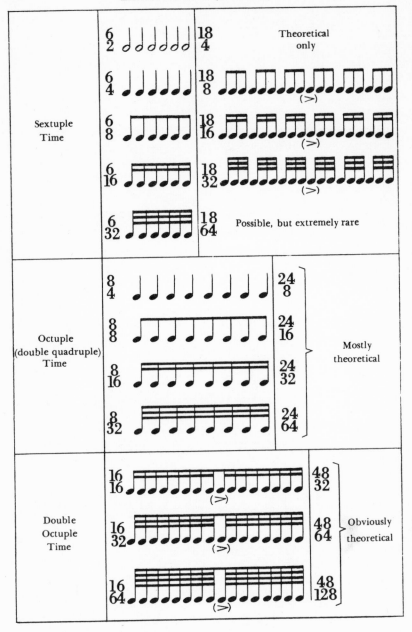

EXAMPLE 10 · 4 (continued)

IMPERFECT METER		
	Duple plus Triple	Triple plus Duple
Quintuple Time	$\frac{5}{2}$ $\frac{5}{4}$ $\frac{5}{8}$ $\frac{5}{16}$ $\frac{5}{32}$	
	Triple plus Quadruple	Quadruple plus Triple
Septuple Time	$\frac{7}{2}$ $\frac{7}{4}$ $\frac{7}{8}$ $\frac{7}{16}$ $\frac{7}{32}$	
Double Quintuple Time	$\frac{10}{4}$ $\frac{10}{8}$ $\frac{10}{16}$ $\frac{10}{32}$	

EXAMPLE 10 - 4 (continued)

EXAMPLE 10 - 4 (continued)

COMBINED METERS

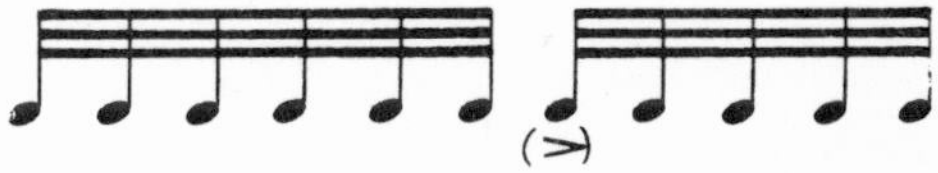

termed "common time" because the **C** is popularly considered an abbreviation of "common." The other sign is **¢**, used to indicate ²⁄₂ (simple duple) meter, misinterpreted as the abbreviation for "cut time." Both definitions result from delusions. Their proper history is as follows:

During the Middle Ages, notational development was in the hands of the monks, who inevitably associated religious and musical phenomena. To them the three-part concept of the Holy Trinity represented religious perfection; therefore to them only triple meter was perfect meter. To express this meter they placed the geometrically perfect circle ◯ (called in Latin a *perfectum*) at the beginning of the plainchant. A compound triple meter (⁹⁄₄ or ⁹⁄₈ in modern notation) was indicated by placing a dot within the circle: ⊙. Representing thrice three, this sign no doubt stood for the ultimate in *triplicum* rhythm!

These church musicians considered all metrical pulsation in two or four *imperfect*. Thus their notation of twos and fours was simplicity itself—a broken or incomplete circle, **C** (*imperfectum* in Latin). As a broken circle is practically indistinguishable from the hand-written letter **C**, the notation of the imperfect meters came to resemble the letter **C** more than the broken circle.

Beyond being the object of popular misconceptions, the sign **C** is ambiguous at best, for it has been used at times to designate ⁴⁄₂ and ⁸⁄₈ as well as ⁴⁄₄. Perhaps it should be discarded as having outlived its usefulness, especially as even ⁴⁄₄ does not always mean today what it did in the past. In older music ⁴⁄₄ (or **C**) invariably meant four quarter-notes to the measure, equally subdivided into eighth notes (upper line of Example 10-5). Today, ⁴⁄₄ might well mean the patterns indicated at the bottom of this example—to give but two current modifications. (See also Example 10-16.)

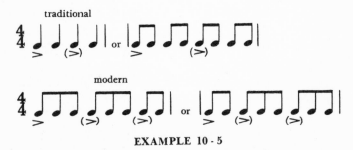

EXAMPLE 10 - 5

As for the symbol **¢** —the imperfect circle bisected by a perpendicular line represents a literal halving of the sign for quadruple meter, and is used for $\frac{2}{2}$ meter, properly termed *alla breve*. $\frac{2}{2}$ is half of $\frac{4}{4}$ in the number of *beats* per measure, although there is the same number of quarter notes in each meter. Again, the symbol seems inadequate for the inner complexity of modern metric pulsation, and perhaps should also be scrapped in favor of more precise time-signatures.

TRADITIONAL PRACTICES

Expert notational practice for meter must be based fundamentally on the concept that meters *change*. Sometimes the change is a simple matter of inner organization of the measure. For whereas quadruple and octuple time are both extensions of simple duple meter, and sextuple time is basically multiplied triple meter—all the *imperfect* meters are capable of several inner patterns. That is to say, quintuple time may be a combination of 3 + 2, or of 2 + 3, or 4 + 1; septuple time may be 4 + 3, 3 + 4, or further broken down into units of 2 + 2 + 3, or 3 + 2 + 2. Double quintuple time is capable of expressing not only 5 + 5, but such subdivisions as 3 + 2 + 2 + 3, or 2 + 3 + 3 + 2—all of which add up to 10 units per measure. The combined meters (5 + 6, or 7 + 6, for example) are all capable of even further fragmentation.

Such metrical complexity—common to the music of all but the most conservative composers of today—will be discussed in detail in the Modern Innovations portion of this chapter. (See Table of Compound Meters, page 169.) But in many cases the notator, with no tool other than correct *beaming* (see Chapter 6), can indicate to the performer the inherent character of these complex patterns.

When, however, there is a change in the *consistent pattern* of the beat groups from one measure to another, it should be indicated by a change in time signature. For example: *one,* two, three; *one,* two, three, four; *one,* two, three—would be expressed as $\frac{3}{4}$; $\frac{4}{4}$; $\frac{3}{4}$. Formerly it was the custom to put a double bar before each meter change. But with the almost constant change of time signature in a large proportion of present-day music, such a practice is tedious and unnecessary. Time-signature changes now are usually prefaced by the single barline only.

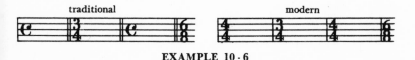

EXAMPLE 10 · 6

Observe one important point: whereas *clef* changes should be indicated *before* the barline, *time signatures* should always be placed *after* the barline (see also page 184). When key signatures are also involved, the meter sign is put *after* the accidentals, not before them.

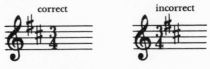

EXAMPLE 10 - 7

When meters (and hence, time signatures) change from perfect *simple* to perfect *compound* time, or vice versa, though the basic unit (or beat) remains the same—the two equal notes of the basic unit are sometimes placed within parentheses just above the new time-signature. The left-hand example below indicates that the eighth note is constant; that is, the $\frac{6}{8}$ measure is not played as two triplets in $\frac{2}{4}$ time, but as six full eighth-notes, each of exactly the same duration as the individual eighth-notes in the $\frac{2}{4}$ measure. A performer studying such a notation might first count the passages below as: *one,* two, three, four; *one,* two, three, four, five, six; and *one,* two three, four, five, six; *one,* two three, four—all at a constant speed. For in the right-hand example the quarter notes of the $\frac{2}{2}$ measure are played at the same speed as those of the $\frac{6}{4}$ measure.

EXAMPLE 10 - 8

MODERN INNOVATIONS

To read contemporary music—to write it, play it, or even listen to it —a musician must first understand the technical elements that set it apart from the historic past. Of these elements, modern rhythmic notation is supremely important.

1. **Unusual Time-Signatures**   A practice so general among twentieth-century composers that it may be safely imitated is the use of written time-signatures that consist only of the *numerator*—notated as a large figure centered on or over the staff. The omitted denominator, or beat unit, must be supplied by the performer, but it should be im-

mediately obvious. There is only one possible denominator—given the
numerator and the written notes of any complete measure.

EXAMPLE 10 - 9

Another intriguing aspect of contemporary rhythmic notation is its
exploitation of the *smaller units*—16th notes and 32nd notes— instead
of the customary half- , quarter- , and eighth-notes. Of the legion of
contemporary works employing the shorter time-units as meter signatures, only a handful can be listed below:

$\frac{2}{32}$
Karlheinz Stockhausen: *Zeitmasse*

$\frac{3}{32}$
Bo Nilsson: *Mädchentotenlieder;*
Karlheinz Stockhausen: *Zeitmasse;*
Anton Webern: *String Quartet,* Op.
28

$\frac{5}{32}$
Karlheinz Stockhausen: *Zeitmasse*

$\frac{7}{32}$
Bo Nilsson: *Mädchentotenlieder;*
Karlheinz Stockhausen: *Zeitmasse*

$\frac{8}{32}$
Karlheinz Stockhausen: *Zeitmasse*
$\frac{21}{32}$
Elliott Carter: *'Cello Sonata*

$\frac{1}{16}$
Giselher Klebe: *Moments musicaux;*
Olivier Messiaen: *Oiseaux ex-
otiques;* Bo Nilsson: *Mädchento-
tenlieder;* Karlheinz Stockhausen:
Gruppen; Zeitmasse

$\frac{2}{16}$
Karlheinz Stockhausen: *Zeitmasse;*
Igor Stravinsky: *Le Sacre du prin-
temps; Symphony in C*

$\frac{3}{16}$
Olivier Messiaen: *Oiseaux exotiques;*

Bo Nilsson: *Mädchentotenlieder;*
Karlheinz Stockhausen: *Gruppen;
Zeitmasse;* Igor Stravinsky: *"Dumbarton Oaks" Concerto; Le Sacre
du printemps; L'Histoire du soldat;
Movements for Piano and Orchestra; Symphony in C;* Anton Webern: *String Quartet,* Op. 28;
String Trio

$\frac{5}{16}$
Luciano Berio: *Serenata I;* Benjamin
Britten: *War Requiem;* Leon
Kirchner: *Duo for Violin and Pi-
ano;* Olivier Messiaen: *Trois petites
liturgies;* Henri Pousseur: *Sym-
phonies à 15 Solistes;* Silvestre
Revueltas: *Planos;* Karlheinz Stock-
hausen: *Gruppen; Zeitmasse;* Igor
Stravinsky: *Agon; Canticum sa-
crum; Capriccio for Piano and Or-
chestra; "Dumbarton Oaks" Con-
certo; Le Sacre du printemps; L'-
Histoire du soldat; Movements for
Piano and Orchestra; Symphony in
C;* Anton Webern: *String Trio*

$\frac{6}{16}$
Benjamin Britten: *Nocturne;* Leoš
Janáček: *Mladi;* Henri Pousseur:
Symphonies à 15 Solistes; Arnold
Schönberg: *Variations for Orches-
tra;* Igor Stravinsky: *Symphony in
C*

$\frac{7}{16}$

Leonard Bernstein: *Serenade for Solo Violin, String Orchestra, Harp and Percussion;* Pierre Boulez: *Improvisation sur Mallarmé,* No. 1; Olivier Messiaen: *Trois petites liturgies;* Henri Pousseur: *Symphonies à 15 Solistes;* Silvestre Revueltas: *Sensemayá;* Roger Sessions: *Duo for Violin and Piano;* Karlheinz Stockhausen: *Gruppen;* Igor Stravinsky: *Agon; Canticum sacrum; "Dumbarton Oaks" Concerto; L'Histoire du soldat; Movements for Piano and Orchestra; Symphony in C*

$\frac{8}{16}$

Pierre Boulez: *Improvisation sur Mallarmé,* No. 1; Karlheinz Stockhausen: *Zeitmasse;* Igor Stravinsky: *Canticum sacrum; L'Histoire du soldat*

$\frac{9}{16}$

Luciano Berio: *Serenata I;* Pierre Boulez: *Improvisation sur Mallarmé,* No. 1; Roy Harris: *Concerto for Piano, Clarinet, and String Quartet;* Leon Kirchner: *Duo for Violin and Piano;* Henri Pousseur: *Symphonies à 15 Solistes;* Arnold Schönberg: *Variations for Orchestra;* Karlheinz Stockhausen: *Gruppen;* Igor Stravinsky: *"Dumbarton Oaks" Concerto; Movements for Piano and Orchestra*

$\frac{10}{16}$

Pierre Boulez: *Improvisation sur Mallarmé,* No. 1; Elliott Carter: *8 Etudes and a Fantasy; String Quartet No. 1; String Quartet No. 2;* Roy Harris: *Concerto for Piano, Clarinet, and String Quartet;* Igor Stravinsky: *Movements for Piano and Orchestra*

$\frac{11}{16}$

Leon Kirchner: *Duo for Violin and Piano; String Quartet No. 1;* Roger

Sessions: *Piano Sonata No. 2;* Karlheinz Stockhausen: *Zeitmasse;* Igor Stravinsky: *"Dumbarton Oaks" Concerto*

$\frac{12}{16}$

Alban Berg: *Lyric Suite;* Elliott Carter: *String Quartet No. 1; String Quartet No. 2;* Roy Harris: *Concerto for Piano, Clarinet, and String Quartet;* Leon Kirchner: *String Quartet No. 1;* Roger Sessions: *Piano Sonata No. 2;* Igor Stravinsky: *Movements for Piano and Orchestra*

$\frac{13}{16}$

Alan Hovhaness: *October Mountain;* Leon Kirchner: *String Quartet No. 1;* Roger Sessions: *Piano Sonata No. 2*

$\frac{14}{16}$

Elliott Carter: *8 Etudes and a Fantasy; String Quartet No. 1; String Quartet No. 2;* Roy Harris: *Concerto for Piano, Clarinet, and String Quartet;* Igor Stravinsky: *Movements for Piano and Orchestra*

$\frac{15}{16}$

Elliott Carter: *String Quartet No. 1; String Quartet No. 2;* Roy Harris: *Concerto for Piano, Clarinet, and String Quartet;* Charles Ives: *Robert Browning Overture;* Leon Kirchner: *String Quartet No. 1*

$\frac{16}{16}$

Roy Harris: *Concerto for Piano, Clarinet, and String Quartet;* Karlheinz Stockhausen: *Zeitmasse*

$\frac{17}{16}$

Roy Harris: *Concerto for Piano, Clarinet, and String Quartet;* Alan Hovhaness: *October Mountain;* Leoš Janáček: *Mladi*

$\frac{18}{16}$

Arnold Schönberg: *Five Piano Pieces,* Op. 23

By no means, of course, are such time-signatures exclusive with the twentieth century. Precedent goes back to J. S. Bach—the *Gigue* of the sixth *English Suite*, for instance, has a signature of $\frac{12}{16}$; *Prelude No. 15* in *The Well-tempered Clavier* is prefaced by a signature of $\frac{24}{16}$. Beethoven's *Piano Sonata*, Op. 111 has a signature of $\frac{12}{32}$ for one movement. But these are exceptional meters in the music of the eighteenth and nineteenth centuries; they are much more frequently found in contemporary music, as the foregoing list well illustrates.

At the opposite extreme of the scale of note values we find the *larger units*—the whole note or even the double whole-note—occasionally used as a basic unit of time. Historically, this also is not a brand-new practice. The celebrated piano pedagogue Muzio Clementi employed the time signature of $\frac{3}{1}$ (the 1 standing for a whole note) in one piece from the *Gradus ad Parnassum;* the same signature was used by Camille Saint-Saëns in the final movement of his *Symphony No. 3,* and by Nicolai Rimsky-Korsakov in his *Russian Easter Overture.* Alexander Borodin wrote the *Scherzo* movement of his *Symphony No. 2* in $\frac{1}{1}$ (four very fast quarter-notes—but only one beat—in each measure). But a good many composers in our own time have used whole or half notes as time signatures, as demonstrated below:

$\frac{1}{1}$

Pierre Boulez: *Improvisation sur Mallarmé,* No. 2

$\frac{2}{1}$

Pierre Boulez: *Improvisation sur Mallarmé,* No. 2; Arnold Schönberg: *Five Piano Pieces,* Op. 23

$\frac{3}{1}$

Carl Orff: *Carmina Burana*

$\frac{4}{1}$

Pierre Boulez: *Improvisation sur Mallarmé,* No. 2

$\frac{5}{1}$

Pierre Boulez: *Improvisation sur Mallarmé,* No. 2

$\frac{8}{1}$

Pierre Boulez: *Improvisation sur Mallarmé,* No. 2; Carl Orff: *Carmina Burana*

$\frac{1}{2}$

Pierre Boulez: *Le Marteau sans maître;* Benjamin Britten: *Cantata Academica; War Requiem;* Luigi Dallapiccola: *Il Prigioniero;* Paul Hindemith: *Der Schwanendreher;* Carl Orff: *Carmina Burana;* Arnold Schönberg: *Chamber Symphony; String Trio;* Karlheinz Stockhausen: *Zeitmasse;* Anton Webern: *Quartet,* Op. 22

$\frac{5}{2}$ *

Samuel Barber: *Adagio for Strings;* Pierre Boulez: *Improvisation sur Mallarmé,* No. 2; Henry Cowell: *Suite for Violin and Piano; Symphony No. 15;* Luigi Dallapiccola: *Volo di notte;* Carl Orff: *Carmina Burana*

$\frac{6}{2}$

Samuel Barber: *Adagio for Strings;* Benjamin Britten: *Gloriana;* Paul

---

* $\frac{2}{2}$, $\frac{3}{2}$, and $\frac{4}{2}$ are too common to justify inclusion here.

Hindemith: *Kammermusik No. 4;* $\frac{8}{2}$
Carl Orff: *Carmina Burana*   Carl Orff: *Carmina Burana*

$\frac{7}{2}$ $\frac{12}{2}$

Henry Cowell: *Suite for Violin and*   Roy Harris: *Concerto for Piano,*
Piano; Carl Orff: *Carmina Burana;*   *Clarinet, and String Quartet*
Anton Webern: *Cantata No. 1*

In other unusual time-signatures we observe a reversal of the foregoing practices. That is, while the units of time (the denominators)
are standard quarter- and eighth-notes, there are many beats per
measure (large numerators). A generous sampling of meters from $\frac{7}{4}$ to
$\frac{21}{8}$ is shown here:

$\frac{7}{4}$

Béla Bartók: *String Quartet No. 5;*
The Miraculous Mandarin; Leon-
ard Bernstein: *The Age of Anxiety;*
Benjamin Britten: *War Requiem;*
Paul Hindemith: *Symphonia Se-*
rena; Charles Ives: *Violin Sonata*
No. 2; Carl Orff: *Carmina Burana;*
Arnold Schönberg: *Variations for*
Orchestra; Roger Sessions: *Duo for*
Violin and Piano; Igor Stravinsky:
Agon

$\frac{8}{4}$

Béla Bartók: *String Quartet No. 5;*
The Miraculous Mandarin; Charles
Ives: *Violin Sonata No. 2;* Ernst
Krenek: *String Quartet No. 7;* Bo
Nilsson: *Ein irrender Sohn;* Arnold
Schönberg: *Moses und Aron;* Igor
Stravinsky: *Agon*

$\frac{9}{4}$

Samuel Barber: *Cello Sonata;* Béla
Bartók: *The Miraculous Mandarin;*
Leonard Bernstein: *Suite from "On*
the Waterfront"; Arthur Honegger:
Le Roi David; Charles Ives: *Violin*
Sonata No. 2; Ernst Krenek: *String*
Quartet No. 7; Bo Nilsson: *Ein ir-*
render Sohn; Carl Orff: *Catulli*
Carmina; Arnold Schönberg: *Violin*
Concerto; Igor Stravinsky: *Agon*

$\frac{10}{4}$

Lukas Foss: *Time Cycle;* Alan Hov-
haness: *Mysterious Mountain;* Ernst
Krenek: *String Quartet No. 7;* Bo
Nilsson: *Ein irrender Sohn*

$\frac{11}{4}$

Lukas Foss: *Time Cycle;* Nicolai
Rimsky-Korsakov: *The Snow*
Maiden; Igor Stravinsky: *Le Sacre*
du printemps

$\frac{12}{4}$

Luigi Dallapiccola: *6 Carmina Alcaei;*
Lukas Foss: *Time Cycle;* Arthur
Honegger: *Le Roi David;* Ernst
Krenek: *String Quartet No. 7;* Wil-
liam Walton: *Belshazzar's Feast;*
Violin Concerto

$\frac{10}{8}$

Béla Bartók: *Music for Strings, Per-
cussion, and Celesta; String Quar-
tet No. 5;* Aaron Copland: *Violin
Sonata;* Roy Harris: *Trio;* Paul
Hindemith: *When Lilacs Last in
the Dooryard Bloom'd;* Olivier
Messiaen: *Les Offrandes oubliées;*
Igor Stravinsky: *Threni*

$\frac{11}{8}$

Béla Bartók: *Music for Strings, Percussion, and Celesta;* Roy Harris:
Symphony No. 7; Paul Hindemith:

Symphonia Serena; André Jolivet: *Concerto pour ondes Martenot;* Leon Kirchner: *String Quartet No. 1;* Olivier Messiaen: *Les Offrandes oubliées*

$\frac{13}{8}$
Leoš Janáček: *Sinfonietta*

$\frac{14}{8}$
Elliott Carter: *8 Etudes and a Fantasy*

$\frac{15}{8}$
Elliott Carter: *String Quartet No. 2;* Claude Debussy: *Fêtes; Rondes de printemps; String Quartet;* Paul

Hindemith: *When Lilacs Last in the Dooryard Bloom'd*

$\frac{18}{8}$
Samuel Barber: *Cello Sonata;* Charles Martin Loeffler: *2 Rhapsodies;* Ottorino Respighi: *Vetrate di chiesa*

$\frac{19}{8}$
John Vincent: *Consort for Piano and Strings*

$\frac{20}{8}$
Igor Stravinsky: *Threni*

$\frac{21}{8}$
Elliott Carter: *String Quartet No. 1*

Conversely, the quarter note and the eighth note have been used as denominators with exceedingly small numerators—such as $\frac{1}{4}$, $\frac{1}{8}$, and $\frac{2}{8}$. A few representative examples follow:

$\frac{1}{4}$
Pierre Boulez: *Improvisation sur Mallarmé,* No. 1 and No. 2; *Le Marteau sans maître;* Aaron Copland: *Short Symphony;* Luigi Dallapiccola: *6 Carmina Alcaei;* Leoš Janáček: *Sinfonietta;* Olivier Messiaen: *Les Offrandes oubliées;* Bo Nilsson: *Mädchentotenlieder;* Luigi Nono: *Incontri;* Carl Orff: *Carmina Burana; Catulli Carmina;* Silvestre Revueltas: *Planos;* Karlheinz Stockhausen: *Gruppen;* Igor Stravinsky: *Symphony in Three Movements;* Edgard Varèse: *Intégrales; Octandre*

$\frac{1}{8}$
Pierre Boulez: *Le Marteau sans maître;* Howard Hanson: *String Quartet;* Leoš Janáček: *Sinfonietta;* Silvestre Revueltas: *Planos;* Karlheinz Stockhausen: *Gruppen; Zeitmasse;* Igor Stravinsky: *Concerto in D for Violin and Orchestra; Le*

Sacre du printemps; Anton Webern: *String Trio*

$\frac{2}{8}$
Béla Bartók: *Piano Concerto No. 2; String Quartet No. 3;* Alban Berg: *Chamber Concerto;* Luciano Berio: *Serenata I;* Luigi Dallapiccola: *Volo di notte;* Olivier Messiaen: *Oiseaux exotiques; Trois petites liturgies;* Carl Orff: *Carmina Burana;* Silvestre Revueltas: *Pianos;* George Rochberg: *Symphony No. 1;* Arnold Schönberg: *Five Piano Pieces,* Op. 23; *Violin Concerto;* Karlheinz Stockhausen: *Gruppen; Zeitmasse;* Igor Stravinsky: *Le Sacre du printemps; Movements for Piano and Orchestra; Symphony in C; Threni;* William Walton: *Symphony No. 1;* Anton Webern: *Cantata No. 1; String Quartet,* Op. 28; *String Trio*

Still other contemporary composers refrain from tinkering with
either the numerators or the denominators of conventional signatures;
instead, they indicate their unusual meters *directly over* the note-
patterns on the staff. An excellent example of this practice is supplied by Nono's *Varianti* for orchestra. Here this contemporary Italian
composer wished to employ a measure-pattern of 28 sixteenth-notes,
for which a correct time-signature would be $\frac{28}{16}$. But since he thought
of this measure in four equal divisions of seven notes each, he chose
to write a conventional $\frac{4}{4}$ signature, and then to indicate the four
groups of seven by the figures directly above them. His procedure, if
compared with the other possible notation in $\frac{28}{16}$, is infinitely simpler
and clearer.

EXAMPLE 10 - 10

2. Alternating Meters   Regular alternating time-signatures
such as $\frac{6}{8}\ \frac{4}{4}\ \frac{6}{8}\ \frac{4}{4}$ are sometimes conveniently notated by means of a
double time-signature placed at the beginning of the movement or
passage: $\frac{6}{8} + \frac{4}{4}$. This would indicate that each pair of measures would
follow this pattern of alternating meters unless otherwise indicated,
thus avoiding repetitive notation of regularly recurring changes. This
practice has been confirmed by successful use in such works as the
following:

$\frac{2}{2} + \frac{3}{2}$ —Aaron Copland: *Sextet for Clarinet and Strings*

$\frac{2}{2} + \frac{3}{4}$ —Leonard Bernstein: *Suite from "On the Waterfront"*

$\frac{6}{4} + \frac{4}{4}$ —Franz Liszt: *A Faust Symphony;* Richard Strauss: *Der Rosenk*

$\frac{5}{4} + \frac{4}{4}$ —Wolfgang Fortner: *Symphony*

$\frac{4}{4} + \frac{5}{4}$ —Gunther Schuller: *Contours for Small Orchestra*

$\frac{4}{4} + \frac{3}{4}$ —Leonard Bernstein: *Serenade; Suite from "On
the Waterfront"; The Age of Anxiety;* Aaron
Copland: *Violin Sonata*

$\frac{4}{4} + \frac{2}{4}$ —Wallingford Riegger: *Symphony No. 4*

$\frac{3}{4} + \frac{4}{4}$ —Richard Strauss: *Der Rosenkavalier*

$\frac{3}{4} + \frac{2}{4}$ —Aaron Copland: *Suite from "The Red Pony"*

$\frac{3}{4} + \frac{3}{8}$ —Leonard Bernstein: *Serenade;* Aaron Copland:
Short Symphony

$\frac{2}{4} + \frac{3}{4}$—Richard Strauss: *Don Quixote*

$\frac{2}{4} + \frac{6}{8}$—Leonard Bernstein: *"Jeremiah" Symphony;* Richard Strauss: *Der Rosenkavalier*

$\frac{2}{4} + \frac{3}{8}$—Leonard Bernstein: *The Age of Anxiety;* Aaron Copland: *Short Symphony*

$\frac{9}{8} + \frac{6}{8}$—Miklos Rozsa: *Violin Concerto*

$\frac{6}{8} + \frac{5}{8}$—Aaron Copland: *Sextet for Clarinet and Strings; Short Symphony*

$\frac{6}{8} + \frac{4}{8}$—Albert Roussel: *Petite Suite*

$\frac{3}{8} + \frac{2}{4}$—Aaron Copland: *Third Symphony*

$\frac{3}{8} + \frac{4}{8}$—Gustav Mahler: *Symphony No. 6*

3. Variable Meters   Variable meters occur when almost every measure needs a new time-signature but when there is no consistent pattern of recurrent meters: $\frac{4}{4}$ $|\frac{3}{4}$ $|\frac{5}{4}$ $|\frac{3}{8}$ $|\frac{4}{4}$ and so on. Some composers in writing variable meters have placed a *single large signature* between the two staves of a keyboard piece, rather than a separate signature on each staff (Example 10-11a). In Claude Debussy's *Préludes pour piano* the composer has written the meter changes directly above the staff, enclosed in parentheses (Example 10-11b). Boulez in his *Sonatine* for flute and piano has put the changing meters on a single line between the flute and piano staves (Example 10-11c).

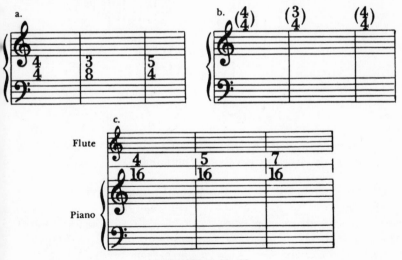

EXAMPLE 10 - 11

Claude Ballif in his *Voyage de mon oreille* (impeccable title!) for orchestra devised a related method of avoiding topheavy numerators.

He simply indicated a *metronome mark,* giving the note-unit (a six-teenth note), but dispensed with any traditional time-signature. Instead, figures are placed *directly over* the staff for each measure to show the number and division of the units within each pair of barlines. Comparison will demonstrate that a more conventional notation is not necessarily more clear:

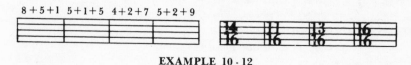

EXAMPLE 10 - 12

It makes little difference, actually, just where these time signatures are placed as long as they are clearly shown. The German composer Boris Blacher solved this problem in his *Orchester-Ornament* by inscribing on the first page of the conductor's score: "In 8ths." For the numerators of his varying meters he then provided a separate line, writing the number of beats above each measure: 2 |5 |9 |7 |6 |4. This work, incidentally, was the first to illustrate Blacher's theory that variable meters should follow a very definite pattern. As a concrete example, the first three score pages followed this pattern of variable meters:

```
|2 |3 |4 |5 |6 |7 |8 |9 |8 |7 |6 |5 |4 |3 |2 |
      |3 |4 |5 |6 |7 |8 |7 |6 |5 |4 |3 |2 |
         |3 |4 |5 |6 |7 |6 |5 |4 |3 |2 |
            |3 |4 |5 |6 |5 |4 |3 |2 |
               |3 |4 |5 |4 |3 |2 |
                  |3 |4 |3 |2 |
                     |3 |2 |
```

The balance of the work was built on similarly elaborate patterns of the eight figures, in every possible permutation.

4. Combined Meters   Combined time-signatures are used in a piece of music to indicate one of two conditions: either a *fixed pattern* of changing meters (such as we have already discussed under Alternating Meters) or a *flexible alternation* of simple and compound meters containing the same number of rhythmic units. A combined signature of $\frac{6}{8}$ ($\frac{3}{4}$) or of $\frac{3}{4}$ ($\frac{6}{8}$) would mean that the measures alternate —freely or strictly—between the simple meter ($\frac{3}{4}$) and the compound meter ($\frac{6}{8}$). (See examples in the left-hand column on page 168.)

Performers beginning their study of works in these combined meters will do well to remember that the *note-values are constant;* only the major stresses change. The first reading of a $\frac{6}{8}$ ($\frac{3}{4}$) meter is best counted throughout as six exactly equal eighth-notes to a measure; the first reading of the $\frac{6}{4} = \frac{3}{2}$ is best counted throughout as six quarter-notes to a measure. Then, with the constant note-value established, the position of the varying stresses may be indicated.

A different type of combined signature marks the shift from triplet measures notated $\frac{3}{8}$, $\frac{6}{8}$, $\frac{9}{8}$, or $\frac{12}{8}$ changing to $\frac{2}{4}$, $\frac{3}{4}$, or $\frac{4}{4}$—in cases where the three eighth-notes (or dotted quarter) of the triplet measures are to have the same time-span as the quarter note of the simple-time measure. We could notate this combined meter as $\frac{2}{4}$ ($\frac{6}{8}$) or $\frac{2}{4} = \frac{6}{8}$.

EXAMPLE 10 - 13

Examples of this type of combined meter may be seen in the right-hand column on page 168.

The combined meter is especially adapted to notating complex patterns that would be cumbersome in a constant $\frac{2}{4}$. But the wary performer will keep firmly in mind that when this $\frac{2}{4}$ becomes $\frac{6}{8}$, there are still *two* beats to a measure, of exactly the same length, whatever the signature; that there are *three* beats in every measure of $\frac{3}{4}$ ($\frac{9}{8}$); and *four* beats in every measure of $\frac{4}{4}$ ($\frac{12}{8}$). Still more complicated alternations become simple to the performer who remembers that in all cases the quarter-note beat of the simple measure equals the three-eighth-note beat of the compound measure (see Example 10-14).

less awkward

more awkward

EXAMPLE 10 - 14

Combined meters may be studied in such works as:

$\frac{3}{2} = \frac{6}{4}$
or
$\frac{6}{4} = \frac{3}{2}$

Luigi Dallapiccola: *Il Prigioniero;* Claude Debussy: *La Cathédrale engloutie;* Alberto Ginastera: *Variaciones Concertantes;* Charles Ives: *Violin Sonata No. 2;* Arnold Schönberg: *Moses und Aron*

$\frac{3}{4} = \frac{6}{8}$
or
$\frac{6}{8} = \frac{3}{4}$

Aaron Copland: *El Salón México;* Alberto Ginastera: *Pampeana No. 3*

$\frac{4}{2} = \frac{12}{4}$ Alban Berg: *3 Orchestra Pieces*

$\frac{3}{2} = \frac{9}{4}$ Paul Hindemith: *When Lilacs Last in the Dooryard Bloom'd*

$\frac{2}{2} = \frac{6}{4}$ Luigi Dallapiccola: *Il Prigioniero*

$\frac{4}{4} = \frac{12}{8}$
or
$\frac{12}{8} = \frac{4}{4}$

Arthur Honegger: *Jeanne d'Arc au bûcher;* Goffredo Petrassi: *Partita for Orchestra*

$\frac{9}{8} = \frac{3}{4}$
or
$\frac{3}{4} = \frac{9}{8}$

Igor Stravinsky: *Concerto in D for String Orchestra*

$\frac{2}{4} = \frac{6}{8}$ Maurice Ravel: *Une Barque sur l'océan*

$\frac{2}{4} = \frac{12}{16}$
or
$\frac{12}{16} = \frac{2}{4}$

Leonard Bernstein: *The Age of Anxiety;* Claude Debussy: *Collines d' Anacapri;* Peter Racine Fricker: *Symphony No. 1*

$\frac{3}{8} = \frac{9}{16}$ Easley Blackwood: *Symphony No. 2*

5. Compound Meters

Compound time-signatures * point out that within the measures there will be *unorthodox groups* of the basic units of time (the beats). We have previously viewed these unorthodox groups as beaming problems (see Chapter 6) because correct beaming makes them accessible. To review—in the examples below we see the eight eighth-notes of a $\frac{4}{4}$ measure first in conventional groups and then in unorthodox groups with a compound signature.

EXAMPLE 10 - 15

Any traditional pattern in any meter may of course be altered to a compound meter, the only limit being the mathematical law of permutation. The Table of Compound Meters lists most of the feasible possibilities in measures from $\frac{4}{8}$ to $\frac{12}{8}$.

---

* Compound *time-signatures* and compound *time* (see page 150) must be considered completely different terms.

EXAMPLE 10-16. TABLE OF COMPOUND METERS

METER	COMPOUND		METER	COMPOUND		METER	COMPOUND	
4/8 (2/4)	1+3/8	1+2+1/8	**8/8 (Cont.)**	1+4+3/8	5+3/8	**11/8**	2+3+2+4/8	5+2+2+2/8
	3+1/8	2+1+1/8		2+1+5/8	6+2/8		2+3+4+2/8	2+3+6/8
	1+1+2/8			2+5+1/8			2+3+3+3/8	2+6+3/8
5/8	1+1+3/8	3+1+1/8	**9/8**	1+2+6/8	3+5+1/8		3+2+2+4/8	3+3+5/8
	1+2+2/8	2+3/8		1+6+2/8	3+2+4/8		3+2+4+2/8	3+5+3/8
	2+1+2/8	3+2/8		1+3+5/8	3+4+2/8		3+2+3+3/8	3+4+4/8
	2+2+1/8			1+5+3/8	4+1+4/8		4+2+2+3/8	3+6+2/8
6/8 (3/4)	1+2+3/8	2+3+1/8		1+4+4/8	4+4+1/8		4+2+3+2/8	4+2+5/8
	1+3+2/8	3+1+2/8		2+1+6/8	5+1+3/8		4+3+2+2/8	4+5+2/8
	2+1+3/8	3+2+1/8		2+6+1/8	5+3+1/8		4+3+4/8	5+3+3/8
7/8	1+2+4/8	3+1+3/8		2+2+5/8	5+2+2/8		4+4+3/8	6+2+3/8
	1+4+2/8	3+3+1/8		2+5+2/8	2+7/8		5+2+4/8	6+3+2/8
	1+3+3/8	3+2+2/8		2+3+4/8	4+5/8		5+4+2/8	7+2+2/8
	2+1+4/8	2+5/8		2+4+3/8	5+4/8	**12/8 (6/4)**	2+3+7/8	3+5+4/8
	2+4+1/8	3+4/8		3+1+5/8	7+2/8		2+7+3/8	4+3+5/8
	2+2+3/8	4+3/8	**10/8 (5/4)**	2+2+3+3/8	2+5+3/8		2+4+6/8	4+5+3/8
	2+3+2/8	5+2/8		2+3+2+3/8	3+2+5/8		2+6+4/8	5+2+5/8
8/8 (4/4)	1+2+5/8	2+3+3/8		2+3+3+2/8	3+5+2/8		2+5+5/8	5+5+2/8
	1+5+2/8	3+2+3/8		3+2+2+3/8	3+3+4/8		2+8+2/8	5+3+4/8
	1+3+4/8	3+5/8		3+2+3+2/8	3+4+3/8		3+2+7/8	5+4+3/8
				3+3+2+2/8	4+3+3/8		3+7+2/8	7+2+3/8
				2+2+6/8	5+2+3/8		3+4+5/8	7+3+2/8
				2+6+2/8	5+3+2/8			
				2+3+5/8	6+2+2/8			

The Table of Compound Meters works just as well with smaller beat-units such as 16th and 32nd notes. Stockhausen's *Zeitmasse,* for instance, employs $\frac{1+6+2}{16}$. And in Boulez' *Improvisation sur Mallarmé,* No. 1 we find:

$$\frac{4+6}{16}, \quad \frac{2+3+2}{16}, \text{ and } \frac{3+2+3}{16}.$$

6. Polymeters (simultaneous meters)

Many composers of our day, writing for large ensemble or orchestra, actually conceive music in which various instruments or instrumental groups play simultaneously in different meters. Obviously there is one constant—a *common unit* of time (or beat)—fundamental to the entire ensemble. This beat the conductor must establish and retain, even though all the barlines do not coincide.

Although polymeters *per se* are largely a twentieth-century manifestation, a striking example of this device may be found in a chamber work by—of all composers—Mozart. In the third movement of his *Oboe Quartet* (K. 370) the oboe part is notated in **C** and the accompanying strings in $\frac{6}{8}$. Because of the fairly rapid tempo of the movement, the meter of **C** is in actuality **¢**; the $\frac{6}{8}$ meter, of course, is also felt in two beats to the measure. Even more noteworthy is the polymetric scheme at the end of Act I of *Don Giovanni:* three orchestral groups—one in the pit and two on stage—each plays in a different meter, combining $\frac{3}{8}, \frac{2}{4}$, and $\frac{3}{4}$.

It is sometimes possible to notate polymeters clearly without actually writing different time-signatures for the different meters. This is still another function of unconventional beaming, especially when one of the individual lines is in the nature of an *ostinato* (a constantly repeated figure). A reiterated figure of three in a basic pulsation of four could be notated as follows:

EXAMPLE 10 - 17

Such a pattern may be found in Stravinsky's *Chant du rossignol* (at No. 24) and in Schönberg's *Five Pieces for Orchestra* (No. 1). A repeated pattern of *two* within the framework of a triple meter, as seen in Copland's *Dance Symphony* (second movement at No. 32), would be notated this way:

EXAMPLE 10 - 18

An outstanding example of a repeated pattern of *four* notes, carried over many measures of changing time-signatures, is to be found in Stravinsky's *"Dumbarton Oaks" Concerto* (the final movement).

Another way of indicating polymeters without changing meters and barlines is as follows:

EXAMPLE 10 - 19

Here a $\frac{5}{8}$ pattern is superimposed on a basic $\frac{2}{4}$ meter. Instead of a $\frac{5}{8}$ signature and displaced barlines for the upper part, a bracket encloses the groups of five notes. In the hands of a proficient performer, the result will exactly duplicate the rhythmic pulse of an actual $\frac{5}{8}$ meter against the $\frac{2}{4}$.

When the composer, however, wishes to heighten the drama—even the conflict—of the contrasting meter-patterns, he frequently prefers to write his simultaneous meters with their individual time-signatures. No contrasted time-signatures are necessary for the *cross rhythms* of the example at the left below, where two different patterns are used within a single meter. But a true polymeter, as illustrated at the right, needs opposing time-signatures.

EXAMPLE 10 - 20

As is usual with polymeters, the unit of pulsation—in this case the quarter note—agrees in the two parts, but the primary stresses come at different places. One could, it is true, always notate such patterns within the framework of one inclusive meter, as shown below, but the performance would lack the aural and emotional impact of a true polymeter (see Example 10-21).

EXAMPLE 10 - 21

One of the most familiar instances of two simultaneous meters is the final section of the first movement of Hindemith's symphony *Mathis der Maler*. Here the Gregorian theme of the trombones is in $\frac{3}{2}$ time, while the balance of the orchestra progresses in $\frac{2}{2}$. As will be seen below, the barlines coincide after every two measures of the $\frac{3}{2}$ and after every three measures of the $\frac{2}{2}$ meter.

EXAMPLE 10 - 22

An unusual example of polymeter is found in the concluding pages of Benjamin Britten's *War Requiem*—an alternating meter of $\frac{2}{2}$ $\frac{3}{2}$ for the boys' choir set against an underlying $\frac{2}{4}$ time-signature in the accompanying orchestra.

Another contemporary example is drawn from Dallapiccola's *6 Carmina Alcaei,* in which overlapping meters of $\frac{3}{4}$, $\frac{9}{4}$, and $\frac{6}{4}$ are used.

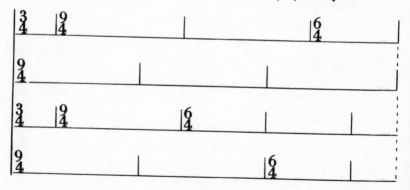

EXAMPLE 10 - 23

A similar example of changing polymeters may be found in Webern's *Cantata No. 2,* in which the meters for each part of the chorus change canonically.

Other examples of polymeters may be found in the following twentieth-century works:

Béla Bartók: *String Quartet No. 3*— $\frac{2}{4}$ / $\frac{4}{4}$

Leonard Bernstein: *Serenade*— $\frac{9}{8}$ / $\frac{3}{4}$

Arthur Bliss: *Quintet for Oboe and Strings*— $\frac{6}{8}$ / $\frac{7}{8}$

Benjamin Britten: *Gloriana*— $\frac{6}{4}$ / $\frac{4}{4}$

—— *Nocturne*— $\frac{4}{8}$ / $\frac{12}{16}$

Aaron Copland: *Suite from "The Red Pony"*— $\frac{4}{4}$ / $\frac{6}{8}$

Henry Cowell: *Exultation*— $\frac{4}{4}$ / $\frac{3}{4,4}$ / $\frac{4}{4}$

Heimo Erbse: *Impression for Orchestra*— $\frac{2}{4}$ / $\frac{3}{4}$

Paul Hindemith: *Der Schwanendreher*— $\frac{3}{2}$ / $\frac{9}{4,2}$ / $\frac{6}{4,4}$ / $\frac{6}{8}$

—— *Symphonia Serena*— $\frac{2}{2}$ / $\frac{4}{8}$

Charles Ives: *4th Symphony*— $\frac{6}{2}$ / $\frac{4}{4,2}$ / $\frac{4}{4,4}$ / $\frac{6}{8}$

Carl Nielsen: *Symphony No. 6*— $\frac{2}{4}$ / $\frac{6}{8,8}$ / $\frac{3}{8}$

Serge Prokofiev: *Violin Concerto No. 2*— $\frac{12}{8}$ / $\frac{4}{4}$

Arnold Schönberg: *Five Pieces for Orchestra*— $\frac{3}{8}$ / $\frac{4}{8}$

Gunther Schuller: *Contours for Small Orchestra*— $\frac{15}{4}$ / $\frac{5}{2,4}$ $\frac{12}{2}$

William Schuman: *Symphony No. 6*— $\frac{3}{2}$ / $\frac{3}{4}$

Richard Strauss: *Der Rosenkavalier*— $\frac{3}{4}$ / $\frac{4}{4}$

The most astounding example of all is the *Fourth of July* movement from Ives's orchestral *Holidays,* in which nearly every instrument plays in a different meter. No doubt the almost insurmountable difficulty of keeping everyone together has prevented frequent performances of this work.

7. **Mixed Meters**   When meters consist of unequal units (simultaneous denominators) grouped within the measure, mixed time-signatures are produced:

EXAMPLE 10-24

This signature may be found in Tippett's *Symphony No. 2.* For the composer, the performer, and the audience this is *not* the same as writing $\frac{11}{16}$, as shown above at the right. The $\frac{11}{16}$ signature implies that a constant sixteenth-note is the beat unit, and this is not what the composer conceived. The mixed meter combines a quarter-note unit with a dotted-eighth unit (or $\frac{3}{16}$), and the metrical feeling is quite different. Such careful distinctions between varying notations is a vital part of contemporary musical expression. It is not our purpose to advocate one method over another, but to help composers say what they mean, and to assist performers in reading this clear notation.

Significant examples of mixed meters may be found in:

Béla Bartók: *Piano Concerto No. 2* – $\frac{3}{4} + \frac{1}{8} =$ ♩♩♩♪

Luciano Berio: *Serenata I* – $\frac{6}{8} + \frac{1}{16} =$ ♫♫ ♫♫ ♪
$\frac{3}{8} + \frac{1}{16} =$ ♫♫ ♪

Pierre Boulez: *Improvisation sur Mallarmé*, No. 1 – $\frac{3}{16} + \frac{4}{8} =$ ♫♫ ♫♫♫
$\frac{2}{4} + \frac{5}{8} =$ ♩♩ ♫♫♫♫

Pierre Boulez: *Improvisation sur Mallarmé*, No. 2 – $\frac{3}{2} + \frac{1}{4} =$ 𝅗𝅥 𝅗𝅥 𝅗𝅥 ♩

Pierre Boulez: *Le Marteau sans maître* – $\frac{3}{16} + \frac{3}{8} =$ ♫♫ ♫♫
$\frac{1}{4} + \frac{1}{16} =$ ♩ ♪

Bo Nilsson: *Mädchentotenlieder* – $\frac{7}{4} + \frac{1}{16} + \frac{3}{4} =$ ♩♩♩♩♩♩♩♪♩♩
$\frac{3}{4} + \frac{3}{32} =$ ♩♩♩ ♬
$\frac{1}{8} + \frac{4}{4} =$ ♪♩♩♩♩

Silvestre Revueltas: *Sensemayá* – $\frac{2}{4} + \frac{3}{8} =$ ♩♩ ♫♫
$\frac{3}{4} + \frac{3}{8} =$ ♩♩♩ ♫♫

Roger Sessions: *Piano Sonata No. 2* – $\frac{3}{4} + \frac{1}{16} =$ ♩♩♩♪
$\frac{5}{8} + \frac{1}{16} =$ ♫♫♫ ♪

Igor Stravinsky: *Threni* – $\frac{1}{8} + \frac{3}{4} =$ ♪♩♩♩

Michael Tippett: *Symphony No. 2* – $\frac{3}{8} + \frac{2}{4} =$ ♫♫ ♩♩
$\frac{3}{8} + \frac{2}{8} + \frac{3}{16} =$ ♫♫ ♫ ♫♫

Edgard Varèse: *Ionization* (for percussion ensemble) – $\frac{2}{4} + \frac{3}{8} =$ ♩♩ ♫♫

8. Fractional Meters

Our final category in the roster of unusual contemporary meters can only be called *fractional meters*. These are of two kinds: meters in which a fraction *is added* to the numerator—such as $2\frac{1}{2}$; and those in which a fraction of a musical entity *is* the numerator—$\frac{2}{4}$, for instance.

The first classification is actually only another way of writing a mixed meter. The $\frac{2\frac{1}{2}}{4}$ could also be notated as $\frac{2}{4} + \frac{1}{8}$, for the complete measure contains $2\frac{1}{2}$ times the value of a quarter note. The meter could also be written as a compound signature: $\frac{4+1}{8}$, although the rhythmic feeling is not precisely the same.

Examples of this first variety of fractional meter may be found in:

$\frac{2\frac{1}{2}}{2}$ Gardner Read: *Piano Quintet*

$\frac{5\frac{1}{2}}{4}$ Gardner Read: *Driftwood Suite*

$\frac{4\frac{2}{3}}{4}$ { Toshiro Mayuzumi: *Nirvāna-Symphonie*

$\frac{4\frac{1}{2}}{4}$ { Charles Ives: *4th Symphony;* Toshiro Mayuzumi: *Nirvāna-Symphonie;* Gardner Read: *Driftwood Suite*

$\frac{3\frac{1}{2}}{4}$ { Toshiro Mayuzumi: *Nirvāna-Symphonie;* Gardner Read: *Driftwood Suite;* Edgard Varèse: *Intégrales; Octandre; Offrandes*

$\frac{2\frac{1}{2}}{4}$ { Toshiro Mayuzumi: *Nirvāna-Symphonie;* Gardner Read: *Touch Piece;* Wallingford Riegger: *Study in Sonority;* Edgard Varèse: *Octàndre*

$\frac{1\frac{1}{2}}{4}$ Edgard Varèse: *Octandre*

$\frac{5\frac{1}{2}}{8}$ Silvestre Revueltas: *Sensemayà*

$\frac{3\frac{1}{2}}{8}$ { Toru Takemitsu: *Masque for 2 Flutes*

$\frac{2\frac{1}{2}}{8}$ { Toru Takemitsu: *Masque for 2 Flutes*

Fractional meters are well justified when the rhythmic pattern begins or ends with the half-beat, for a $\frac{5}{8}$ divided as $4 + 1$ or $1 + 4$ makes good sense notated as $\frac{2\frac{1}{2}}{4}$. Because the problem of fractional meters may be new to many notators and performers, a Table of Fractional Meters has been included.

The *second* classification of fractional meters (such as $\frac{2}{4}$) is more complicated—both to devise and to explain. In order to have two-thirds of a figure we must first find its whole, or three-thirds. To divide a quarter note into thirds means thinking of it as a triplet in which the three segments are tied together: ♩♩♩   Two-thirds of this triplet equal: ♩♩(♩) . Therefore $\frac{2}{4}$ means the time-duration of two eighth-notes of a triplet figure, without accounting for the "lost" third note. The diagram on page 176 (Example 10-26) may show more clearly than words what takes place metrically.

EXAMPLE 10-25.   TABLE OF FRACTIONAL METERS

$\frac{4\frac{1}{2}}{2} = \frac{4}{2} + \frac{1}{4}$ = ♩♩♩♩♩	$\frac{4\frac{1}{2}}{4} = \frac{4}{4} + \frac{1}{8}$ = ♩♩♩♩♪
$\frac{3\frac{1}{2}}{2} = \frac{3}{2} + \frac{1}{4}$ = ♩♩♩♩	$\frac{3\frac{1}{2}}{4} = \frac{3}{4} + \frac{1}{8}$ = ♩♩♩♪
$\frac{2\frac{1}{2}}{2} = \frac{2}{2} + \frac{1}{4}$ = ♩♩♩	$\frac{2\frac{1}{2}}{4} = \frac{2}{4} + \frac{1}{8}$ = ♩♩♪
$\frac{1\frac{1}{2}}{2} = \frac{1}{2} + \frac{1}{4}$ = ♩♩	$\frac{1\frac{1}{2}}{4} = \frac{1}{4} + \frac{1}{8}$ = ♩♪
$\frac{4\frac{1}{2}}{8} = \frac{4}{8} + \frac{1}{16}$ =	$\frac{4\frac{1}{2}}{16} = \frac{4}{16} + \frac{1}{32}$ =
$\frac{3\frac{1}{2}}{8} = \frac{3}{8} + \frac{1}{16}$ =	$\frac{3\frac{1}{2}}{16} = \frac{3}{16} + \frac{1}{32}$ =
$\frac{2\frac{1}{2}}{8} = \frac{2}{8} + \frac{1}{16}$ =	$\frac{2\frac{1}{2}}{16} = \frac{2}{16} + \frac{1}{32}$ =
$\frac{1\frac{1}{2}}{8} = \frac{1}{8} + \frac{1}{16}$ =	$\frac{1\frac{1}{2}}{16} = \frac{1}{16} + \frac{1}{32}$ =

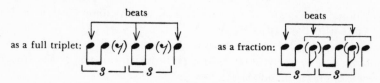

as a full triplet: beats   as a fraction: beats

EXAMPLE 10-26

The ⅔ signature just discussed, as well as ⅔, appear in *Le Marteau sans maitre* by the French composer Boulez—foremost practitioner of this type of fractional meter. Curiously, the fractional figure occupies an entire measure; the measure, then, is actually complete-but-incomplete by one-third of a triplet.

The Swedish avant-garde composer Bo Nilsson has used several forms of fractional meter in his *Mädchentotenlieder*. In addition to the "conventional" use of $\frac{3}{4}$, $\frac{2}{2}$, $\frac{4}{4}$, $\frac{2}{4}$, and $\frac{1}{4}$, (!) in the manner of Boulez, he has combined fractional and mixed meters as follows:

$$\frac{1}{32} + \frac{2}{4}; \ \frac{3}{4} + \frac{1}{8}; \text{ and } \frac{2}{4} + \frac{1}{4}.$$

It is not the purpose of this manual to give a verdict of right or wrong for any technical innovation. Yet one cannot help question whether or not these extreme subleties are actually perceived in performance. Mathematically, the concept of such fractional meters may be explained, and to a degree understood, by the performing musician. But unless produced by a machine (and such music exists, of course, in tape-recorder composition) it is extremely doubtful if the highly complex metric organization of these fractional meters can be justified by what is actually heard.

9. Decimal Meters   Fractional meters may also be expressed by using decimals. For example, we may notate $\frac{2\frac{1}{2}}{4}$ also as $\frac{2.5}{4}$, as the Japanese composer Yoshiro Irino does in his *Music for Violin and Violoncello*. Or, in place of $\frac{4\frac{1}{2}}{4}$ we may substitute $\frac{4.5}{4}$, or write $\frac{3.5}{2}$ in place of $\frac{3\frac{1}{2}}{2}$. Although found in a few recent avant-garde scores, decimal meters are even rarer than their fractional counterparts.

10. Conducting Patterns   Not all contemporary composers who create complex rhythms are indifferent to the problems they create. Many of them have devised various methods to help the performer (instrumentalist, vocalist, or conductor) clarify their asymmetrical meters or inner rhythmic complexities. One of the most helpful devices is placing brackets or other signs over the metrical figures (or units of time), thus graphically making intelligible their varying patterns.

Rhythmic or metrical patterns that might ordinarily require changing meters are sometimes notated with elongated brackets over the uppermost staff:

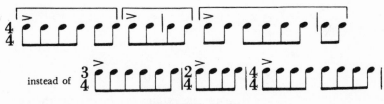

EXAMPLE 10 - 27

Alternating irregular patterns within a single meter are also marked in this way:

EXAMPLE 10 - 28

The Italian composer Dallapiccola has solved this problem by notating a brief meter-change above the staff in the following way:

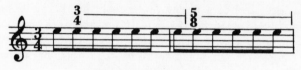

EXAMPLE 10 - 29

Even more graphic are the conducting signs placed over the top staves to indicate subdivisions of the measure—first extensively employed in Messiaen's published works.

$\mid$ or $\llcorner$ = 1 beat		$\sqcup$ or $\sqcap$ = 2 beats	
$\triangle$ or $\triangle$ = 3 beats		$\square$ = 4 beats	

$$\frac{3+2+3}{8} =$$

$$\frac{4+2+3+1}{8} =$$

EXAMPLE 10 - 30

Dotted barlines also serve the same function; these will be discussed in detail in the next chapter.

SUGGESTED REFORMS

Our century has advanced many suggestions for increasing the effectiveness of meter notation and for new methods of indicating time signatures. Many proposed time-signature reforms substitute a note-symbol for the denominator. This is very reasonable, for the lower figure has always stood for the basic unit of the measure: 2, for a half note; 4, for a quarter note; 8, for an eighth note; and so on. The upper number (or numerator) of course indicates the number of units per measure. By using notes instead of figures as the metric unit, we achieve simple time-signatures such as the following:

Perfect meter – Simple time

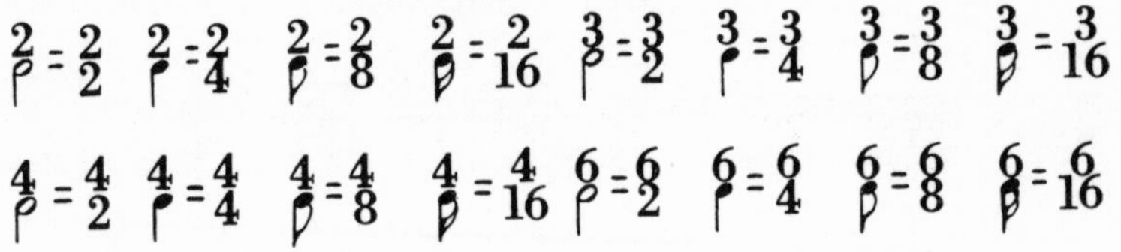

EXAMPLE 10 - 31

Signatures in compound time would be notated in the following forms:

Perfect meter–Compound time

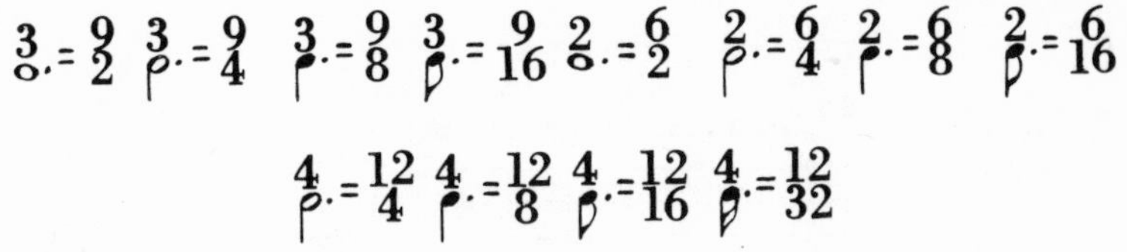

EXAMPLE 10 - 32

Orff in his *Catulli Carmina* has used this system of indicating meters, but has modified it by separating the numerator and denominator with a heavy line and placing the signature just above, rather than on, the top staff, as shown below. In his *Carmina Burana* the composer has slightly altered the symbol by slanting the line between numerator and note-denominator, while still placing the meter sign above the uppermost staff (bottom example, below). Credit for inventing this

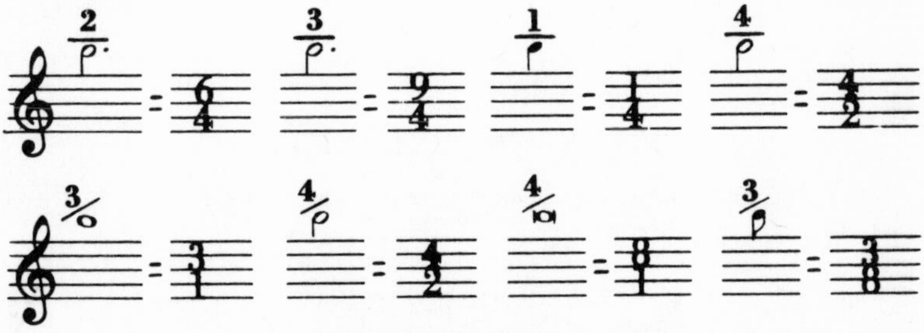

EXAMPLE 10 - 33

simple yet effective form of meter-signature goes to the noted theorist
Jacques Dalcroze.

The American composer Elliott Carter has also employed these
modernized forms in his *String Quartet No. 1*. At one place in the
score he has written the first signature shown at the left, below. This
is far more logical than presenting the pattern conventionally in $\frac{3}{8}$
(center example) or as a quadruplet in triple meter (shown at the right).

EXAMPLE 10 - 34

At another place in the quartet this composer has used the signature:

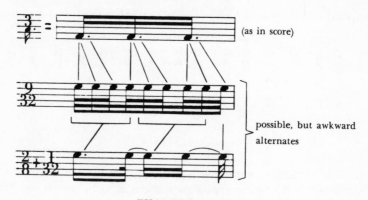

EXAMPLE 10 - 35

There would seem to be no other way of expressing this pattern, which
is highly irregular and can be made to fit into conventional notation
only by the most awkward groupings. Carter has also used the meter
signature of 2 over a half note, in the manner of Orff.

NOTATION EXERCISES

1. Re-notate the following example, using changes of time signature
at the indicated accents:

EXAMPLE 10 - 36

2. Write an original example illustrating: a. variable meters; b. alternating meters; c. combined meters; d. compound meters; e. polymeters; f. mixed meters.
3. What types of meters are illustrated in the examples below? Renotate each example in at least one alternative form:

EXAMPLE 10 - 37

4. Draw conducting patterns for each indicated unit of the example below, and re-beam for greater visual clarity:

EXAMPLE 10 - 38

11

Barlines and Rhythm

THE THIN VERTICAL LINES DRAWN THROUGH THE staff to set off the time-length of each measure (see page 149) are called barlines (Fr. *barre*, pl. *barres;* Ger. *Taktstrich,* pl. *Taktstriche;* It. *stanghetta,* pl. *stanghette*). They enclose, so to speak, the requisite number of beats or pulsations, whether in unchanging sequence (when the time signature is unaltered) or in changing sequence (when the meter is variable).

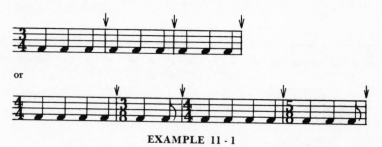

EXAMPLE 11 - 1

In their earliest forms, barlines had more the character of breathing-points, of places of brief rest for the singers, than of fixed indications of metrical pattern. In the plainchant music of the thirteenth to sixteenth centuries we find three degrees of such pauses. The shortest, a line drawn through the top staff-line, corresponded to the comma. The next degree, the equivalent of the semicolon, was a vertical line through the two center staff-lines. The third version, in appearance like the modern barline, was analogous to a period, and indicated the end of a verse. (Compare with Example M.)

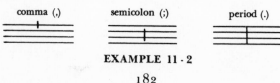

comma (,)   semicolon (;)   period (.)

EXAMPLE 11 - 2

At a somewhat later date, a complete barline was used to ensure the vertical alignment of vocal or instrumental parts written on a number of staves—a guide for the eye rather than a mark of metrical division.

Regularly recurring barlines in the modern sense first appeared in the keyboard tablature notation of the fifteenth century (see page 22), though not until the early sixteenth century did they function to indicate recurring metrical stress in other notation. A curious *Practicum Musicum* for voices with lute accompaniment was published as late as 1584 with soprano and bass parts unbarred, but the lute part —in tablature notation—barred. By the mid-seventeenth century— which saw both the development of the opera and the embryonic beginnings of the orchestra—barlines of the modern type had become basic to all music, vocal and instrumental.

The changing duties of the barline were implicit in every paragraph of Chapter 10, for this symbol now functions to define the meter in two ways: it marks the *primary stresses,* as the first beat following any barline normally receives the strongest pulsation of the measure; and it divides the basic pulse into convenient groups, or *units of time.* Whether the groups are regular (one basic time-signature) or irregular (changing time-signatures), the barlines serve as convenient guideposts to the metric flow. (See Example 11-1.)

When the guideposts are notated for two staves or more—for keyboard instruments, ensembles, and orchestras—the question arises: Where is the barline to stop? Does it go only through each staff separately? or through both staves when there are only two? through all the systems of an entire score page? or through only one system? These questions may be answered by these guiding principles:

1. Keyboard instruments (piano, celesta, harpsichord) and harp—the barline goes through *both staves.*
2. Organ—the barline goes through the two manual staves and stops; then separately through the pedal staff (see Example 18-21).
3. Ensembles (string quartet, woodwind trio, brass quintet, and so on)—the barlines go unbroken through *all staves* (see Example 11-38).
4. Orchestra and band scores—the barlines go through *each section* (woodwinds, brasses, percussion, and strings), breaking between the separate choirs (see Examples 26-1, 26-2, 26-3, and 26-5).
5. Chorus and vocal ensembles—the barlines go through *each voice staff* only, and are not joined (see Examples 17-3, 17-5, and 26-6). This is to avoid running the barlines into the text, placed between the staves.

Imprecise musicians use the terms *bar* and *measure* synonymously, but—strictly speaking—they are not the same. A bar is the barline itself, not the measure set off by two barlines. Instead of speaking loosely of starting "two bars after letter **A**" it would be more accurate —and more professional—to say "beginning with the third measure after letter **A**."

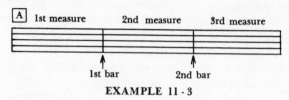

EXAMPLE 11 - 3

THE DOUBLE BAR

It has been pointed out that older music used various forms of the barline roughly equivalent to punctuation marks: the comma, semicolon, and period. Modern music notation also has its semicolon and period in the two forms of the *double bar* (Fr. *double-barre;* Ger. *Doppeltaktstrich;* It. *doppia barra*). As a "semicolon" the double bar consists of two vertical lines of equal size, placed very slightly apart on the staff and used principally to indicate the end of a section of music. The simple double-bar has also been used to set off a change of key (see Chapter 9), or a change of time when the metric scheme is fairly orthodox and time changes are few and far between (see Chapter 10).

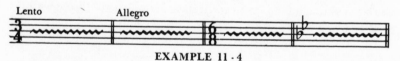

EXAMPLE 11 - 4

In music of a constantly fluctuating meter it would be cumbersome to put a double bar before every single time-change. Modern notation, therefore, has all but dispensed with this traditional usage, and frequently also indicates a brief change of key by accidentals rather than by formal change of signature. Note that both key- and time-signature changes come *after* the double bar, when used, not before it. When such a change of key or time occurs at the end of a line or system, the staff is left open, with no barline of any kind coming after the new signature. (See also Example 9-29.)

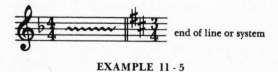

EXAMPLE 11 - 5

The "period" form of double bar, used at the end of a composition or of a movement within it, consists of a thin vertical line followed by a thicker one. In itself this double bar means "the end." It is redundant, then, to put *Fine* (Italian for "the end") over or under the final double bar.

EXAMPLE 11 - 6

The final measure of any piece of music—a completed work or a movement or detached section within an extended composition—should always contain a *complete* time-value. That is to say, the full number of beats should be present, regardless of how the piece began in the metric sense. If the time signature is $\frac{4}{4}$, and the music begins on the fourth beat as an upbeat, the final measure should still contain the full four beats required, either in notes or their equivalent rests (example at the left, below). The practice of making the final measure complete the number of beats in an incomplete first measure was justified in the Classical era (Haydn and Mozart, for example) for movements that repeated the section immediately before the final double-bar (right, below).

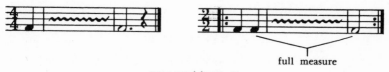

full measure

EXAMPLE 11 - 7

In this case, the final measure had to fill out any missing beats of the first measure. One would still observe this practice today when writing music in a strict classical pattern. But literal repetitions of whole sections are comparatively rare in today's music, so that incomplete final measures seldom have to be balanced off.

RHYTHM

Barlines—as we have just set forth—frame metrical patterns established by time signatures, creating units of time known as measures. Meter —as we established in the preceding chapter—is the recurring pattern of musical pulsations so organized. *Rhythm* (Fr. *rhythme;* Ger.

Rhythmus; It. *ritmo*) is the division of the larger metrical pattern into smaller units of stress and release within the measure-design.

We have learned that meter may be *regular,* with the same time-signature in every measure, or it may be *irregular,* with changing time-signatures. In the same way, rhythm may be regular within a meter (as at the left, below) or irregular (as at the right).

EXAMPLE 11 - 8

Rhythm may be synonymous with the over-all meter (as in the music of the eighteenth and nineteenth century) or the one may be at variance with the other (as in much of the music of our century). In the Classical minuet and in the waltz, the rhythmic patterns parallel the metric flow; both forms bear a $\frac{3}{4}$ signature, and both have a duplicating rhythmic pattern, with the first beat stressed and the other two basically unstressed.

EXAMPLE 11 - 9

But rhythm and the over-all meter may also be sharply contrasted. If we write a time signature of $\frac{3}{4}$, we are saying in effect that the meter is *triple*—three beats to the measure. If we then write $\frac{3}{4}$ ♩. ♩. , we are indicating that the rhythm is *duple,* for it takes only these two equal notes to fill out the time-value of the measure. Reversing the procedure, we may write a $\frac{6}{8}$ time signature, meaning *compound duple* meter (two beats per measure) and within this meter write $\frac{6}{8}$ ♩ ♩ ♩, which makes the rhythm *simple triple.*

In twentieth-century music we no longer have inflexible time-signatures, unvarying barlines, or rigid four-measure phrases. Yet today "the tyranny of the barline" is just as strong as before—in exact reverse. In his eagerness to "fight the barline" the contemporary composer has felt compelled to alter the position of *every* barline. This compulsion has produced only a different kind of tyranny. But it has irretrievably altered the importance of the barline, this very simple device for keeping time, to the point where it now indicates primary stress and pulsation only by coincidence. The notation of *inner rhythm* is now more significant than the positioning of barlines.

NOTATING UNEQUAL GROUPS

Notated rhythm serves the composer and the performer in two spheres: it exists not only for the ear alone, but also for the eye *plus* the ear. The eye helps to clarify rhythmic subtleties that the ear alone cannot distinguish. As our primary concern is the process of notation, rather than composition, we shall concentrate here on the notation of those situations where the eye must especially assist the ear.

Notating unequal groups—triplets against duplets or quadruplets, quintuplets against triplets, and so on—is one of the musician's most perplexing problems. He debates what note-values to employ; he is uncertain of the proper vertical alignment. Where *does* the ninth note of a group of eleven come in relation to the tenth note in a group of fifteen?

Yet the choice of *note-values,* at least, is a comparatively simple decision. The note-values of the extraordinary group are always determined by the note-values of the ordinary group against which they are set. If, for instance, we pit an irregular three against a normal two— the most common of all unequal units—the note-values of the triplet will always be the same as those of the duplet. If the notes of the duplet are quarter notes, then the triplet will also be in quarter notes. If the note-values of the duplet are eighths, the triplet values will be eighths also.

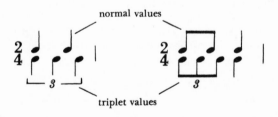

EXAMPLE 11 - 10

When, however, the number of notes in the irregular group exceeds *twice* the number of note-values in the regular group, the uncommon group must employ the next smaller note-value. In Example 11-10 (above) there are two quarter-notes in the normal unit of the measure; if we should place five notes against these two quarters, we would ex-

ceed twice their number (in this case, four). We would then need to
write our quintuplet in eighth notes rather than in quarters.

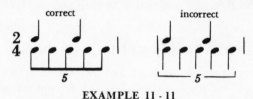

EXAMPLE 11 - 11

These same principles govern the choice of note-values even when
there is no normal melodic line (or another irregular line) pitted
against the irregular note-group. The choice of note-values is still
governed by the note-values of an *ordinary measure* in the given meter.
If the time-unit is a quarter note (as in $\frac{5}{4}$, $\frac{4}{4}$, or $\frac{3}{4}$), then an irregular
group of 11 notes occupying three beats (equivalent to six eighth-notes)
would be beamed as eighth notes. In the same measure, an irregular
group of 13 notes covering three beats would be beamed as sixteenth
notes. (See also Example 11-21, 10. and 11.)

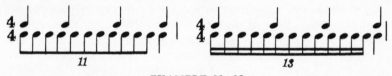

EXAMPLE 11 - 12

The same principle holds also for *compound time-values*. In a $\frac{6}{8}$,
$\frac{9}{8}$, or $\frac{12}{8}$ meter, the normal measure-unit is three eighth-notes. A duplet
set against these three would be written as eighths, or as two dotted-
eighths minus the duplet figure (♪. ♩.). A quintuplet set against one
of these eighth-note groups would also be written in eighths, because
five is less than twice three (left, below). But if we should wish to write
a septuplet (seven notes) against the three, we would use sixteenth
notes, for seven does exceed twice three (right, below. See also Example
11-21, 8. and 9.)

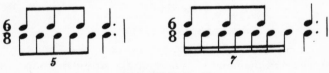

EXAMPLE 11 - 13

Composers and publishers are by no means consistent in this matter
—certainly not infallible. In the published copy of Charles Ives's *Violin*

Sonata No. 4, to quote one example, we find the following beaming in an arpeggiated figure for the piano:

EXAMPLE 11 - 14

The septuplet above should be beamed as 16ths, not 32nds, as from four to seven notes per quarter note would be 16ths, and from eight to fifteen notes, 32nds. But if all composers and all publishers were consistent in the elements of notation, we would have Utopia! In music—as in all endeavors of man—that is a bit too much to hope (and we must sympathize with the problems of getting Ives into print at all—in his own time).

The second phase of notating unequal units—that of *vertical placement*—is more complicated than the choice of note-values. But the infallible solution of the problem is a graph to figure out the mathematical relationship—and hence the exact alignment—between the groups. The first step toward the graph is to multiply the *regular number* of the smallest notes included in the *normal* note-group by the number of notes in the irregular group (or, in the case of large note-groups, to find their least common multiple). Taking again as an obvious example the common two-against-three pattern (see Example 11-10) we multiply the number of notes in the normal group (two, and both quarter-notes) by the number of notes in the triplet (three). With this answer (six) we proceed to think of each group in six units.

Now we graph the relationship between the two note-groups by drawing six evenly spaced vertical lines, each representing the beginning of one unit. We first place the two notes of the normal note-group —evenly spaced in the six units—at lines one and four, for the first unit of any measure begins at the left-hand barline. We next place the triplet notes—again evenly spaced in the six units—at lines one, three, and five. Immediately we see that the second quarter of the two-note group comes midway between the second and third notes of the trip-let.*

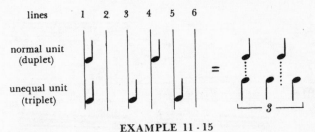

EXAMPLE 11 - 15

If the basic unit of two quarters is subdivided into eighth notes (♫♫ or ♩♫ or ♩♪ and so on), we need to increase the number of graph lines in order to obtain an accurate picture of note align-ment. As we must consider four eighth-notes in relation to the three quarters in the triplet, we multiply four by three, getting twelve as the number of lines to graph. Again we evenly space out the notes of each group. (This may be done quickly by dividing the total number of units—twelve in this case—by the number of notes in each group. Twelve divided by four—the number of eighth notes—shows that each occupies three of the twelve units. Twelve divided by three—the notes of the triplet pattern—shows that each occupies four of the twelve units.)

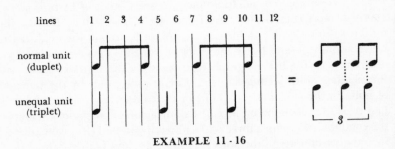

EXAMPLE 11 - 16

The twelve-line graph would also show us the division of the triplet into smaller units (eighth notes and sixteenth notes) because the twelve units of the measure are divisible by six (eighth-notes in a triplet) and by twelve (sixteenth-notes in a triplet).

---

* A very simple short-cut is always available when the first note of the triplet is dotted, as ♩.♫♫ or ♩.♪♪ . In this case only, the second note of the duplet may be aligned exactly with the second note of the triplet. The dotted note is exactly half the time-value of the triplet group. (See Example 11-20.)

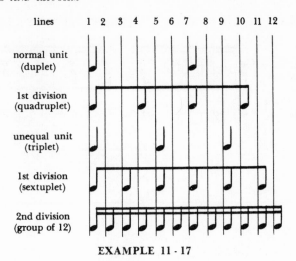

EXAMPLE 11 - 17

A word of explanation regarding the terms *1st, 2nd,* and *3rd division* —used in Example 11-17—is in order here. Every note-value can be divided into smaller portions of itself: a whole note, for instance, can be divided into two half-notes (the "first division"), into four quarter-notes (the "second division"), and into eight eighth-notes (the "third division"). Further divisions are possible, of course, but in plotting out unequal note-groups we shall not go beyond the third division.

If the normal two-quarter-note unit is subdivided into 16th or 32nd notes, more graph-lines will be required, because 12 units cannot be equally divided by eight (the equivalent number of 16th notes) or by 16 (the equivalent number of 32nd notes). To diagram a pattern using 16th notes—as ♩. ♪ ♫ ♪ —against the quarter-note triplet means multiplying eight (the number of 16th notes contained in the normal unit of two quarter-notes) by three. This gives us a total of 24 lines for our graph. By first diagraming all eight 16th-notes—each needing three of the 24 units—and then tieing the necessary ones to obtain the pattern given above, we get the vertical placement of the two rhythmic groups shown in Example 11-18.

By graphing in this manner the most complicated irregular rhythmic figures may be accurately aligned with other patterns equally complex —whether usual in their notation or completely irregular. We need only to follow this orderly process:

1. Find the number of smallest note-values in the normal group.
2. Find the number of smallest note-values in the extraordinary group.

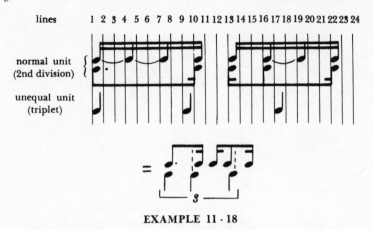

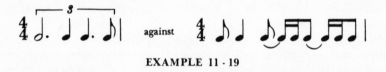

EXAMPLE 11 - 18

3. Find the least common multiple of the two (or in case of small numbers, simply multiply the two numbers).
4. Use as many graph-lines as this multiple, and graph the two note-groups.

As a final challenge, let us plot the complications of the two following patterns, and show their correctly notated alignment:

EXAMPLE 11 - 19

The smallest note-value in the triplet group is an eighth note; there would be four of them to each half-note of the triplet, or a total of twelve to the measure. The smallest note-value in the normal unit is the sixteenth note, and there are 16 of them in the full measure. Twelve times 16 are 192, but we actually need only 48 graph-lines because 48 is the least common multiple for the two figures (12 and 16). Our problem, then, is solved in the manner shown on page 193. ..

Because the pitting of unequal rhythmic patterns occurs so frequently in contemporary music, the Table of Unequal Note-Groups—from duplets to groups of 20—will no doubt solve many notational problems for the young composer or performer. These rhythmic groups are not theoretical combinations, but an actual and vital part of the serious music of our time, so they merit detailed consideration. We preface this Table with a glossary of the terms referring to the rhythmic groups, both normal and extraordinary:

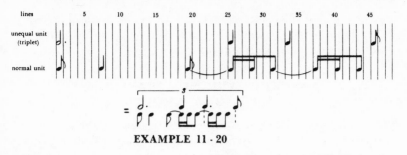

EXAMPLE 11 - 20

English	French	German	Italian
duplet	*duolet*	*Duole*	*duoletta*
triplet	*triolet*	*Triole*	*tripletta*
quadruplet	*quartolet*	*Quatrole*	*quadroletta*
quintuplet	*quintolet*	*Quintole*	*quintupletta*
sextuplet	*sextolet*	*Sextole*	*sestima*
septuplet	*septolet*	*Septole*	*septimole*
octuplet	*octolet*	*Octole*	*ottemole*
nonuplet	*nonolet*	*Nonole*	*novemole*
decuplet	*decolet*	*Decole*	*decimole*
group of 11	*groupe de 11*	*Gruppe von 11*	*gruppetto di 11*
(notes)	*(notes)*	*(Noten)*	*(note)*

And so on --

Each unit of the extensive Table of Unequal Note-Groups shows at the top, numerically, the *unequal groups* to which it applies. Below this listing are given the two opposing *metric units,* each followed by its 1st, 2nd, and—sometimes—3rd divisions. The position of each entire half (metric unit, 1st division, 2nd division, 3rd division) could be *inverted* so that the group now at the top would be placed below; the group now below, placed above. To use the first chart as an example: the group of two is there given *above* the group of three, but their positions could be reversed so that the triplet would be above the duplet. The same process of reversal could be followed for all the other divisions.

The whole note and the dotted whole-note have been arbitrarily used as the basic units. Each separate chart can be adapted by selecting another basic unit: instead of the whole note—a half note, quarter note, or eighth note. The appended divisions of each unit would then be proportionately reduced in note-value. But whether the given unit is to be a whole note or an eighth note, the principle of vertical alignment always remains the same.

As a space-saving device we have charted no unequal figures that require over 80 graph lines (10 against 13, for instance). An enterpris-

ing notator may fill in the gaps in the Tables by availing himself of
large graph paper (or combining two sheets of standard size), and
plotting out the missing groupings.

BRACKETS AND NUMERALS FOR IRREGULAR GROUPS

When an unorthodox note-group is used against a normal one, it is
customary to indicate—over or under the irregular group, depending
upon stem or beam direction—the number of notes therein. Formerly,
printed music used a slur-mark over or under the figure: $\widehat{3}$, $\underset{\smile}{6}$, but
this sign has now been generally replaced by the square bracket. This

(*Text continues on page 212.*)

EXAMPLE 11 - 21. TABLE OF UNEQUAL NOTE-GROUPS

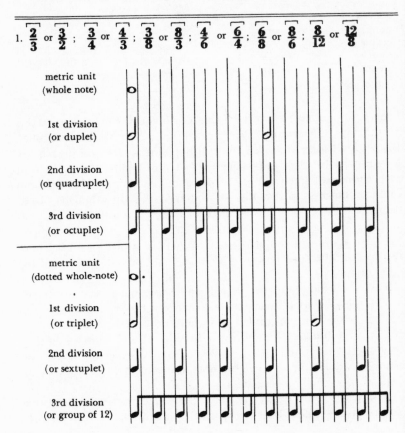

EXAMPLE 11 - 21 (continued)

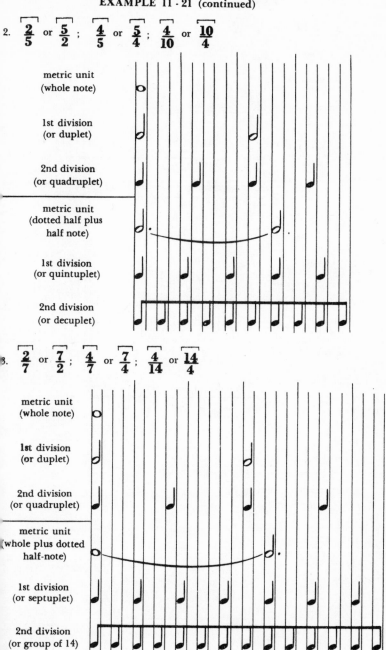

EXAMPLE 11 - 21 (continued)

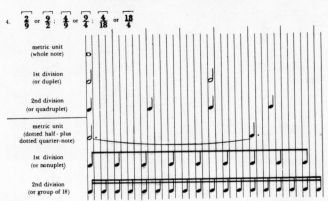

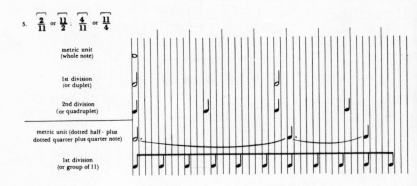

EXAMPLE 11 - 21 (continued)

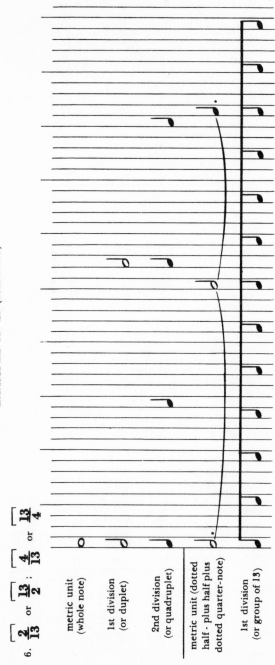

EXAMPLE 11 · 21 (continued)

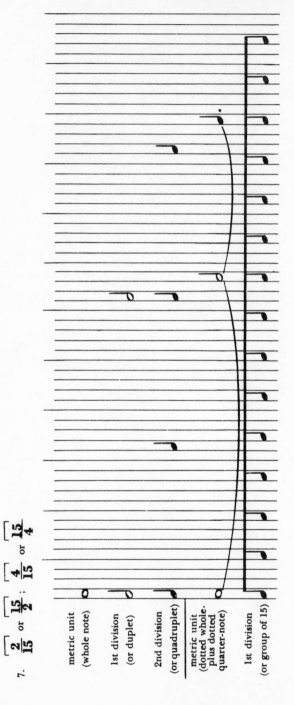

EXAMPLE 11 - 21 (continued)

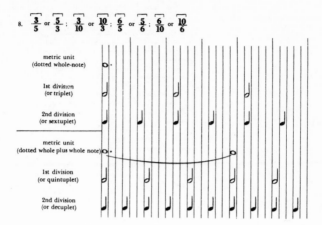

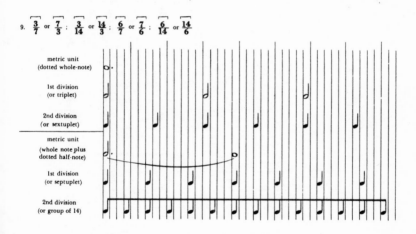

EXAMPLE 11 - 21 (continued)

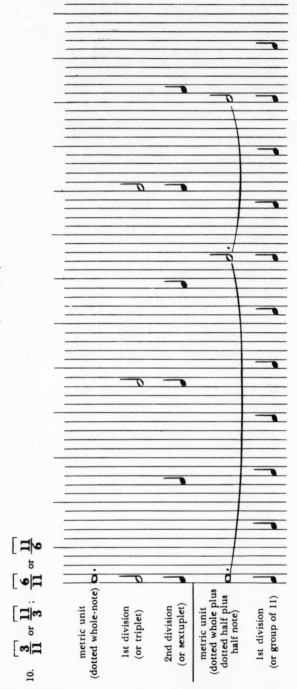

EXAMPLE 11 - 21 (continued)

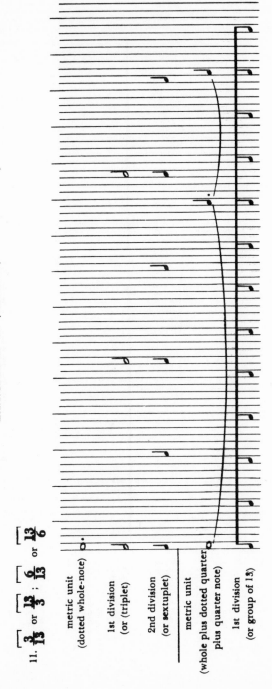

EXAMPLE 11 - 21 (continued)

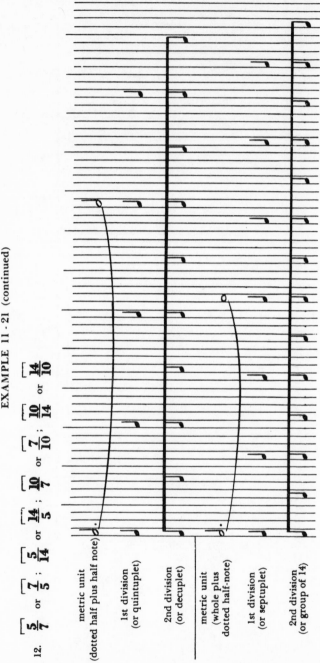

12. $\left[\dfrac{5}{7}\ \text{or}\ \dfrac{7}{5}\ ;\ \dfrac{5}{14}\ \text{or}\ \dfrac{14}{5}\ ;\ \dfrac{10}{7}\ \text{or}\ \dfrac{7}{10}\ \text{or}\ \dfrac{10}{14}\ \text{or}\ \dfrac{14}{10}\right.$

metric unit
(dotted half plus half note)

1st division
(or quintuplet)

2nd division
(or decuplet)

metric unit
(whole plus
dotted half-note)

1st division
(or septuplet)

2nd division
(or group of 14)

EXAMPLE 11 - 21 (continued)

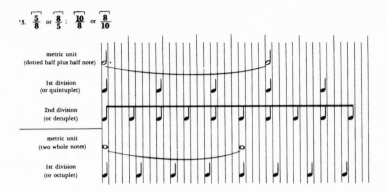

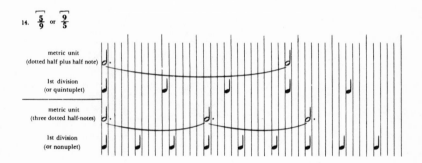

EXAMPLE 11 - 21 (continued)

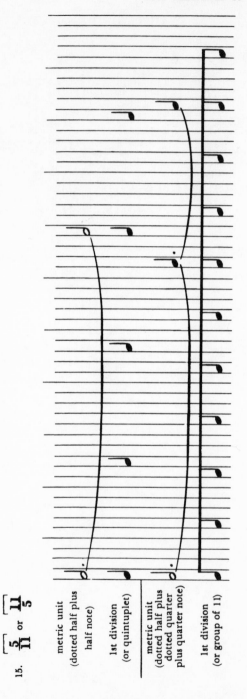

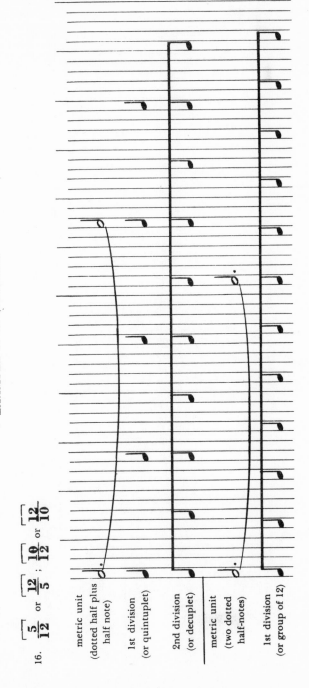

EXAMPLE 11 · 21 (continued)

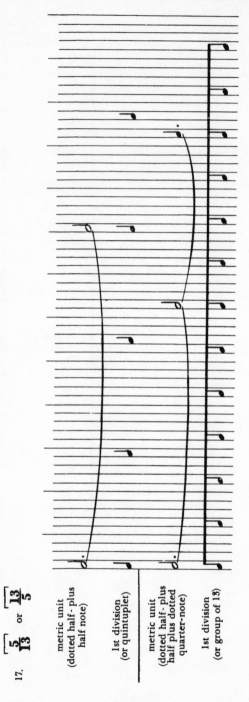

EXAMPLE 11·21 (continued)

17. $\dfrac{5}{13}$ or $\dfrac{13}{5}$

metric unit
(dotted half · plus
half note)

1st division
(or quintuplet)

metric unit
(dotted half · plus
half plus dotted
quarter-note)

1st division
(or group of 13)

EXAMPLE 11 · 21 (continued)

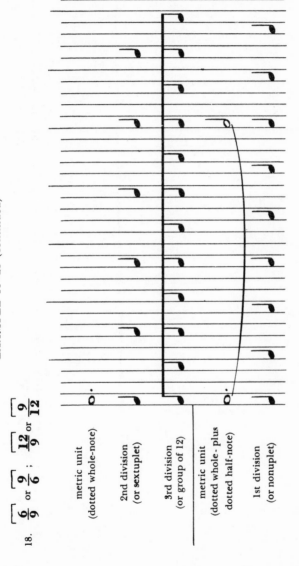

EXAMPLE 11 - 21 (continued)

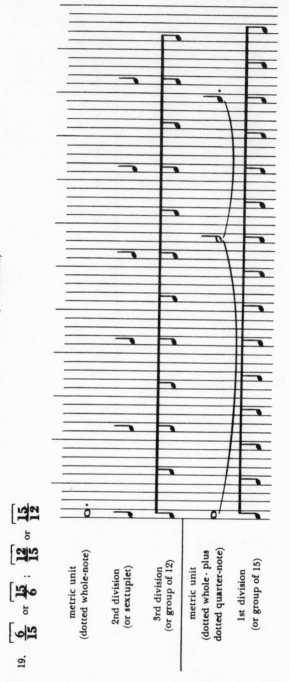

19. $\lceil\dfrac{6}{15}\rceil$ or $\lceil\dfrac{15}{6}\rceil$; $\lceil\dfrac{12}{15}\rceil$ or $\lceil\dfrac{15}{12}\rceil$

metric unit
(dotted whole-note)

2nd division
(or sextuplet)

3rd division
(or group of 12)

metric unit
(dotted whole - plus
dotted quarter-note)

1st division
(or group of 15)

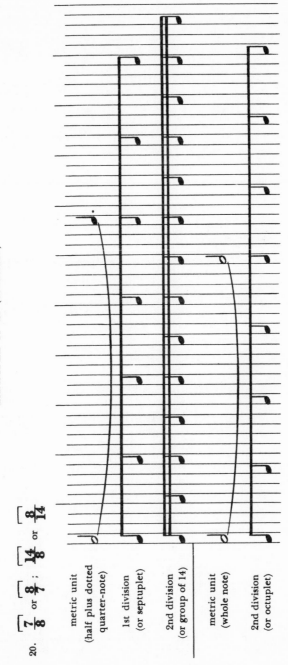

EXAMPLE 11 · 21 (continued)

21. $\dfrac{7}{9}$ or $\dfrac{9}{7}$

metric unit
(half plus dotted
quarter-note)

1st division
(or septuplet)

metric unit
(dotted half · plus
dotted quarter-note)

1st division
(or nonuplet)

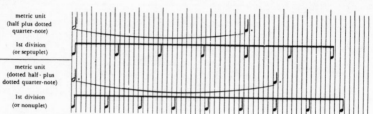

22. $\dfrac{7}{11}$ or $\dfrac{11}{7}$

metric unit
(half plus dotted
quarter-note)

1st division
(or septuplet)

metric unit
(whole plus dotted
quarter-note)

1st division
(or group of 11)

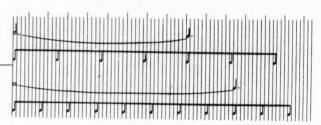

23. $\dfrac{8}{9}$ or $\dfrac{9}{8}$

metric unit
(whole note)

3rd division
(or octuplet)

metric unit
(dotted half · plus
dotted quarter-note)

1st division
(or nonuplet)

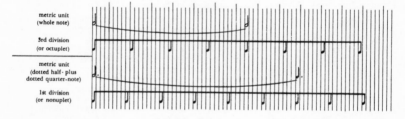

24. $\dfrac{9}{15}$ or $\dfrac{15}{9}$

metric unit
(dotted half · plus
dotted quarter-note)

1st division
(or nonuplet)

metric unit
(dotted whole · plus
dotted quarter-note)

1st division
(or group of 15)

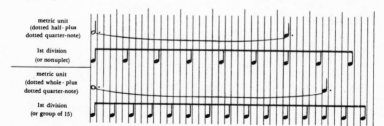

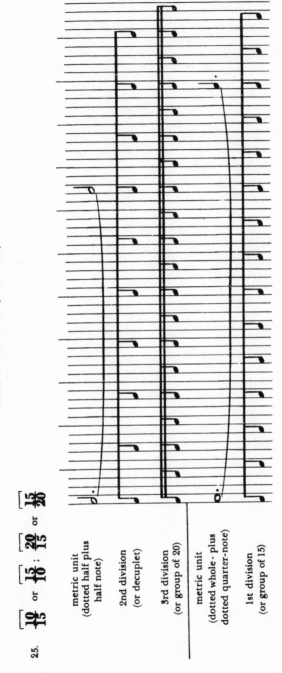

EXAMPLE 11 · 21 (continued)

may go entirely over (or under) the number, or be broken, as shown below.

EXAMPLE 11 - 22

The bracket, when used, is always slanted in the direction of the note-group it affects, whether placed above the group or below it. Note in Examples 11-23 and 11-24 that the figure is always placed directly over or under the primary beam, and is always aligned with the note of the figure that is central in *time* (and not with the center in *space*). For example, the quintuplet in Example 11-23 is subdivided at two points, and the first three notes carry accidentals. If the figure 5 were to be centered in space, the 5 would come beneath the **e''**. The central rhythmic note of the figure, however, is the **g''**, third of the five primary eighth-notes in the quintuplet. Therefore the figure 5 should be placed under **g''**.

EXAMPLE 11 - 23

One exception to the rule illustrated in Example 11-23: in cases where the irregular note-group consists of only two notes—a short and a long—the numeral should be centered *between* the two notes ♪ ♩ , rather than placed over the note covering the rhythmic mid-point of the group: ♪ ♩ . If an irregular group carries within it a further uncommon division requiring a second figure and bracket, these are drawn parallel to the primary figure and bracket.

EXAMPLE 11 - 24

When the unorthodox note-group consists of both beamed notes and single-stemmed notes, as in the second part of the preceding example, the bracket should definitely be used for visual clarity. If rests are included either at the beginning or at the end of the uncommon note-group, the bracket is essential for the same reasons. If the rests are covered by the beams, however, the bracket is not imperative.

EXAMPLE 11 - 25

Ordinarily, no bracket is required when a primary beam clearly shows the metrical relationship of the unequal group to the measure. But if no beams are present, or the group consists mainly of stemmed or flagged notes, the bracket is obligatory (see Examples 11-19 and 11-27, for instance).

In beaming irregular groups that contain sixteenth notes or smaller values, it is extremely important to break the secondary beaming so as to conform to the pattern expressed by the orthodox note-group. If a sextuplet, for example, is paired with a duplet (left, below), the secondary beam should be broken to show that the sextuplet consists of two units of three notes each. If, on the other hand, the sextuplet is paired with a triplet, the secondary beam will be divided into three units of two notes each (center example). Only when the sextuplet is paired with a quarter note, or with an even group that contains eighths and sixteenths, will the secondary beam be unbroken (right, below).

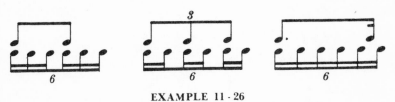

EXAMPLE 11 - 26

The broken beaming should always agree with the basic division of the opposing group, even when this is subdivided unequally. For instance, if the sextuplet were paired with a triplet divided between an eighth note and a quarter note, the secondary beam would still be broken into three units of two, as in Example 11-27.

When an extended passage requires the constant use of unequal groups (triplets, sextuplets, and so on) in all the parts or voices, it is

EXAMPLE 11 - 27

better to change the meter accordingly. If one were to notate the pattern below in a duple meter for a lengthy section, it would be far more sensible to change the time signature to $\frac{6}{8}$, thus avoiding the necessity of indicating triplets on every beat.

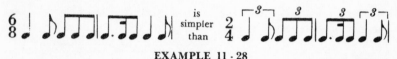

EXAMPLE 11 - 28

In this case, the unit-value changes from a quarter (in $\frac{2}{4}$) to a dotted quarter (in $\frac{6}{8}$); in other words, the previous quarter now equals a dotted quarter. The aural effect will be the same in both notations, but the first version is simpler to read.

If the use of irregular note-groups is confined to one part only (such as an arpeggiated accompaniment in the left-hand part of a piano piece), the groups are marked as triplets, sextuplets, or whatever they may be,

EXAMPLE 11 - 29

rather than with the signature of a polymeter. Usually it is sufficient to put the required numeral over (or under) only the first group or so of a series; it will be clearly understood that the ensuing groups are to be the same.

MODERN INNOVATIONS

1. **Barline Practices**   In much twentieth-century music the barline has been placed in unorthodox locations, such as between the two staves of a keyboard composition. (See also Example 2-7.) This practice can have some validity if it is used to relate polymeters, as illustrated at the right, below.

EXAMPLE 11 - 30

Certain composers, such as Stravinsky (see Example 2-7), have placed the barlines between the contiguous staves of related instruments, rather than through each staff separately or all joined together as a complete system.

Final barlines have sometimes taken the following forms in recent avant-garde scores:

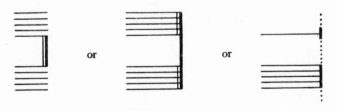

EXAMPLE 11 - 31

A number of contemporary composers have dispensed with the barline altogether—not out of willfulness, but as a means to a completely free and fluid rhythmic expression. It is one way, at least, of avoiding the "tyranny of the barline". Among the composers who have written

works without barlines are Erik Satie (*Gnossienne No. 2* for piano),
Roy Harris (*Piano Quintet*), and Charles Ives (*Concord Sonata,* final
movement; *Violin Sonata No. 4,* second movement).

All of the works cited use conventional note-heads, flags, and beams
for rhythmic duration, regardless of the fact that the music is meterless.
Music written in analog or proportional notation (see Example 5-23)
likewise dispenses with metric barlines. If barlines are present in such
notation they do not function in the traditional sense; instead, they
indicate chronological time, or are used as guidelines of coordination.
Many avant-garde works using such barlines space them a centimeter
apart, each representing one second of clock time. The various proportional note-heads then are extended through these lines according
to their individual duration.

The most prevalent modification of barline use in present-day music
is the *dotted barline,* employed to depict inner subdivisions of complex
rhythms or to show the structure of compound meters. Dotted barlines,
therefore, act as secondary pulsation signs, and they help the eye to
comprehend intricate or unusual patterns.

EXAMPLE 11-32

Dotted barlines are particularly helpful in showing the division of
five-beat, seven-beat, and other irregular meters. In the example at the
left, below, the dotted barline indicates the division of a $\frac{5}{4}$ measure
into 2 + 3. At the right, the division is shown to be 3 + 2 + 2 in a $\frac{7}{8}$
metric scheme.

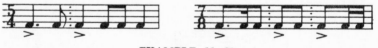

EXAMPLE 11-33

Such complex patterns as one finds in Igor Stravinsky's *"Dumbarton
Oaks" Concerto* benefit enormously from the use of dotted barlines.
Compare the following two versions—the clear upper notation as

EXAMPLE 11-34

Stravinsky wrote the passage, and the obscure lower version as a more conservative composer might have attempted to approximate the pattern.

Another use of the dotted barline is to clarify asymmetrical note-groupings in the individual parts of an ensemble score. In such cases the dotted barlines will not agree between the different parts. Béla Bartók in his *String Quartet No. 5*, for instance, used dotted barlines to contrast the pattern of the upper three instruments with the 'cello pattern, and vice versa:

EXAMPLE 11 - 35

Dotted lines—extended slightly above and below the staff because they serve as "guidelines" as well as inner barlines—are sometimes employed on a single staff or a group of related staves to make the reading easier. With the dotted lines extended to the same level as the following notes, stems, or beams, the eye more quickly takes in a note-combination or wide melodic leap.

EXAMPLE 11 - 36

Such combined bar- and guidelines are invaluable in pointillistic music, where the notes of an instrumental theme or even the word-syllables of a vocal line are tossed from one voice to another. They

EXAMPLE 11 - 37

are positioned as follows: if they go *above* the staff, they are extended
upward from the fourth staff line to the level of the highest note-
element—whether note-head, stem, or beam; if they go *below* the staff,
they are extended downward from the second staff line to the level of
the lowest note-element (note-head, stem, or beam).

Dotted guidelines are also employed in dodecaphonic (twelve-tone)
music to show the progress of the "row" from one instrument to another:

EXAMPLE 11-38

2. Notation of Irregular Groups

The conventional method
of indicating an irregular note-group, whatever the basic meter, has
been to write a single figure over the group (as in the left-hand notation of Example 11-39). In many modern works this method has been
somewhat modified, in that two different figures are sometimes given
—the irregular one and a figure showing the normal number of notes
for that time-span.

EXAMPLE 11-39

The validity—even the necessity—of this practice is determined by
the complexity of the irregular figure. In the straightforward septuplet
at the left in Example 11-40, the double figure is superfluous. But for
the complex notation at the center the 7:8 figure makes sense, indicat-

ing as it does that seven sixteenths—divided between notes and rests—
are to be played in the time-span of eight. Certainly the unusual arrangement at the right would benefit from the double figures to show
that four of the five sixteenth-notes are tied together as a quarter note,
the final sixteenth appearing as a rest.

EXAMPLE 11 - 40

This double-figure method can also be used to mark unequal groups
(called *die irrationalen Dauerwerte* in German texts) within complete
units of time. Below, at the left, we see a triplet included within a
beamed normal group, and then in the traditional notation. A slight
modification of the double-figure practice is exemplified in recent
works by French composers. The terms *pour* ("for") or *de* ("of") mean
the same thing as the colon (:) in the left-hand example below; all
three figuratively mean "in the duration of."

Any device for clarity is welcome in this field, where notation seems
to become more complex by the hour. Irregular groups, for instance,
are now written to begin on the *weak part* of the beat. This spreads

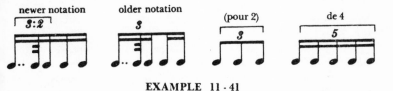

EXAMPLE 11 - 41

the figure over the second half of one beat and the first half of the
following beat. Such an extraordinary group must be carefully notated so as to show its precise metrical location in the measure. In the
example at the left below, observe that the eighth note following the
triplet is flagged separately instead of being beamed with the following two eighth-notes. This is done to show more clearly its relation to
the triplet, and also to avoid having two beamed groups of three notes
each, one of which is a triplet (example at the right).

EXAMPLE 11 - 42

Not all contemporary composers are unmindful of the problems created by such rhythmically distorted notation. In his *Woodwind Quintet* Milton Babbitt has indicated above the measure in question a simplified solution of the following unusual figure:

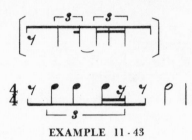

EXAMPLE 11 - 43

In certain rhythmic complexities, irregular groups are also spread *over barlines.* When this occurs, the principle involved is to split the central note-value of the uncommon group into two halves, one tied to the other over the barline.

EXAMPLE 11 - 44

In the above, the second half-note of the triplet is divided into two quarter-notes tied over the barline. This device places one written half of the figure in each measure—exactly the way the pattern would be heard. When irregular figures are stretched over two full measures, the same principle is observed in notation: divide the center note-value of the group into two equal notes, and tie them across the barline.

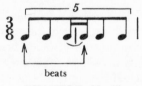

EXAMPLE 11 - 45

Possibly the most striking contemporary innovation in notating free rhythm is the device known as "frame notation." This is a box or rectangle that encloses a group of pitches—free or specified—which are to be played in a random and aperiodic manner (see Example

27-1). When the note-heads are linked together with lines, solid or
dotted, the performer is free to begin with any note but must then
follow the indicated sequence. The length of the "frame" indicates
the relative duration of the note-group.

NOTATION EXERCISES

1. Graph the following combinations of regular note-groups against
   irregular figures:

EXAMPLE 11 - 46

2. Correct the note-values in each of the following irregular note-
   groups:

EXAMPLE 11 - 47

3. Write an original passage for snare drum, illustrating *compound meters* and *dotted barlines.*

12

Repetition Signs

REPETITION IS ONE OF THE MOST VENERABLE DEVICES for unifying a musical composition. Its ancient status has so well consolidated notational practice that the few symbols are easy to learn and unmistakable in their meaning.

Repetitions may affect single units of time (beats), whole measures of any length, and groups of measures. Each length of repetition has its own distinctive symbol and employs this symbol exclusively.

Measured and unmeasured repetitions of single notes or chords as *tremolos* will be discussed in Chapter 13, as such repetition qualifies as ornamentation.

When a *single beat* is repeated—this beat consisting of but one note, or a unified group like a chord—it may be indicated by a single thick, slanting slash placed between the second and fourth staff-lines (upper line, below). If the beat is subdivided into simple eighth-notes alone, the same slash is used again (lower line, below).

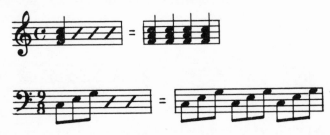

EXAMPLE 12 - 1

If the beat is made up of even sixteenth-notes, two slashes are required (thus corresponding to the two flags of sixteenth notes). Thirty-second notes would require three slashes; 64th notes, four; and 128th notes, five. These slashes are drawn very close together, and always slant upward from left to right.

EXAMPLE 12 - 2

Beats consisting of mixed values are abbreviated by using double slashes accompanied by two dots:

EXAMPLE 12 - 3

The same symbol may be used for the repetition of figures that do not vary, even though a new meter-signature may change the number of *beats* in each measure. The sign represents a unit of time—a full beat, regardless of whether the beat is a half note, a quarter note, or any other value. The example below shows how the repeat symbol may be used under these conditions.

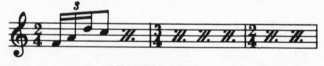

EXAMPLE 12 - 4

The repetition of an *entire measure* (whether it consists of uniform note-values or of mixed values) is indicated by using the sign in the example below. The single slash—slanted as steeply as the previous signs—suffices for any meter and for any combination of rhythmic values. Note the position of the two dots wherever used: on either side of the slash—the upper in the third space, the lower in the second space, and both touching the staff lines.

When there are many such measure-repetitions, it is very helpful to the performer to number the repeated measures, using small figures

EXAMPLE 12 - 5

centered between barlines just above the staff. As the written-out measure constitutes number 1, the measures bearing repeat signs properly
begin with 2, as in the example above. This is not a universal practice,
however, as many notators begin with the figure 1 over the first repeat
measure. The principal disadvantage of this procedure is that the
figure over the final measure of repeat will not equal the actual total
of measures played alike. For maximum convenience to the performer,
the last measure of repeat ought to show by number the total of measures played, not merely repeated.

If a *two-measure pattern* is repeated, it may be correctly notated
according to either of the two versions below. The first notation places
a bracket over the two measures, with the word *bis* ("twice") centered
over the barline. The alternate version uses the slanting slash (or two
slashes) through the barline, the two dots each in a separate measure.
It is helpful to the performer (although not absolutely essential) to
put the figure 2 over the barline, reminding him that the repetition
affects two full measures.

EXAMPLE 12 - 6

Only on rare occasions will there be repeated a three- or four-
measure pattern simple enough to justify the use of the bracket over
the measures, again with the word *bis* centered over the group. It is
not possible to use the elongated slash or slashes to indicate a repetition of more than two measures.

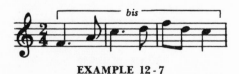

EXAMPLE 12 - 7

When a repetition involves *more than two measures* that are at all complicated in their inner rhythm, the best plan is to use the conventional repeat bars at the beginning and end of the passage to be repeated. Here the heavy bar is now vertical, and extended to the full height of the staff, followed by a thin bar and by dots in the second and third spaces. The sign is literally reversed at the end of the final measure.

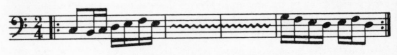

EXAMPLE 12 - 8

Although the repeat bars in the example above coincide with barlines, they must *not* be thought of as synonymous with barlines. They may occur within a measure and on any beat—even bisecting a beat, as shown on the lower line below. Occasionally the single thin line of the repeat mark (the barline proper) is omitted (illustrated at the upper right), but this practice is not recommended.

EXAMPLE 12 - 9

A repeated section frequently has different *first* and *second endings,* as shown at the left below. The first ending is marked with a figure **1** and enclosed by a level bracket with an initial downward jog, ending with a similar jog at the repeat sign. The second ending is marked with a figure **2**, and is also set off with a horizontal bracket—this time beginning with the down-jog and extended without termination, usually as far as the first barline thereafter.

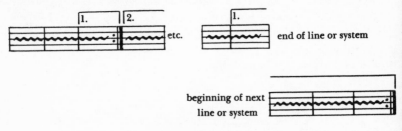

EXAMPLE 12 - 10

If a first ending (also known as a *prima volta* or "first time") continues onto another line or system, the bracket minus a downward jog
is not given the concluding downward jog until the repeat mark is
reached (example at the right).

Should there be a third, or terminating, ending (*ultima volta* or
"final time"), the second ending (*seconda volta* or "second time") is
notated in the manner of the usual first ending.

When two sections follow one another, both of them to be repeated,
the repeat marks take the form below. Notice that the single thin line
is used before and after a single thick bar between the sections, and
that the dots are retained in their usual position.

EXAMPLE 12 - 11

When a change of meter or key signature comes at the beginning of
a section to be repeated, the change is indicated on the staff *before*
the position of the first repeat-bar, as shown below. The notator must
once again observe that repeat signs are not actually barlines, and so
do not follow the same rules of notation.

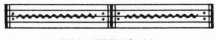

EXAMPLE 12 - 12

When repeat signs come within a measure, note-values or rests must
be carefully indicated to ensure the presence of the full time-value.

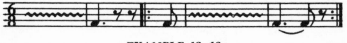

EXAMPLE 12 - 13

Needless to say, none of the repetition signs so far discussed and
illustrated—for one beat, one measure, two measures, or an entire
section—can be used if there is the *slightest deviation* in the pattern
repeat. The alteration of so much as a single note, rhythm, accent,
slur, or dynamic mark affecting anything but the *entire* repeated
pattern makes it imperative that the measures be written out again
in full. If, however, the only change between the first time and the
second time is a change in dynamics affecting the entire pattern, the

repeat signs may be used and the new dynamic mark (see Chapter 14)
given at the appropriate place (lower line, below).

EXAMPLE 12 - 14

A further illustration of this significant technical variation may be
seen in the examples below. As notated at the left, the repetition sign
indicate that each measure is to be played *sfp*. But if the composer
should wish only the first measure to be attacked *sfp*, and the follow
ing measures played *p*, he would have to notate the passage as at the
right.

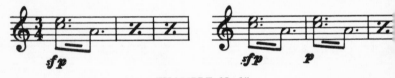

EXAMPLE 12 - 15

Here is proof of the importance of careful notation: indifferent or
slipshod methods only produce confusion or lead to misinterpretation.

When long sections of a composition are to be repeated exactly—or
returned to after a diversion—the abbreviations *D.C.* or *D.S.* are fre
quently used instead of other repeat marks. These symbols need not
be confusing if one will remember that they *are* abbreviations. *D.C.*
stands for *Da Capo* (Italian for "from the beginning"—literally, "from
the head"), while *D.S.* means *Dal Segno* (Italian for "from the sign").
To heed the direction *D.C.*, then, is to go back to the very beginning of
the music and repeat; to follow the direction *D.S.* means to go back
only as far as the sign ℅ or ⊕ , and then repeat. *D.S.* was first em
ployed by composers in the keyboard tablature notation of the six
teenth and seventeenth centuries, and has not changed its basic func
tion to this day.

Both *D.C.* and *D.S.* are sometimes accompanied by modifying direc
tions such as *D.C al Fine* or *D.C. al segno e poi la Coda*. The precise

meaning of all the terms commonly used can best be indicated by the
following diagrams:

1. *Da Capo* alone

2. *Da Capo al Fine*

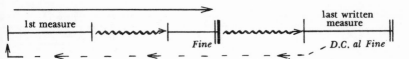

3. *Da Capo al Segno*

4. *Da Capo al Segno e poi la Coda*

5. *Dal Segno* alone

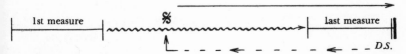

6. *Dal Segno al Fine*

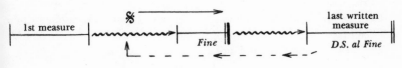

EXAMPLE 12 - 16

Finally—for convenience in writing orchestral scores a very useful sign may be notated on the double-bass staff to signify that the part is an exact *written* duplication of the 'cello line just above it (although the bass sounds, as usual, an octave lower than written). This time-saving symbol may also be used on the staff of one of a family pair of instruments—piccolo and flute, bassoon and contrabassoon, or Violin I and Violin II, for instance—accompanied by the direction *with*, plus the instrumental name. (Italian terms may also be used: *col* with the masculine singular noun, *coi* with masculine plural, *colla* with feminine singular, or *colle* with feminine plural.)

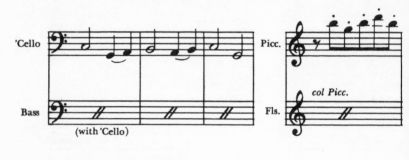

EXAMPLE 12 - 17

The sign illustrated above could also be used when a divided string section (violas or 'cellos on two staves each, for example) has measures of duplicate *written* material. It could be employed for clarinet and bass clarinet only if the latter instrument were reading from the treble clef, its notes duplicating those of the clarinet. It cannot, however, be used for related instruments when one transposes (as oboe and English horn), or for such different instruments as trombone and tuba, even though both are brass members.

Concise and undeviating though they may be—and by very nature unimaginative—the repetition signs merit early mastery for their contribution to time-saving and notational clarity.

MODERN INNOVATIONS

For repeated-note figures that are not true tremolos some contemporary composers have utilized the following abbreviated notation:

EXAMPLE 12-18

Aperiodic repetitions of single notes or short rhythmic figures are common in avant-garde music today. To indicate such repetitions, which are to be played as fast as possible and generally in random order, composers have invented the following notations:

EXAMPLE 12-19

NOTATION EXERCISE

Prepare in table form, with musical illustrations as brief as possible, a complete review of every type of repetition covered in this chapter.

13

Ornaments

Musical devices that literally "ornament" or decorate the melodic line, instrumental or vocal, are called *ornaments* (Fr. *agréments* or *broderies;* Ger. *Verzierungen;* It. *fiorette* or *fioriture* or *abbellimenti*). They are essential features of Baroque music (end of the sixteenth to the mid-eighteenth century), and figure prominently in the era of Classical music (mid-eighteenth to early nineteenth century). Except in keyboard works by such composers as Chopin and Liszt, they are much less frequent in the Romantic nineteenth century. Today, ornaments indicated by special signs are a comparative rarity; if used, they are—with the sole exception of the trill—almost invariably written out in full.

It is not within the scope of this book to go into the historical development of ornaments, or the musicological reasons for this or that interpretation. There are literally dozens of ways in which ornaments have been—can be, or are—written using specific signs. There are scores of ways in which they have been—and are—interpreted and performed. Lengthy books have been written about embellishments in old music, and in a recent edition of Grove's *Dictionary of Music and Musicians* the article on ornamentation covers sixty-four pages! Our concern must be to master—not historical background but traditional practice, which is relatively limited in the number of signs used, and fairly consistent in their rendition.

TRILL

The ornament in most common use today is the trill (Fr. *tremblement;* Ger. *Triller;* It. *trillo*)—the very rapid alternation of two notes a second apart. This interval may, of course, be a half step or a whole step, but it is generally understood that the trill takes in the diatonic (natural scale) step above the written note, unless altered by an accidental. The sign for this ornament is the abbreviation *tr* (without a period) placed over the staff directly above the note affected (the principal note), and usually followed by a wavy line on the same level as the top of the *r*.

EXAMPLE 13 - 1

Note (above) that any required accidental sign is put *after* the **tr**, and *before* the extended wavy line if one is used; if the wavy line is omitted, any accidental is placed *above* the **tr** sign (left, below). Occasionally one will find the accidental placed over or under the wavy line or enclosed in parentheses before it (see Example 13-4); neither variant is an improvement over the version shown in Example 13-1, which is to be preferred.

If the trill is relatively short—a single beat or a beat fraction—the wavy line may be omitted to save space (left, below). Or if such a short trill should be one of a series, the entire series may be notated with a single wavy line, as shown at the center below. It is also permissible, though uncommon, to notate a trill by writing the upper note smaller and in parentheses, without stem or flag (right, below).

EXAMPLE 13 - 2

In actual execution, a trill customarily has a termination group of three notes, as shown at the center, below. This allows the trill to end on the principal note—especially necessary when the trill is to be followed by a note at a different pitch level. The terminal group, however, is seldom actually notated, though understood; if written down, as at the right in Example 13-3, it is given as two grace-notes.

A trill that extends through several measures should have the principal notes tied, unless a pronounced accent is desired at the beginning

EXAMPLE 13-3

of each measure. The portion at the left in Example 13-4 would be continuously trilled without special accents; that at the right would be noticeably accented after each barline.

EXAMPLE 13-4

As a point of information for performers of Baroque and Classical compositions, we must also mention two of the many early trill notations seldom found in modern music. In keyboard music of the seventeenth and eighteenth centuries, the trill sometimes began on the higher note, went once through the principal note to the step below it, and thereafter trilled only the original pair (as detailed on the upper line, below). Another variant began on the note below the principal, so that again three different tones were involved instead of two (as on the lower line, below).

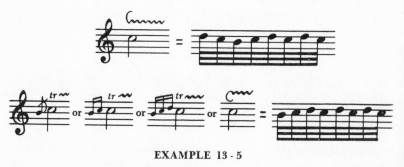

EXAMPLE 13-5

Occasionally even a modern composer may have in mind a trill going from the higher to the lower of two notes. For complete clarity, such

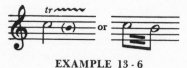

EXAMPLE 13-6

a downward trill is best written as a tremolo (as illustrated in Example 13-6, and as analyzed in the section immediately following).

TREMOLO

The *tremolo* (derived from the Italian word for "tremble"—Fr. *trémolo;* Ger. *Tremolo;* It. *tremolo)* is actually a kind of trill: a very rapid alternation of two or more notes that are further apart in pitch than a major second.

EXAMPLE 13 - 7

On string instruments this alternation may be between two notes on the same string or on adjacent strings, though with somewhat different effect. (See Chapter 23 for a more detailed discussion, with material also on bowed tremolo.)

There are basically two kinds of tremolo—measured and unmeasured. In *measured tremolo* the hearer will consciously perceive the note-values of the alternating notes. In a moderate tempo he would hear sixteenth notes *as* sixteenth notes; in a faster tempo, he would be able to hear eighth notes *as* eighth notes. (See Chapter 16 for a clarification of tempo indications.)

EXAMPLE 13 - 8

In an *unmeasured tremolo,* no specific number of alternations is heard. For very fast tempos, a tremolo written in sixteenth notes would ensure that no precise note-values would be distinguished. In most moderate tempos, the same result would be achieved with 32nd notes. Should the tempo mark be on the very slow side, then the tremolo must be written as 64th notes to be "unmeasured," but even in an Adagio it is not necessary to use 128th notes for proper effect.

EXAMPLE 13 - 9

Examples 13-7 through 13-9 all show tremolos in half notes, with the required beams joining the two stems. Note that the two parts of a written tremolo *duplicate* the note-value involved. Thus in Example 13-8 the half note, which is the *full value* of the $\frac{2}{4}$ measure, is written *twice*. With other note-values the same principle holds good: the entire value must be duplicated in the two written segments of the unmeasured tremolo. Given below, in table form, are the proper notations for unmeasured tremolos from the whole note to the eighth note, in fast, moderate, and slow tempos.

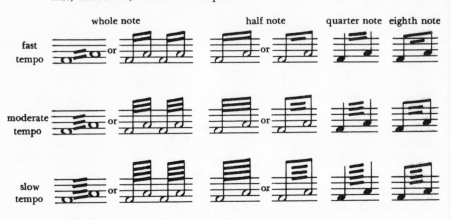

EXAMPLE 13 - 10

Notice that only in the case of an unmeasured tremolo in quarter notes is the primary beam broken, so that it does not connect the two stems. This is a visual matter; there is no other way of setting the quarter note apart from the smaller values. The half (or dotted half) notes can always be joined by a primary beam, as they are set apart by being open, white notes.

It is imperative that the secondary beams be broken when the eighth, sixteenth, 32nd, or 64th note is the basic unit; otherwise the notation looks like a simple succession of two smaller units. When smaller note-values are required, the number of primary beams increases, making it necessary to add more secondary beams in order to indicate the tremolo effect.

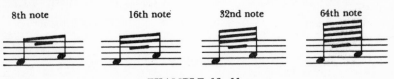

EXAMPLE 13 - 11

Recent practice requires a special notation to distinguish between the measured and the unmeasured tremolo when successive quarter-notes are involved—as in $\frac{4}{4}$ or $\frac{3}{4}$ measure, or a group of $\frac{2}{4}$ measures. Formerly all tremolo figures—whether measured or unmeasured—were written as shown at the left, below. Today the *measured version* (even in sixteenth notes) is notated as at the right, below. When the primary beam is connected to the stems, both notes become eighths, and the single broken secondary beam is a shorthand way of writing four sixteenths.

traditional notation   modern notation

EXAMPLE 13 - 12

When two whole-notes are used with the tremolo beams, and the measure space is quite small, the beam-ends go not quite to where an imaginary stem would be placed (left, below). If the measure space is quite wide, the beams are centered between the two whole-notes, their length being determined by the over-all space available (right, below). It is not necessary to lengthen the beams themselves unduly.

EXAMPLE 13 - 13

When the primary beam of a tremolo is placed between two staves, as in a keyboard piece, the secondary beams are usually (but not exclusively) placed below it (left, below). When tremolo beams for whole notes are placed between the staves, they slant in the direction of the notes they are joining (right, below).

EXAMPLE 13 - 14

The placement of the *second* note of any tremolo figure is of great importance. As the note-values of any tremolo are written twice, the

second note must be located at the exact *metric center* of the beats
involved. The table below shows where the second note of a variety
of tremolo figures is placed in relation to beats, and the meters in
which they occur.

EXAMPLE 13 - 15

GRACE NOTES

Grace notes (Fr. *petites notes;* Ger. *kurz Vorschläge;* It. *appoggiature*)
are literal reductions of full-sized note-forms, without actual rhythmic
value in a measure, as the time in which they are to be performed must
be subtracted from an adjacent beat. If *unaccented*—their most familiar guise—they exist by "grace" of the beat preceding, as in the
example at the left, below. If *accented* (right, below) they exist by
"grace" of the beat following.

unaccented   accented

EXAMPLE 13 · 16

Accented grace-notes are properly appoggiaturas, further illustrated in Examples 13-18–13-21 of the section below. Grace notes are also used frequently in notating arpeggiated chords, as in Example 13-22.

Single grace-notes are usually written as small eighth-notes, with an oblique slash through stem and flag: ♪ ♪. Double grace-notes carry two small beams, as shown below and in Example 22-23. Grace-note groups of three notes customarily have two beams also (as in Examples 6-27, 13-16, and 22-23), but occasionally carry three. Groups of four or more grace-notes generally require three beams. If accidentals, accents, or slurs accompany them, their size must be proportionate to that of the grace notes. The stems, flags, and beams of the single grace-note or grace-note group are usually drawn *up*, regardless of their position on the staff, although publishers are by no means consistent in this practice. Regardless of the number of notes involved, the entire grace-note group should always be written *before* the beat; no note of it should coincide with other voices written on the beat.

correct   incorrect

EXAMPLE 13 · 17

APPOGGIATURA

Appoggiaturas (Fr. *ports de voix* or *notes d'agrément;* Ger. *langer Vorschläge;* It. *appoggiature*), a special classification of grace notes, are of two general kinds: the true appoggiatura (now of interest solely to performers of early music), and the occasional short appoggiatura. The true appoggiatura' (from the Italian *appoggiare,* meaning "to lean") is always *accented;* it occurs *on* the beat and gets its time-value from the note it precedes.

During the nineteenth century the term *appoggiatura* was unfortunately confused with the term *acciaccatura* (from the Italian verb *acciaccare,* meaning "to crush"). The *acciaccatura* is no ornament at all, but a manner of playing, then releasing part of, a chord in keyboard music. It has, then, no real connection with the ornament under consideration.

The appoggiatura is indicated, after the manner of all grace notes, with a small note in the value of a quarter, an eighth, or a sixteenth—but without the slash. As a rule it has half the time-value of the note it precedes (its "principal"), as shown below.

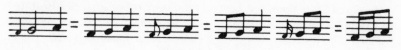

EXAMPLE 13 - 18

Of the vast array of complicated appoggiaturas in music of the Baroque and Classical periods, we can describe only a few situations as a preliminary guide to performers. When, for instance, the principal note of the appoggiatura (the note that follows the small grace-note) is dotted, the grace note receives two-thirds the total value of the dotted note. In the example at the left, below, the principal note is a dotted quarter, or the equivalent of three eighth-notes. Two-thirds of its length would be two eighth-notes, or one quarter-note; thus the grace note is performed as a quarter note. Should the appoggiatura precede a tied note, the same principle holds true, for the tie in this case (right, below) is the equivalent of dotting the principal note. Hence the grace note is again performed as a quarter note.

EXAMPLE 13 - 19

Some versions of the early appoggiatura employ two grace-notes. One—sometimes called the *disjunct double appoggiatura*—normally uses the scale degrees just above and below the principal. This figure is accented, and thus takes part of the beat, as shown at the left, below. Another version is known as the *slide,* and has two grace-notes that rush up, so to speak, to the principal note (right, below).

EXAMPLE 13 - 20

The so-called *short appoggiatura*—notated as a small eighth-note with a tiny slash through stem and flag—is the only form of appoggiatura common in modern music. It is treated in one of two ways: if it follows a note that is *slurred* to the appoggiatura (left-hand example), it is unaccented and takes its time-value from the preceding note. If, on the other hand, the small note is *slurred into* a following note, it is accented, taking its value from the succeeding note (right-hand example). In either case, the appoggiatura "steals" its time-value.

EXAMPLE 13 - 21

Except for the short appoggiatura, this ornament is today unfamiliar and ambiguous; such patterns are more safely written out in appropriate time-values.

ARPEGGIO

Obviously, the word *arpeggio* (Fr. *arpègement*, pl. *arpègements;* Ger. *Brechung*, pl. *Brechungen;* or *Arpeggio*, pl. *Arpeggios;* It. *arpeggio*, pl. *arpeggi*) derives from the Italian *arpeggiare*, meaning "to play on the harp." To *arpeggiate* is to play the tones of a chord successively rather than simultaneously, rolling the notes, usually from bottom to top, in the manner of traditional harp-playing. Some arpeggiated chords are completely written out in rhythm; others are indicated with the assistance of grace notes or by the use of the standard arpeggio-sign (see Example 13-24).

The grace-note group before the arpeggiated chords below indicates that all the notes of the chord but the top one are to be played quickly *before* the beat, with the result that the top note is inevitably emphasized.

EXAMPLE 13 - 22

If the *first* note of the arpeggio is to be accented (played on the beat), then it is best to write the arpeggio in regular notes with proper time-values. Note in the correct illustrations at the left and center, below, the manner in which the notes are tied. The highest note has its tie-mark looped above; the lower notes are connected by loops that go below the note-heads. In order not to conflict with the beams, the note

stems are elongated so as to provide the room necessary for the ties. At
the right, below, is shown an old-fashioned way of notating such arpeggio ties. Each note was given a double stem and separate flag—
exceedingly awkward, and now supplanted by the correct version at
the left.

correct   awkward

EXAMPLE 13 - 23

The arpeggio sign—used when the arpeggiated notes are neither
written out successively nor indicated as graces—is a wavy vertical line
placed before the notes of the chord, in appearance rather like a
perpendicular trill-sign. This standard sign is far more graphic than
the occasional curved line, similar to a vertical slur-mark, used by a
few composers.

standard   dubious

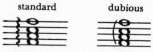

EXAMPLE 13 - 24

A *reverse* (downward) *arpeggio*—first used in the lute music of the
sixteenth and seventeenth centuries, then neglected for two centuries
thereafter—has been revived in the present century by such composers
as Béla Bartók and Arnold Schönberg. As the term implies, the notes
of the chord are rolled from top to bottom rather than the reverse.
The sign for such an arpeggio, if the notes are not actually written out
in full, is the standard wavy line with an arrowhead attached at the
bottom (below, left). In a few foreign editions one may find the reverse arpeggio notated with the wavy line and a vertical wedge (center,
below), or with a downward arrow-sign (right, below).

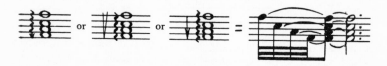

EXAMPLE 13 - 25

Because the wedge symbol in the second example above commonly
relates to dynamic fluctuation (see page 251 and following), and

furthermore is increasingly used by composers in such a vertical position, this notated form of the reverse arpeggio can no longer be recommended. If, however, a *decrease* in intensity is desired from highest to lowest note of the arpeggio, the wedge may be used as illustrated. An *increase* in dynamic strength would call for the position of the wedge to be reversed:

In keyboard music, arpeggiated chords for the two hands are often extended across the two staves. If the chord is to be rolled as a succession of single notes from the very bottom to the very top, the arpeggio sign is *unbroken* (Example 13-26, left). If, on the other hand, the bottom notes for both hands are to be struck simultaneously, and the top notes are to coincide, the wavy line must be *broken* between the staves (Example 13-26, right).

EXAMPLE 13 - 26

It is quite possible, of course, to notate both forms as reverse arpeggios, with an arrowhead at the bottom of the one or the two wavy lines (upper line of Example 13-27). Also possible is a combination of the two forms between the two hands, as on the lower line of Example 13-27. In this case an arrowhead is also placed on the normal arpeggio sign, pointing up.

GLISSANDO

In effect, the *glissando* (Fr. *glissement,* pl. *glissements;* Ger. *Glissando,* pl. *Glissandos;* It. *glissando,* pl. *glissandi*) is a rapid swoop up or down at a tempo so fast that the intermediate pitches are not heard individually. Even on keyboard instruments the actual notes are heard not separately but only as a swift glide between two far-flung pitches.

Traditionally, glissandos have been written with a straight or a wavy line connecting the note-heads of the bottom and top pitches, as shown at the left of Example 13-28. On occasion the notation takes

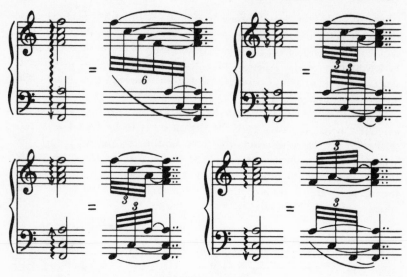

EXAMPLE 13 · 27

the form shown at the right, below; note the incomplete beams, and the fact that three are usually employed.

EXAMPLE 13 · 28

Sometimes glissandos must end just before a barline or before a strong beat, but not on any clearly defined portion of the beat. In this case it is customary to extend the line to a grace note or to a stem placed at the approximate pitch where the glissando is to end. The word *approximate* should be emphasized, for the concluding pitch is often indefinite. If it is important that a certain final note be heard, the glissando should be notated in one of the ways shown in Example 13-28 (above).

EXAMPLE 13 · 29

Because the problems of both tone-production and notation for glissandos are individual to the various instrumental groups and voices, they will be considered in detail in the appropriate chapters to come.

MORDENT

The etymology of the word *mordent*—from the French *mordre*, "to bite"—is singularly apt, for the mordent sign resembles a segment of a trill-sign, literally "bitten off": ∿. A mordent (Fr. *mordant* or *pincé*; Ger. *Pralltriller* or *Mordent*; It. *mordente*) may therefore be considered as the first three notes of a downward trill, beginning on the beat. In duration the notes are measured—the first two rapid, and the third somewhat longer—in proportion to the 'general tempo of the music. In a slow tempo the final note would have a somewhat longer duration than in a fast tempo (upper examples, below).

A double, or "long," mordent consists of five notes—the first four quick and the fifth longer. Again the exact speed and duration of the component notes would be determined by tempo (lower examples, below).

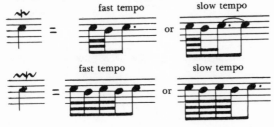

EXAMPLE 13 - 30

Both forms of mordent may be inverted—that is, turned upside down so that the middle note of the group of three (or second and fourth notes in a group of five) would lie *above* the principal note. The inverted mordent-sign is minus the short vertical line drawn through the jagged sign at mid-point.

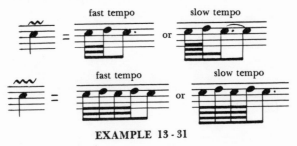

EXAMPLE 13 - 31

Some theorists and music scholars have defined mordents and inverted mordents as just the reverse of the above definitions. As it is possible to write out mordent like figures in full (as demonstrated in Examples 13-30 and 13-31), modern notators might gratefully follow the frequent example of J. S. Bach in notating exactly what is desired.

TURN

The *turn* (Fr. *brisé* or *groupe* or *doublé;* Ger. *Doppelschlag;* It. *gruppetto*) usually consists of four notes, rather like the concluding four notes of a trill (see Example 13-3). Its symbol is ingeniously pictorial: ∼ or ∾ . When this sign is placed directly *over* a note, the turn begins on the beat, but starting with the tone above (first example, below). When the sign comes *after* a note, the figure also begins on the tone above, but on the second half of the beat instead of the first half (second example, below).

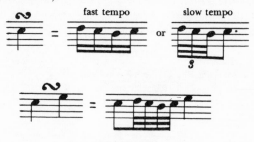

EXAMPLE 13 - 32

It is quite common to find accidentals used with the turn-sign. If the accidental is placed *above* the turn-symbol, it refers to the upper note (top line, below). If the accidental is placed *below* the turn-sign, it refers to the lower note (bottom line, below). A turn may also include accidentals above and below (right-hand example, bottom line).

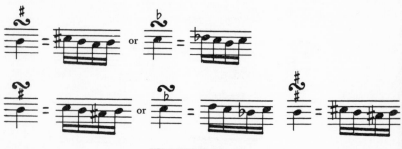

EXAMPLE 13 - 33

Like the mordent, the turn-figure is best written out so that no mis-interpretation can occur.

MODERN INNOVATIONS

Although the reverse arpeggio previously discussed and illustrated (Examples 13-25 and 13-27) might qualify as a modern innovation in ornamentation, its notation follows traditional practice with but slight modification. Further removed from conventional writing would be the notation devised for a kind of indefinite rumble in the bass register of the piano (or any other keyboard instrument). This effect, lying under three, four, or five fingers of the left hand, is a kind of indeterminate tremolo in which the sequence of notes may be random. Given below are the forms of notation covering three-note, four-note, and five-note patterns. There is no reason, of course, why such an effect—with its correlative notation—should not be used by the right hand in a higher register of the keyboard instrument.

EXAMPLE 13 - 34

EXAMPLE 13 - 35

Contemporary variations on the standard tremolo-sign are shown in Example 13-35. The final example indicates an extremely fast and aperiodic tremolo.

As a corollary to these signs, the following variants have been used in place of the traditional trill-sign:

EXAMPLE 13 - 36

NOTATION EXERCISES

1. Notate an *unmeasured tremolo* using dotted half-notes in:
   a. A fast tempo; b. A moderate tempo; c. A very slow tempo.
2. Notate an *unmeasured tremolo* using dotted quarter-notes in a moderate tempo, and showing the alignment of the second note against:
   a. Three quarter-notes; b. Six eighth-notes; c. Twelve sixteenth-notes.
3. Write out in actual note-values the following arpeggiated chords, all in a moderately slow tempo:

EXAMPLE 13 - 37

14
Dynamic Markings

A NOTATOR WITH AUTOMATIC COMMAND OF THE technical materials of the previous 13 chapters should be able to inscribe almost any desired note or combination of notes. Even so, the result will not be a *musical expression* without all the indications of an emotional connotation, for the composer cannot expect even the best performers in the world to be clairvoyant. The imagination was his, and he must be explicit in his directions for reproducing—if not the original aura of creativity, a reasonable image thereof. The first of these directions are his *dynamic marks.*

Originating in a Greek term meaning "power," the term *dynamic markings* refers to all the *indications of power* desired in the performance of the music—to the words used, and to their abbreviations and symbols. This power may be described scientifically, as in the phrase defining volume as the "amplitude of tonal vibrations," by such an emotional word as "intensity," or quite adequately by the simple terms "loudness" and "softness." For this is the aim of dynamic markings—the accurate indication of the relative loudness or softness of individual notes, phrases, sections, and entire movements.

Dynamic markings first appeared in music at the beginning of the seventeenth century, when the prevailing compositional technique—which featured contrasting instrumental groups—suggested the parallel of capitalizing on contrasts of volume. At first the indications were merely the Italian *piano* ("soft") and *forte* ("loud"). Then, as all the implications of symphonic writing began to develop in the eighteenth-century works of Haydn and Mozart, dynamic marks came to be qualified as to *degree: forte* was sometimes *mezzo forte; piano* might also be *pianissimo* (see page 250). In the two intervening centuries, dynamic gradations have become more and more rarefied. The subtleties demanded by the nineteenth-century Romantics (Wagner, Tchaikovsky, Mahler, and Scriabin) have been atomized by the twentieth-century avant-garde (such as Stockhausen, Berio, Pousseur, Nono, and Boulez).

SCALE OF DYNAMIC MARKINGS

In terms of its markings, the *dynamic scale* (Fr. *dynamiques;* Ger. *Lautstärken* or *Tonintensität;* It. *dinamice*), or *gamut,* may be considered to extend from *pppppp* (Tchaikovsky: *Pathétique Symphony,* measure 160 of the first movement) to *ffff* (Tchaikovsky: *1812 Overture,* page 81). In actual notation the lengthy terms—such as *pianississimo*—would be cumbersome, so abbreviations are correctly and universally used instead. The scale of dynamic markings given below shows the average level as *mp* or *mf;* from this midway point the volume level rises to the maximum *(ffff)* and falls to the minimum *(pppppp).*

EXAMPLE 14·1. SCALE OF DYNAMIC MARKINGS

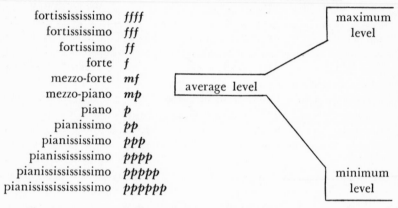

fortississississimo	*ffff*	maximum level
fortississimo	*fff*	
fortissimo	*ff*	
forte	*f*	
mezzo-forte	*mf*	average level
mezzo-piano	*mp*	
piano	*p*	
pianissimo	*pp*	
pianississimo	*ppp*	
pianissississimo	*pppp*	
pianississississimo	*ppppp*	minimum level
pianissississississimo	*pppppp*	

DYNAMIC TERMS

In addition to the terminology of the scale above, the most important terms in the vocabulary of dynamic markings are *crescendo* (abbreviated *cresc.*) and *diminuendo* (*dim.*)—or *decrescendo* (*decresc.*). One also finds such directions given thus:

```
cre _____scen _____do
de _____cre _____scen _____do
di _____min _____u _____en _____do
```

A *crescendo* is a gradual increase in intensity, or loudness. It does *not* connote an increase in speed—which would be correctly indicated as *accelerando*—even though many performers make this mistake. *Diminuendo* (or *decrescendo*) commands a gradual decrease in loudness or intensity—exactly the opposite of *crescendo*. It does *not* signify a slow-ing-down of the tempo; this would correctly be indicated as *ritardando*. No well-grounded musician may be excused for confusing these ex-plicit terms.

DYNAMIC SIGNS

When the increase or decrease in volume is brief, the symbol ━━━━ is often employed to indicate *crescendo,* and the symbol ═══► to indicate *diminuendo.* Both these signs—first used in English lute music around the beginning of the seventeenth century—are popularly known as *hairpins* or *wedges.* Wedges are often accompanied by the terms *molto* ("much") and *poco* ("little"). These terms are usually placed within the wedge sign itself, although there is no good reason why they could not be placed over the sign. It is important, however, that they be located precisely: in, between, or over the wedges, but *exactly* where the *molto* or *poco* is desired.

EXAMPLE 14 - 2

Forte-piano signs have long been combined to produce a special kind of accent or note-attack at all general dynamic levels (see also Chapter 15). The sign *fp* directs that the note or chord be attacked at *forte* (nearly always with an accent) followed by an immediate *piano.* It is almost the equivalent of writing a note or chord tied to itself, the first fraction (the *f* note) being made short, and the second part (the *p* note) made longer.

EXAMPLE 14 - 3

The *fp* marking does not signify a *diminuendo* from *f* to *p,* but an immediate softening (as shown in Example 14-4). This is particularly

EXAMPLE 14 - 4

important to remember in a tremolo or trill, which involve repetitions of notes (see Chapter 13).

The notation of the *fp* may be modified in various ways to indicate increased loudness of attack, softer release, reduced attack, or increased level for the second note. Some of the variants are *ffpp; ffmp; mfp; fppp.*

Various accent terms are also combined with dynamic marks in the manner of the preceding examples. Thus we have *sforzando (sf)*, or *forzando (fz)*, or *sforzato (sfz)* used in place of *f* or *ff*, followed by *p* or its modification. This gives us such markings as: *sfp; sfmp; fzp; fzpp; sfzp; sfzmp*—all being extensions or modifications of the *fp* sign, implying a more specific attack.

NOTATIONAL PRACTICES

In general, dynamic marks should be placed *as close as possible* to the notes they affect—if this position is consistent with over-all visual clarity. They should not, of course, be crowded into a small space, or written in any way that makes them illegible.

In keyboard music, a single dynamic-mark placed in the center *between* the two staves will suffice for both hands, providing the volume level is to be uniform (left-hand example). If either hand has a different dynamic mark from the other, the two separate marks should go just above (or below) the individual staves (center and right-hand examples).

EXAMPLE 14 - 5

In vocal and choral music it is the practice to place the dynamic marks *over* the staff rather than under it. This is done to avoid confusion with the text, which is always placed beneath the staff (see Examples 17-3 and 17-5).

Instrumental music—both ensemble and orchestral—usually has the dynamics placed *beneath* the staff to which they refer (see left-hand

part of Example 14-6). This general rule is, of course, altered should
there be inadequate room because of elements (note-heads, beams, slur
signs, and the like) related to the staff just below, or when different
dynamic markings affect two voices written on one staff, as in Example
26-17. In visually crowded scores, dynamics are sometimes placed even
on the staff itself.

Once correctly placed, the dynamic markings must be checked for
exactness. It is extremely important to include the sign for the proper
dynamic level after every *crescendo* and *diminuendo* (or *decrescendo*).
If a passage begins *mp*, followed by a *crescendo* over several measures
with no further dynamic marking given, the performer has no way of
knowing the intensity level the composer wants. Does the *crescendo*
go to *f*? or only to *mf*? or up to *fff*? It is a cardinal rule in music notation that precise dynamic markings be used at all times; one should
never take it for granted that the performer will know what level is
required. We must reiterate the absolutely infallible principle of music
notation: *Assume nothing; be explicit.*

For this reason, it is best to indicate extended increases of intensity
by writing the abbreviated term, followed by widely spaced dashes or a
dotted line to the indication of maximum or minimum volume:

> *mf*   *cresc.*   -   -   -   -   *fff*
> *f*   *dim.* . . . . *pp*

If wedges (or "hairpins") are substituted for the spaced dashes or
dots suggested above, they are generally placed *beneath* the staff rather
than over it (see example at the left, below). If space is crowded under
the staff, then the signs can be placed *over* the notes and staff (right,
below).

EXAMPLE 14 - 6

In keyboard compositions wedges may be put *between* the staves
(as in the example at the left, below), but if they refer to *one staff only*,
they must be placed directly over or under that staff (center, below).
But over, under, or between—*crescendo* and *diminuendo* wedges must
never be separated from their accompanying dynamic-marks.

Elongated wedges are occasionally used for *crescendos* or *diminuendos* that extend through a series of instruments in a score or through the two staves of a keyboard piece. They must be drawn, if possible, so as to avoid conflicting with notes, beams, slurs, and other notational elements on the separate staves. For greater visual clarity the wedge is placed close to the note-heads, the slur going above it, as in the example at the right:

EXAMPLE 14 - 7

It is sometimes impossible to avoid running wedge-signs into note-stems, especially when they must be placed between two staves and there are beams connecting notes in both staves. The only solution, if there is no room over the top staff or below the bottom one, is to draw the wedges *through* the stems, avoiding the beams. If other elements block the way, the wedges must be broken as in the example given below.

EXAMPLE 14 - 8

If a wedge-sign is to extend from the last measure of one line or system to the first measure of the line or system below, it is broken as illustrated below. Note that the wedge is left open at its resumption

when the *crescendo* is used, and at the end of the first staff when the
diminuendo wedge is employed.

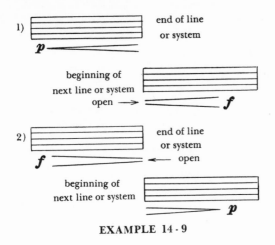

EXAMPLE 14 - 9

MODERN INNOVATIONS

Some listeners to contemporary music may feel that today's composers
have added appreciably to the scale of dynamics—particularly at the
louder end of the gamut! But as a practical matter it is dubious if there
would be any *musical* result of adding another *forte* to *ffff*, or another
piano to *pppppp*. There is a point of loudness beyond which sound
moves into sheer noise, and a point of softness at which it moves into
inaudibility. Anton Webern and John Cage have composed their
silences, and electronic composers their noise, but neither field is part
of this discussion of musical dynamics, which must inevitably remain
within the framework of the scale of humanly *controlled* and *audible*
musical sound.

But if their extremes have no place here, today's composers merit
our present attention as they exploit to the utmost every minor grada-
tion and subtle nuance of the dynamic scale, until the gradations
assume a hypermicroscopic invisibility (see Example 14-14). At the
same time, some contemporary composers have devised new ways of
designating successive dynamic markings, as shown below:

f —— *mp* —— *mf* —— *p*   or   *f* - - - *mp* - - - *mf* - - - *p*

both meaning: *f*   *mp* subito   *mf* sub.   *p* sub.

EXAMPLE 14 - 10

Other composers—mostly European avant-gardists—have created entire new dynamic codes and scales. Karlheinz Stockhausen, for instance, has devised a personal set of signs to grade dynamic increases. Each of his three signs (below) increases by one degree the level of the prevailing dynamic mark.

EXAMPLE 14 - 11

Quite apart from the difficulty of accurately grading an increase from *mf* to *f*, the system has the further drawback of using signs traditionally associated with accent (see Chapter 15).

More logical—as well as more graphic—is Earle Brown's method of incorporating dynamic intensity into the note-shape itself: that is, the degree of note-thickness equals the degree of loudness (see Example 5-23). However, the fact that the same symbol has been used by certain other avant-gardists to denote an increase or decrease in the density of a tone-cluster makes its uniform adoption problematical.

Other contemporary composers, we might add, have followed the same procedure of equating note size with dynamic strength but have used conventional note-heads for this purpose. The examples below, as found in the scores of Berio, Stockhausen, and others, use black note-heads minus stems, usually in proportional notation (refer to page 72).

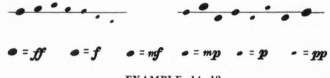

EXAMPLE 14 - 12

For unpitched percussion instruments—or even for various pitched orchestral instruments—playing "noises" such as tapping or clicking sounds, certain composers have organized dynamic scales on three-, four-, or five-line staves, as shown in Example 14-13.

Many twelve-tone composers have graded the dynamic scale so as to produce twelve degrees of intensity (see the Scale of Dynamic Markings, page 250). These twelve degrees are organized serially, just as the notes of the basic tone-row are organized, to be used inverted, in retro-

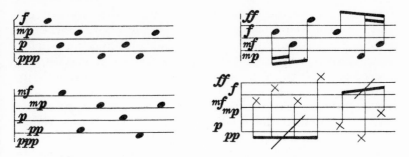

EXAMPLE 14 - 13

grade (backward), in retrograde inversion, fragmented (in irregular order), and in every conceivable permutation.

The Swedish composer Bo Nilsson, on the other hand, has ranked the scale of dynamics numerically, as follows:

$1,0 = pppp$	$3,5 = pp+$	$6,0 = mf$	$8,5 = ff+$
$1,5 = pppp+$	$4,0 = p$	$6,5 = mf+$	$9,0 = fff$
$2,0 = ppp$	$4,5 = p+$	$7,0 = f$	$9,5 = fff+$
$2,5 = ppp+$	$5,0 = mp$	$7,5 = f+$	$10,0 = ffff$
$3,0 = pp$	$5,5 = mp+$	$8,0 = ff$	

As notators we have learned to ask certain basic questions about such an innovation: Does it answer a genuine need? Is it truly accessible to the performer or reader of music? Does it have effective results in actual performance? To apply these tests to Nilsson's scheme, we may inspect a short passage from his *Frequenzen,* which uses his numbered dynamic scale.

EXAMPLE 14 - 14

By referring to the composer's scale we see that the vibraphone performer is required to play, at the rapid tempo suggested by the composer, the following sequence of dynamics: *ppp* - *mp* - *ppp* - *ppp*+ - *pppp* - *f* - *mp*+ - *f*+ - *p* - *f* - *mf*+ - *ff* - *mp*. As the vibraphone—a mallet percussion instrument—is utterly incapable of making such wide and constant fluctuations of intensity at any speed whatsoever, the actual aural result must be left to the imagination.

Now the substitution of numbers for letters makes perfectly good sense, especially since varying dynamic indications affect almost every note of much contemporary music (see almost any composition of Anton Webern or the late works of Arnold Schönberg). It is not, then, the system itself that is at fault, but the composers' unrealistic conception of the performers' ability to produce such kaleidoscopic changes. Add to dynamics a dozen or more varieties of accent, a multiplicity of articulation for wind instruments, and of bowing patterns for string players; add to these the complex rhythmic formations, fractional meters, unorthodox beaming, and drastic changes of tempo—the result for the poor performer can only be a kind of stupor in which all musical sensitivities are numbed. The science of music notation would be immeasurably advanced were the composers to seek universal simplicity and clarity in their expression, rather than a spurious profundity that is only obscure.

NOTATION EXERCISES

1. Correct and revise the following excerpts from a Beethoven piano sonata with regard to the placement of dynamic markings, wedges, and terminology:

EXAMPLE 14-15. Ludwig van Beethoven: From *Piano Sonata,*
Op. 14, No. 1

2. Construct an original example for an instrument of your own
choice, illustrating the numerical scale of dynamic marks given on
page 257.

15

Accents and Slurs

Early in chapter 14 we affirmed that notes on a staff—properly stemmed, flagged, and beamed; with all necessary dots, ties, rests, accidentals, key- and time-signatures—still do not constitute a musical idea completely realized. To give these individual notes their ultimate meaning, expressive indications must be supplied. These indications are sometimes called *ancillary* ("auxiliary") *signs* because they are not such basic symbols as the staff, clefs, and notes.

In the previous chapter we gave attention to dynamic markings; in this we consider notations setting forth fine points of stress, and the unification of the melodic idea; in the following we conclude with indications of the tempo desired in performance, and of the mood and quality of sound to be evoked. Without these indications music is an unfinished art—as though a painter should stop halfway through his canvas, or a novelist abruptly terminate his book midway through the story.

ACCENTS

All traditional music has a natural pattern of accent (Fr. *accent;* pl. *accents;* Ger. *Akzent,* pl. *Akzente;* It. *accento,* pl. *accenti*) or stress, even without extra markings. Normal emphasis is provided by meter —the rhythmic pulse set up by placing barlines; the initial beat of any measure, regardless of the time signature, always receives a primary accent. In fact, the real justification for a barline is that it provides this stress, so that it is not necessary to mark the measure accent unless it is to be especially emphasized.

Accent marks are symbols for *special* or exaggerated *stress* upon any beat, or portion of a beat. They are divided into two categories: those for *percussive* attack, and those for *pressure* attack. Usually the percussive accents are restricted to the higher dynamic levels (*mf* and louder), while the pressure accents are mainly used at the lower levels (*mp* and softer).

1. **Percussive Accents** The two principal signs for percussive accent are ➤ and Λ . The first symbol is made identically whether it is placed above or below the note-head (it is *never* written: ＜). The second sign is inverted (that is, written: **V**) when it is placed below any note-head, stem, or beam. Note the heavier shading on one side of the symbol in both versions. Choice between the two is governed by the degree of force and intensity desired. The sign Λ implies the stronger attack, so is suitable only at a fairly high dynamic level (*f*, *ff*, *fff*). The sign ➤ signifies a moderately sharp attack, and can be used at any dynamic level from *pp* to *ff*.

Although it is not an accent in keyboard music, the *staccato mark* must be discussed here because it has become associated with the percussive accent in orchestral instruments. The staccato mark—a *dot* placed directly over or under the note-head ♩ ♪ —was first used by the keyboard composers of the seventeenth century (Rameau, Couperin, J. S. Bach, Vivaldi, and others) to indicate a short, detached note-production. In order to create this detached effect the notes are shortened in value, an actual (although unwritten) rest separating one note from another. The degree of separation is usually determined by the tempo of the music and by the general style or mood—slow, formal, and

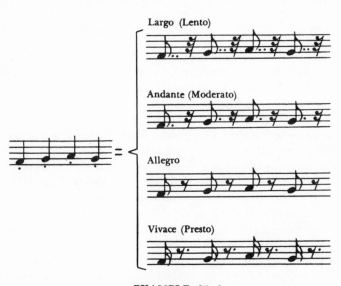

EXAMPLE 15-1

elegant, for example; or fast, gay, and spirited. In a slow to moderate tempo the value of the unwritten interpolated rest is small. When the tempo is fairly fast, however, the rest-value is larger, although still relative (see Example 15-1).

Another form of the staccato mark is the solid, small *"wedge"* ▾ used by C. P. E. Bach, Haydn, Mozart, and Beethoven. In modern usage this implies an exaggerated degree of staccato (*staccatissimo*)—the maximum shortness possible, illustrated below.

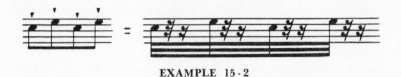

EXAMPLE 15-2

Modern orchestral composers use the solid wedge-sign to mean a combination of the strong percussive attack indicated by the **Λ** with the effect of the staccato dot. In addition, the solid wedge-sign is used in string notation—principally in orchestral music—to indicate *martellato,* a "hammered" effect uniting the sounds indicated by the percussive accent and the dot (**Λ̣** or ⟩̇). This effect, which is produced by the player using the heel of the bow—where maximum wrist strength is achieved—qualifies as an intense form of marcato bowing (see page 403).

2. **Pressure Accents**   The second degree of percussive accent, written ⟩, can serve as a pressure mark if the dynamic level is fairly soft. It is obvious that one cannot play sharply and forcefully when the note or chord is marked *pianissimo;* the accent then becomes more a matter of sudden pressure than of sharp attack.

But the principal symbol for pressure accent, regardless of dynamic level, is a short, heavy *dash* placed over or below the note-head: **p̄ ♩** —the same symbol we met in Chapter 7 as a *tenuto* mark. This symbol implies a kind of "leaning" on the note, giving it special stress without noticeably attacking it; at the same time, it indicates that the note is to be held full value as well as stressed. For this reason the pressure accent could be used at almost any dynamic level, loud or soft.

The Table of Accents (below) points out the relative degree of force implied by each of the four accent-symbols, and by their various combinations.

EXAMPLE 15 - 3.   TABLE OF ACCENTS

strong	Λ Λ̲ Λ̇ Λ̣ or V V̄ V̇ V̂
medium	> ≥ >̣ >̣ – -̣ or >̄ >̇ >̂ -̄
light	• ▼ ▲

3. Combined Accents

Increasing complexity of musical expression has forced composers to invent new symbols, or to combine in various ways the traditional signs. Many of these combinations are found, of course, in the music of the nineteenth century; the culmination of the Romantic period saw an exaggeration in every aspect of the expressive elements of music, and accentuation is but one of these elements. But the present century has expanded unbelievably the permutations of expression marks. In some music almost every individual note has its personal dynamic mark, accent sign, or other ancillary marking. A brief excerpt from the *Five Piano Pieces,* Op. 23 of Arnold Schönberg will illustrate this point:

EXAMPLE 15 - 4. Arnold Schönberg: From *Five Piano Pieces,* Op. 23 (1923)

The following table summarizes the possible combinations of the various percussive, pressure, and staccato accents. Some combinations are not feasible (the wedge and dot used together are redundant; the Λ, standing for the maximum of >, precludes their being used together).

Accent marks of all kinds—with the sole exception of the maximum percussive accent symbol (Λ)—are notated just above or below the

EXAMPLE 15 - 5.   TABLE OF COMBINED ACCENTS

Λ̣ V̇	very percussive, but short
≳̣ ≐	moderately percussive and short, equal to ▼
Λ̲ V̄	very percussive, but receiving full value
≧ ≳̄	moderately percussive with full value
ī ▾̲	stressed, but quite short
⊤̇ ≐	stressed and moderately short, separated from next note

note-head. They should not be placed over stems, flags, or beams unless there is no room available by the notes themselves. Also, the written accents should accompany the rise and fall of the note-heads, rather
than persevere in a straight line.

EXAMPLE 15 - 6

In intervals of the second, and in chord structures with "added"
notes, accent marks must be placed just above or below the note-head
that determines the stem direction. The accent of a whole-note sonority
would be aligned by an imaginary stem.

EXAMPLE 15 - 7

4. **Accent Terminology**   In addition to the accent marks
themselves, a number of accent terms are widely used, and always in
their abbreviated form. No one today writes out the word *piano* or
forte for "soft" and "loud"; neither does one write *sforzando* when
sf serves as well. The appended chart shows the three principal degrees of these accent terms, graded in intensity and force, and with the
equivalents in terms of accent marks at various dynamic levels. In
reality, many of these accent terms are combinations of words *and*
dynamics: *sff* means *sf + f*, or *sf in ff*.

EXAMPLE 15 - 8.   SCALE OF ACCENT TERMINOLOGY

Sforzando	Forzando or Forzato	Sforzato
sf = > in all dynamic levels from $pppppp$ to f	fz = $\wedge$ in mf or f	sfz = $\underline{\wedge}$ in mf or f
sff = > in ff	ffz = $\wedge$ in ff	$sffz$ = $\underline{\wedge}$ in ff
$sfff$ = > in fff	$fffz$ = $\wedge$ in fff	$sfffz$ = $\underline{\wedge}$ in fff

SLURS

Accents affect notes as *individuals,* though there may be a sequence of individually-accented notes. Slurs (Fr. *liaison,* pl. *liaisons;* Ger. *Bindungzeichen,* pl. *Bindungzeichen* or *Bindebogen,* pl. *Bindebögen;* It. *legatura,* pl. *legature*) affect note-*groups* as entities, for their primary function is to unite. Much of this unifying is emotional and visual, as the sweeping curve of the slur-sign catches the eye—insisting that two or many notes be thought of as one group, for a variety of reasons.

In seventeenth- and eighteenth-century practice, the slur might be placed over two notes of fairly short duration (quarters or eighths) to indicate that the first note was accented and also sustained into the attack on the second, which would be played short (left, below). If, however, a similar slur were placed over two notes of longer duration than a quarter note, the rule of accent and release did not apply—only that of slightly prolonging the first note into the second (right, below).

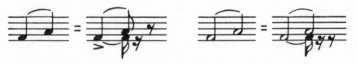

EXAMPLE 15 - 9

In keyboard music of the eighteenth century (Haydn and Mozart, for example) the slur was first employed to indicate that all the notes beneath it were to be played *legato*—smoothly connected, without any perceptible break between them. Slurs so employed gradually took on their most significant general function—that of guiding the performer to consider a note-sequence as a *unified melodic idea.*

EXAMPLE 15 - 10

Most other duties of the slur—although its large musical implication of unifying the material it covers is universal—are associated closely with the performance techniques of vocal, keyboard, and orchestral music. In vocal music, the phrase-slur indicates a passage sung in one breath, the end of the slur marking the point where the singer is to take a breath. The singer will find the slur also under the note-heads when a single word or syllable is to be sung through several notes (see Chapter 17). In keyboard music the slur sign frequently refers to the legato fingering pattern mentioned above, with the notes bound together as closely as possible (see Chapter 18). In instrumental music the slur marks tonguing patterns in woodwinds and brasses, and bowing patterns in strings (see Chapters 20–23 for a fuller discussion).

SLUR PLACEMENT

Markings indigenous to single classifications of performance will be treated in later chapters, but others of more general character can be discussed here. In general, the slur mark is placed next to the note-heads, but may go over stems, flags, and beams when there is no other room—especially when the slur is a long phrase-mark. (See Examples 18-15 and 18-24, for instance.)

When the slur is used in conjunction with *tied notes,* it may be placed over or under the note-heads tied together, but the tie mark always loops according to the note position on the staff (refer to page 110).

EXAMPLE 15 - 11

When slurs are placed over a passage that ends in a tied note, the slur sign should extend as far as the *second note* of the tie, rather than end on the first note. The principle involved should be obvious; the breath of the singer or wind instrumentalist, the bow of a string player, cannot stop at the first note if it is to be prolonged by a tie.

EXAMPLE 15 - 12

Whether ending on a tied note or not, the phrase sign should always be carefully terminated (see examples above) and not left hanging in the air (left, below) or extended into blank space (right, below). Careless slurring inevitably betrays the amateur notator.

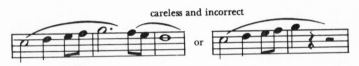

EXAMPLE 15 - 13

If a series of notes affected by a legato slur have stems going both up and down, it is best to put the legato slur *over* the notes rather than under them.

EXAMPLE 15 - 14

Unison notes expanding to intervals may also be affected by legato slurs. Two slur-marks are required in such cases, as the double stem on the unison notes signifies two voices. The reverse procedure—an interval contracting to a unison note—also requires a double slur.

EXAMPLE 15 - 15

In addition to showing the use of two slur-marks for unisons slurred to intervals, the above examples also illustrate the proper placement of all slur-marks *between two notes only*. Unless beams are involved, these slurs always extend from note-head to note-head rather than from stem-top to stem-top, as they do in Example 15-16, left.

On occasion, slurs affect consecutive intervals or chords in which the top or bottom note remains the same for both sonorities. In such cases the legato slur must be placed next to the notes that *move*—not next to the stationary note-heads. The latter practice would look as if a tie were meant.

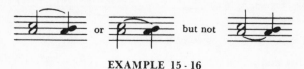

EXAMPLE 15 - 16

Legato slurs affecting *parallel chord-structures* are treated in various ways. If no notes are tied between the chords, one slur-mark is used—preferably beneath or over the chord structures (but sometimes next to the stems if the space between staves is crowded). It is not necessary to put a slur mark for each of the note-heads when their movements are parallel; one slur does the work for all the notes.

EXAMPLE 15 - 17

When one or more pairs of notes are tied between chord structures notated also with a legato slur, the tie marks loop in a direction *opposite* that of the legato mark (top line, below). This same principle is observed if the chords are beamed as groups of eighths, sixteenths, or smaller values (bottom line, below). Ordinarily the tie slur loops *away* from the beam, but this rule is bypassed when a legato slur is present. The theory is that curving the tie-mark and slur-mark in opposite directions makes their respective functions more clearly observed.

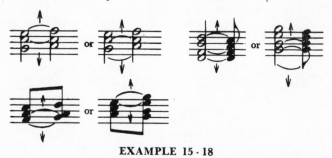

EXAMPLE 15 - 18

ACCENTS AND SLURS COMBINED

When accent marks are combined with slurs, the result is more psychological than actual—that is, the combination *suggests* a quality of sound, rather than indicating it exactly. To combine the slur, which implies legato, with the staccato dot, which means "short," would seem a paradox. How can a note be short and long at the same time? The answer is that the dot does indeed shorten the note, but that the slur "carries over" the phrasing and minimizes the note-separation. In this way the performer is guided by the slur to shorten not the notes but the implied rests between them. The resulting interpretation will vary somewhat with the tempo:

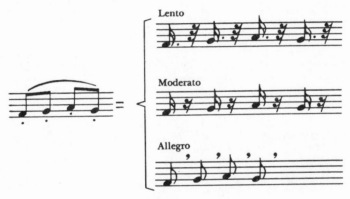

EXAMPLE 15 - 19

This combined *legato-staccato* indication was first used by Mozart in his piano sonatas. Today it is employed for other instruments and voices as well, still with its original implications.

The slur and the dot are sometimes used in partial combination: in a two-note group, for instance, only the first will be marked staccato (left, below) or only the second (right, below). When the first of the two notes has the dot, it is shortened and receives the accent, the second being unaccented. When the second note has the staccato dot, it is shortened and somewhat accented at the same time. The stress in both cases is more pressure than percussive.

EXAMPLE 15 - 20

The two tables given below show the relative note- and rest-values of accented notes—combined with slurs and without slurs.

EXAMPLE 15 - 21.   TABLE OF ACCENTS PLUS SLURS

Written	Played
♩ ♩ ♩ ♩ (slurred) > > > >	♪... 𝄾 ♪... 𝄾 ♪... 𝄾 ♪... 𝄾 > > > >
♩ ♩ ♩ ♩ (slurred)	♪. 𝄾 ♪. 𝄾 ♪. 𝄾 ♪. 𝄾
♩ ♩ ♩ ♩ (slurred)	♪ 𝄾 ♪ 𝄾 ♪ 𝄾 ♪ 𝄾 . . . .

EXAMPLE 15 - 22.   TABLE OF ACCENTS WITHOUT SLURS

Written	Played
♩ ♩ ♩ ♩ > > > >	♪. 𝄾 ♪. 𝄾 ♪. 𝄾 ♪. 𝄾 > > > >
♩ ♩ ♩ ♩	♪ 𝄾 ♪ 𝄾 ♪ 𝄾 ♪ 𝄾
♩ ♩ ♩ ♩	♪ 𝄾. ♪ 𝄾. ♪ 𝄾. ♪ 𝄾. . . . .

The notation of combined accents and slur marks requires careful consideration. In order that the slur mark may not be mistaken for a tie, any accent marks for repeated notes are placed close to the note-heads, with the slur marks *outside* of them. Slur signs are also placed consistently outside any staccato dots or tenuto dashes—whether repeated notes are involved or not.

correct   incorrect

EXAMPLE 15 - 23

On the other hand, percussive accents, because of their larger size (Λ >), are usually placed *above* the slur mark, which in this case goes close to the note-heads. It is rare, of course, to see these symbols used together because of their opposing functions.

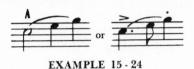

EXAMPLE 15 - 24

When two notes affected by both accents and slurs have stems in different directions, the slur mark usually goes *above* the staff, regardless of whether the accent goes below or above the note.

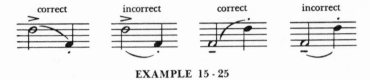

EXAMPLE 15 - 25

MODERN INNOVATIONS

Although the various combinations of accent signs are to be found almost exclusively in twentieth-century music, they cannot be listed as innovations, as their use merely extends a long-standing tradition. Some, significant modifications, however, are unique in form and so deserve mention here. Chief among these are two symbols invented by Arnold Schönberg and used to command a strong accent where none is metrically indicated (on a weak beat, or on the second half of any beat) or to cancel out a normal accent on a strong beat. These symbols are used to alter the normal (unwritten) accents produced by barlines or by the natural position of strong and weak beats in any measure, as in the passage on the bottom line:

/ or 𝈩 = accent, as on a *strong* beat

∪ or 𝈈 = no accent, as on a *weak* beat

EXAMPLE 15 - 26

Another accent symbol is the ♂ invented by Stockhausen, inveterate fabricator of notational devices. This sign is a slight modification of the ♂ or ♀ created by Béla Bartók for the "snap" pizzicato in string instruments: an explosive effect in which the string actually strikes the fingerboard with great force (see page 400). Stockhausen devised his variant for woodwind and brass instruments, to command the hardest attack (or accent) possible. But with sublime disregard for practicalities, in his *Zeitmasse* he has used this sign on three different notes played by the English horn in fairly rapid succession:

EXAMPLE 15 - 27

If Stockhausen's symbol means what he says, one can only ask: What is the difference between the three versions? Why are they necessary?

Equally incomprehensible is Bo Nilsson's combination of three contradictory accent-marks for the vibraphone in his *Reaktionen:*

A third recent innovation is the *dotted slur-sign,* used when rests of any kind are included in a group of notes slurred together. (Compare with the dotted tie-sign, page 121.) The usual unbroken phrase-mark means, of course, that each note is connected to the next note, with no audible separation between them. Should rests come between the notes, they obviously cannot be bound together, yet a dotted or broken slur can give visual logic to the phrase sense.

EXAMPLE 15 - 28

The dotted slur is also used for a phrase mark over double- and triple-tonguing effects, flutter-tonguing, trills, and tremolos in woodwind and brass instruments. It is effective also in delineating phrases for string instruments playing tremolo or pizzicato, or over bowing patterns subdividing a long phrase. (See Chapters 20–23 for more detailed discussion.) In all instances, the broken slur-sign serves a psychological function; hence it may be considered one of the most logical and successful of contemporary notational devices.

Two further innovations in the use of phrase-marks might be described as *overlapping slurs* and *double slurs*. The first of these involves a kind of chain-sequence in which successive short slurs link a melodic or rhythmic idea by an overlapping process: the end of one slur becomes the beginning of the next, and so on throughout the passage. The slur marks may be notated entirely on one level, as shown at the left, below, or they may alternate between a position above the staff and a position below, as at the right.

EXAMPLE 15 - 29

Double slurs result from the simultaneous appearance of two slur-signs—a long phrasing mark, either unbroken (left, below) or dotted (right, below) and a number of shorter "breathing" slurs affecting but a few notes at a time.

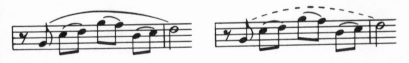

EXAMPLE 15 - 30

Both overlapping and double slurs serve the same kind of psychological function as the dotted tie or single dotted slur-mark. By their use the notator increases the flexibility of familiar and tested symbols, so that they enhance the qualitative aspects of his notation.

NOTATION EXERCISES

1. In the following example correct all the erroneously placed *slurs* and *tie-signs:*

EXAMPLE 15 - 31

2. Indicate the appropriate *accent-sign* or combination of accents for the following:

EXAMPLE 15 - 32

3. Write for a woodwind instrument of your choice an original melody which will illustrate the various uses of the *dotted slur-sign*.

16

Tempo and Expression Marks

THERE WAS A TIME IN MUSICAL HISTORY WHEN IT WAS
something of a miracle to command an indubitable printed indication
of exact pitches in definite rhythm. In the music of the Middle Ages
and Renaissance the expressive aspects enhancing this essential nucleus
were the personal province of performers, and depended on their
religious fervor or momentary high spirits far more than on any dis-
cipline imposed by musical notation. Today, however, the music itself
is more nearly in command, and we have devoted the two previous
chapters to notations by which a composer can request power, emphasis, and a musical line. This chapter completes the notator's gamut
of expressive indications, adding *tempo marks* to designate the rate of
speed desired in performance, and *expression marks*—indications of
the mood, quality of tone, and all the other subjective elements of a
total musical expression.

Not until the seventeenth century, with the advent of harmonic
music, did composers begin to introduce signs or terms directing first,
a certain tempo and later, dynamics or mood. At that time, also, performers first received idiomatic directions for keyboard touch, string
bowing, or vocal phrasing and breath control. Terms for mood or
tempo were by the mid-eighteenth century appearing at the beginning
of a composition, but qualifying adjectives or adverbs for tempo markings arrived only in the early nineteenth century. At the romantic
peak of the late nineteenth century, expressive directions had reached
such formidable proportions as: *Lo stesso movimento, ma più sostenuto quasi andante* ("in the same tempo, but more sustained and moderate"). Today's composer, it would seem, operates at the poles of the
expressive scale—almost no markings at all, or over-fastidious indications for every single note.

TEMPO MARKS

Tempo—a condition as exactly measurable as car speed is measurable by a speedometer—would appear the least subjective of all the attributes of a musical performance. Yet most performers would testify that tempo is not only personal, but often the hardest aspect of music to control. They would indeed confess that they are swayed from concert to concert by the size of a concert hall, by its acoustics, or by atmospheric conditions—to say nothing of such intangible factors as their state of mind and the emotional pitch of the audience. Arturo Toscanini once said that any piece of music had three different tempos: the *first* tempo—felt when the conductor or performer first read the music at his desk; the *second* tempo—established at rehearsals; and the *third* tempo—heard at actual public performance!

There exists, nonetheless, an irrefutable type of marking made available by Johann Nepomuk Maelzel, a German inventor of the early nineteenth century. Maelzel's *metronome* utilizes a double pendulum (a rod with a weight on either end) that can oscillate to produce from 40 to 208 regular ticks per minute. M.M. 72, then, instructs the performer to set his Maelzel's Metronome (not "metronome mark") for 72 ticks per minute. If a quarter note is the beat-unit, there will be 72 quarter-notes per minute; if the beat-unit is a half note, there will be 72 half-notes—or 144 quarter-notes—each minute.

If only this instrument had been available to Bach, Handel, Haydn, and Mozart, we might have been spared endless disagreements regarding the proper tempos for their music. Only beginning with Beethoven —first serious composer to make use of the metronome—can we be reasonably sure of the tempo desired by the composer.

Exact as they are, however, metronome marks are seldom used as the only *tempo indications* (Fr. *signes de temps;* Ger. *Zeitmasse* or *Tempobezeichnungen;* It. *segni di tempo*). Most composers add a descriptive word, either in Italian—the international language of music —or possibly in one of the other standard languages: French, German, or English. Because the musician will frequently encounter tempo indications in all of these languages, the following Table of Tempo Indications—scaled from the slowest to the quickest tempos—is given in four parallel forms.

When a notator adds one of the descriptive indications in the table above to a specific tempo marking, he has combined directions for speed with those for a subjective quality. A number of these terms have some emotional connotation, and it is amusing to recall that in a very literal sense the word *allegro* did not originally signify any tempo. The

EXAMPLE 16·1. TABLE OF TEMPO INDICATIONS

M.M. =	Italian	English	French	German
40	Larghissimo Adagissimo Lentissimo }	Extremely slow	Très lent	Sehr langsam; Ganz langsam
	Largo Adagio Lento }	Very slow	Lent; Large	Langsam; Breit
	Larghetto Adagietto }	Rather slow	Un peu lent	Etwas langsam
60	Andante Andantino }	Moderately slow	Allant; Très modéré	Mässig langsam; Gehend
	Moderato	Moderately	Modéré	Mässig; Mässig bewegt
	Allegretto	Rather fast	Un peu animé	Etwas bewegt
120	Allegro	Fast; quick	Animé	Bewegt; Schnell
	Vivace Vivo Presto }	Quite fast	Vif; Vite	Lebhaft; Eilig
208	Allegrissimo Vivacissimo Prestissimo }	Very fast	Très vif	Ganz schnell; Ganz lebhaft

word means "cheerful" in Italian, was first used in that sense, and only later took on its present meaning of "fast." Why one cannot be cheerful in a slow or moderate tempo is left unexplained.

The tempo indications listed above may be made more precise by the addition of such brief qualifying expressions as are cited below:

These terms, together with the Glossary that follows, are basic equipment for composers, notators, and performers. To this list it is expected that the thoroughgoing musician will add constantly, both in variety and exactness.

A cautionary note is in order regarding the usage of *cédez* (see preceding list) in some French scores. Printed thus: *cédez* - - - - - - // *Tempo*—the slanting dashes do not indicate a pause (see Chapter 7), but merely signify the end of the ritardando. The usual pause-sign is placed *on* the staff, while the end of the *cédez* is always placed well *off* the staff.

Actual *notation* of tempo marks involves few problems. The general terms are placed over the uppermost staff—well above beams, flags,

EXAMPLE 16·2. TABLE OF TEMPO QUALIFICATIONS

Expression	Meaning	As in	Signifying
It. *a poco a poco* Fr. *peu à peu* Ger. *allmählich*	little by little	*accelerando poco a poco* *accélerez peu à peu* *allmählich schneller werden*	becoming faster little by little
assai, molto *très* *sehr, ganz*	very, much, quite	*presto assai* or *molto presto* *très vif* *sehr schnell* or *ganz lebhaft*	very fast
con *avec* *•_____*	with	*con brio* *avec verve* *schwungvoll*	with spirit
meno *moins* *weniger*	less	*meno vivace* *moins vif* *weniger schnell*	not so fast
non troppo *pas trop* *nicht zu*	not too much	*largo non troppo* *pas trop lent* *nicht zu langsam*	slow, but not in excess
più *plus* suffix *er*	more	*più vivace* *plus vite* *eileger* or *lebhafter*	faster
pochissimo *un peu* *etwas*	a very little	*pochissimo rit.* *cédez un peu* *etwas zuruckhalten*	a slight retard
poco, un poco *un peu* *ein wenig*	a little, somewhat	*poco adagio* *un peu lent* *ein wenig langsam*	somewhat slow
quasi	like, almost	*moderato quasi andante*	moderately, like an andante

* In German, the expression itself is altered to embody the idea of *mit* ("with").

slurs, and accents—at the beginning of the composition or at appropriate points during the course of the music. The initial letter of the term (usually a capital) customarily is aligned over the meter signature, or—if none is present—over the first notational element of the measure, such as note-heads, accidentals, repeat signs, and so on. (See Example 16-1, and Examples 17-3, 18-24, 26-1, 26-2, 26-15, and 26-17 as well.) In older music the metronome mark in parentheses

EXAMPLE 16 - 3. GLOSSARY OF TEMPO TERMINOLOGY

accelerando (accel.)	Quickening; a gradual speeding-up of the tempo
alla breve	Duple time with a half note as the unit; same as ¢
allargando (allarg.)	Broadening; sometimes interpreted as a combination of *ritardando* and *crescendo*
ancora	Still more; used generally with tempo indications, as *ancora meno mosso* ("still more slowly")
a tempo	In tempo; reestablishes original speed after *accelerando* or *ritardando*
cédez	French for *poco ritardando;* a slight holding-back
come prima	As at first
come sopra	As above; much the same as *come prima*
doppio movimento	Twice as fast; usually used in conjunction with C changing to ¢
l'istesso (or *lo stesso*) *tempo*	The same tempo, indicating that the beat remains constant when the meter changes, as: $\frac{2}{4}$ to $\frac{6}{8}$ —previous ♩ now equals ♩.
meno mosso or *più lento*	Less motion; slower. May be qualified by *poco* (a little less)
più allegro *più animato* *più mosso*	Faster
pressez	French term for "quicken"; same meaning as *accelerando*
rallentando (rall.)	Same as *ritardando;* a gradual slowing-down of tempo
ritardando (rit.)	Slowing down; a gradual holding-back of the tempo
ritenuto (rit., riten.)	Frequently confused with *ritardando;* means a sudden slowing-down, in contrast to the gradual holding-back of *rallentando*
rubato	Literally, to "rob" the time-values by holding back or speeding up at will to color a phrase
stringendo (string.)	Pressing forward; sometimes erroneously interpreted as a combination of *accelerando* and *crescendo*
tempo giusto	In strict tempo (*non-rubato*)
tempo primo (*Tempo I°*)	Original tempo
trattenuto (tratt.)	Holding back (same as *rallentando*) with the addition of a sustained quality (*sostenuto*)

followed the tempo indication, as: *Allegro moderato* (M.M. ♩ = 80). Today the tendency is to write this as: *Allegro moderato* ♩ = 80.

Metronome marks are sometimes given in pairs when the unit of time may fluctuate—between a half note and a quarter note, for example. In ²⁄₂ meter, for instance, we might see: **M.M.** ♩ = 60 (♩ = 120). This practice is especially desirable in slow tempos, where the next smaller denominator might in actuality be the prevailing unit of time.

When, however, there is a change of time signature in which the new unit of time is twice as fast, or twice as slow, as the previous metric beat, it is customary to indicate the fact by means of two small notes placed over the meter of the new section, as shown below. The left-hand example makes clear that the *previous quarter-note* had the same duration as the *present half-note*. The right-hand example indicates that the *former eighth-note* had the same duration as the *present sixteenth-note*. The small notes may be written in parentheses, as in the left-hand example, or remain unenclosed. Also, the small arrows shown in the right-hand example may be omitted at will, although they are very graphic and unequivocal in meaning.

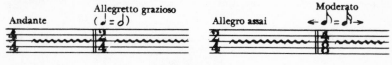

EXAMPLE 16 - 4

Finally, metronome markings recognize the human difficulty of controlling an exact tempo, and are occasionally written in one of the following flexible forms: *Allegro* (♩ = about 112); or *Allegro* (♩ = 108–116); or ♪ = ca. 160. The *ca.* is the abbreviation for *circa* ("about"), so that the third variant means that the speed should be *about* 160 eighth-notes to the minute—give or take a few degrees one way or the other.

EXPRESSION MARKS

Few experiencd composers expect even a superb performance to be the exact image of their original thought, but it is a foolish composer who makes sympathetic performance impossible by his omission of detailed expression marks (Fr. *signes d'expression;* Ger. *Vortragszeichen;* It. *segni d'espressione*). His creative cycle, then, is not complete until he has found distinctive expressions for the mood and quality of tone closest to his concept. If he begins his notations with Italian expressions, he should continue in Italian; if he begins in English or another language, he should continue in that language, for it is not good form to mix the terminology of his directions.

A basic glossary of expression terminology should comprise a vital segment of any notator's or performer's technical knowledge. An authoritative and up-to-date music dictionary ought to be in the possession of any practicing musician; the *Harvard Dictionary of Music* and *A Dictionary of Musical Terms in 4 Languages* (see Bibliography) are especially recommended.

Expression marks are notated *as close as possible* to the notes they affect, avoiding conflict with beams, slurs, wedges, or other ancillary markings. In keyboard music they generally go between the staves if the term affects both hands; in instrumental and vocal music they are related to the individual staves.

Though they are not strictly expressive terms, a few performance directions should supplement any expression glossary. They are:

attacca	Begin the following section or movement without pause
colla (*col; coll'; colle; cogli; coi*)	With the, as in *colla voce* ("with the voice"), meaning to adjust the accompaniment to the voice part; or *colla parte* ("with the part"), meaning to follow the *rubato* of the solo part
segue	Begin the following section or movement without pause; also, continue a repeated figure in the same manner
sempre	Always, continually; as *sempre f* ("continually loud")
simile (*sim.*)	Continue a repeated figure in the same manner; or, continue an established pattern of accenting, slurring, or bowing

The term *sempre* (listed above) is often used for special emphasis of expression and dynamic marks, and of all forms of ancillary devices. Should the composer mark an *accelerando* passage with a *diminuendo*, for instance, he would do well to warn the performer in no uncertain terms by marking it *sempre diminuendo*. This is only a sensible precaution, for many performers have the habit of getting louder as they increase tempo.

On occasion, any ancillary device may be enclosed in parentheses, as: (═══ ═══), or (*rit.*). So marked because they represent editorial additions, or corrections of music previously printed, they are common in modern editions of early music. They may also be found in works by modern composers, such as Béla Bartók's *3rd Piano Concerto*—barely finished before his death, and completed by Bartók's publisher from an unedited manuscript.

MODERN INNOVATIONS

Many contemporary composers prefer to leave subjective expression to the discretion (or the mood) of the performer. Avoiding such terms as *Grave e molto mesto, con espressione assai* ("gravely and very sadly, with much expression"), the present-day composer will often merely place an impersonal metronome-mark above the first measure: ♪ = 44, and leave it at that.

Other cliques are prone to extreme over-marking, quite beyond the technical skill of their performers or the conscious hearing of their audiences. (See Example 14-14.) While this extreme is to be avoided, fastidious notators could well emulate the careful metronome indications shown in the example below, typical of much current practice. Here the *ritardando* from ♪ = 114 to ♪ = 93 is pinpointed on one note of the second measure. Likewise, the *accelerando* following the *a tempo* reaches a new tempo-mark at a clearly specified point in the measure following. We cannot always be sure that the performer does follow directions, but at least he cannot blame the composer for vagueness.

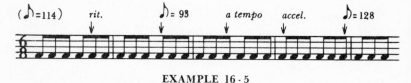

EXAMPLE 16 - 5

For *accelerandi* and *ritardandi* of brief but precise effect, some contemporaries (Boulez, in particular) have used an elongated arrow-sign in conjunction with specific metronome markings or degree numbers. In the center example below, zero would represent the basic speed; 4 would be used as the equivalent of a higher metronome mark in a graded scale of speeds. For non-constant dynamic "ups and downs," curved or angled lines are used (right, below).

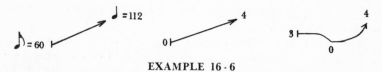

EXAMPLE 16 - 6

One of the most sensible, and at the same time successful, of all contemporary notational devices is that invented by Arnold Schönberg to set off a principal thematic line in his music. Using the German word *Hauptstimme* ("principal part") as the basis for his sign, Schönberg placed this symbol—H⌐—at the beginning of each principal melodic line. The final note of the passage was marked: ⌐ , indicating the end of the theme. As a corollary to this sign, Schönberg marked the other melodic lines with: N⌐ (*Nebenstimme,* meaning "secondary part"), identifying them as secondary voices. The end of a part in this secondary capacity was marked with: ⌐ , a thinner version of the sign used at the conclusion of the *Hauptstimme* part.

Certain American composers writing in the twelve-tone technique have modified Schönberg's signs to correspond to English terminology. Thus H⌐ becomes ⌐P⌐ (Principal part), and N⌐ becomes ⌐S⌐ (Secondary part). Other composers have devised such variants as: ⌐ ⌐ for H⌐ , and: ⌐ ⌐ for N⌐ .

In music of a predominantly contrapuntal character, where all the parts (whether vocal or instrumental) are thematic to some degree, the adoption of these signs is of immediate help to the performer. Without their aid one would frequently find it difficult to determine which of the many polyphonic strands is most important at any given moment. Schönberg's symbols end the guesswork, and precisely indicate the composer's intent.

NOTATION EXERCISE

1. Imagine yourself with a commission to write a musical score for a television production of Shakespeare's *Macbeth.* Make a condensed scenario of each scene in Act I and indicate the tempo and expression marks most suitable for the background music you are to compose.

PART III

Idiomatic Notation

17

Vocal Notation

Generally speaking, vocal notation is not so complicated as that required for instruments. The limited gamut of vocal color-effects and the narrower range of technical devices available to the singer minimize the notational problems of traditionally conceived vocal music. Avant-garde music for the voice requires, of course, a more extensive repertory of unusual vocal effects and hence a more specialized notation (see page 299).

TRADITIONAL PRACTICES

Because vocal music is essentially the singing of *words*—or their component syllables—divided according to speech rhythm or metrical pulsation, the characteristic notational problems relate to flags and beams. All the principal elements must be considered, however, and will be referred to in the same order they assumed in the detailed treatment in Chapters 1 through 16. If certain elements have no special application in vocal notation, they will be passed over, and the same plan will be followed in Chapters 18 through 24.

Staves   In music for *solo voice* the single staff for the singer is always placed above any accompaniment (piano, organ, string quartet, and so forth) except in the case of orchestral accompaniment. When included in an orchestra score, the vocal staff is put just above the string choir. It is important that enough room be allowed below the vocal staff for the words of the text. For this reason, and because the first violins are apt to have many notes on ledger lines above their staff, the copyist is wise to leave a blank staff below the vocal part in an orchestra score (see Example 17-1).

Adequate *vertical space* is also necessary between the vocal staff and the staves of piano, organ, or any other accompanying instrument. And—one might add parenthetically—*horizontal space* is also an essen-

EXAMPLE 17 - 1

tial in vocal notation: that is, room must be allowed for the spacing out of words and syllables, without cramping them or having to split the levels on which the words are written out.

uncrowded, professional

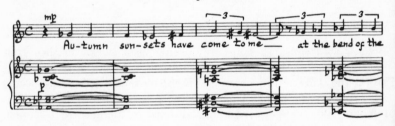

crowded, unprofessional

EXAMPLE 17 - 2

As a rule, *chorale* and *hymn notation* require only two staves, although the chorales in the Bach Passions and Cantatas are written on four staves. When two staves are used, the soprano and alto voices share the upper staff, and the tenor and bass the lower one. The words are then written between the two staves—sometimes several lines of words, when second and third verses are included. When there is room for only a verse or two, the remaining verses are printed at the bottom of the page. (See any standard hymnal for illustrations of hymn format.)

In full-scale (four-staff) choral music, when either the sopranos and altos or the tenors and basses sing the same words at the same time, the text is sometimes put between their pairs of staves (as in Example 17-3). It is not always necessary to duplicate the words underneath each separate staff; one line of text serves two voices simultaneously, although many publishers prefer to give the duplicated text in full for each of the four voices (see Example 17-5).

Choral music—in contrast to hymn notation—uses a separate staff for each type of voice required. A standard S.S.A. arrangement (Soprano I, Soprano II, Alto) would have three staves; an S.A.T.B. arrangement (Soprano, Alto, Tenor, Bass) would have four staves (see

EXAMPLE 17 - 3. Gardner Read: From *A Mountain Song* (1963)

Example 17-3); a male-voice arrangement, T.T.B.B. (Tenor I, Tenor II, Bass I, Bass II) would require four staves, and so on.

Ordinary *divisi* in choral parts usually needs only one staff. If the sopranos, for instance, divide into two parts for a few notes or even a few measures, the two parts can uusually be accommodated on the one staff (see Example 17-5). Where the complexity of either part makes it undesirable to share the staff, the two voices must be put on separate staves.

At the beginning of any choral score, the *names* of the voices are written out in full, as in Example 17-3. After the first page, the simple letter abbreviations S., A., T., B. may be used, or not. If the four-staff pattern continues without change, it is unnecessary to continue the voice identifications.

In *operatic scores,* separate staves are used for each chorus part and for each solo voice. The solo lines are placed at the top of the vocal score, the female voices first (soprano, mezzo, alto, contralto), followed by the male voices (tenor, baritone, bass). The same plan is observed in sacred or secular choral works with orchestra—the Verdi *Requiem,* for example, or Vaughan Williams' *A Sea Symphony.* Always the vocal parts in an orchestral score—solo and choral—are put just above the string section. They thus act as a divider between the percussion group (including harp, celesta, and piano) and the strings. (In older choral-orchestral scores—Brahms's *A German Requiem,* for instance—the choral parts were inserted between viola and 'cello staves, but this practice is no longer followed.)

Because space is at a premium in full operatic scores, the choral parts are sometimes condensed by putting the sopranos and altos on one staff. The tenors and basses must still have their own staves because of different clefs (see page 293).

Systems   A bracket ([ ) rather than a brace ({) encloses the staves of vocal parts. A single vocal line is usually not set off in this manner, but a duet would be. Two or more vocal staves, therefore, are joined by the bracket. When solo voices and chorus are together on the page, two separate bracket-signs are used. If a *double chorus* is called for, two brackets are also employed, one for each complete choral unit. (See Example 17-4 and also Example 2-2.)

If extensive *divisi* requires the use of two staves for each vocal division, braces are used to enclose the two staves occupied by like voices (divided altos or divided basses, for example). The brace signs are placed outside the main bracket linking all the vocal staves.

The four or more staves of an *a cappella* choral work would com-

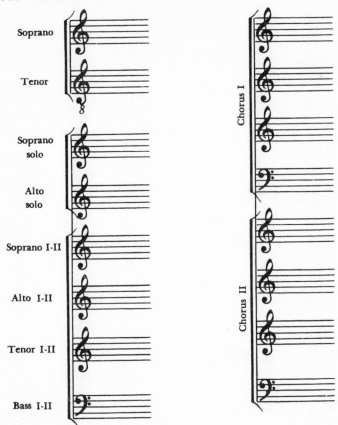

EXAMPLE 17 - 4

prise a system. A separate system would be indicated for the customary *reduction* of the vocal lines, to be used in rehearsal by piano or organ (but not ordinarily in performance). The reduction, put on the two staves for the keyboard instrument, is generally printed in small notes, with only a minimum of dynamic markings, accents, and phrasing. Usually the soprano and alto notes are given to the right hand and the tenor and bass notes to the left. If the tenor goes rather high and the bass somewhat low, the tenor part can be included with the right hand. Actually, the division of notes should be arranged for playing convenience, not as a literal transcription onto two staves from four. If one wishes to show voice-leading in these reductions—tenor notes going into the treble keyboard-staff, for instance—a line may be drawn from note to note to show the progression. The words "For rehearsal only" are customarily placed at the beginning of the keyboard reduction, either centered in front of the brace or between the staves of the first measure (see Example 17-3).

In an accompanied choral work the system would include the instrumental as well as the choral staves. When *a cappella* passages occur in accompanied music, they are cued in by small notes in the accompaniment, usually enclosed in brackets. Rest signs for the keyboard instrument are not necessary in these cases, as the small notes serve to fill out the time requirement (see Example 17-5).

EXAMPLE 17-5. Gardner Read: From *Though I Speak With the Tongues of Men* (1960)

Ledger Lines, Octave Signs   Ledger lines are used for all voices whenever required. More than two or three added staff-lines are rarely necessary; the restricted range of the voices keeps them fairly well on their staves.

It is a cardinal rule in vocal notation that *octave signs are never used.* As they merely substitute for excessive ledger lines—which are practically non-existent in vocal music—there is really no need to employ *8ᵛᵃ* or *8ᵛᵃ bassa* signs.

Clefs   Three clefs are used in modern vocal notation—two, if one considers the modern vocal tenor clef as a simple modification of the treble clef. All female voices use treble clef only; tenor voices use the treble clef sign—with or without an appended *8*, a double treble clef, or a combination of treble and C-clef (see below); baritone and bass voices use the bass clef only.

EXAMPLE 17·6.   TABLE OF VOCAL CLEFS

The use of treble clef for tenor voice, sounding an octave lower than written, makes this part an actual transposition. All other vocal parts sound exactly as written.

Beaming, Stems   Vocal notation—while still observing the customary placement of stems, dots, rests, and accidentals—has traditionally employed a personal manner of handling flags and beams. Unlike instrumental notation, in which large groups of small note-values are beamed together as a beat-unit (see page 81), vocal notation has heretofore marked each note with a separate flag to correspond to the syllable division (upper staff in Example 17-7). Only when a single word or syllable was sung on several notes of small value (eighths and smaller) were beams used.

This practice was logical and clear to the eye in music of simple metric and rhythmic texture; the separate flagged notes could quickly and easily be related to the large metric units as well as to the proper syllables. But with increasing rhythmic complexity in the music of the present century—vocal as well as instrumental—the tradition of flagging vocal notes has become outmoded. Practically all progressive vocal

EXAMPLE 17-7. Paul Hindemith: From *When Lilacs Last in the Dooryard Bloom'd* (1946)

294

publications now print the voice parts with beams instead of individual flags, a much-needed revision in notational practice. Far from objecting to this, singers in general have welcomed the clarity of this new practice (as shown in the lower staff of Example 17-7 and in Example 6-2). It seems fairly safe to predict that vocal beaming will become standard in the very near future.

Note-elements are handled conventionally in vocal music except when special *stemming* is used for chorale notation and for some hymns. Chorales, being essentially contrapuntal and therefore having more rhythmic independence between the voices, must use separate stems for each of the two voices sharing a common staff. Conservative hymns, on the other hand, are basically homophonic (a melody in four-part harmony) and require only one stem for the two notes on one staff unless the time-values differ. When the harmonization is more independent, however, many hymns are notated with separate stems for each vocal part.

Rests, Pauses   In addition to all the standard rests and *fermata* signs, vocal music employs two special signs that signify breathing places. These signs are the comma (❜) placed just over the staff (see Example 7-18), and the small, elongated "v" (∨) or its variant (ⱱ). Both symbols indicate the point for a breath, but too short a pause for a rest sign of definite value.

Key Signatures   In predominantly tonal music, voice or choral parts would carry key signatures. In much contemporary music for voices, key signatures are dispensed with, just as they are in instrumental music.

Time Signatures   As a general rule, vocal parts are each given a time signature, although the four choral staves in a work for chorus with orchestra may have one large meter-sign for all the staves. (See Example 26-6.)

Barlines, Rhythm   In order not to interfere with the written text of vocal music, placed beneath the staff, barlines do not usually extend through all the voice staves as a group. With each staff— whether for a single solo voice or for a whole chorus—barred separately, the text may be more easily read; in this way slurs, wedges, and expression marks are not bisected by barlines. (See Examples 17-3 and 17-5.)

In vocal music the rhythmic patterns shown on the staff may involve several notes for a single word or syllable, which must then be indicated as drawn out. When a word or syllable is to be so extended, a straight, unbroken line called an *extender* is drawn from the end of the one word (or syllable) to a position under the last note on which it is sung.

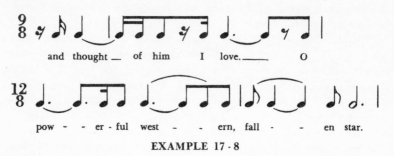

and thought ＿ of him   I   love.＿＿＿   O

pow - - er - ful west - - ern, fall - - en star.

EXAMPLE 17 - 8

If *punctuation marks* come after a word, the extender begins immediately after the comma (period, semicolon, or colon). When a word is divided into syllables, any one of which is drawn out in time-values, a long *hyphen* is used, or a number of widely-spaced hyphens if required by space (see Example 17-8). The extender and the hyphen must be clearly differentiated in level: the hyphen centered, the extender drawn on a level with the bottom of the word it follows.

Allowing always for variations and exceptions when space requirements so dictate, the alignment of note-heads with words or syllables is generally as follows: *single* short words or syllables (three or four letters) are *centered* under the note. A two-letter word or syllable is almost always centered beneath the note-head. Longer words are generally aligned by the first vowel; otherwise, they are centered under the note. When either a word or a syllable is spread over several notes (or one note tied to another), the first letter is usually aligned with the first note. (Refer to Examples 17-7, 17-8, and 17-9 for illustrations of these principles.)

Ornaments   Many ornaments are primarily instrumental, and so unsuited to vocal manipulation. The vocal tremolo, in fact, is a phenomenon peculiar to voices alone—an exaggerated vibrato, rather than the purposeful alternation of two or more notes of fixed pitch that characterizes the instrumental tremolo. All vocal ornaments save the trill are best written out in complete detail.

Dynamic Markings   It is customary to put dynamic marks, including "hairpins" and terms for crescendo or decrescendo, *above* each vocal staff rather than below, to avoid conflict with the words placed beneath the staff. Because vocal crescendos and diminuendos are as a rule of shorter duration than instrumental ones, "hairpins" are more effective than written terms. They must be accurately positioned over the notes they affect, and as close to the note-heads, flags, or beams as possible without undue crowding (see Example 17-3). If the increase or decrease of volume is spread over a number of measures, the terms *cresc.* and *dim.* may of course be used.

Accents, Slurs   Accent marks in vocal music are usually limited to three: >, − , and • (or ▼)—meaning a forceful attack, a moderate emphasis, and a light one. The strongest form of accent sign (Λ) is rarely used, as voices cannot produce the same degree of percussive attack as most instruments. Combinations such as ⧸ or ⧽ are not really feasible for voices.

When required, accent marks are placed *over* the notes or stems, to get them away from the written text. The same is true of long phrase-marks, although short slurs affecting only two or three notes are usually placed next to the note-heads (see Example 17-7).

Slur marks in the sense of instrumental phrasing are seldom found in vocal music. Phrasing for voices is usually achieved by breathing; therefore, vocal phrases must on the whole be shorter than instrumental phrases. Instead of long, curved phrase-marks such as one finds in keyboard music or orchestra scores, vocal phrasing is indicated either by actual rests, or by the pause signs discussed on page 105. Actual slurs, then, should be used only for a series of notes sung to one word or syllable.

Slurring is more complicated when vocal music is printed with a translation in another language beneath the original words. As the division of words and syllables will vary at times, there will be held notes instead of the repeated notes of the original, and vice versa. Phrasing and slurs must then be shown in two ways—one for the original text, and one for the translation. For the original text, a normal, solid slur-sign is used; for the alternate, translated version there will sometimes be a dotted slur-sign. If both slurs are unbroken, one will go above the notes, stems, and flags, and one below, as shown here. Moreover, separate stems must be used, with different flagging or beaming to correspond with the altered text. (See Example 17-9.)

Tempo, Expression Marks   One tempo indication placed above the topmost staff of choral or vocal ensemble music will suffice. Any further general directions—*ritardando, accelerando, allargando,* and so on—are also put only above the topmost staff. But individual

EXAMPLE 17 - 9. Frederick Delius: From *Sea Drift* (1904)

directions, and all expressive indications (*dolce, cantabile, con espressione,* and so forth) are put above each vocal staff at the required place.

Successful writing for voices proceeds from the composer's awareness of the peculiar gifts—and limitations—of that medium. Good vocal notation will assist the performers by aiming for impeccable clarity, and by requesting the possible—not the improbable—achievement.

MODERN INNOVATIONS

Some new note-shapes have originated in twentieth-century music that utilizes the human voice as an instrument of color and special effect rather than as the conventional organ of song. One such unorthodox approach is the half-spoken, half-sung effect known as *Sprechstimme.* Arnold Schönberg's method of notating *Sprechstimme* was to write an approximate pitch with a small x through the stem of the note. Other composers have used the x alone, flagged or beamed, to show time duration.

EXAMPLE 17 - 10

Other new note-shapes invented by avant-garde composers for various vocal effects include the following:

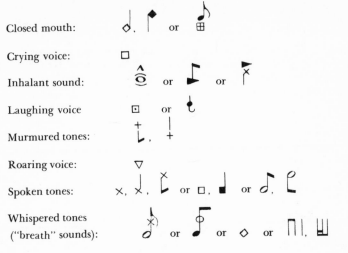

EXAMPLE 17 - 11

Cluster-effects (diatonic or chromatic) in divided choral voices are generally notated as follows:

EXAMPLE 17 - 12

18

Keyboard Notation

JUST AS THE PECULIAR PROBLEMS OF VOCAL NOTATION relate to the setting of words, so the notational principles for keyboard instruments relate to the use of hands and fingers (and feet as well, in organ music.) Keyboard notation, then, is basically geared to the division of labor between the hands, with every notational element affected in some way by this consideration.

TRADITIONAL PRACTICES

Staves   All keyboard instruments use a minimum of *two* staves. The organ makes almost constant use of *three* staves: two for the hands on the two to five manuals, and one for the feet on the pedals (see Example 18-3). On small two-manual instruments the organist would have available the *Swell* (*Sw.*) on top, with the *Great* (*Gr.*) below. A three-manual instrument would add the *Choir* (*Ch.*) or *Positif* (*Pos.*) below the *Great* manual. Additional keyboards would be the *Solo* (top manual in a four-manual organ) and the *Echo* (top in a five-manual instrument). To designate any manual, however, no new staves are employed; instead, the notator will indicate any special choice of manual above either staff at the proper point.

When the organ is an accompanying instrument for choral music, its part is often printed on *two* staves only, as a space-saving device. The pedal part then shares the bass staff with the left-hand manual part. The two lines are labeled at the beginning of the first bass staff, and further distinguished by up-stems for the bass manual and down-stems for the pedal.

Three or even *four* staves may be occasionally encountered in piano music when the complexity of the written notes demands it. If three staves are used, the middle staff serves both left and right hands; if four staves, the upper two are for the right hand and the lower two for the left (see Example 18-3). Music for celesta and harpsichord rarely requires more than two staves, but the same principle would apply if more were needed.

Four staves are uniformly needed in music written for four hands at one or two pianos, but the staves are arranged in different ways for the two media. For two-piano works, the four staves are combined into a *system* (see below), Piano I using the upper two staves and Piano II the lower two. For four-hand music on one instrument, the two parts are placed on facing pages, with each measure in a position exactly parallel to that of the corresponding measure on the facing page. The first player (*primo;* top part) reads from the right-hand page (*Prima Parte*); the second player (*secondo;* bottom part) reads from the left-hand page (*Seconda Parte*).

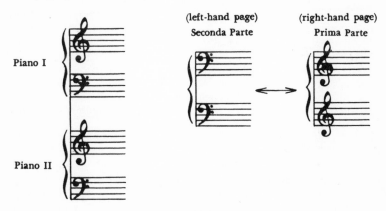

EXAMPLE 18 - 1

Braces, Systems   The two staves of all the keyboard instruments, including the manual staves in organ music, are connected by a brace. The organ pedal-staff is not included in the brace, but stands apart from it. For all the keyboard instruments the brace precedes a single long barline, which joins the two, three, or four staves (see Example 18-3).

The two or more component staves of celesta, harpsichord, and piano music and the three staves of organ music comprise a single system. A printed page of piano music may contain anywhere from three to six systems, five being the average number; an organ page will usually contain three or four systems.

The four staves of two-piano compositions also constitute a system; usually there are not more than three such systems to a page.

The straight bracket also appears in a function additional to its use in systems. A thin bracket with one terminal jog is used to show notes taken by the one hand in a staff normally occupied by the opposite hand—the jog showing the note (or notes) to be taken by the unusual hand.

EXAMPLE 18 - 2

An alternative marking for this situation is the standard abbreviation for the correct hand, placed over the initial notes affected. The abbreviation chosen should correspond to the language in which other directions are given throughout.

Right hand (**R.H.** or **r.h.**); Fr. *main droit* (**m.d.**); Ger. *rechte Hand* (**R.H.**); It. *mano destra* (**m.d.**)

Left hand (**L.H.** or **l.h.**); Fr. *main gauche* (**m.g.**); Ger. *linke Hand* (**L.H.**); It. *mano sinistra* (**m.s.**)

Ledger Lines, Octave Signs   Because the over-all ranges are relatively great, all of the keyboard instruments freely and constantly use both ledger lines and octave signs. If the ledger lines become excessive, *8ᵛᵃ* or *8ᵛᵃ bassa* signs are used, and occasionally even the *15ᵐᵃ* sign. But not all the keyboard instruments use *all* of the signs. The restrictions for each are as follows:

Celesta:	uses *8ᵛᵃ* only above treble clef; *8ᵛᵃ bassa* is not necessary, as the lowest written note for the instrument is **c** in bass clef.
Harpsichord:	*8ᵛᵃ* above treble clef and *8ᵛᵃ bassa* beneath bass clef are both possible, but rarely needed, as the highest written note is **f'''** and the lowest is **F,**; ledger lines are thus more commonly used.
Organ:	*8ᵛᵃ* is occasionally used over treble staff; *8ᵛᵃ bassa* is never used because the lowest written manual and pedal notes are **C**.
Piano:	uses *8ᵛᵃ* and *15ᵐᵃ* above treble clef only; uses *8ᵛᵃ bassa* beneath bass clef only.

Clefs Only *two* clef-signs—treble and bass—are employed today by any keyboard instrument. Normally the disposition is: treble clef for the upper (right-hand) staff, and bass for the lower (left-hand) staff. This arrangement may be reversed, of course, for "crossed hands" effects, or both staves may use the same clef momentarily. The pedal part for organ music is always notated on the bass staff. These usual dispositions are shown in the table below, with clef signs in parentheses indicating alternate usages.

EXAMPLE 18 - 3. TABLE OF KEYBOARD CLEFS

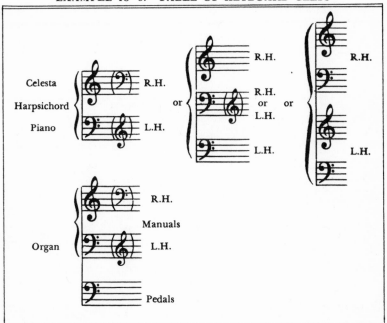

Notes, Stems Some stemming problems are personal to piano, organ, or other keyboard instruments. For instance, on occasion the right-hand part goes into the lower staff momentarily, to avoid changing the clef sign of the upper staff. In such a case, the stems of all notes to be played by the right hand go *up*, and those of the left hand all go *down*, regardless of the staff position of any of the notes. The same principle holds true for transferring the left-hand part to the upper staff. No rests are required for the measure portions thus vacated (see Example 18-4).

EXAMPLE 18 - 4

Sometimes *chord notes* played by either hand are divided between the two staves. When this occurs, the stems of the right-hand notes again go *up,* and those of the left hand go *down,* regardless of the position of the notes on either staff.

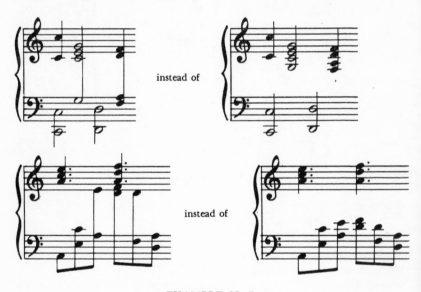

instead of

instead of

EXAMPLE 18 - 5

If in addition to the chord division discussed above *inner voices* are required, they must be notated with separate stems going in the *opposite direction* from the chord stems. Rests necessary for the inner voice must be placed *under* the right-hand staff or *over* the left-hand staff. Should the normal vertical placement of the rest get in the way of note-heads or stems, it may be moved slightly to the left.

EXAMPLE 18 - 6

It is sometimes necessary—because of contrapuntal complexities—to involve three, or even four, stems in one vertical relationship on a single staff. In such a case, several separate stems on notes of unequal duration must go in the same direction; to make the situation absolutely clear the notator must place one of the notes slightly to the side of the vertical alignment (as shown in Example 18-7). Whatever the arrangement, the separate identities of the various contrapuntal lines must be clearly shown, as though two staves rather than one were being used.

EXAMPLE 18 - 7

Admittedly the second measure of this example presents an extreme illustration of the problem, but comparable instances will be encountered in reading highly polyphonic keyboard music. The challenge is always to notate in the clearest possible manner. If multiple stems must be used, one has to find such a placement for them that each individual voice may be easily traced. Whatever its notational complexity, Example 18-7 does just that.

With stemming, as with all other notational problems, sound common sense may occasionally dictate that the way to be clear is to contravene the usual rules. A typical instance is a passage from Debussy's *Minstrels,* where inner voices are divided between the two staves, with the common stem touching the opposite sides of the notes involved.

EXAMPLE 18 - 8

Here Debussy wished to clarify the ascending chromatic line in both hands: **d**, **e♭**, **e♮**, **f**, **f♯**, and **g**. Their vertical alignment made it necessary to use unorthodox stemming, and attach the stems on the opposite sides of the two inner notes. The rule of interval placement is also by-passed here, for the seconds are notated in reverse order: the higher note is placed to the left rather than to the right. (Compare with page 71.)

Flags, Beams   When the two hands in a keyboard composition play in succession on a *single staff*, we must make—in addition to the adjustment of stems mentioned above—adjustment of flags and beaming as well. Notes taken by the right hand will obviously have flags and beams going *up,* while the notes played by the left hand will have them going *down.* In the example below, the first separately flagged sixteenth-note is necessary to show that it belongs to the right-hand group, even though metrically it is part of the left-hand group. Likewise, the next two separately flagged sixteenth-notes show that they are taken by the left hand.

EXAMPLE 18 - 9

Most keyboard beaming problems, however, arise because there are two staves in keyboard notation rather than the single staff used by singers or orchestral instrumentalists; beaming over or between these two staves must make clear the duties of either hand. Single-line figures

(arpeggios or broken chords) may be beamed—as demonstrated below
—in any of three ways, depending on staff space available. At the far
left, beams are over the entire sequence; at the left center, beams are
between the staves, and at the right center, under the entire sequence.
In such figures it is not necessary to include rests on either staff for the
portions of the beat during which one hand does not play. The two
levels—thanks to the common beam—fill out each beat in the metric
sense (lower line, below).

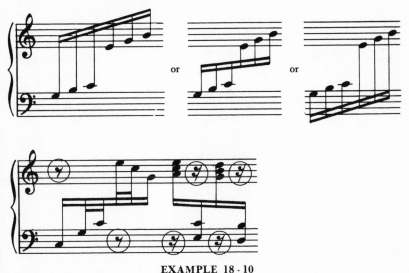

EXAMPLE 18 - 10

On rare occasions a common beam is shared by the two hands playing at the same time. In the example below, the notes also share a common stem. Upper and lower note-heads are placed on the correct
side of the stem—the right-hand side for the upper note, and the left-
hand side for the lower note. This makes it necessary to move the lower
note slightly to the left in order that the stem may be perfectly perpendicular. Admittedly, such a notational device is rare.

EXAMPLE 18 - 11

On other occasions, a single beam must be positioned for chords played by a single hand, but notated on the two staves. If the chord is to be played by the right hand, the beams are drawn *above* the note-heads (left, below); if the chord is to be played by the left hand, the beams are drawn *below* the note-heads (center, below). Occasionally seen, though not recommended because it is less clear, is the common beam between the staves, joining horizontally the common stems of the notes (right, below).

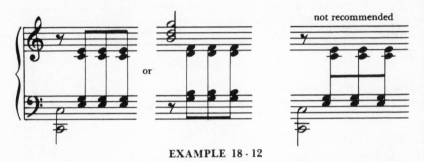

EXAMPLE 18 - 12

Contrapuntal lines may occasionally bring both hands to an *identical note*. Included in the left-hand beaming of the example below is a note in parentheses, indicating that **d'** is part of the melodic progression in the left hand. At this same moment the contrapuntal line in the right-hand part also comes to rest on **d'**; as obviously only one hand can play the duplicated note, the unison in the other hand is enclosed in parentheses. The choice of hand to play and to rest in such situations depends largely on context—on hand position and the surrounding fingering patterns. If the composer makes an awkward choice, he may be sure that the performer will alter the notation to suit himself!

EXAMPLE 18 - 13

If the first note of a beamed group of eighth or sixteenth notes is to be *sustained* through two quarter-note beats, it may be written as a half note, even though it is beamed with the group of shorter values (left, below). If it lasts for three beats, it may be notated as a dotted half-note (right, below). For four beats duration, the note would be written as a whole note placed at the left of a duplicating eighth or smaller unit in the beamed group (bottom line, below).

EXAMPLE 18 - 14

Probably the most perplexing problem relating to flagging and beaming occurs when one set of notes serves a *two-fold* function: the music outlines a melody and its harmonic figuration simultaneously. This kind of musical texture is widely prevalent in the keyboard works of such Romanticists as Schumann, Mendelssohn, Chopin, and Liszt. In order to clarify the melodic threads—sometimes several at the same time—as well as the incorporated accompaniment figures, a complicated system of separate stems, flags, and/or beams must be written. The following short excerpt well illustrates the problem.

EXAMPLE 18 - 15. Frédéric Chopin: From *Nocturne,* Op. 15, No. 2

We see here that the right hand actually carries on a four-fold role: a main thematic idea at the top (left, below); two inner figures (center, below); and an accompanying pattern in quintuplets (right, below).

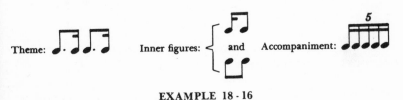

EXAMPLE 18 - 16

All of this is set against an independent chord part for the left hand. Truly this illustrates the necessity for the left hand to know what the right hand is doing!

Flag-and-beam quandaries could be expounded indefinitely, but we shall cite only one further serviceable example. Under certain circumstances, separate flags rather than a beam have to be used when the placement of stems and notes provides no room for a beam without its bisecting note-heads or stems. For example, in the following excerpt the melodic line in eighth notes must be separately flagged, as a beam joining the three notes would conflict with the note-heads or stems of the figurated sixteenth-notes.

EXAMPLE 18 - 17. Franz Liszt: From *La Campanella*

Theoretically, the passage above could be notated with the sixteenth-note beams above the staff, and the melodic eighth-note beam below; but this alternative would not be practical because of the immense amount of space it would require over the staff, especially as the *8va* sign still must be placed above the passage.

Ties, Dots   Tie-signs and augmentation dots are used for keyboard instruments according to the general principles discussed in Chapter 8. There are times, however, when one may find tied together two notes usually written as one (left and center examples below). This form of notation is used to show a change of fingering on the sustained note, the object being to shift the finger in an imperceptible manner. Nearly always the fingering will be given just above the notes or stems (right, below).

EXAMPLE 18 - 18

If no fingering is shown, the change is optional or the choice of finger is left to the player's discretion.

When two hands play on one staff and there are *tied notes* present, the tie-slurs are always looped in opposite directions—those of the right hand going up, and those of the left hand going down. This principle is observed regardless of the number of vertically placed notes being tied or their individual position on the staff.

EXAMPLE 18 - 19

A curious kind of tieing occurs when a single tone or chord in one hand is tied over a barline but into the *other staff*, meaning a transference to the opposite hand (below). The tie(s) must curve from note-head to note-head, and it is important to allow plenty of room so that the ties do not bisect clef signs, other notes, or dynamic markings.

EXAMPLE 18 - 20

Key Signatures   When the nature of the music demands it, all keyboard instruments make use of conventional key-signatures. These are placed—as previously described in detail (see pages 135–140) —on each staff directly following the clef sign, and are repeated on each successive system until canceled or otherwise altered. When changes of key signature are infrequent, they are usually preceded by a double bar (see Examples 9-28–9-31).

Time Signatures   Time signatures for the keyboard instruments are normally located on the staff itself, but frequently one will find them centered between the staves, or a single meter-sign will be placed directly over the uppermost staff. (See Example 10-11.) A piece of music that does not alter its initial time-signature is well served, of course, by the conventional placement of the meter sign on the two staves. But in music that continually changes its meter, the use of a single large time-signature between the staves (rather than over the top staff) is recommended as logical and efficient.

Barlines   Two methods are used in barring *organ music:* one separates the manuals from the pedal staff, and the other joins all three staves with an unbroken barline. The first method is the more logical, and is generally preferred to the second. In other keyboard music—with the exception of two-piano works—barlines usually are drawn continuously through all the staves of the system.

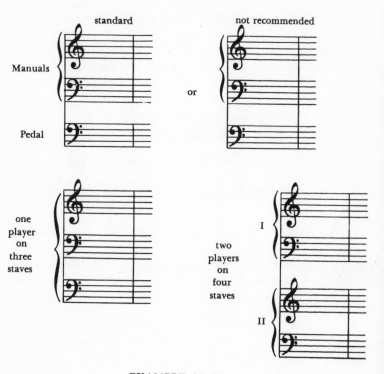

EXAMPLE 18 - 21

Dotted barlines are freely used to clarify metric patterns. Occasionally such dotted barlines may be found centered between the staves and not on them—as indeed the regular unbroken barlines are sometimes notated in contemporary keyboard literature.

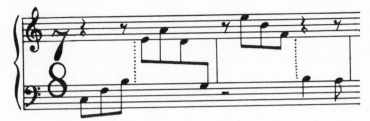

EXAMPLE 18-22

It frequently happens in piano or other keyboard music that—because of florid passage-work or rhythmically extended arpeggios, runs, cadenzas, and the like—the end of the system is reached part-way through a measure. When this happens, the staves at the end of the system must be left open, and the concluding barline of the measure must come in the system below. Usually such breaks in a measure are spaced so that they come at a convenient—or, at the very least, logical —point in terms of beat or rhythm. The following example indicates the logical place where the pattern should be broken for the end of the system, and resumed in the one just below.

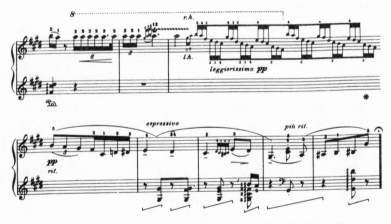

EXAMPLE 18-23. Franz Liszt: From *The Nightingale*

Dynamic Markings   Keyboard notation follows the universal principle for dynamic markings: place them as close as possible to the note (or group of notes) they affect. This is also true of the wedge, or "hairpin," signs. Depending on the space available, they may be located above, below, or between the staves—or even on the staff if other notational elements crowd the spaces above or below. (See Examples 14-5, 14-7, 14-8, 15-4, 18-15, and 18-24 for accepted placement.)

Slurs   Prime functions of the slur in keyboard music—as detailed in Chapter 15—are to delineate the extent of a phrase line and to indicate the legato performance of melodies or arpeggiated chords. In keyboard music of a single texture (a simple melody with harmonic accompaniment) a single phrasing-slur over the top staff suffices for the entire system. Chopin's *Prelude in A major*, Op. 28, No. 7 affords a good illustration of such a use. If a more complex structure requires separate slurs for the right and left hands, it is best if the right-hand slur extends *over* the staff, and the left-hand slur *under* the lower staff.

EXAMPLE 18-24. Claude Debussy: From *La Cathédrale engloutie* (1910)

Legato arpeggio figures are a bit tricky to slur, particularly when they are divided between the two hands. When separate beams are used for groups divided between the two hands, the slur may go over, under, or between the groups according to the available room. The rule of thumb here is that when stems and beams are *up* for both hands, the phrasing slur goes *below* the groups; when stems and beams are *down,* the slur goes *above.* When the left-hand beams are below and the right-hand beams above, the phrasing slur is put between the groups (first three examples, below).

If, however, the arpeggiated figures or melodic passages are beamed together, the slur must go either over the entire group or below the entire group—provided room is available (far right, below).

EXAMPLE 18-25

Though it is not truly desirable, the notator cannot avoid on occasion having phrase-slurs cross each other in transferring a melodic line from one staff to the other (left, below). Slurs also have to be "bent" in various ways to avoid conflicting with note-heads, ties, and so on (top line, right, and lower line, below).

EXAMPLE 18 - 26

Tempo, Expression Marks   Tempo marks, including metronome indications, are always placed above the uppermost staff. Both may be put on one line, or the metronome mark may be placed directly beneath the tempo indication.

CORRECT: Allegro vivace ($\downarrow$ = 126)   CORRECT: Allegro vivace
M.M. $\downarrow$ = 126

All other terms referring specifically to tempo (including ritardandos and accelerandos) or to any kind of expressive indication are put either above the top staff or between the two staves. Occasionally, owing to lack of room, they may be found below the lower staff. Because only one person is performing, a single direction is all that is necessary, wherever the term or symbol is placed. For two-piano works, and for one piano four-hands, duplicate signs must of course be used in both parts.

Fingering   When any specific fingering is to be given, the
small figures are placed as close as possible to, and directly above or
below, the note-head, stem, or beam. Special fingering indications must
often be given to illuminate an unusual notational problem, as when
one hand plays on a staff normally employed by the other (as in Example 18-9) or when a finger is silently changed on a sustained note
(see page 310). Fingering for technically difficult passages, on the other
hand, tends today to be left to the individual performer to adjust to
his physical limitations. When fingering is needed for intervals and
chords, it is given vertically; in the right hand the figures read *down*
from fifth finger to thumb, and in the left hand they read *up*.

EXAMPLE 18 - 27

Certain older editions of keyboard music indicate the thumb with an
x or a cross (**+**) instead of the small figure **1**; but modern editions almost universally use the figure.

Organ Pedal Markings   Two symbols are used in notating
the staff for organ pedals: ∪ (or o) for the heel, and ∧ (or ∨) for
the toe. The pedaling for the right foot is put *above* the staff, and
for the left foot *below* the staff. If a change of foot on a tied note is
required—from left to right, or right to left—one puts the necessary
signs above and below the two note-heads:

EXAMPLE 18 - 28

Other changes are indicated as follows:

∧　⌣　=　　　from toe to heel, right foot

∧　⌣　=　　　from toe to heel, left foot

⌣　∧　=　　　from heel to toe, right foot

⌣　∧　=　　　from heel to toe, left foot

EXAMPLE 18 - 29

Other Pedal Markings　　　　　Pedal indications are one of the most important notational aspects of piano music. The most commonly used of the three piano pedals is the one at the right, called the *damper pedal* (to the perpetual confusion of music students). When pressed down, the damper pedal *raises* the dampers (small felted blocks resting on the strings), and so allows the strings to continue vibrating after being struck. Various signs, placed always below the bass staff, may correctly be used to show where the damper pedal is to be depressed and where it is to be released. The most commonly employed are these:

full-pedal markings

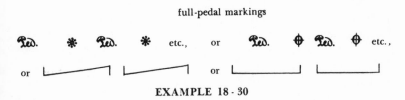

EXAMPLE 18 - 30

Whether the asterisk or its substitute form is used to indicate the release of the pedal, it is essential that the sign be placed *precisely under* the beat or fraction of the beat where the foot is to allow the pedal to rise, thus stopping (damping) the vibration of the strings (as in Example 18-15). If the slanting line is used, the initial and terminal jogs must also coincide accurately with the moments of pedal depression and release. (See Example 18-23.)

The damper pedal is often deliberately released only half-way, so that some of the vibrations from the previous tones continue into the next pedal-group. This effect is called *half pedal,* and the sign is usually a horizontal line drawn from the abbreviation **Ped.**, with a "dip" in the line at each place where the half pedal is to be used. The line terminates either with a jog or with an asterisk, both indicating a complete release of the damper pedal.

half-pedal markings

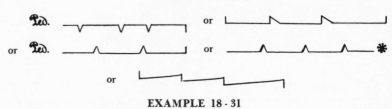

EXAMPLE 18 - 31

The left piano pedal is correctly called the muting or *soft pedal* (*una corda*). This Italian term for "one string" indicates that depressing the soft pedal shifts the entire keyboard slightly to the left, so that the hammers strike only two of the three strings for each piano key (one string only in the bass register—and in early piano history the *una-corda* was literally one string throughout). This of course produces a softer sound than when all three of the strings are struck by the hammer.

To request the use of the soft pedal, the notator writes *una corda* below the bass staff at the point required. When normal use of all three strings is to be restored by the release of the soft pedal, the indication *tre corde* (Italian for "three strings") is put below the bass staff.

On concert grands and other large models there is a third pedal placed between the soft and the damper pedals. This is the *sostenuto pedal* (*S.P.*); its function is to prolong only the tones of certain preselected strings. When the pianist strikes a single key, an octave, or perhaps a closely spaced sonority (in the bass register only), the sostenuto pedal acts as a damper pedal on those notes alone. The use of this pedal is usually indicated by *S.P.* below the notated sonority, followed by a slanting line and downward jog for the release of the pedal: *S.P.*

Most celestas have a single damper pedal (none have muting or sostenuto pedals), but its effectiveness varies considerably with different instruments. In terms of lasting sonority, even the best-made celesta cannot duplicate the sustaining ability of the piano using the damper pedal. Pedaling for the celesta may be written in the same way as for the piano, using the standard signs shown in the examples above.

Because of the unique principle of tone production on the harpsichord (the strings are plucked rather than struck) the instrument does not have damper or sostenuto pedals. Most modern harpsichords do have a number of pedals, knee levers, or draw knobs that work somewhat on the principle of organ stops: that is, they affect timbre rather than duration. Employment of these mechanical devices, however, is best left to the harpsichordist's discretion, as neither the devices nor their notational symbols are systematized.

MODERN INNOVATIONS

Of all the keyboard instruments, the piano has been the principal object of recent experimentation. Some effects such as John Cage's "prepared piano" require no new symbols, but only elaborate directions as to how certain piano strings should be "prepared" by inserting pencils, erasers, or bits of wood, rubber, or metal between the strings. Others are creations of solo or ensemble performers and have not entered the general notational stream. Still other new keyboard devices require new notational signs, notably those standardized for harmonics and tone-clusters.

Harmonics (or overtones) for one piano string can be achieved by silently pressing down the key of the pitch desired, then forcefully striking the key one or two octaves lower (or higher) and immediately releasing it (example at the left). The silently depressed key will allow the resulting overtone vibrations to sound very clearly. For a similar result, a chord may be played loudly with the damper pedal down, the same keys an octave higher or lower then inaudibly depressed, and the damper pedal released (example at the right). The overtones of the entire chord will sound out, then gradually die away.

To indicate the key or keys to be silently depressed, Arnold Schönberg adapted to keyboard notation the diamond-shaped notes used for string harmonics, as shown below.

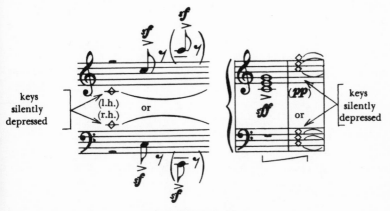

EXAMPLE 18 - 32

Tone-clusters—the invention of Henry Cowell—are an innovation
that was first applied exclusively to keyboard instruments. They are
now found as well in music for various combinations of orchestral
instruments, including the mallet percussion, and for voices (see pages
299 and 408). Piano clusters composed of a large number of adjacent
notes can be constructed on white keys only, black keys only, or on
both simultaneously. The notations for each type will differ, and all
will depend for notation on the outer extent of the cluster.

If a cluster covers a relatively small area, all the notes may be written in, with a common stem running through the middle (left, below).
If it stretches over a rather wide area, only the bottom and top notes
are actually written, with either a thick stem joining the two note-heads
at their center or two regular stems—one on either side of the two notes
(right, below). In the absence of any accidental-sign it may be assumed
that the examples below consist only of white keys.

EXAMPLE 18 - 33

When the cluster is to be on the black keys, a large sharp or a large
flat is placed just at the left of the cluster-notation, or a normal-sized
sharp or flat just above the cluster-notation. It does not matter which
accidental is used, but if black keys are wanted then the outer notes
indicated must be those that would be black keys when flatted or
sharped.

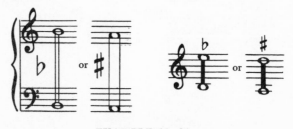

EXAMPLE 18 - 34

A few of the many variant forms of the cluster-symbol devised by contemporary composers for white-note and black-note tone clusters are given below. It would seem that a standardized notation for this effect is a necessity; there is little logic or reason to have so many symbol-variations for this pianistic device.

White-note clusters:

Black-note clusters:

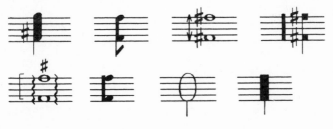

EXAMPLE 18-35

For chromatic clusters—structures that contain both black and white keys—the following variant forms have been used in current experimental piano music:

EXAMPLE 18 - 36

As the technique of producing harmonics can be applied to cluster-formations as well as to single tones and simple chords, their notations usually take the forms shown below:

EXAMPLE 18 - 37

Today's avant-garde composers have thoroughly explored—and ex-ploited—the varied and unorthodox effects obtained by playing inside the piano, directly on the strings. A number of ingenious symbols have been devised to direct the performer to: rub the indicated string or strings with his finger (**a.** below), or with the fingernail (**b.**); pluck the string with the nail (**c.**), or with a plectrum (**d.**); strike the string(s) forcefully with the fingers or palm (**e.**), with the fingernails (**f.**), or with various kinds of mallets (**g.**); dampen the string with one finger while playing on the key (**h.**).

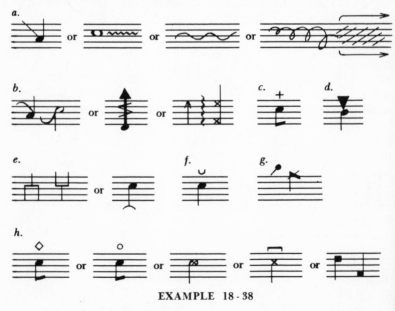

EXAMPLE 18 - 38

19

Harp Notation

TOO MANY COMPOSERS THINK OF THE HARP IN TERMS of piano technique. Ignorant alike of its unique potential and of its technical limitations, they obviously cannot write adequately for this instrument. The extensive peculiarities of harp notation, however, are such as to preempt a chapter of their own.

TRADITIONAL PRACTICES

Staves   The harp, like the keyboard instruments, generally uses two staves. They are made into a system in the same way as piano staves: with a single line preceded by a curved brace (see Example 2-1).

Ledger Lines, Octave Signs   Because the over-all range of the harp is quite extensive (C♭,–g♯′′′′), it freely uses both ledger lines and the standard *8ᵛᵃ* signs. *15ᵐᵃ* would not ordinarily be found in harp music unless space above its top staff were at a premium in full score.

Clefs   Like the keyboard instruments, the harp employs only the treble and bass clefs. Either staff may bear either of these two clef signs.

Beams   Because of the nature of "harpistic" writing, beamed groups of notes often cross from staff to staff, as in keyboard notation (see Examples 18-10 and 18-25). The same rules apply to their make-up and direction.

Ties   Ties are seldom used in harp notation unless the value of the notes is fairly short. This is because the instrument does not possess a damper pedal, as does the piano, and hence cannot prolong the sounds of the plucked strings. *Incomplete* ties are commonly used, however, to indicate *laissez vibrer* (*l.v.*), meaning that the strings are not to be muffled in any way, but the tone allowed to ring through as long as physically possible.

EXAMPLE 19 - 1

Key Signatures   Key signatures are used for harp music when appropriate. Because the strings of the instrument sound better in flat keys than in sharp keys, enharmonic key-signatures are frequently substituted. If the tonality of an orchestral work were F♯ major, for instance, the harp part ought to be written in G♭ major; instead of B major, requiring five sharps, the harp would sound better in C♭ major, seven flats. This reasoning will become clearer in the following section.

Accidentals   Accidentals in harp music invariably relate to the indication of pedal settings. There are seven pedals—three on the left side of the instrument, and four on the right side—and each pedal is connected to *all* the strings of one letter pitch. For instance, the C pedal is attached to all the C strings.

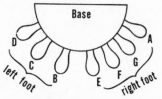

EXAMPLE 19 - 2

Normally the left pedals are operated by the left foot, the right pedals by the right foot. Obviously, one foot can manage only one pedal at a time, as each must be depressed or raised to fit into one of three different notches. Only when two adjacent pedals are both to be placed in corresponding notches can both be changed simultaneously by one foot (E♮ and F♮ to E♭ and F♭; G♭ and A♭ to G♮ and A♮, for example). When the pedal is in the top notch, it is in its "flat" position; that is, the string vibrates at its maximum length, so is lowest in pitch. In the second notch the string is in the "natural" position, and in the bottom notch it is in the "sharp" position. When the pedal is depressed so as to fit into the middle and bottom notches, a mechanism shortens the string by a half-step for each notch. Both feet, of course, may simultaneously operate the pedals, creating such combinations as **C** and **E**, **D** and **F**, **B** and **G** or **A**.

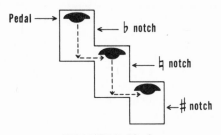

EXAMPLE 19 - 3

The pedal settings must always be given at the beginning of any harp music. These are shown in one of two ways: either the letter pitches are given (in the order of the pedals from left to right), or the setting is graphically indicated on an ingenious diagram invented by Carlos Salzedo.

EXAMPLE 19 - 4

As one can see, the Salzedo diagram visually indicates the position of each pedal—the top level showing the flat settings; the bottom level, the sharps; and the midway horizontal line, the naturals. Harpists the world over know this manner of indicating pedal settings, and it is rapidly becoming standard even in orchestra scores.

Because chromatic indications in harp music must be related to the pedals, changes ought to be shown as *far in advance* as possible; the harpist cannot alter a pedal setting when the string is being plucked without a resulting disagreeable "buzz." In other words, it is not sufficient merely to place the accidental sign before the note itself; it must also be displayed *ahead* of the actual beat it affects. Letter pitches to be changed, together with the impending accidentals, are indicated below the bass staff (or centered between the staves). A glance at the harp parts of almost any Ravel or Debussy orchestral score will illustrate the proper method and timing for indicating pedal changes.

One word of caution: double flats and double sharps ought never to be used in harp notation. As any one string can be set only in a flat, natural, or sharp position, it is obvious that a double flat or sharp must be taken on an adjacent string as an enharmonic note. Thus **F×** should be notated as **G** natural; **B♭♭** as **A** natural, and so on.

Time Signatures, Barlines   Meters are shown just as in keyboard music, by a signature on both staves or a single one placed between the staves. Barlines are drawn through both staves, and all problems of rhythmic notation are solved in the same manner as has been previously discussed (see Chapters 10 and 11).

Ornaments   Ornaments and special effects on the harp comprise glissandos, trills, tremolos, arpeggios (naturally!), harmonics, and two special effects: "sons étouffés" and "près de la table."

Glissandos—called "fluxes" by advocates of the Salzedo school of harp playing—have become one of the most abused clichés in music, but must still be notated. They may be played by either hand or by both together, passing over every string without exception. Because they cannot be selective—in the way a keyboard glissando can be "black key" or "white key"—the pedal setting for every string must be indicated. Many glissandos are comprised of chords containing enharmonic duplications. The pedal setting shown in Example 19-4 (above) will produce a diminished-seventh chord glissando: **F♯ – A♮ – C♮ – E♭**, the other three pedals being set enharmonically for one of these four pitches. The glissando itself would be notated in one of the following manners:

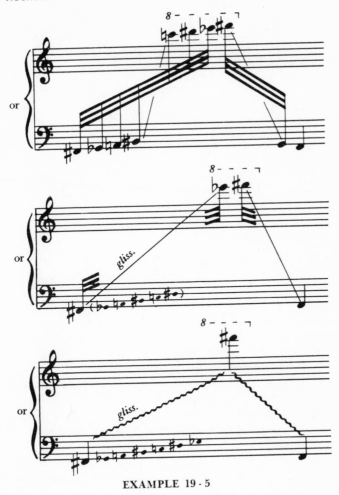

EXAMPLE 19 - 5

As illustrated above, the seven notes are written out in full, usually with the value of 32nd notes. The word *glissando* (or *gliss.*) is usually written over the beamed group, and a straight or wavy line connects the last note-head of this group with the note-head indicating the top limit of the ascending glissando; another straight or wavy line connects this top note-head with the final note of the downward glissando. The direction of the glissando may be reversed, of course, so that it starts on top and goes down (upper line, below; note the variant notation employed here). A simultaneous up- and down-glissando may also be written, the two hands sweeping the strings in opposite directions (lower line, below).

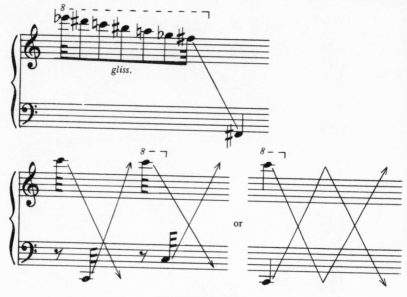

EXAMPLE 19 - 6

Notice that termination notes are not given in the lower examples above, and that the directional arrow is put at the end of each line. The top or bottom note of any rapid glissando on the harp is variable: that is, the finger may or may not reverse its direction on any one particular string, but some note must be given to show at least the *approximate* extent of the glissando. When no pitch is shown at all, the glissando freely covers the entire span of the instrument.

If a two-hand glissando begins quite low, the first notes for both hands are written in the bass clef, the right hand with stems *up* and the left hand with stems and beams *down* (left, below). If the two hands begin the glissando high in the treble clef, the first notes are both written on that staff, the same principle of stem and beam direction applying (right, below). It should be observed that only one seven-note pattern has to be written out in such cases, a single beginning note for the other hand being sufficient. (See Example 19-7.)

Chord glissandos are possible in either hand, but are limited to not more than four notes, as the little finger is never used in harp playing. Note that in a chord glissando the seven different pitches must be shown in two vertical structures, rather than as a scale (compare with Example 19-5). Alternating up and down chord-glissandos are usually taken by alternating hands, although one hand may be responsible for both. (Refer to Example 19-8.)

EXAMPLE 19 - 7

EXAMPLE 19 - 8

It is possible to produce a half-step or a whole-step glissando on the harp by using the pedal mechanism. The string is plucked forcibly, and the pedal is immediately pushed down, or raised into another notch; the mechanism that tightens or loosens the string causes the sliding effect. The notation for a *pedal glissando* is merely the pitch letter of the pre-set string, joined by a line to the altered pitch, with a slur over the two notes (example below). The effect is best in the middle to lower range of the instrument, where the strings have greatest natural resonance.

EXAMPLE 19 - 9

Trills are usually played on the harp with the two hands alternating on the notes involved. The trill is written in one of two ways: the hands alternate in playing on the two trilled notes, one of the repetitions being written as an enharmonic note if possible (left-hand example, below); *or* either hand plays only one of the notes being trilled (example at the right). In the latter case, the trill is written as a tremolo, with double stems and beams.

EXAMPLE 19 - 10

Rapid *repeated notes* are played like a trill. When possible, the pitch is tuned enharmonically on an adjacent string, and the two hands alternate on the two strings.

EXAMPLE 19 - 11

The *chord tremolo* is known as *bisbigliando* in harp terminology. It is played by the two hands alternating as rapidly as possible on the given notes in a soft, indefinite manner.

EXAMPLE 19 - 12

Arpeggiated chords (limited, as are the regular chords, to four notes in either hand) are notated with the familiar vertical wavy line. They may be rolled upward (the normal way) or downward; or the hands may arpeggiate the chord in opposite directions. (See also Examples 13-25–13-27.)

Chords may also be played *non-arpeggiato;* the notation is a thin vertical bracket enclosing the notes to be so played (right, below).

Staccato chords are written either with the dot or the solid wedge, and are frequently marked *sec* or *secco* ("dry") to ensure that the

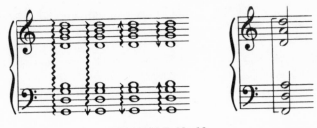

EXAMPLE 19 - 13

strings are quickly damped (with the palm or the flattened fingers)
after being sounded (left example, below). An allied effect is called
by its French term, *sons étouffés*. This also is a very dry kind of
staccato sound, but the term usually applies to single notes rather
than to chords. The notation calls for dots or wedges, with the term
sons étouffés (right example).

EXAMPLE 19 - 14

A related device is also notated by its French term, *près de la table*
(near the sounding board). The harpist plays low on the strings
instead of in the normal middle area. The effect is somewhat metallic,
very similar to the tone of a guitar. In fact, the Italian term *quasi
chitarra* is often substituted for the French in calling for this effect.
Près de la table passages should not carry on for too long a time, as
the resistance of the string just above the sounding board causes the
fingers to tire and to blister more easily than usual.

Harmonics (see page 385) are produced by stopping the harp string
at its midway node, thus dividing the vibrations into halves and raising
the pitch one octave. There is some confusion, even among harpists,
as to the correct manner of notating these harmonics. Some prefer the
actual pitch to be given, but it is more accurate to show the actual
string to be played, remembering that the resultant sound will be
an octave higher. In either case, a small zero is put over the note-
head.

The right hand is able to play only one harmonic at a time, but the left hand—thanks to its position on the string—can play double, triple, or (very rarely) quadruple harmonics if the interval between the outer notes does not exceed a fifth. *Double harmonics* on two adjacent strings are easy to play (see below). Note that for double, triple, and quadruple harmonics the zero signs are placed vertically above or below the note-heads.

EXAMPLE 19 - 15

Dynamic Markings   All levels of dynamic markings are used in harp notation, but the resulting power is relative. The harp's *ff* is not comparable to that of the piano, and most assuredly not to that of the organ. In fact, the harp tone is not capable of subtle distinctions in dynamic strength, and writing *fff* or *ppp* is more psychological in its effect than actual. The marks themselves, including crescendo and decrescendo wedges, are normally placed between the two staves.

Accents, Phrase Marks   Both accents and phrase marks are freely used in harp music, but again the aural effect is relative to the tonal capacity and the nature of the instrument. In other words, the harp cannot make certain accents such as the tenuto (–) because the sound of the string is produced by plucking rather than by striking. As the harp string lacks the normal sustaining quality of the piano or harpsichord string, the staccato dot is generally redundant. It is used, as previously explained, primarily for the exaggerated staccato of *sons étouffés*. The maximum percussive accent (∧) also makes little sense when applied to harp sound. All of these accents, however, may be found in harp literature; their effective application is the problem of the performer.

Phrase marks to indicate *legato* may also be considered an anomaly in harp notation, as a true legato is literally impossible on this instrument. They are commonly used, however, for arpeggios and broken-chord figures, and for outlining melodic ideas—in the same way one phrases piano music.

MODERN INNOVATIONS

For modern harp literature that is colorful and imaginative we are indebted to the eminent harpist Carlos Salzedo—as teacher, performer, and composer. Foremost among his contributions are his invention and novel notation of special performance effects for his instrument. Though there are far too many for individual description, we must mention a few that have become standard in modern harp writing.

One unusual effect is obtained by playing isolated chords or single notes with the *fingernails* rather than with the fleshy tips of the fingers. Naturally, this effect must not be overdone—out of consideration for the player if for no other reason! The sign devised by Salzedo is a horizontally placed half-moon over the chord or note (top example, below).

For a glissando near the *sounding board* (termed by the composer an "oboic flux") the notation is shown in the lower left example below. A glissando played with the fingernails, called the "falling-hail" effect (again, not to be overused) is written as at the lower right. In the examples below, the pedal settings are not shown, but they would be pre-set and indicated in the manner explained on page 325.

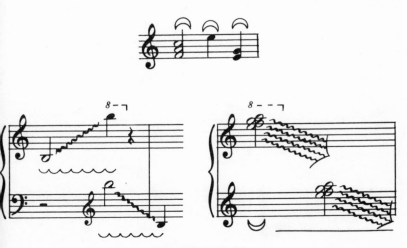

EXAMPLE 19 · 16

A combination of these two effects—a glissando with the fingernails played close to the sounding board, picturesquely termed a "xyloflux" —has the notation shown at the left, below. "Gushing chords," short and violent bursts of glissando, are notated as at the right.

EXAMPLE 19 - 17

For anyone especially interested in the details and unique notation of many other equally intriguing sound-effects devised by Salzedo, his book, *Modern Method for the Harp,* is highly recommended. It is a "bible" to harp players—in the United States, at least—and well worth consultation by the composer or orchestrator anxious to enlarge his knowledge of harp potential in solo or in the orchestra.

Because the harp strings, especially those in the middle to low register, vibrate strongly after being plucked, they must be dampened by the hand in order to muffle any unwanted prolongation of sound. To indicate such purposeful muffling Salzedo invented the basic symbol shown at **a.** below, together with the illustrated modifications at **b.** (for muffling certain selected strings), and at **c.** (for muffling all the strings).

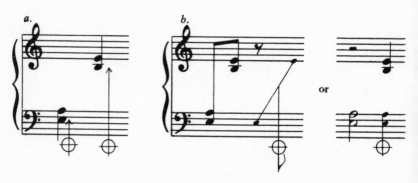

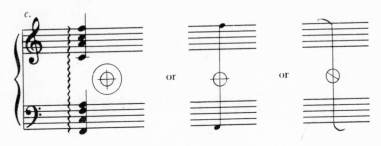

EXAMPLE 19 - 18

20

Woodwind Notation

Mᴏʀᴇ ᴛʜᴀɴ ᴀɴʏ ᴏᴛʜᴇʀ ᴘᴇʀꜰᴏʀᴍɪɴɢ ᴍᴇᴅɪᴀ, ʙᴀɴᴅ and orchestra instruments create special problems of notation. Though certain principles of notation—note-heads, flags, beams, staves, rests, and so on—are applicable to all the instruments, others require individual modifications. Each of the many different instruments has its peculiar possibilities and limitations that directly affect the notation used, and a few even have their own unique symbols.

It must be remembered that this manual deals primarily with notation, and is not a treatise on orchestration. Many instrumental techniques, then, are but briefly explained, and others barely mentioned. Our concern here is with notational problems—their origin and their proper solution. For full discussion of scoring problems the reader may easily refer to standard texts on instrumentation.

TRADITIONAL PRACTICES

Staves In most orchestra and band scores it is the practice to combine *pairs* of instruments on one staff. If three family instruments (such as three flutes or three clarinets) are required, two staves should be used. Player 1. and player 2. may share a staff, with 3. on a separate staff; or player 1. may occupy the upper staff alone, with 2. and 3. on the lower. The best arrangement will be determined by the composer's handling of the parts involved.

Related instruments (piccolo and flute; oboe and English horn; clarinet and bass clarinet; bassoon and contrabassoon) are always written on separate staves. One should *never* combine transposing and nontransposing instruments on the same staff. Note that the name of the instrument (or its abbreviation) is centered before the staff (left, below)

336

or placed midway between the staves, parallel to the point of the brace sign (right, below).

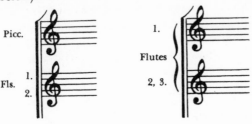

EXAMPLE 20 - 1

It is immaterial whether one uses Roman numerals to identify instrumental parts (I, II, III) or Arabic numerals (1, 2, 3). It *is* important, however, that one type of indication be used consistently. Names of the instruments must also be consistently given in one form: singular (Flute I – II) or plural (Flute*s* 1. and 2.). When two instruments are involved, the plural form makes more sense, even though the instruments are identical.

The first page of any score gives the names of individual instruments in full (see Example 26-1); from the second page to the end of a movement the names are usually abbreviated. Again, consistency in abbreviation should be the rule. It is not professional to put *Cl.* on one page, *Cls.* on another, and *Clars.* on still another. If only one of a pair of instruments is to play on an entire staff-line, the identifying number should be used at the beginning of the staff: Cl. 1. (I) or Cl. 2. (II), for example.

In *band scores,* the clarinets occupy three staves, as in band works these instruments are customarily divided into three parts, with a number of players on each part. One separate staff is assigned to the E-flat clarinet, one to the alto, and one to the bass clarinet even when several players are on each part. In addition, band scores include two or three staves for saxophones. Note particularly that the clarinet and saxophone groups are separated from the rest of the woodwind choir, and are placed at the bottom of the section, just over the brasses. (See Example 26-2.)

Braces, Systems   In *orchestra scores,* the woodwind section as a whole is customarily joined at the left-hand page margin by an elongated bracket, the curved ends extending above the highest staff (piccolo) and below the lowest staff (contrabassoon). The individual braces or brackets lie outside this all-inclusive bracket. (Again, see Example 26-1.)

A pair of staves occupied by *family instruments* (Fl. 1. and Fl. 2., or Picc. and Fls., for example) are connected at the left-hand margin of the score page by either a brace or a bracket. Identical instruments should use the brace; related instruments should use the bracket (see Example 20-1 and Example 26-2).

Unless it stands alone as a self-contained performing unit, the woodwind choir does not in itself constitute a system. Only in such works as Richard Strauss's *Symphony for Winds* would the combined woodwind staves create a complete system. When it is not performing alone, the woodwind section is a part of the larger system that takes in all the orchestral choirs at once.

Band scores differ slightly from orchestra scores in the use of braces and brackets. Commonly, piccolo, flute, oboe, English horn if used, and bassoon are linked with one bracket; the group of saxophones is similarly enclosed (see Example 26-2). The E-flat, alto, and bass clarinets are bracketed together as a family group, but the B-flat clarinets are set apart with an additional brace-sign. If, moreover, flutes, oboes, and bassoons each require two or more staves, braces are then used to enclose each related pair of staves.

Ledger Lines, Octave Signs   All of the woodwinds freely use ledger lines when required, but not all use the octave signs. Piccolo, flute, and clarinet frequently employ the 8va sign; the oboe uses it rarely, and the remaining woodwind instruments not at all. No woodwinds make use of the 8va *bassa* sign, and only under the most extraordinary circumstances would piccolo or flute employ the 15ma sign. Such rare instances would affect only the score; the player's part would have to be written with ledger lines plus the 8va sign.

It should be pointed out that the very reason for having transposing instruments (see pages 340 to 342) is to avoid the necessity for excessive ledger-lines or for constant use of any of the 8va signs.

Clefs   Certain woodwinds use only one clef; others make occasional use of two, but none employs more than two. Piccolo, flute, alto flute, oboe, clarinet, and saxophone are written only on the treble staff.

Normally, the English horn is also written only on the treble staff, but many Russian scores notate it in the alto clef exclusively. It must be admitted that this practice has certain theoretical justification, as the English horn is in effect an alto oboe. Still, the alto clef does not solve the problem of high notes on the instrument, for they lie well above even the treble staff.

In ordinary practice the contrabassoon is found only in the bass clef, but in a few rare instances it has been notated in the tenor clef. There seems little reason for so doing, as the highest written note for the instrument is only **g′**, three added lines above the bass staff.

This leaves two woodwind instruments that commonly use two clefs —the bass clarinet, notated either in the treble ("French system") or in the bass clef ("German system"), or alternating between them; and the bassoon, which uses both bass and tenor clefs.

Mention must also be made here of the recorder family, even though these instruments are not members of the modern band or orchestra. Indispensable in serious concerts and recordings of early music, recorders have experienced a popular revival in this century—as one aspect of a current interest in folk music and for performance in the home and in social groups. Four of the five family members play from the treble staff —the tiny sopranino, the soprano (or descant), the alto (or treble), and the tenor; the impressive-appearing bass reads from the bass staff. Both the sopranino and the soprano may be called transposing instruments,

EXAMPLE 20 - 2. TABLE OF WOODWIND CLEFS

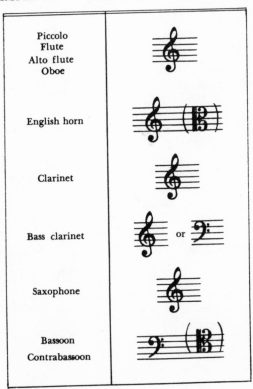

as they sound an octave *higher* than their notated pitch. In some moderns editions of recorder music the clef sign for these two is marked with a superimposed 8-sign. (Refer to the earlier discussion of this clef sign on page 56.) The tenor recorder sounds an octave *lower* than the written notation.

For convenient reference, the table on page 339 shows the clefs normally used for each standard woodwind instrument; alternate clefs are given in parentheses.

Transpositions   The orchestral woodwind choir normally consists of three non-transposing instruments (they sound exactly as written), and seven that sound pitches other than those written. The non-transposing (or **C**) instruments are the flute, oboe, and bassoon. Two of the transposing members are octave instruments—that is, they merely sound up or down by an octave from the notated pitch. The piccolo sounds *8va*, and the contrabassoon is pitched *8va bassa.*

The actual transposing woodwinds of the symphony orchestra are as follows:

Instrument	*Transposition*
Alto flute (in **G**)	
English horn (in **F**)	
Clarinet in **B♭**	
Clarinet in **A**	

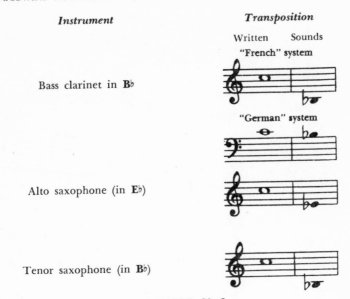

EXAMPLE 20 - 3

Additional transposing woodwinds, usually found in band scores, are the following:

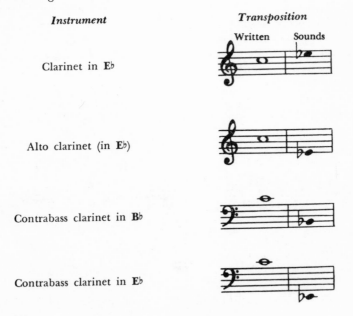

Instrument	Transposition

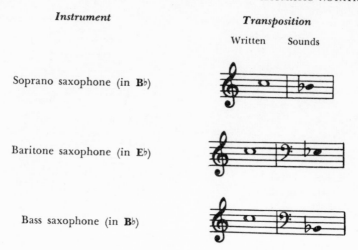

Soprano saxophone (in B♭)

Baritone saxophone (in E♭)

Bass saxophone (in B♭)

EXAMPLE 20 - 4

Any up-to-date text on orchestration will furnish detailed information on the techniques of transposition, together with the complete
ranges of all the instruments.

Stems, Beams   Because pairs of like instruments (flutes, oboes,
clarinets, bassoons) normally share the same staff, special effort must be
made toward clear notation of the independent parts. Traditionally,
the upper of two written notes on the staff is taken by the first player,
the lower by the second player. When the time-values of both parts
coincide, a single stem—together with any necessary flags or beams—
is sufficient (left, below). If the rhythmic values are different in any
way, however, separate stems, flags, or beams must be used (right,
below).

EXAMPLE 20 - 5

When melodic lines cross—that is, when the first instrument plays
below the part of the second instrument, and vice versa—separate stems
must also be written. Furthermore, the notes must be aligned in such

a way that the pairs of stems do not conflict with note-heads. Should the voice-crossing become too complicated for this simple form of notation, separate staves will have to be employed.

EXAMPLE 20·6

A single part written on a staff shared by two players requires one of these three accompanying directions above the staff:

a2—symbol for the Italian *a due*, meaning both instruments play in unison
1st (alternate symbols: **I. - 1. - I° - 1°**)—indicating only the first player performs
2nd (alternate symbols: **II. - 2. - II° - 2°**)—signifying that the notes are to be taken by the second player

The *alternate notation* for the three symbols above is to write all the stems, flags, and beams *up* for the first player, with whole rests placed *beneath* the staff for the second player (top left, below); or—if the part is to be taken by the second player—all the stems *down* and whole rests placed *above* the staff (top right, below). If both are to play the same line, double stems, flags, and beams would then be used for each note (lower line, below). These alternative solutions are more fussy and space-consuming than the first suggested notations, so are not enthusiastically endorsed.

EXAMPLE 20·7

If, on the other hand, unison notes occur in a passage predominantly in two voices, upward and downward stems, flags, and beams must be put on all the notes, or double note-heads must be used for the unisons. It would be much too pretentious to write *a2* for only a note or two; this direction should be reserved for lengthy—or, at least, consistent—unison passages. (See Example 20-8.)

When one instrument enters on the second note of a tied unison, a *separate stem* is required even if the passage continues in unison. Usu-

EXAMPLE 20 - 8

ally the *a2* sign is brought in after the first full beat, in which case the
single stem then suffices.

EXAMPLE 20 - 9

However one chooses to notate, a specific and clear indication must
always be given; it should never be taken for granted that any notational choice is clear if it is not precisely indicated. A *ff* passage for the
flute, for instance, might suggest that *both* instruments were to play.
But it is quite possible that only *one* flute is meant on the part, so the
proper direction above the staff is an absolute necessity. A cardinal
rule for all composers, orchestrators, and copyists might well be: *Take
nothing for granted!*

Rests   The placement of rests on the individual woodwind
staves presents no special problems if the rest sign applies to *both*
instruments simultaneously. Rests are written in the normal staff position (refer to the table on page 96) when a single sign suffices. Even
though separate stems have been employed for the two voices, a single
rest-symbol may be used when both voices are to rest for the same time-
duration (left, below).

When there is more than one rest-symbol—when, in other words,
only *one* of the instruments rests on a certain part of the measure—
separate stems are required for both parts, and individual rest-signs for
each part must be placed in appropriate positions. A single stem, inci-
dentally, should not join the notes on the first beat of the second
measure in the right-hand example below, even though their value
is the same. (See Example 20-10.)

The amount of space available on the score page will determine the
exact location of rest signs placed above or below the staff. It is important not to crowd the rest symbols, or merge them with adjoining note-
heads, beams, dynamic signs, or any terminology. (Example 20-11.)

EXAMPLE 20 - 10

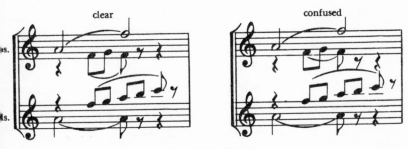

EXAMPLE 20 - 11

The inflexible rule to remember here is that each instrument must be accounted for at all times—either with rests, or by virtue of marking the part 1. or 2. (meaning that the other player rests), or with *a2*.

Dots, Ties   No particular problems exist for the notation of augmentation dots and ties in woodwind parts. When two separate instruments are involved on one staff, tie-slurs are looped *up* for the first player, and *down* for the second player (see Examples 20-5 and 20-9).

Key Signatures   Key signatures are required for all woodwind instruments if the music is tonal and signatures are used for the other orchestra or band instruments. Because of the various transpositions involved (see pages 340 to 342) the signatures will not all agree, but no woodwind lacks some kind of signature in tonal music unless its transposition puts it into the written key of **C**.

The writing of accidentals follows the standard procedures set forth in Chapter 9. The special point to be emphasized is the necessary *repetition* of an accidental affecting one part, if the other part later plays the same note (see Examples 9-16 and 20-8). The use of the *8va* sign also necessitates a repetition of any required accidental, even though the same written note occupies a line or space previously affected by the same accidental. (See Example 9-17.)

Time Signatures   In older scores, ensemble as well as orchestral, it was the practice to put a meter signature on every single staff of a section—brass, percussion, and string, as well as woodwind. In music that seldom changed its time signatures—save from movement to movement—this practice was sensible. But in the music written from the late Romantic period (end of the nineteenth century) up to the present, meter changes are so frequent that it becomes tiring to write and to read a time-signature alteration on every score staff. The prevailing score practice today is to use but one meter-signature for each of the four sections of the orchestra (or four evenly spaced in the vertical sense). These meters are written very large, the exact size depending on the number of staves they must encompass and their general position on the page (see Example 26-5).

Barlines   One barline is drawn through all the staves of the woodwind section, from the top staff to the bottom one. The barline break between the orchestral choirs is a visual aid, so that one may instantly relate the instruments to their appropriate section (see Example 26-1).

Ornaments   All ornaments except arpeggiated chords are possible on woodwind instruments. They are, however, usually written out in full, with the exception of trills, tremolos, and glissandos. The notation for these three categories, as discussed on pages 232–238 and 243–245, serves for all of the wind instruments. It is not within the scope of this book to go into the degrees of ease and effectiveness the various instruments bring to the playing of ornaments; in notation, at least, they are identical.

Dynamic Markings   In writing dynamic signs, the most important factor is that *each part* must have its own signs. If six instruments are playing on six staves, there will be six dynamic-marks—one for each staff. If divided parts are present on any staff, requiring the use of separate stems, beams, or rests, duplicate dynamic-markings are required (see Examples 20-9 and 26-18).

Unless two marks are required (one above and one below the staff), the dynamic sign is usually placed *beneath* the staff. The same is true for "hairpins" and *cresc.* and *dim.* indications.

It is essential that an instrument be given a dynamic mark upon entering after more than a measure or two of rest. Even then, it might be advisable to repeat the prevailing dynamic indication. An individual player in the orchestra or band has no way of knowing his relationship to the current dynamic level of the other instruments. As it is not only possible but fairly common that different instruments—even of the same family—are given simultaneous contrasting dynamic-marks, it is all the more important that care be taken to mark all levels exactly.

One of the most effective devices on a wind instrument is the sudden crescendo and diminuendo on a single sustained note, written with a small pair of wedges ($\underline{\hspace{0.3cm}<\hspace{0.3cm}}$ $\underline{\hspace{0.3cm}>\hspace{0.3cm}}$). The player makes a rapid crescendo from a soft dynamic level (usually *p* or *pp*) up to a loud one (*f* or *ff*) and down again. The effect is sometimes referred to as *messa di voce* ("placing the voice")—a term used to describe a particular kind of vocal ornamentation in older music.

Accents, Slurs   Accent marks for the woodwinds—as for all the instruments—are placed just above or below the *note-head* when only one stem is used, and just above or below a flagged or beamed *stem* when double stems are required (see Examples 20-3 and 20-7).

Phrase marks (slurs) go *above* the staff as a rule, regardless of stem, flag, and beam direction, unless double stems are needed. In that case, the phrasing slurs go both above and below (see example at the left, below). They should *never,* under any circumstance, be placed between the notes (right, below).

EXAMPLE 20 · 12

Because both accents and slurs relate directly to woodwind articulation, it is important that the correct form of each be used. Woodwind instruments (and brass as well) employ a variety of tonguing effects, each of which requires a special kind of notation—as discussed below.

Legato tonguing may affect as few as two successive notes, or a large group of notes covering several measures. Whatever the number of notes involved, a slur sign is placed over or under them to show that they are to be connected in one breath. Slurs and phrasing may or may not coincide. For that reason, it is sensible—though regrettably uncommon—to use the normal slur-sign for legato tonguing, and a dotted slur for the over-all phrasing (left, below). A *semi-legato* effect can be had by writing a slur over tenuto dashes or staccato dots (center and right, below).

EXAMPLE 20 - 13

Staccato tonguing, which is a non-legato form of single tonguing, requires a sharp articulation on each note. Dots (not wedges) are traditionally used over the note-heads.

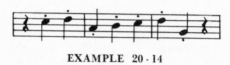

EXAMPLE 20 - 14

Single tonguing is called for when there is no slur or any other kind of mark written above the notes. Each tone is articulated separately by the tongue, with varying degrees of emphasis depending upon the dynamic level. Staccato tonguing is one form of single tonguing; *marcato* and *tenuto* effects can be produced by the joint action of tongue and breath, or what is called the *attack.* The conventional signs for tenuto (−) and for marcato (>) are commonly used. The superlative marcato mark (∧) and combinations of accents (>̣ or ∧̣) are also employed by the woodwinds.

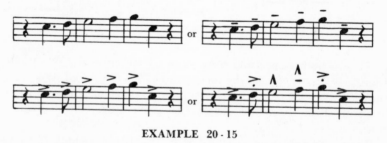

EXAMPLE 20 - 15

Double tonguing requires two rapid articulations under one breath-impulse, somewhat akin to speaking quickly the syllables *tu-ku.* The notation calls for two notes, each marked with a staccato dot, and a short slur over the dots (below). The double notes may be abbreviated after a beat or two by writing a single slanted slash midway through the stem of the note. In this case, each note-head receives two dots, together with the tiny slur-mark.

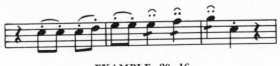

EXAMPLE 20-16

Double tonguing, of course, may also relate to successive pitches played rapidly and articulated in groups of two. This, however, is a matter of performance technique rather than a problem of notation; each note-head receives a single staccato dot and no slur-marks are usually indicated.

Triple tonguing—an extension of the principle that produces double tonguing—combines three rapid articulations (*tu-tu-ku* or *tu-ku-tu*) in one breath impulse. The notation requires three notes (written as a triplet if the time is not compound), each with a dot and all three under one slur-mark.

EXAMPLE 20-17

Again, the technique may be applied to successive pitches rather than to repetitions of one note. In this case only dots and not accompanying slurs are usually put above the note-heads.

Flutter-tonguing—a unique color effect easily achieved by performers who have learned to roll a Spanish *r*—is much less employed by the woodwinds in older music than the other varieties of tonguing illustrated. In contemporary music—especially in avant-garde scores—flutter-tonguing is a constant staple in the department of unusual timbre effects demanded by today's composers. The conventional notation is to put two or three slashes through the note stem (similar to bowed tremolo in the strings; see page 393). The alternative notation would be to write the word or its abbreviation, followed by a wavy line similar to a trill, extending to the final note to be so tongued.

EXAMPLE 20-18

Tempo, Expression Marks   In orchestra and band scores it is the custom to place one *tempo mark* above the top staff of each main section of the ensemble, or—as a minimum number—one tempo indication above the woodwind section and one above the string choir. This includes any qualifying terms or metronome marks that might be necessary. Expression marks, on the other hand, are handled in the same way as dynamics, accents, and phrase indications: they are placed in relation to each staff or instrumental part.

Although the terms *Solo* and *Soli* (It.) are not, strictly speaking, expression marks, they do have expressive connotations for wind instruments. *Solo* (applied to one instrument) and *Soli* (applied to more than one) draw attention to a passage of melodic importance, and request that it be given special emphasis in performance.

These two terms as just defined apply only to the woodwind and brass sections; their meaning is quite different when used with the string instruments. *Solo* in a string part designates *one* player, and only coincidentally means a melodically prominent passage. The word *Soli* would in the strings also be qualified by a specific number of players—*6 soli, 8 soli, 3 soli,* for example. (Because the word *viola* in Italian is feminine—the other strings are "masculine"—*sola* and *sole* are the correct terms for violas.)

MODERN INNOVATIONS

Every orchestra and band instrument is capable of producing certain special effects that are among the composer's prime resources for instrumental color, though they require a specific notation, symbol, or terminology. They should be commandeered only with discretion by composer and player alike.

In a manner of speaking, flutter-tonguing, mentioned above, would be such an effect. Other woodwind devices that would qualify in this special category are muting, harmonics, quarter-tone glissandos, breath sounds, and key clicks.

Although the notational forms of flutter-tonguing as illustrated in Example 20-18 are still commonly used by most composers, a few variant forms are to be found in avant-garde music that relies on proportional or "time-notation" (see page 72).

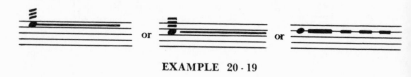

EXAMPLE 20 - 19

Muting is a standard procedure with the brass and string instruments, but it is much rarer in the woodwinds. Because of their construction these instruments, generally speaking, do not lend themselves to the use of mechanical mutes. When used, the mute—for oboe, clarinet, and bassoon only—is some kind of cloth pad or cardboard cylinder inserted into the bell of the instrument. Its use creates intonation problems, and in terms of aural results is perhaps not worth the effort. But if one is determined to call for muted oboe, clarinet, or bassoon, the direction *muted, with mute,* or the Italian *con sordino (con sord.)* is put at the outset of the muted passage. For the resumption of the instrument's normal tone, the direction *senza sord.* ("without mute") is put at the appropriate point.

Harmonics—a staple device of the string instruments—are rarely used in the woodwind choir. They are produced by overblowing, and are notated at pitch with a small zero above the note-head.

EXAMPLE 20 - 20

The use of this device is limited to the flute family and to the oboe. As only certain notes on these instruments can be produced as harmonics, the notator is advised to consult one of the reliable orchestration texts for more detailed information.

With an ever-increasing emphasis being placed on microtonal intervals in contemporary musical expression, today's avant-garde composer has utilized quarter-tones and even smaller intervals in wind-brass music as well as in that for strings. Portamento or quasi-glissando effects using these microtones have been notated as shown below:

EXAMPLE 20 - 21

Experimental composers have also explored the novel sound-effect created by blowing forcefully into the mouthpiece of a wind or brass instrument without producing a definite tone. To requisition these effects, the following notations have been devised:

EXAMPLE 20 - 22

As a postscript to our discussion of modern innovations for the woodwind instruments we must mention "key clicks." A favorite device of such avant-gardists as Pierre Boulez and Luciano Berio, this is an effect produced by the player's forcefully striking the keys of his instrument with his fingers, so that a sharp metallic click is heard. The notational symbol most frequently used for this effect is a small cross (+) placed over or under the note to be audibly fingered. It would be wise, however, for the composer-notator to append a footnote describing this effect, as the notational symbol is not yet standardized.

EXAMPLE 20 - 23

21

Brass Notation

Few digressions from standard notation exist for the brass instruments. Except for the special format of the required staves, discussed below, both band and orchestra brasses are affected by identical notational procedures.

TRADITIONAL PRACTICES

Staves   As a rule, the brass instruments of the *orchestra* occupy a total of six score-staves. The horns almost invariably are put on two staves—1. and 2. on the upper, and 3. and 4. on the lower—although three, or even four, staves may be used for exceptionally diversified horn parts. The trumpets are normally written on two staves, but may be notated on one staff if the nature of the parts warrants. Trombones and tuba commonly share two staves—trombones 1. and 2. on the upper staff, and trombone 3. and tuba on the lower. A separate staff may sometimes be required for the tuba; or, more rarely, the trombones may share a single staff.

In *band* scores the cornets are frequently placed on two additional staves above the trumpets, and one extra staff is used for the baritone, or euphonium. Because the basses (tubas) in a band usually number two or more, they are always written on a separate staff and not combined with the third trombone, as in many orchestral scores.

The order of staves in the brass section is somewhat different in band and orchestra scores (compare Example 26-1 with Example 26-2). In band scores the cornets and trumpets are always placed above the horns, rather than below them as in the orchestra. The baritone or euphonium staff is inserted between the horns and trombones, with the basses occupying the bottom staff of the section.

Braces, Systems   In both orchestra and band scores the brass section is enclosed with an elongated bracket. The curved ends extend above the uppermost staff and below the lowest staff. As with the woodwind instruments, family or related brasses on two staves are linked by a brace placed outside the section bracket (see page 337).

The normal disposition of the horns in orchestra and band scores is 1. and 2. on the upper staff and 3. and 4. on the lower staff. Should this arrangement be changed at any time during the course of the work, enclosing brackets to point up the change may be used just before the new format.

EXAMPLE 21 - 1

Only when it is placed alone on a score page, independent of any of the other sections, does the brass choir constitute a complete system. On the other hand, the joined staves of any composition for brass choir alone would qualify as a system on the score page.

Ledger Lines, Octave Signs   All of the brass instruments— orchestra or band—resort to ledger lines when needed, but none uses the octave signs. When parts in the horns go so low as to require excessive ledger lines, they are put into the bass clef (see Example 21-2); trombone parts that would require many extra lines above the bass staff are notated in the tenor clef.

Infrequently one may find an *8va bassa* sign written in the fourth horn part—in score only—when limitations of space prevent ledger lines, and context on the staff prohibits a change of clef. The instrumental part, however, still must be notated with the ledger lines or clef changes (see section below), as the player does not read the *8va* sign.

Clefs   Two of the four orchestral brass instruments employ only one clef—the trumpet (treble clef) and the bass tuba (bass clef). Horns and trombones make use of two clefs; the horns are primarily in the treble, but occasionally go into the bass clef for very low notes.

The trombones freely alternate between bass and tenor clefs. (The tenor tuba is notated in the treble clef, but this instrument is not standard in either orchestra or band.)

In many older scores calling for the now-obsolete alto trombone, one will find the part notated in alto clef. Some contemporary scores—mainly by Soviet composers—put the tenor trombones in this clef. The early Stravinsky works (*Firebird* and *Fireworks,* for example), as well as more recent symphonic compositions by Serge Prokofiev and Dmitri Shostakovich, all notate the trombones in the alto clef. All of Samuel Barber's recent orchestral works, including the *Piano Concerto,* likewise resort to this clef for the horn parts (and English horn as well). But while Russian performers are still trained in the tradition of the now-obsolete alto instrument, few trombonists elsewhere—even in major symphonic groups—are adept at reading in the alto clef. The practical notator, therefore, will use bass and tenor clefs for trombones.

In scores of the late Romantic period one will sometimes find the simultaneous use of treble and bass clef on one of the horn staves. This situation arose when one of two horns sharing a staff (usually 3. and 4.) had rather high notes, and the other horn, quite low pitches. To avoid an excessive number of ledger lines for either instrument—or the necessity of employing two separate staves—a small bass clef was written for the lower horn just below the treble staff. Needless to say, the transpositions for each instrument remained the same as though each occupied a separate staff. (See page 356 for an explanation of bass-clef transposition.)

EXAMPLE 21 · 2

The symphonic band generally uses two additional brass instruments —cornets and baritones (euphoniums). Cornets are notated precisely as one notates trumpets—always in the treble clef. The baritone or euphonium is notated in bass clef in the score, but band publishers often include a duplicate part notated in the treble clef in **B-flat**. The reason is that the instrument is frequently played by a cornetist, the fingering problems being very similar on the two instruments.

The table below is for ready reference. Alternate clefs are shown in parentheses.

EXAMPLE 21 - 3.   TABLE OF BRASS INSTRUMENT CLEFS

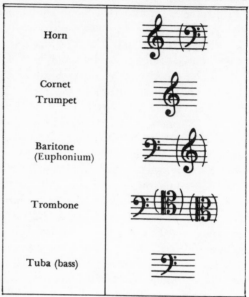

Transposition   Of the six principal brasses, three are non-transposing and three transpose. The **C** instruments (non-transposing) are the trombones, baritones (as notated in score) and tubas or basses. Those that transpose are the horns (almost universally now in **F**, sounding a perfect fifth lower than written) and the trumpets and cornets (both in **B-flat**, sounding a major second lower than written). In many contemporary scores, however, trumpets written in **C** are becoming more common than the **B-flat** instruments.

In older scores (up to the turn of the last century, at least) a change to bass clef for the horn necessitated a change in normal transposition. Instead of sounding a *fifth lower* than written, the horn reversed its transposition in the bass clef so that the sounding pitch was a *fourth higher* than written (see Example 21-2). Today, composers are more and more ignoring this outmoded convention, and continue the *same* direction of transposition in both treble and bass clefs. The horn tone, in other words, always sounds a fifth lower than written, whether the instrument is reading from the treble or the bass clef.

Accidentals, Key Signatures   For the brasses as for other winds, an accidental must always be given for each instrument needing it, even though another instrument sharing the staff has already had an accidental on the same line or space (see Example 9-16). As a rule, double flats and double sharps are not written for brass instruments; the enharmonic spelling ought always to be used.

Key signatures (when required by the music) are normally employed only by trombones and tuba; horns, cornets, trumpets, and baritone do not use them. This is a matter of tradition, and tradition is not always logical. Many band publications and school-orchestra editions put in signatures for these latter instruments, especially when the music they are to play is very tonal (it usually is!) On the other hand, the tendency among serious symphonic and ensemble composers has been to get away from key signatures altogether—not only for the brasses, but also for the orchestra as a whole. At least this newer practice removes one reading hazard in music of a complex and non-tonal nature.

Time Signatures   One large time-signature centered on the brass staves is the current practice in manuscript and published scores. Example 26-5 illustrates a few of the variant forms found in the notation of today.

Barlines   As with the woodwind section, one barline is drawn through all the staves of the brass choir.

Ornaments   When mordents, turns, and appoggiaturas are assigned to the brasses, they should be written out in full. Tremolos, however, and both conventional and downward trills are notated as described on pages 232–238. Trills are played by using the lip or by the action of the valves. It is not essential, though, that the orchestrator know which is which, as this is properly the concern of the player, and identical notation is used for both varieties.

Glissandos are possible on all the brass instruments, but are more effectively performed by the horn than by the other choir members. Because the true glissando on the horn is produced by the overtones of any finger-position, the actual notes are usually written out (left, below). There is also a "faked" glissando—a combination of overtones and lip action; a straight or wavy line from the first to the last notes usually suffices as notation (right, below).

Observe in the right-hand example below that the notes are joined by a single primary beam, and that two incomplete sets of secondary beams are put on the stems. This is a shorthand way of indicating the

EXAMPLE 21 - 4

rhythmic value of the group. If written out in full, there would be nine notes—a nonuplet in 32nd notes, in other words.

Trombone glissandos, which have become a tedious cliché in commercial orchestration, are produced by the slide. As only seven chromatic notes—a diminished fifth, which is the extent from seventh to first position on the instrument—are possible as a true slide-glissando, care must be taken not to exceed that written interval. A somewhat wider range can be obtained by combining a lip slur with the slide glissando. The notation for trombone glissandos is usually the actual notes written out, with the abbreviation *gliss.* put over the group, plus the indication of the slide position (left, below). As an alternative, only the beginning and ending notes may be notated, joined by a straight or a wavy line (right, below).

EXAMPLE 21 - 5

Dynamic Markings   Because family pairs of brass instruments commonly occupy two staves, and dynamic markings usually apply equally to both staves, many composers now write a single dynamic-mark centered between the two staves, preceded by a small brace (see Example 2-4).

Accents, Phrase Marks   Brass instruments employ the same articulation devices as do the woodwinds; therefore, all the points discussed in the previous chapter in relation to woodwind tonguing are equally applicable to the brasses (see pages 347 to 349).

In some ways the brass instruments are actually superior to the woodwinds in the production of very soft single-tongued effects. As might be expected, they are also more successful in producing sharp and forceful *sfz* attacks. But—effective or otherwise—the basic notation required for any articulation does not alter throughout the wind instruments.

Special Effects   Muting is as commonplace for the brasses as it is rare for the woodwinds. Furthermore, the effect is used for *f* and *ff* quite as much as it is for *p* and *pp*—for its special color, and not solely to reduce the volume of the instrument.

Formerly it was sufficient to write merely the direction: *muted, with mute, con sord.,* or any other commonly used term for the effect. But brass players today are equipped with several varieties of mutes, each with its own unique quality; therefore the sensitive orchestrator calls specifically for cup mute, solo-tone mute, Harmon mute, straight mute, or any one of the other types in current use.* When the natural, open sound is wanted after the muted passage, the directions *senza sord., open, unmuted,* or their foreign equivalents must be used. (See page 405.)

An effect allied to muting, called *hand-stopping,* requires a different notational symbol. The device is more or less limited to the horn because of the relation of the player's hand to the bell of this instrument; by thrusting the clenched fist hard into the opening of the bell, the player obtains a snarling "brassy" effect.

The sign for this effect was the invention of Richard Wagner; it is a small cross put over the note to be stopped. A series of stopped notes may be notated with the cross over each note (left, below) or one over the first note only, followed by an unbroken line to the final note, ending in a downward jog (center, below). A passage of stopped notes may also be notated with the direction "stopped" (or the French *bouché,* German *gestopft,* or Italian *chiuso*). When the natural, open tone is wanted after a stopped passage, a small zero is put over the first open note (right, below).

EXAMPLE 21 - 6

Flutter-tonguing is possible on all the brass instruments, including the tuba. The notation for this effect is no different from that used for the woodwinds, including the variant forms for proportionately-notated music (see Examples 20-18 and 20-20).

---

* Refer to pages 104–105 of the author's *Thesaurus of Orchestral Devices* for a listing of the many kinds of brass mutes.

Both the horn and the trumpet are able to play natural tones: that is, notes that exist as the overtones or harmonics of the fundamental tone of the instrument. The horn in **F**, for example, can play the overtone series on **F** without recourse to valves. The zero sign is used to designate such notes; the context of the passage would clearly show whether overtones were desired or whether the zero merely stood for open notes following a muted passage.

MODERN INNOVATIONS

The composer's request for a specific kind of brass mute (see page 359) is distinctly a twentieth-century innovation. Such requisitions, however, are indicated by terminology rather than by new symbols. Special brass effects that do make use of newly-invented notational symbols are largely covered in the chapter on jazz notation (pages 415–416), and so need not be included here.

Certain composers of avant-gardist inclination have used "key clicks" (described on page 352) for the horn, which with its lever mechanism is the only brass instrument capable of producing this unusual effect. The small cross (+) used to requisition key-clicking from the wood-winds is impractical for the horns, however, as in brass notation this symbol is called upon to indicate stopping or muting. The device is best explained by a footnote in the player's part, with asterisks over the notes involved, or by using one of the alternate notations shown in Example 20-23.

Breath sounds, illustrated in Example 20-22, and the percussive device of sharply striking the mouthpiece or the bell of the instrument with the open hand, are to be encountered in many experimental compositions for the brass instruments. The latter effect has been notated as follows:

EXAMPLE 21 - 7

22

Percussion Notation

PERCUSSION INSTRUMENTS HAVE BEEN A PART OF THE composer's instrumental resources since antiquity, but their importance in the total fabric of orchestral sound has grown phenomenally in the past century. Had this text been offered to notators contemporary with Haydn and Mozart, the present chapter would have treated only the correct notation for two timpani, with occasional bass drum, cymbals, and triangle. In contrast, a notator of the late nineteenth century would have needed procedures for a long list of diverse percussion instruments, demonstrating that the percussion section was assuming equal status with woodwinds and brass, if not with strings. No twentieth-century composer, however, is adequately equipped without the techniques of writing for the contemporary percussion orchestra (see pages 379–380).

TRADITIONAL PRACTICES

Staves   The percussion instruments of the orchestra and band are of two categories: those of *definite pitch,* and those of *indefinite pitch.* For the instruments that sound an actual pitch, a standard five-line staff must be used; those with sound indeterminate in pitch use either a five-line staff or a single line that replaces the staff.

The only advantage of the five-line staff over the single line is that two instruments may share the same staff without undue crowding. It is not advisable, however, to notate more than two percussion instruments on any staff, because of the complexity of stems, flags, and beams. Usually the top and bottom spaces of the staff are used for the shared parts, with stems up and down, although any clear arrangement is permissible. Whatever lines or spaces are chosen for the note-heads, the plan must be consistent throughout.

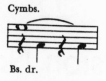

EXAMPLE 22 - 1

Also consistent should be the *pairing* of unpitched percussion instruments—whether on a five-line staff or a single line. As a rule, instruments related in use (such as bass drum and cymbals) share a single staff; suspended cymbal and gong or tam-tam are frequently paired, or triangle and snare drum.

In orchestra scores the percussion staves are put *between* the brasses and the strings (or above the harp and keyboard instruments, when used). In band scores the percussion section is always placed *at the bottom* of the score page (see Example 26-2).

Braces, Systems   There seems to be no hard and fast rule regarding the use of braces or brackets for the percussion section. The group as a whole is usually enclosed with an elongated bracket, though sometimes with a large brace. Generally, related instruments are not set apart with separate braces. The unpitched instruments are ordinarily placed immediately beneath the timpani staff (which always heads the section), followed by the instruments of definite pitch. Whether the bracket or the brace is used, it normally encloses the entire group, instead of separating the pitched from the unpitched instruments (**a.** of Example 22-2).

If there is only one staff or single line in addition to the timpani, a thick bracket sometimes sets it apart from the timpani staff (**b.** and **c.** of Example 22-2). If two single lines are used in addition to timpani, they will be linked in one of the ways shown at the right (**d.**, **e.**, and **f.**).

When one player is responsible for a number of instruments, each notated separately on a single line, his group of single lines is usually set off by a brace (see Example 22-9).

Ledger Lines, Octave Signs   Few ledger-lines are necessary for the pitched percussion instruments—first, because of range limitations; and second, because octave transpositions for two of the mallet instruments obviate the use of extra staff lines. The xylophone sounds

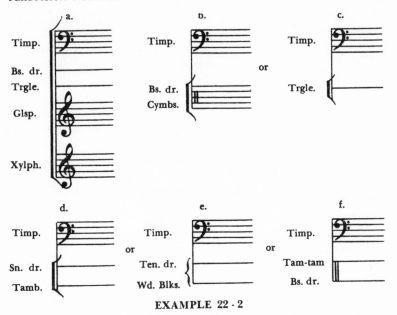

EXAMPLE 22 - 2

one octave higher than written, and the glockenspiel, two octaves.

The only pitched percussion that might conceivably need an 8va sign would be the largest xylophone, with a written range up to c''''. Because of crowding between score staves, the highest notes might have to be written with an 8va sign (remember, in this case, that the actual pitch will then be *two octaves* higher than written).

As the glockenspiel normally sounds 15ma and its highest written note is only c''', it does not use an 8va sign.

Unfortunately, there exists a certain amount of confusion regarding the transposition of both xylophone and glockenspiel, although the majority of instrumentation texts agree on the transpositions indicated above. It is best to explain in the score exactly the transposition desired. A simple statement at the beginning of the xylophone part: "Sounds 8va," and over the glockenspiel staff: "Sounds 15ma" should suffice. (See also the clef-sign suggestions on page 56.)

Clefs   A wide variety of clefs exists for the percussion. The pitched instruments use only two clefs: xylophone, marimba, vibraphone, glockenspiel, chimes, and antique cymbals—all are normally in treble clef, though occasionally marimba and vibraphone may use bass clef for consistently low passages; timpani alone are traditionally in bass clef. But when we come to the instruments of indefinite pitch, we are faced with an extensive array of clef signs. Though treble and bass clefs have been—and are still—widely used for unpitched percussion, in this function they have no significance as *clefs*. Because tradition-minded composers have hesitated to write percussion parts on an un-cleffed staff, they have put instruments having a "high" sound (triangle, cymbals, and snare drum, for example) on a treble staff and the "low-sounding" percussion (bass drum, gong, and tam-tam) on a bass staff. The distinction is perhaps academic, for advanced percussion techniques and devices can sometimes make high instruments sound low, and vice versa.

The more progressive composers use other clef-symbols for the un-pitched percussion instruments, reserving treble and bass clefs for the pitched variety. These clef-symbols range from no sign at all to fancy variations of the alto clef-sign (see the table below). It is impossible to give any kind of qualitative evaluation of these hybrid clef-symbols, or to advocate one over another. The composer or arranger must choose the one that appeals to him most, and then use it consistently.

EXAMPLE 22 - 3.   TABLE OF PERCUSSION INSTRUMENT CLEFS

PITCHED PERCUSSION		UNPITCHED PERCUSSION		SPECIAL CLEFS	
Timp.	𝄢	Bass drum Bongos Castanets Claves Cymbals Gong Maracas Snare drum Suspended cymbal Tambourine Tam-tam Temple blocks Tenor drum Triangle Wood-blocks	*[various percussion clef symbols, with "or" between several alternatives]*	Cymbal	*[clef symbol]*
Antique cymbals Chimes (Tubular bells) Glockenspiel Marimba Vibraphone Xylophone	𝄞			Gong (Tam-tam)	*[clef symbol]*

Note-heads   In no other instrumental notation is there such a variety of note-heads as are used for the unpitched percussion instruments. Crosses, x's, diamonds, squares, triangles—all have been used at one time or another. Unfortunately, whatever their merits, there exists no standardized system for their use, although one or two of the note-shapes are found universally for certain specific instruments—as the triangle-shaped note for the triangle.

The triangle, square, and diamond can—by virtue of their shape—be given specific time-values, but the cross and the x are more difficult to make identifiable. The cross and the x can be given stems, and any number of flags joined to the stem, but any visual distinction is limited to eighth notes and smaller denominations. From their shape alone it would not be possible to tell whether a half- or a quarter-note is intended. Without any stem at all, these two symbols tend to be lost on the staff; at best, they are ambiguous in meaning. In the example below, the notator has opportunity to examine and compare the effectiveness of these various symbols—the form and color of the note-heads and the position of stems and flags.

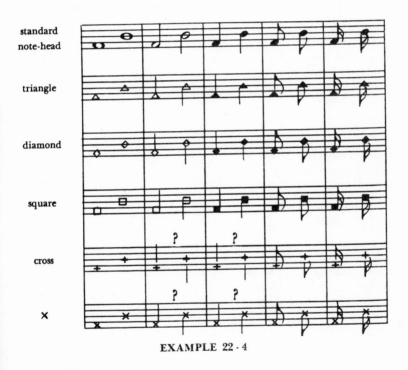

EXAMPLE 22·4

A number of related symbols denoting certain instruments are written by some composers in addition to regular note-heads. Illustrated below are a few of these symbols, as well as some of the unconventional note-heads as they might appear in instrumental parts.

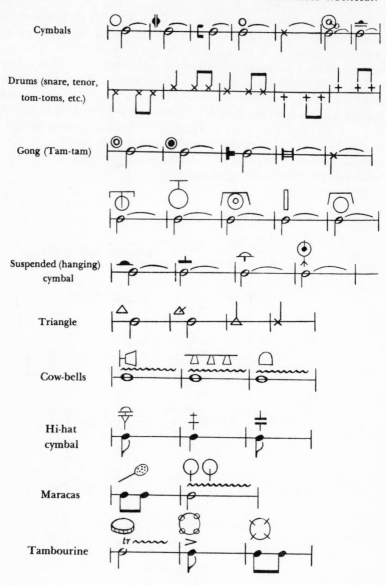

EXAMPLE 22·5

Because the cymbals are basic to the percussion section (if overused at times) composers have devised various special "cymbal symbols." For the clash effect (the two plates struck together forcibly) there is

a choice of those at the left, below. For the use of a drumstick or
mallet on the hanging plate, the symbol may be one of those at the
right.

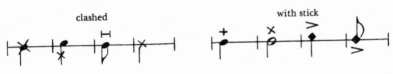

clashed   with stick

EXAMPLE 22 - 6

More orthodox notations, however, continue to be essential in percussion notation. *Up-* and *down-*stems must be used to differentiate between two parts sharing a staff or a single line. Such notes are flagged
and beamed according to the customary principles discussed in Chapter 6.

Double stems (or double note-heads and stems) are written for the
various drums, including timpani, when two sticks are to be struck
simultaneously on the drumhead. For the bass drum, double stems
would indicate that both heads are to be struck at once.

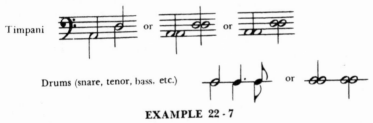

Timpani   or   or

Drums (snare, tenor, bass, etc.)   or

EXAMPLE 22 - 7

Chords (or more properly, *intervals*) of two notes can be played
on two timpani simultaneously, one note with either hand. The two
notes are indicated either by a single stem, or by separate stems.

or

EXAMPLE 22 - 8

Three- and four-note chords can be played on the various mallet
instruments (xylophone, glockenspiel, and so on) by a performer hold-
ing two mallets in either hand. One stick is held between thumb and
forefinger, the other between forefinger and index finger. By slightly
spreading his fingers and tilting his hand forward, the performer may

position the four mallet-heads over a structure of three or four notes. It is usually unnecessary to notate such chords with up- and down-stems; if the division of labor between the hands is not obvious, the player will determine the easiest manner of playing the chord.

In a small orchestra or chamber ensemble, one percussion player is often called upon to play a variety of instruments—almost literally all at the same time. Consequently, it is common to see the percussion parts organized in the following way:

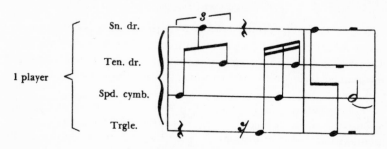

EXAMPLE 22 - 9

Note in the example above that the stems and beams extend from staff line to staff line. Time-values are written for each beat as an *entity* on the entire group of staves, and separate rests are not required unless they are necessary to show the division of the measure.

Rests   When the five-line staff is used, the usual placing of rests is observed (refer to Chapter 7, and to page 344). The use of the single line requires the rest-signs to be placed, as a rule, directly on the line (top left, below). If two instruments are written above and below the one line, the requisite rests are also placed above and below. Whole- and half-rests then require a ledger line for their notation; the other symbols are placed with one end not quite touching the continuous line (top right and lower examples).

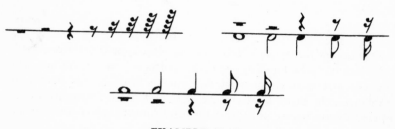

EXAMPLE 22 - 10

Dots, Ties   For percussion notation, the one problem involving either augmentation dots or ties relates to notes placed on a single line. If the note-stem goes *up,* the dot and the tie go *below* the line; if the stem is *down,* dot and tie go *above* the line (left-hand examples). If two instruments share a single line, dots and ties of the *upper* instrument go *above;* those of the lower instrument go *below* (right-hand example).

EXAMPLE 22 - 11

Incomplete ties are commonly used for cymbals, suspended cymbal, and gong when their tone is to ring through after they are struck or clashed. This is the standard indication for *let vibrate* (*l.v.*), and the term frequently accompanies the incomplete tie. Conveniently enough, *l.v.* is also the abbreviation of the French *laissez vibrer* ("allow to vibrate").

l.v.

EXAMPLE 22 - 12

Incomplete tie-signs are also written for the vibraphone with motor on, as the tone(s) can be prolonged beyond the moment of striking the bars. They may be used as well on glockenspiel, marimba, or xylophone for single notes or intervals that require the *illusion* of being prolonged.

Accidentals, Key Signatures   Key signatures are rarely used even for pitched percussion, as their music is not so continuous as for other instruments. Even the timpani, which contribute more as a rule than any of the other members, do not take a key signature except in some school-orchestra editions.

In scores of the Classical and early Romantic periods it was the custom to indicate the tuning of the timpani at the outset of the music, using accidentals as needed, thereafter writing the pitches as they occurred, but without the accidentals (left-hand example, below). This practice was then entirely feasible, as the timpani never changed pitches within movements, only between them. Furthermore, the custom was more logical than that used in Baroque scores (Handel and Bach, for example), where the notes were always written as **C** and **G**, representing tonic and dominant pitches of the music, *regardless of key*. Thus we find such strange notations as the example at the right, below:

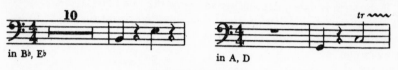

in B♭, E♭   in A, D

EXAMPLE 22 - 13

With the chromatic resources of the modern pedal-timpani available to today's composers, tuning may change almost from measure to measure, so that the proper accidentals must *always* be written in. Timpani accidentals must be repeated even when it would seem obvious that the same pitch is to be repeated (right-hand example). Remember the notator's cardinal rule: *Take nothing for granted!*

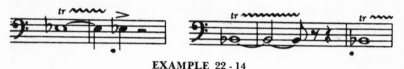

EXAMPLE 22 - 14

Time Signatures   Time signatures are placed in a variety of ways on the percussion staves. For the five-line staff, meters are written just as they are on any other staff; on the single line, they are notated so that the numerator goes *above* the line and the denominator *below* it (left-hand example). Sometimes a single figure will suffice for two single-line parts (center and right-hand examples).

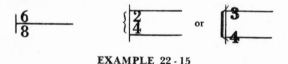

EXAMPLE 22 - 15

Barlines, Rhythm   Barlines are usually extended through *all* the percussion staves, from the timpani staff through the lowest staff used—five-line or single. If only single lines are used, the barline connects them (see Example 22-9). If only one single line is used, a small barline is extended slightly above and below the line (see Example 22-12).

Triplets, sextuplets, and all other unequal groups that require marking with a figure, have this number placed *over* the single line as a rule, and set off by a horizontal bracket (left, below). If two instruments share the line, and the unusual figure is given to the lower instrument, the figure and bracket must of necessity be put *beneath* the staff (right, below).

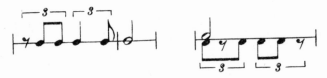

EXAMPLE 22 - 16

Ornaments   The pitched mallet-instruments in the percussion choir can execute, of course, any of the standard ornaments described in Chapter 13, even the effect of an arpeggiated chord. The unpitched instruments are limited to the tremolo (or *roll*, as it is called in the vernacular) and the various forms of grace notes.

1. *Tremolo (roll, trill)*   The tremolo effect, available to the entire section, is sometimes called a trill because the standard trill-sign (*tr* 〰〰) is one of its common notations.

EXAMPLE 22 - 17

For the unpitched instruments the roll is not a trill in the usual sense, yet the trill sign is probably the better of the two possible notations. The alternate notation—the standard tremolo-sign—might sometimes be mistaken for a measured reiteration rather than a free repetition.

On the other hand, it is incorrect to use the trill sign for the *pitched* percussion (with the sole exception of timpani) unless an actual alternation between two notes is meant. For the xylophone, glockenspiel, vibraphone, and marimba (example at the right, below) the trill notation would mean something very different from the same notation in a timpani part (left, below).

Timpani   other pitched percussion

EXAMPLE 22 - 18

A roll between *two* timpani may be notated in the forms shown below, the example at the left being preferable.

EXAMPLE 22 - 19

For rolls employing a pair of cymbals, as well as those on the hanging cymbal struck by various kinds of sticks, the trill sign is used. A two-plate roll, done by rubbing the two cymbals together, is notated with a wavy trill-sign and the indication *a2*.

EXAMPLE 22 - 20

If an actual *tremolo* is wanted for pitched mallet-instruments other than the timpani, slashes must be written through the stem of the note (see Example 22-32). As in all tremolos previously discussed, the number of such slashes is determined by the tempo of the music. For a fast tempo, two slashes (equivalent to creating sixteenth notes) are sufficient; for a moderate tempo, three slashes should be used (equivalent to 32nds); and for a slow tempo four stem-slashes.

EXAMPLE 22 - 21

In notating an extended roll for any percussion instrument (timpani, drums, suspended cymbal, tam-tam, and so on) it is important to indicate by the manipulation of ties whether the roll is to be periodically accented or played without any measure stresses. Tied notes with a trill sign over them (left, below) will be played without special accent; without the ties (center, below), each note will receive a certain amount of initial stress. When the trill sign is repeated over each measure (right, below), a more pronounced accent will be given by the player.

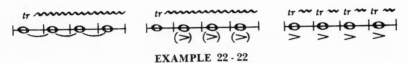

EXAMPLE 22 - 22

2. Grace Notes   For unpitched percussion, grace notes are used to designate types of strokes with the two sticks. They function as true grace-notes in that they precede the actual beat and are not accented to the same degree as the note they precede. The following notations using grace notes apply to timpani and to all the other drum-types—snare, tenor, bass, tom-tom, tabor, and so on.

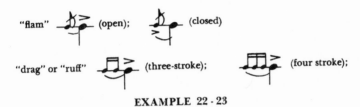

EXAMPLE 22 - 23

Note, above, that the stems and beams of the grace notes are usually put in the direction opposite that of the regular note-stems and beams, as a reading aid to the performer.

3. Arpeggio   The arpeggiated-chord effect ( ) is impossible to execute on a mallet percussion instrument unless it is limited to two notes fairly close to each other in either hand. The player can quickly (within reason) sound two different pitches in either hand, giving the illusion of an arpeggio, in this manner:

EXAMPLE 22 - 24

The farther apart the notes are, the more difficult it is to play them accurately. The correct notation uses grace notes for the arpeggiated notes—those played by the left hand with stems and beams *down*, those by the right hand with them *up*.

A *measured arpeggio*, with notes having regular time-values, can be executed by any of the keyed instruments. Obviously, the speed cannot be extreme without making the arpeggio too difficult to manage.·

4. **Glissandos**   Glissandos are possible on all pitched percussion. For the keyed members the effect is limited to "white" notes alone or "black" notes alone, as on the piano and other keyboard instruments. (A simultaneous "black" and "white" glissando would best be made by two players standing on opposite sides of a mallet instrument. One player would "glissando" from right to left, on the lower level of bars, and the other player from left to right, on the upper level.) The notation for all these instruments is a straight or wavy line extending from lowest to highest note (example below; see also Example 13-28). If the beginning pitch is a natural note, the glissando is assumed to be "white-note"; if the first note is a flat or sharp, it is assumed to be "black-note."

"white-note" glissando   "black-note" glissando

EXAMPLE 22 - 25

With the advent of the *pedal timpani*, glissando effects became staple devices for this instrument. Two kinds of glissando, each with slightly different notation, are possible. The *first* is executed by playing a roll with two sticks on the drumhead, while depressing or raising the pedal mechanism (see Example 22-27). Pressing the pedal down raises the pitch; raising the pedal lowers the pitch.

As the effective over-all compass of any one *timpano* (the singular form of *timpani*) is only a fifth, no pedal glissando should exceed that interval. Furthermore, if the beginning or ending pitch of the glissando is other than the very highest or lowest pitch possible on that particular drum, the range will be even smaller. As an illustration of this problem let us imagine we are using the 25″ drum (usually the third in a set of four, extending from the player's left to right—from deepest to highest). The range of the 25″ timpano normally is:

EXAMPLE 22 - 26

We have pre-tuned this timpano to **c-sharp**, so we must write the glissando beginning on this pitch. But because the highest note available to us on this drum is only **f**, our glissando cannot go higher than this pitch (upper line, below). This passage could also be notated using, instead of the trill-sign, tremolo slashes through the note-stems (lower line, below). The first version is to be preferred, however, if a true unmeasured glissando is wanted. The second version, particularly in a very slow tempo, might be misinterpreted as measured 32nd-notes.

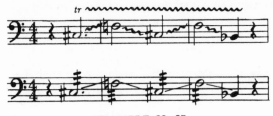

EXAMPLE 22 · 27

The *second* type of pedal glissando is executed by striking the drum forcibly, and then immediately depressing the pedal (if the glissando is to go *up*) or raising the pedal (if the glissando is to go *down*). Usually this approach makes use of the extremes of pitch on the individual drum: that is, the effect ascends to the highest note available, or descends to the lowest possible pitch—owing to the difficulty of halting the pedal mechanism quickly on an accurate in-between pitch. The concluding note of the glissando may be written as a grace note, as in the illustrations on the top line, below, or as a short note-value, if it is rhythmically possible (examples on the lower line).

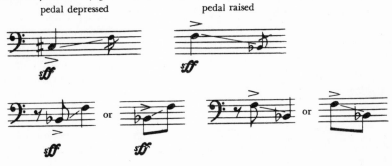

EXAMPLE 22 · 28

An actual chromatic scale can be played in measured rhythm by one timpano, the performer raising or lowering the pedal mechanism in tempo. The extent of such a scale cannot, of course, exceed the total range available on the one drum. This effect may be seen in the initial movement of Ernst Toch's *Second Symphony* (pages 15–18 of the study score).

Regrettably, there exists no standard indication that the player should produce successive chromatic notes on one timpano, rather than divide them between several timpani. One possible method is that shown on the top line, below; another, on the bottom line. Both forms use numbers to identify the specific pre-tuned drums; both have logic and visual clarity. Composers and percussionists should agree to standardize, and employ exclusively, either of these styles of indication for chromatic notes on a single drum.

EXAMPLE 22 - 29

Dynamic Markings   While there is no unusual place to write the dynamic signs for percussion instruments, nor unusual forms of presentation, the *accurate* notation of these symbols is of paramount importance. The dynamic level of every entrance, of every crescendo and diminuendo—however notated—of every attack and special accent should *always* be indicated in the percussion instruments. One cannot emphasize this point too strongly. *Improper or insufficient dynamic markings can ruin an otherwise competent piece of orchestration.* The example below illustrates the kind of meticulous notation that should go in every percussion part, regardless of the specific instrument or the musical style.

EXAMPLE 22 - 30

Accents, Phrase Marks   Accent marks of all kinds are used for percussion. Those that imply a strong or sharp attack are the most suitable, of course, as the percussion on the whole are not effective in a *tenuto* type of accent (–). On the other hand, staccato dots are freely used; to the percussionist these mean a very "dry" note (*secco*), one that is struck and immediately damped. Both the dot and the standard accent mark (➤) are used to denote such damped tones.

EXAMPLE 22 - 31

Phrase marks are somewhat rare in this section, as the very nature of its tone production precludes a true legato. A phrase *effect* can be notated by using a broken slur-sign, as seen in this passage for xylophone:

Xylph.

EXAMPLE 22 - 32

This once again illustrates the psychological attributes of the broken slur in contrast to the realism of the standard phrasing-slur: by "thinking legato" the player will minimize the detached tone-production peculiar to the instrument.

Tempo, Expression Marks   If tempo marks (including a metronome indication) are put above the top staff of each orchestral choir, they will also go directly above the timpani staff. But when the section as a whole is small, requiring but two or three staves in all, tempo marks above the section may be omitted. Naturally, they must be included in the separate instrumental parts.

On the other hand, expression marks are always included below the required staves, along with dynamic markings—"hairpins," *cresc.* and *dim.*, accents, and all other descriptive terminology. In addition to the standard indications just mentioned, the percussion frequently are affected by special symbols or written directions. Basically, these indicate methods of striking or playing upon the instrument, or designate a type of mallet or stick to be used. Without digressing into a detailed description of all the possible effects (to be found in any competent orchestration text), the following are the notational symbols most commonly used:

a. Play in center of instrument (gong, suspended cymbal, etc.)

b. Play at or near rim (drums, gong, suspended cymbal, etc.)

c. Rim-shots (snare and tenor drums, tom-toms, etc.)

d. Strike with handle of stick (on drums, suspended cymbal, timpani, etc.)

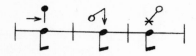

e. Symbols for tambourine

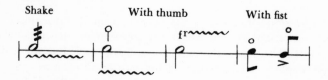

f. Mallet symbols

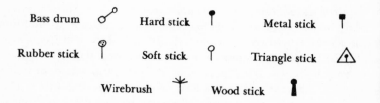

Bass drum   Hard stick   Metal stick

Rubber stick   Soft stick   Triangle stick

Wirebrush   Wood stick

EXAMPLE 22 - 33

MODERN INNOVATIONS

The contemporary percussion orchestra is a separate performing unit of four to a dozen players commanding the ensemble sound of ten to a hundred different percussive instruments. To write for this challenging group, the composer must supply from his background in instrumentation a knowledge of the various instrumental techniques involved. The conventional (and not-so-conventional) notational symbols he needs were detailed earlier in this chapter; the new element at this point must be the actual format of the score for percussion ensemble.

On the score-page for percussion ensemble, each *system* will have as many *staves* as there are individual performers: three staves for three players; seven staves for seven players. *Never* would two performers share one staff, even though this is correct in orchestra and band scoring. Conversely, it is most unlikely that any player will be responsible for more than one staff.

As each performer plays many instruments, no instrumental names precede the first system. Instead, each player is assigned an arbitrary number that has nothing to do with his importance in the group. Player 1. simply follows the top staff, Player 2. the second staff, and so on.

Above the first measure for each performer is written the name of the instrument he plays *first;* each player in the course of the work will perform on a variety of instruments.

In the example at the left, page 380—using a typical combination of instruments—the pitched instruments initially employed are placed at the top, unpitched instruments in the middle, with timpani—as is customary in ensemble—at the bottom. In the example at the right, all the instruments—again simply chosen as typical, and in arbitrary order—are unpitched, and hence need only single-line notation.

Once Player 1. has begun to play from the top staff, he continues to read from this staff throughout the composition. Player 2. continues on the second staff, Player 3. on the third. When any of them changes instruments, the direction above his staff will read *Take triangle* (or tambourine, or maracas, or anything small enough to be "taken") or *To xylophone* (or chimes, or bass drum, or anything so large one must go "to" it).

While it makes little difference which score-position is assigned to any instrumental line, it does make a difference that specific instruments are kept in *one* player's part, rather than haphazardly assigned. For example, if Player 2. were to begin the work playing xylophone, he should normally be responsible for all the xylophone passages; they should not be given to Player 4. at one point, to Player 5. at another, and then to Player 2. again.

In planning this division of labor the composer must at the same time devise a "floor-plan" for the performance. A player cannot have, say, 16 different instruments and 16 well-lighted music stands within easy reach of his hand. Percussion performances well plotted-out are often as intriguing to the eye as to the ear, but the composer who fumbles his little ballet will be mortified by a resounding collision of his players—added to his composed effects.

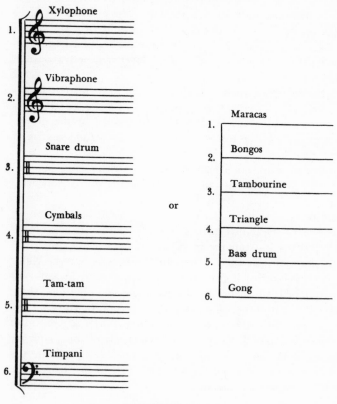

EXAMPLE 22 - 34

23

String Notation

Whenever there are individual methods of tone-production, there are individual problems of notation. The string family produces its musical tone by two methods—*arco* (Italian for "bow") and *pizzicato* (plucking a string or strings with the finger). These two techniques, added to the disposition of the four strings over a curved fingerboard, create the special considerations for all string notation.

TRADITIONAL PRACTICES

All unmarked passages for string instruments may be assumed to be played *arco*. If *pizzicato* is desired, the abbreviation *pizz.* appears above the staff. When the normal method of playing is to be resumed, it is indicated by the word *arco* over or under the first bowed note (see Example 23-18).

Staves Unless greatly divided, the orchestral strings occupy five staves—one staff each for Violin I, Violin II, Viola, Violoncello, and Double bass (see Example 26-1). In Classical scores the 'cellos and basses were usually combined on one staff, as the basses merely reinforced the 'cellos at the lower octave. In modern notation, however, these two instruments are always placed on separate staves, even when they play duplicate parts. In extensive *divisi* passages, moreover, the strings may expand to two, three, four, or even more staves for each of the five members. (See Richard Strauss's *Don Quixote*, for example.)

Separate staves should be used for solo instruments within the string choir. These solo staves go above the staff (or staves) used by other

family members. A typical arrangement of staves to include solo parts
is shown in Example 23-1.

Solo

Violin I

*gli altri**

Violin II

Viola

Solo

Violoncello

*gli altri**

Bass

*"the others"

EXAMPLE 23 - 1

When a solo instrument concludes its part before the end of a line
or system, either:

1. Rests may be used to fill out the remaining measures, or
2. The part may duplicate that of the other players, or
3. The staff may be terminated at the point of rest for the solo player.

Usually the words *cogli altri* ("with the others") are written in at that
point.

Brackets, Systems   A single, elongated bracket is normally
used to set off the string choir of the orchestra (see Example 23-1).
Outside this bracket is put the brace (when used) that joins the two

staves of Violins I and II. Occasionally the 'cello and bass staves are also linked by a brace, but it is more usual not to do so.

The five or more string staves comprise a system when used alone on the score page, or in a work for string orchestra.

A small bracket with straight terminal jogs is used in string notation to designate *non-divisi* or *non-arpeggio*. An interval or chord to be played as a double-, triple-, or quadruple-stop (see page 389) rather than with the players divided on the notes, is marked as shown at the left, below. The same symbol serves for a chord to be played as unbroken as possible across the four strings. The bracket may be put after the notes, but it is preferable to write it as in this example. Observe that the bracket always precedes any accidentals before the notes. Only if all the notes had accidentals and the space were crowded would it be advisable to place the bracket following the notes (right, below).

standard   less usual

and
not

EXAMPLE 23-2

A similar bracket is placed before *pizzicato* notes to be played with *two fingers*, rather than with one as ordinarily. The sound is very sharp and dry, so that the effect is advisable only at a loud dynamic level.

Ledger Lines, Octave Signs

Of all the string family, only the violins resort as a rule to extensive ledger-lines. When viola parts get so high as to require many ledger-lines, the music is notated in the treble clef (see section below). For high notes in the 'cello, the tenor or the treble clef is used; for the bass, the part is notated in the tenor clef unless written extremely high, in which case the part is put in treble clef. Whether in tenor or treble clef, the bass part is still written an octave higher than actual pitch.

Only the violins make extensive use of the *8va* sign; a change of clef is the usual solution for viola, 'cello, and bass passages that would require an *8va* sign. None of the strings uses the *8va bassa* indication, though the *8va bassa* device is "built into" the double bass, and none requires the *15ma* sign.

Clefs

Violins I and II use one clef only; violas, two clefs; and 'cellos and basses, three different clefs. (See the table which follows.)

EXAMPLE 23 - 3.   TABLE OF STRING INSTRUMENT CLEFS

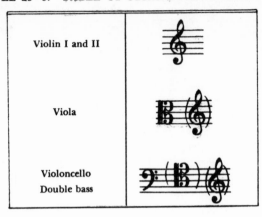

Notes Two problems of note-formation are indigenous to string instruments: the notation of *harmonics,* and the correct indications for *multiple stopping* (or chords).

1. *Harmonics* Just as white light is actually made up of many colors, so any musical tone is actually constituted of many *partials*—higher frequencies related to the audible pitch, though not consciously heard. When a vibrating string is touched lightly at certain strategic points—known as *nodes*—these partials (termed *harmonics* or *overtones*) become audible. The pitch of the harmonic depends on the point at which the string is touched; on a 'cello **C** string, for instance, the first harmonic would be **c** an octave higher, followed by the successively higher **g**, **c′**, **e′**, and **g′**.

Harmonics for string instruments are designated by one of two special symbols—a small zero over a conventional note-head ○ or a diamond-shaped note-head ◇ . The *zero* should designate only natural harmonics; the *diamond* may be employed for either artificial or natural harmonics if notated with meticulous care.

When the zero is used over a note-head to indicate a natural harmonic, it is written at the *actual sounding pitch* of the harmonic, as shown at the left, below. If the note can be produced in several ways, the string player determines the string on which the harmonic will be obtained—unless the composer specifically indicates the string, as shown at the right, below.

EXAMPLE 23 - 4

To clarify the two new symbols in the above examples—the roman numeral followed by a small vertical dash refers to a specific string. The four strings are numbered in order from highest to lowest, so that on the violin the highest string (**E**) would be numbered I; the next lower (**A**) would be II; the next (**D**), III; and the lowest string (**G**) would be IV. The small dash is shorthand for *string*.

The other new terminology above is the Italian manner of designating the specific strings. *Sul* (with the Italian masculine singular) means "on"; hence, *sul* **D** signifies "on the **D**-string." Sometimes only the letter name of the string will be given, minus the *sul*. Both methods are quite clear; it is up to each notator to choose one form and use it consistently.

The table below, for convenient reference, gives the various specific string symbols and terminology for the four different string instruments.

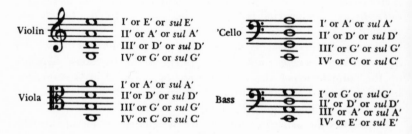

Violin
I' or E' or *sul* E'
II' or A' or *sul* A'
III' or D' or *sul* D'
IV' or G' or *sul* G'

'Cello
I' or A' or *sul* A'
II' or D' or *sul* D'
III' or G' or *sul* G'
IV' or C' or *sul* C'

Viola
I' or A' or *sul* A'
II' or D' or *sul* D'
III' or G' or *sul* G'
IV' or C' or *sul* C'

Bass
I' or G' or *sul* G'
II' or D' or *sul* D'
III' or A' or *sul* A'
IV' or E' or *sul* E'

EXAMPLE 23 - 5

The diamond may also be used to indicate a *natural* harmonic, but in this case the position of the diamond note is *not* the sounding pitch of the harmonic. Instead, the diamond merely indicates the point where the player is to touch the string lightly with his third or fourth finger (the "node," as indicated above). The fundamental tone—if it is not shown—is the nearest open string below the diamond, and the notations shown on the upper line, below, when played as harmonics result in the pitches diagrammed just below.

sounding pitch →

finger on string →
open string →

EXAMPLE 23 · 6

More commonly, the diamond is used to indicate an *artificial harmonic*, notated as shown below. Again the small diamond—written a perfect fourth (easy to play) or a fifth (more difficult) above the fingered (solid) note on the string—is *not* a sounding pitch. It is merely the symbol for the point where the performer lightly touches the string with his fourth finger (to make the harmonic), while firmly pressing down the lower note with his first finger (to create a fundamental that is *not* the open string).

EXAMPLE 23 · 7

It will be noticed in the above example that the diamond note is always an open, "white" symbol, regardless of the note-value. Only the stopped (lower) note is filled in as necessary to distinguish rhythmic values, supplemented of course by the proper flags or beams. When the diamond is used alone, the distinction between a quarter note and a half note is clearly demonstrated by the diamond's metric position and by any supplementary notes or rests. The interval of the fourth must always be properly spelled by using the required accidentals. These are written small, before the diamond note. If a key signature is involved one must be careful to add or subtract accidentals before the harmonics as necessary.

EXAMPLE 23 · 8

Understandably, composers are sometimes unsure of the notation for harmonics, or else are unduly cautious, and so resort to such unnecessary notational duplications as the addition of a small note (at the actual pitch of the desired harmonic) above the diamond and stopped notes (example at the left, below). The small note is really superfluous, as no other pitch can possibly sound—given the correct notation of the lower note-symbols. A few composers (Arnold Schönberg is a conspicuous example) even go so far as to put a zero over the small note, and add the word *flageolet,* the German term for a harmonic! This is redundancy with a vengeance.

EXAMPLE 23 · 9

Double harmonics (natural harmonics only) can be sounded on two adjacent open strings. Their notation is two zeros over or at the side of the notes, written at the actual pitch of the harmonics. (This notation is correct whenever the zero is used, as explained above.) Just as the fundamentals—the open strings—are a fifth apart, so will the sounding harmonics be a perfect fifth apart.

EXAMPLE 23 · 10

As demonstrated in Example 23-6, above, the small zero, or "o" sign, is also used in manuscript writing to designate the open strings. In printed music the symbol for open strings is somewhat larger and more oval in shape. For this function the zero is over, under, or at the side of the note-head, depending upon available space. Ordinarily there should be no danger of confusing the signs for open strings with those for natural harmonics, as the context of the music will indicate which is required. Then, too, only the pitch of the highest of the four strings on violin, viola, and 'cello *could* be played both as a harmonic and as an open string.

A zero with a small appended vertical dash is used to designate thumb position on the 'cello. When the sign is placed *over* the note-head, the dash is at the bottom of the zero; when the sign is put *under* the note, the dash extends above the zero. This symbol is rarely—if ever—notated in orchestra music; it is primarily a pedagogical device, so is found only in methods and studies for the 'cello.

EXAMPLE 23·11

2. *Multiple Stopping*   Chord notation for string instruments often appears incorrect to the non-string player. The unorthodox image is a necessary adjustment to the fact that only the top note or two can be sustained in a triple-stop (three notes) or a quadruple-stop (four notes). The first example below shows various notations for sustaining only the *topmost* note of three- and four-part chords; the second example shows indications for prolonging the upper *two* notes. Black note-symbols—with or without flags—are used for the notes that must be released, but no rests are required to fill out the beat.

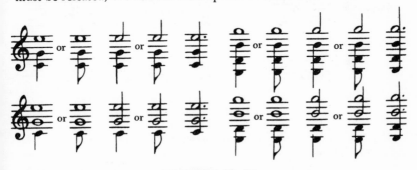

EXAMPLE 23·12

A further modification of chord notation occurs when the top two notes of a triple- or quadruple-stop momentarily have *different rhythmic values,* as in the example below. In this case, the lower of the two top notes must have its stem put *down,* but in order not to conflict with the bottom note (or notes) of the chord, it must be moved slightly to the *left.* The highest and the lowest notes are aligned, and

again no rest-symbol is necessary after the lowest note (or notes) is
released.

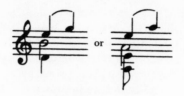

EXAMPLE 23 - 13

Double-stopped unisons are played by combining with an open string
the same pitch produced by fingering on the string below. These are
limited to the upper three strings of each instrument, and the notations
for each follow:

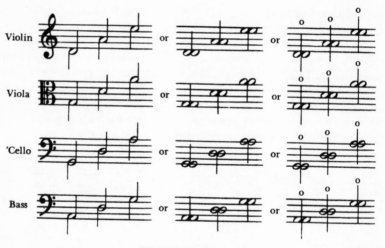

EXAMPLE 23 - 14

Repeated notes that alternate between the open string and the
fingered version of the same note are written as at the left, below.
A double-stopped unison incorporated into a chord is notated as at the
right.

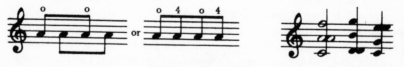

EXAMPLE 23 - 15

Ties, Slurs   *Incomplete tie-signs* (see examples below) are used in string notation to designate *pizzicato vibrato,* meaning that the note is to be plucked and allowed to vibrate. The sound is most effective on the lower instruments—'cellos and basses—though it is called for in violins and violas as well. Such notes are usually written as whole, half, or quarter notes, depending upon the meter (top left, below). Writing an incomplete tie-sign for an eighth note followed by a rest is contradictory (top right, below).

To indicate a *pizzicato vibrato* that begins even before the note is plucked, I have utilized two small tie-curves, one on either side of the note-head. This tells the player that he is to begin a pronounced vibrato on the string prior to actually plucking it, and to continue the vibrato after the note has been sounded (example on lower line).

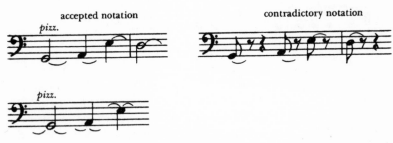

EXAMPLE 23 · 16

The *dotted tie-sign*—apparently the invention of Béla Bartók—is used in several ways. Among them is the indication to prolong a single pitch produced as a *harmonic* (left, below); another function is to tie the notes of a *tremolo* (right-hand example)—a psychological effect rather than an actual one. In the case of harmonics, a regular tie is used for the lower, stopped note; the dotted tie connects only the diamond symbols.

EXAMPLE 23 · 17

A broken or dotted *horizontal* line is common and effective for showing the extent of special color effects, such as: for the direction to play on a specific *string* (top left, below); for the employment of *non-vibrato* (top right), and for the devices of *sul tasto, sul ponticello,* and *col legno* (lower examples). Further description of these effects will be found on pages 404–405. Even though the termination of the broken line would indicate a return to normal sound or bowing, the verbal direction must also be written (final example).

EXAMPLE 23 · 18

Accidentals, Key Signatures   All of the strings make normal use of accidentals, although *double flats* and *double sharps* are usually avoided. This restriction is imposed because of practical problems of fingering and position on the strings; a string player does not read a doubly-affected accidental in terms of harmony or voice-leading, but only in terms of finger and position. For example: c′ played by violin would require the third finger in first position on the G-string. c′-sharp would also require the third finger, but slightly moved up on the string into what is known as half-position. c′ **double-sharp**, on the other hand, is enharmonic with **d′-natural**, which would be played in first position by the fourth finger, or by the third finger moved up to second position. The visual aspect of this string problem is demonstrated in the example below.

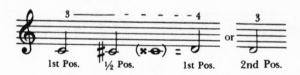

Quarter-tones—pitch distinctions between two such notes as **F-sharp** and **G-flat**—have been notated by composers in various ways, as illustrated in Chapter 9 (see page 145). Their use, however, is not common; hence the lack of a standard notational system. If any one of the previously illustrated notations for quarter-tones is used, a brief footnote of explanation would be in order.

Key signatures, when required in the orchestra, are used by all the strings. For the proper placement of sharps and flats on alto and tenor staves, refer to the Table of Key Signatures on pages 136 to 138.

Time Signatures   Time signatures are notated either on each separate staff or—as in the other orchestra choirs—by a single large meter-sign centered on the five (or more) staves of the section. (See Example 26-5.)

Barlines   One barline connects the five or more staves of the string choir, as in the example cited just above. Even when extensive *divisi* necessitates many extra staves, or solo parts are required, the single barline suffices.

Ornaments   Particularly suited to the ornamentation of string writing are tremolos of several kinds, glissandos, arpeggio figures, and many forms of the characteristic pizzicato.

1. *Tremolos*   Bowed tremolo, fingered tremolo, and the combination of the two—all require special forms of notation. As its name implies, the *bowed tremolo* is produced by rapidly alternating up- and down-bows (see page 401) on the string—(or strings, if there are two notes). When the tremolo is to be *unmeasured* (when no specific note-values are to be heard), the notation requires slanted slashes—usually three or four—through the note-stem, and the word *tremolo* (or its abbreviation, *trem.*) over the passage. For notes with flags or beams, one slash less per flag or beam is required. For whole notes the slashes (also slanted) are centered above or below the note. Tremolo slashes are drawn only slightly thinner than the normal thickness of a beam.

EXAMPLE 23 - 20

The *measured* tremolo articulates its notes in a clearly perceived rhythmic pattern, and the number of stem slashes in bowed tremolo represents the exact note-values desired: one slash would call for eighth notes; two slashes, sixteenth notes; and so on. The table below gives the correct notation for each unit required.

EXAMPLE 23·21.   TABLE OF MEASURED BOWED TREMOLO

WRITTEN	PLAYED

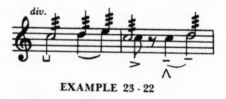

If—owing to space limitations—*divisi* strings playing both bowed tremolo and non-tremolo use a single staff, separate stems must be written, and all necessary bowing-marks carefully indicated for the non-tremolo part.

EXAMPLE 23·22

The *fingered tremolo*—as shown in the table on page 395—is notated in the same manner as the keyboard tremolo: the two fingered notes are written as duplicated time-values, and broken beams are used to indicate the tremolo effect—measured or free. The half note, eighth note,

EXAMPLE 23·23. TABLE OF MEASURED FINGERED TREMOLO

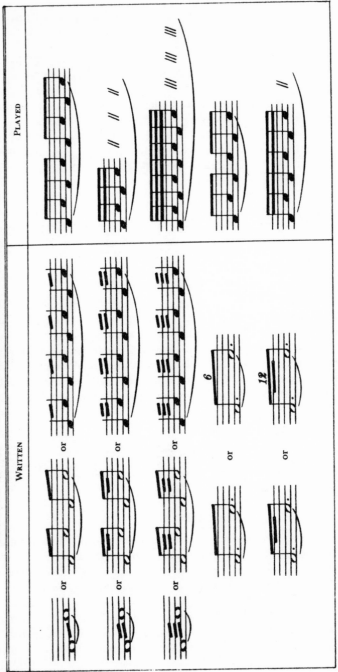

and all smaller units have a primary beam joining the two stems; the quarter note has all beams broken, in order to distinguish between the value of the quarter and the smaller units. Exact note-values for the measured version are indicated by the total number of beams—one for eighth-note values, two for sixteenth-note values, and so on.

Note particularly in the examples just given that the fingered tremolo always has a *bowing slur* over or under the notes. Without the slur, a different effect would be produced—the *bow-finger tremolo,* or *détaché trill.* This is a very nervous sound, with the tremolo produced both by the action of the alternating fingers and by rapid up- and down-bows on the two strings. To avoid any misunderstanding, this effect, when desired, is usually marked *non-legato,* or *détaché.*

EXAMPLE 23 - 24

Divisi fingered tremolos comprising *three* notes are frequently written as at the left, below. In the notation one note is duplicated, but the listener will hear only the three notes sounding as a blur. Even two-note fingered tremolos are sometimes written as duplications, each of the two string-parts moving in a different direction (center, below). This effect is more visual than actual, for the resulting sound will be indistinguishable from the more conventional form of notation (right, below).

EXAMPLE 23 - 25

A true fingered tremolo cannot exceed the interval of a fourth unless the bottom note is an open string. This is because the fingers on one string and in one position cover only that interval. Tremolos exceeding the fourth (but not taking in an open string) have to be played as an undulating double-stop: the fingers stop the two notes on adjacent strings, and the bow rocks back and forth across the two strings. The notation for this category, however, is not diffierent from that of the normal fingered-tremolo. The interval cannot exceed an octave, because this is the span encompassed by first and fourth fingers on two adjacent strings.

2. *Glissandos*   On string instruments, glissandos are produced by sliding the finger up or down the string while one long bow is drawn. If the finger slides slowly, the chromatic tones will be apparent; if the slide is rapid, it is difficult to hear individual pitches, and the effect is a "swoop." An ordinary glissando is notated in one of the several ways shown below:

EXAMPLE 23 - 26

In all notations of string glissando it is best to write the abbreviation *gliss.* over the straight or wavy line to distinguish the effect from the less-pronounced sliding device known as *portamento.* If the portamento is wanted rather than a true glissando, the abbreviation *port.* should be written in.

A glissando *to a harmonic* is written in the same way as an ordinary glissando, except that the final note has a zero over it (the natural harmonic at actual pitch), or will be the fingered (black) note of an artificial harmonic. In this latter case, the glissando line goes only to the fingered note, not to the diamond symbol above it.

EXAMPLE 23 - 27

A glissando *in harmonics* is notated in the two forms shown below. The first example is a glissando on the overtone series, or in *natural* harmonics. By sliding the fourth finger very lightly up and down the string, the player will touch the successive nodes and sound the series of harmonics. In this case, the glissando does not produce scale-notes but intervals. Such a glissando may be produced on any of the four strings of each instrument. The second example below shows the notation for a glissando in *artificial* harmonics. An unbroken line connects the two stopped notes (played by sliding the first finger), and a dotted line connects the diamonds (played by lightly sliding the fourth finger).

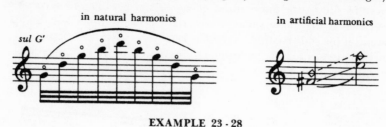

EXAMPLE 23 - 28

Tremolos can be combined with glissando, with harmonics, or with a combination of both—as shown in the examples below.

EXAMPLE 23 - 29

3. *Chord Figures*   Performed by string instruments, chord figures (as previously discussed in the section on notes) are of necessity arpeggiated. A triple- or quadruple-stop will be broken in various groupings from the bottom to the top notes, as shown at the top left and right below (see also Examples 23-12 and 23-13). Effective and idiomatic is the broken-chord figure played as an *arpeggio* across the four strings, as shown on the bottom line, below. The notes are stopped as for a quadruple-stop, and the bow undulates across the four strings.

EXAMPLE 23 - 30

4. *Pizzicato* Pizzicato chords, if they are to be deliberately arpeggiated, are notated as shown at the left below. Notice the use of the slur as a phrase-mark, *not* as a bow-sign! A chord (either arco or pizzicato) to be played as non-arpeggiato as possible is marked, as previously pointed out, with a straight bracket or a curved line before the notes (right, below).

EXAMPLE 23 - 31

Rapidly repeated pizzicato chords, strummed *a la guitarra* over three or four strings, are played in a somewhat non-arpeggiated manner. Brackets are not necessary for such chords, but the chords are notated with up- and down-arrows, "borrowed" bow-signs, or alternating opposite stems and beams (examples on the top line). A tremolo effect can be obtained by rapidly plucking two strings, notated as on the lower line.

EXAMPLE 23 - 32

In addition to plucked chords played arpeggiato and non-arpeggiato, pizzicato effects include *glissando,* as shown below. As the tone of the plucked string fades rather quickly, the glissando can extend only the distance of a fourth or fifth. The initial note is usually marked with an accent, and a slur is placed beneath the note-heads. Straight lines go from note to note, as in all other types of glissando.

Pizzicato notes taken with the *left hand,* alternating with normal pizzicato notes or bowed notes (or even played simultaneously with them), are notated with a small cross over or under the note. If the

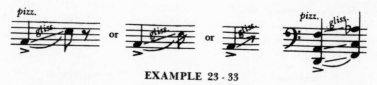

EXAMPLE 23 - 33

cross is not used, one of the various abbreviations for left hand (see page 302) may be put beside the note-head. This device is usually limited to the open strings.

EXAMPLE 23 - 34

A master of every instrumental device, the composer Bartók invented two unusual pizzicato effects (with correlative symbols) that have become standard in modern string notation. One is the so-called *"snap" pizzicato*, notated (left, below) with what looks like a **Q** that has a straight "tail" either at the bottom or at the top. To produce this effect the player plucks the string with such force that it literally rebounds off the fingerboard with a loud snap. The other device is the *"nail" pizzicato*: the string is plucked not with the fleshy part of the finger end but with the fingernail itself, giving a metallic *twang*. The symbol for this device is a small circle with a thick dot in its center (sometimes a small open dot), as shown at the right, below.

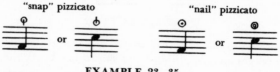

EXAMPLE 23 - 35

Frequently pizzicato and arco, notated on one staff, are combined in one family group of strings (as in divided Violin I, for instance). *Double note-heads* are then used, with up- and down-stems. In addition, different values have to be given the notes, as the pizzicato cannot sustain as long as the arco notes. In a fast tempo, longer note-values may be used for the pizzicato than in a moderate to slow tempo.

EXAMPLE 23 - 36

Accents, Phrase Marks (Bowing Patterns)   Because accents
and phrasing in the strings are achieved by bowing patterns, bowing
notation is of paramount importance. For the sake of simplicity we
shall confine our analysis to problems most frequently encountered.
Orchestrators and composers will expect to avail themselves of far
more specialized material.

1. *Basic Strokes*   When the bow-arm is moved away from the
body, the performer is using the down-bow; the sign is ⊓ . When the
bow-arm is moved toward the body, the performer is using the up-bow;
the sign is ⋁ .

Normally, these two basic bow-signs are placed above the note-head,
stem, or any beams. If they must be put below the staff because of
insufficient room above it (or in *divisi* passages requiring double stems),
the signs are literally inverted. Down-bows are then written as ⊔ ,
and up-bows as ⋀ . In many French publications, down-bows are consistently printed in the inverted form. Other specific bowing-indica-
tions include successive down-bows, notated with a separate sign over
each note (left, below); successive up-bows (center, below); and an
effect known as *reverse bowing* (right, below). Normally, accented
notes are played with down-bow and unaccented notes with up-bow;
in reverse bowing the pattern is deliberately reversed and a correspondingly nervous effect is induced.

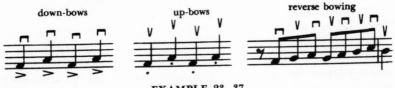

EXAMPLE 23 - 37

2. *Legato Bowing*

A curved slur over or under two or more notes indicates that these notes are to be executed in one bow (up or down), and smoothly connected (example below). Slurs are only partially indicative of phrasing; if an actual phrase-mark is necessary (to unite several bow-strokes into a larger melodic idea), it should be notated above the passage with broken lines (as in measures one and two of the example below). Older scores used regular phrase-marks, and some composers (Wagner, for example) have written only phrase indications rather than bowing slurs—*not* a practice to emulate! As a general rule, bowing-slurs are placed next to the note-heads rather than over stems and beams.

EXAMPLE 23 - 38

3. *Détaché Bowing*

In this type of bowing (the term is French for "detached") each note is well articulated by virtue of being played with a separate bow-stroke. The bow hair, however, does not leave the string in *détaché*. In moderate to fast tempo no special marking is necessary (example at the left); in a slow tempo, dots should be used over or under the notes (example at the right).

EXAMPLE 23 - 39

4. *Staccato Bowings*

Of the various staccato bowings, only group staccato is simple enough to be handled by string players of modest accomplishment. Here three to six notes are separated not by changing the direction of the bow but by slightly stopping or lifting it. Group staccato is indicated by a dot over or under each note, with a bowing-slur beyond the dots (left, below).

True *staccato bowing* is a solo device rather than an orchestral bowing. Though it is notated like the group staccato (right-hand example, below), a great many more notes may be covered by the bow-slur, and the bow is allowed to spring slightly from the string.

staccato bowing
group stacc.

staccato bowing
solo stacc.

EXAMPLE 23 - 40

Spiccato bowing is a form of rapid detached bowing, in that separate bow-strokes are used for each note, but the bow hair actually rebounds off the string so that the separation is more pronounced than in *détaché* bowing. It is notated with a dot over each note, plus the abbreviation *spicc.* for absolute clarity (example at the left, below). Though there ought not to be confusion regarding *détaché* notation in a slow tempo (see Example 23-39) as distinguished from the *spiccato,* explicit terminology in either case is desirable.

Jeté (or *saltando*) is a "bouncing-bow" technique applied to short groups of three to six detached notes, usually on the same pitch. The notation is the same as for group staccato: a slur in conjunction with dots over or under the note-heads, usually with the word *saltando* (right, below).

spiccato bowing

Allegro

saltando or *jeté* bowing

spicc.

EXAMPLE 23 - 41

5. *Marcato Bowings*

Almost any degree of accent may be achieved by bowing. Perhaps the most extreme is the *martelé* (or *martellato*), which literally means a "hammer-stroke" accentuation. This degree of accent is notated with the solid small wedge (or "arrowhead"), as seen at the left, below.

For a heavy accent—a somewhat percussive attack—the horizontal open wedge (>) is used (center, below). The vertical accent-mark (⋀) is seldom used for the strings, as it too closely resembles the inverted sign for up-bow (⋀).

A softer type of *marcato* bowing is known as the *louré;* it implies a leaning or gentle pressure with the bow on the string. The *tenuto* dash is used under the note-head, and groups of two, three, or four notes (usually not more) are executed with one bow-slur (right, below).

EXAMPLE 23 - 42

Tempo, Expression Marks   A single tempo-mark is usually placed above the string section. Ensuing directions for *ritardando, accelerando, più mosso, meno mosso, a tempo,* and the like are also placed above the Violin I line and apply to the section as a whole. Individual expression-marks, however, (*dolce, espressivo, cantabile,* and similar indications) are always put under *each part* they affect. The logic observed here is that tempo indications of necessity refer to all the instruments at one time, but that expressive directions need not apply to all equally—or even simultaneously.

Other Performance Indications   The Italian term *unisoni* (*unis.*), or its foreign equivalents (Fr. *unis;* Ger. *nicht geteilt*) should always be used after a *divisi* (*div.*) passage (Fr. *divisés;* Ger. *geteilt*) to indicate that all the players now perform the same part. The term *non divisi* (*non div.*), or the French *non divisés* or German *Doppelgriff,* is generally reserved for passages that are to be played with multiple stopping (see Examples 23-2 and 23-12). All of these terms should be written over the staff at the beginning of each passage in question.

When only half of a section of the strings is required, the figure ½, or its foreign equivalents (*la moitié; die Hälfte; la metà*) is written above the staff at the outset of such a passage. To signify that all the players of the section join in, the English *all* (*tous; alle; tutti*) is written in at the appropriate place above the staff. Parts divided by desk rather than by individual player are marked *div. by desks* (*par pupitres; pultweise; da leggii*).

Special Effects   Many special effects for the strings do not have notational symbols, but are indicated by a familiar glossary of directions. One group of words covers the use of specific portions of the bow. To indicate the use of the tip of the bow, *punta d'arco* (or its English equivalent) is written over the passage. To command the heel or frog of the bow, the notator may use the French *au* (or *du*) *talon* or the Italian *al tallone;* for the middle (or normal) part of the bow— *metà arco.*

There are likewise no notational symbols for the special playing effects known as *sul ponticello* ("on the bridge"), *sul tasto* ("over the fingerboard"), or *col legno* ("with the wood"). The direction is merely written at the beginning of the passage, usually followed by a dotted or broken line to the final note so affected (see Example 23-18). For a return to normal bowing, the term *modo ordinario (ord.)* or *naturale (nat.)* is given. Both *sul ponticello* and *sul tasto* are ordinarily combined with bowed tremolo for best effect.

Col legno may be treated in two distinct ways, each of which requires a different term. To tap on the string with the back of the bow is indicated as *col legno battuto;* this is the more common form of the device. To draw the back of the bow across the string in the manner of ordinary bowing (or as a tremolo) is indicated by the term *col legno tratto.*

Muting the string instruments requires no special notation other than the direction *muted* or *with mutes* (or the foreign equivalents: *avec sourdines (sourd.); mit Dämpfer (Dpf.); con sordine (sord.).** When mutes are to be removed, one writes *mutes off (sans sourd.; Dämpfer weg* or *ohne Dpf.; senza sord.).*

MODERN INNOVATIONS

Together with the percussion instruments and the piano, the strings have been the object of intensive sonoric experimentation in the music of the avant-garde. Every aspect of string technique has been expanded and every device of tone production has been exploited to the utmost. A number of new effects, fairly standard today, are shown in the various examples that follow.

Frequently encountered is an indication for the highest note possible on the instrument (which varies according to the individual player and, no less, to the instrument itself). The symbol used takes the form of **a.** below when related to the five-line staff; it is notated as at **b.** when put above a single pitch-line.

EXAMPLE 23 - 43

For another effect the string instruments are sometimes required to play *behind* the bridge. Since no actual pitches can be produced on the short length of string from bridge to tailpiece, the effect is notated in one of the several ways shown in Example 23-44.

---

* The Italian word for mute is feminine when applied to the strings and masculine when referring to all other instruments.

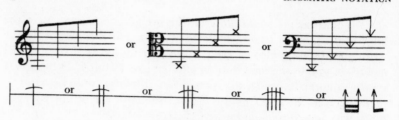

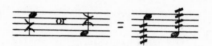

EXAMPLE 23 - 44

The most common modification of the bow-tremolo sign is used for a very rapid, tight, but non-rhythmic repetition of notes:

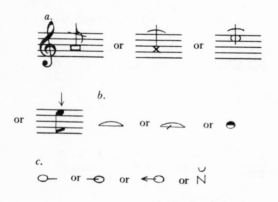

EXAMPLE 23 - 45

To the various methods of producing pizzicato, discussed on pages 399–400, we must now add the following: for a pizzicato behind the bridge (**a.** below); pizzicato with the left-hand finger lightly touching the string (**b.**), and for a strong pizzicato that allows the string to rebound against the left-hand fingernail, placed sideways next to the string (**c.**).

EXAMPLE 23 - 46

As a coloring device, vibratos are frequently exaggerated in contemporary string writing. An extremely slow vibrato that actually produces a quarter-tone pitch variance is notated as shown at **a.** below. An extremely fast or narrow vibrato is indicated as at **b.**

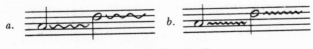

EXAMPLE 23 · 47

With so much emphasis placed today on the percussive potentialities of all instruments, it was inevitable that many new "noise" effects should have been invented for the string instruments. The list of such devices is extensive; those illustrated below are only a few of the more commonly used percussive string effects.

For noises that are produced directly on the strings, the following notations are used: striking the strings with the flat hand (**a.** below); tapping or hitting the string with the finger(s) (**b.**).

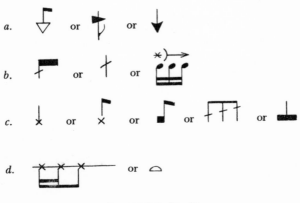

EXAMPLE 23 · 48

For sound effects on the body of the instrument one finds the following notations employed: striking the tailpiece with the bowstick (**a.** below); striking the sounding-board with the fingers or bow (**b.**); tapping on the frame (side, back, etc.) with the fingers (**c.**); with the fingernail (**d.**).

EXAMPLE 23 · 49

The technique of using tone-clusters has been applied more successfully to the string section than to any other orchestral group. This is because of the natural possibilities that exist for massed, homogeneous tonal structures in all the strings—in quarter-tones as well as chromatic and diatonic intervals. The symbols most frequently used for this device are given below. It should be noted that the "solution" of the top-line cluster usually is given in the score as illustrated on the lower line. The length of the thick rectangle represents duration; the arrowhead at the end of the second cluster-symbol indicates that it continues into another system or page.

EXAMPLE 23 - 50

24

Jazz Notation

.

J AZZ IS A POTENT INFLUENCE AT EVERY LEVEL OF AMER-
ican music-making, from the cheapest commercialized popular music
to the most serious expressions of the symphonic composer. It is the
greater paradox, then, that jazz has no standardized, universally accepted forms of notation. When written down at all, the music is often
in the personal shorthand of the composer or arranger; even more
jazz music never risks the hazard of a written form, for fear of dim-
ming the improvisatory spark. Because of these limitations, we can
only indicate briefly the few notational features that are in any way
general in jazz notation. Like the subterranean portion of an iceberg,
the vaster bulk of the jazz idea is never in view of the physical eye, but
stretches out unmeasured and unseen.

STANDARD PRACTICES

Staves   The five-line staff is used by all the jazz instruments
except guitar and ukulele. These two instruments still read from a
tablature notation similar to that used in the sixteenth and seventeenth centuries for lute and keyboard music, including organ (see
page 22). To review briefly: tablature notation does not employ a
staff with notes indicating pitch and duration; instead, it offers a
diagram of finger-position on the frets, strings, or keys of the instrument.

Given below is an example of tablature notation for jazz guitar.
("Classical" guitar is conventionally notated on the treble staff, sounding an octave lower than written.) Note the indicated tuning of the
instrument's six strings, and their visual counterpart on the diagram.

The horizontal lines correspond to the frets of the fingerboard, and the small black dots indicate the position of the fingers in relation to the frets. Each fret marks a half-step interval, so that a finger pressed down in the space before the first fret of the **E**-string would produce **F**; the next fret-space would give **F♯**, the third fret, **G**, and so on.

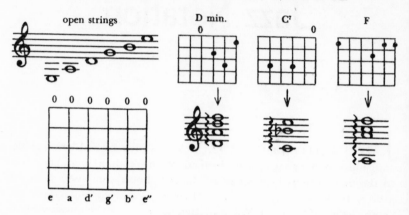

EXAMPLE 24 - 1

The ukulele, while not considered a significant jazz instrument, makes use of the same tablature notation as the guitar. Fingering on each of the four strings is shown in exactly the same way as for the guitar, with small black dots centered in the fret-spaces on each string. In addition, the actual fingering is sometimes given at the bottom of the diagram, **o** standing for the open string.

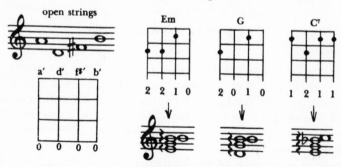

EXAMPLE 24 - 2

It will be noted that a chord-symbol (such as **D⁷** or **C⁶**) is usually placed over the tablature of both guitar and ukulele. Frequently *only* this chord-symbol is used in the notation, the actual spacing (or "voicing") of the chord being left up to the player. The pitch letter is usu-

ally followed by various numerals that indicate extensions of the chord
(sevenths and ninths) added notes, or pitch alterations. Thus **D⁷** means
a seventh-chord on **D**; **C⁶** indicates a C-major triad with added sixth
(**A**); **F⁺⁵** means a chord on **F** with a raised fifth degree (in other words,
an augmented triad); **B°** stands for a diminished triad on **B**; and so on.
The minus-sign (**⁻⁹**, for example) means a lowered form of the interval.
Minor chords are indicated by the abbreviation *min.* after the letter
name (as **D** *min.*).

EXAMPLE 24 - 3

In this kind of notation, further abbreviations are used to indicate
repetitions of the chord on each beat of the measure. These take the
form of heavy, slanted slashes between the second and fourth staff-lines.
This notational device is also used for the piano, the vibraphone
("vibes"), drums, and string bass. The entire page of a jazz score might
consist of nothing but the following abbreviated forms:

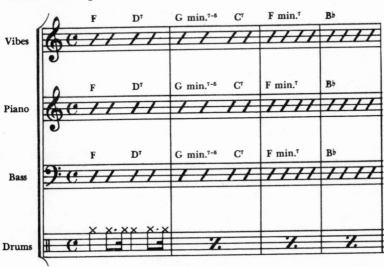

EXAMPLE 24 - 4

Because the five-line staff is used in this modern form of tablature
only as a convenient locale for the abbreviated harmonic and rhythmic
elements of the music, frequently just a single staff is allotted to the

piano (as above). Even when the piano uses two staves, they serve not so much to show precise structures for either hand as to make more room for the patterns usually compressed on one staff.

The percussion part in a jazz score is nearly always notated on a single five-line staff, as one solitary performer is responsible for the "kitchen" department of the jazz ensemble. Sometimes the staff bears nothing but the beat slashes and written instructions to the performer, such as: "light ride cymbal with brushes," or "regular rhythm with sticks," or "improvise break," or merely "ad lib." These directions may baffle the uninitiated, but they are simple a-b-c's to jazz performers.

brushes *ad lib*   add sock cymbal on 4th beat

EXAMPLE 24 - 5

Braces, Systems   Braces or brackets more or less duplicate the forms and uses in orchestra and band music, with one important exception: because the "vibes," piano, drums, and string bass often form a solo-type unit within most jazz groups, these instruments are grouped together in a jazz score and their staves are linked by a bracket (see Example 24-4). In scores that employ this quartet of jazz players with orchestral combinations, the quartet unit is placed between the wind-brass groups and the strings. In purely jazz combinations, the core group is put at the bottom of the page.

Clefs   Jazz performers use the same clefs as their symphonic and band colleagues (see pages 339 and 356). Clef signs are, however, frequently omitted in the separate instrumental parts after the first line, because the players ordinarily do not change clefs. Unlike certain orchestra instruments that read in several clefs (bassoon, trombone, 'cello, for example) jazz instruments are notated solely in one clef. An exception to this practice may be found in a few scores by jazz composers who also write "serious" music. The ingrained habit of thinking in terms of dual clefs for certain instruments reveals itself in the occasional use of tenor clef for the bassoon and trombone. The table on page 413 gives the more commonly used jazz instruments, and their respective clefs.

Notes   Ordinary note-heads are used for all the non-tablature jazz instruments except the percussion. For percussion, x's are employed for wire-brushes on drums or cymbal (see Example 24-4), and dia-

EXAMPLE 24-6. TABLE OF JAZZ INSTRUMENT CLEFS

Flute (Piccolo) Oboe (English horn) Clarinet (Bass clarinet) Saxophone: Soprano in B♭; Alto in E♭; Tenor in B♭ Horn Trumpet (Cornet) Vibraphone ("Vibes")	𝄞
Bassoon Trombone String bass	𝄢
Piano	𝄢 or 𝄞 or { 𝄞 𝄢
Percussion	▦ or ▥

mond-shaped notes for sticks on either. These symbols are nearly always placed in the space directly above the five-line staff or in the top
space. If other percussion instruments are used (bass drum, wood-blocks,
and the like), they are notated with regular note-heads placed on arbitrarily chosen spaces on the staff.

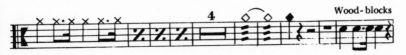

EXAMPLE 24-7

It is a custom in jazz notation and in popular music arrangements
to omit the actual notes of a duplicating or doubling part, and to

write on the staff *col clarinet* (or whatever the written-out part may be) followed by a wavy line through the staff center.

EXAMPLE 24 - 8

Rests   While jazz notation does not use the standard rest-symbols in any unique way, it does employ multiple rest-signs in a rather unusual manner. In many jazz scores an instrument that rests for, say, six measures at the beginning of a page will have its part marked not with individual whole-rests in each measure but with a figure **6** over a heavy beam put in the initial measure. The remaining measures of silence are then left blank.

EXAMPLE 24 - 9

The multiple rest-symbol is also used for instruments improvising solo "breaks." The sign is slanted on the staff, with heavy ends placed between the first and third staff-lines and between the third and fifth. Over it is written the number of bars (measures!) for the "break" (Example 24-10). The *tacet* instruments have a rest-symbol placed in the normal horizontal manner on the third staff-line.

Key Signatures   When required, key signatures are used for all of the jazz instruments. Some "third stream" * composers prefer to dispense with key signatures and to write in all accidentals as they occur, but they are in the minority.

---

* "Third stream" is a term coined by the American composer Gunther Schuller to describe the fusion of jazz with serious music.

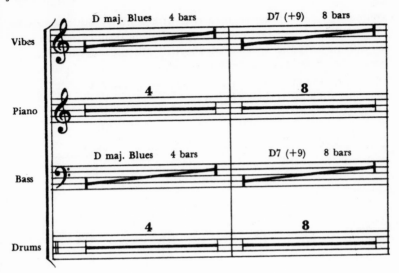

EXAMPLE 24 - 10

Time Signatures   Although time signatures are used in jazz notation, they rarely—if ever—change in the course of a composition. In addition, they are restricted almost without exception to **C** ($\frac{4}{4}$) or possibly $\frac{2}{4}$. For all its rhythmic vitality, conventional jazz seldom operates outside the framework of perfect simple or compound time. Although it may not actually carry a signature of $\frac{12}{8}$, many a jazz composition does function in this meter as far as written note-values are concerned (see Example 24-8). What comes out in performance is not strictly compound time, however, for syncopations and rubatos blur the precision of orthodox pulsation.

"Progressive" jazz and similar expressions outside the main stream of modern jazz often are more daring in their use of unorthodox meters. Don Ellis's *Hindustani Jazz Sextet,* for instance, plays music based on such meters as $\frac{11}{8}$, $\frac{19}{8}$, $\frac{27}{8}$, and $\frac{3\frac{1}{2}}{4}$. Even these more experimental modes of rhythm, however, are seldom notated; instead, they merely form an intuitive part of the players' improvisatory techniques.

Ornaments, Effects   Jazz has its own peculiar forms of ornamentation, some of which resemble but do not literally duplicate the classical ornaments of other music. The trill, for instance, has its jazz permutations: the "growl" or the "bend"—quasi-trill sounds plus a quality that can only be described as "dirty." The "growl" might be explained as a combination of a trill with a brassy flutter-tonguing. The "bend" is like a rapid wavering on indefinite pitches. Older and now somewhat passé versions of the trill are the "smear" and the "wow," the "flare" and the "wah-wah." Still used are the "lip-slur," the "rip," "slap-tongue," and an effect known as "doink." These effects are *sometimes* notated as shown below:

EXAMPLE 24-11

Dynamic Markings   Dynamic markings are usually at a minimum in jazz scores. Frequently an instrument will have no indication of the desired dynamic level; the player is supposed to fit his part into the general ensemble unless he has a solo "break." As a general rule, jazz makes little distinction in dynamic levels beyond loud and soft. Dynamic contrasts are sudden, and subtle crescendos and diminuendos are conspicuously absent.

It is tempting to counterbalance the "minus" picture in this chapter by a discussion of the intricate and demanding notational codes devised by Lukas Foss for his improvisatory ensemble. Except, however, for the sheer fact of improvisation, their high level of compositional skill and intellectual preparation separates such a group from the typical jazz ensembles dealt with here. Their notational code, moreover, is essentially private, and others similarly developed would doubtless also be the personal creative collaboration of the performers.

PART IV

Manuscript Techniques

25

Manuscript Writing

and Proofreading

MOST COMPOSERS ARE FORCED TO CONSIDER PROFESsional copyists an impossible luxury, and must prepare their own manuscripts. The same chore awaits composition students, theory teachers, and even some commercial arrangers. But the prospect of having to write one's own manuscript ought not to strike gloom in the heart of the enforced notator. Writing music manuscript can be a rewarding and even stimulating experience, granted one knows thoroughly the elements of notation and has on hand all the requisite tools. If the notator puts into his copying the same degree of imagination and disciplined skill that went into the making of the music itself, his task should be both enjoyable and gratifying.

MANUSCRIPT WRITING

Beyond the thorough study of notational elements in the foregoing chapters, two very practical phases of manuscript writing remain to be discussed: first, how best to draw certain notational signs and symbols that require special precision; and second, what tools are needed for the complete range of copying work. The suggestions given here—based on long experience—are offered not as hard and fast rules but as reliable methods for doing a praiseworthy job of manuscript writing.

Staves   Staves present no problem, for they are included on all kinds of manuscript paper, from 10- or 12-line paper used for piano or vocal music to 30-line paper required for orchestra or band scores.

Braces, Brackets   Braces or brackets must be written in on manuscript paper as required. Three steps are involved in drawing the brace: a very small dot slightly to the left of the long barline and centered between the two staves (if the brace is to join only two) or at the midway point of any larger numbers of staves to be linked—shown as (1) in the illustration below; the upper half of the brace, beginning at the top and extending to the centered dot (2); and the lower half of the brace, from the dot to the bottom of the lowest staff (3).

EXAMPLE 25 · 1

Ledger Lines   Nothing can be more annoying to a performer than to find a *single* ledger-line written at a higher distance above the staff than *two* lines. All ledger-lines must be properly related to the staff, and evenly spaced. The left-hand version below is correct; the right-hand version is obviously faulty in spacing.

EXAMPLE 25 · 2

Octave Signs   Octave signs must be clearly visible and accurately positioned. The sign itself—*8* or *8ᵛᵃ* or *15,* for example— should go directly above or below the *first note* of the passage affected. It should not start over rests, barlines, tied notes, or—to put it plainly —anywhere else.

correct   incorrect

EXAMPLE 25 - 3

If an *8ᵛᵃ* passage is interrupted briefly by rests, the broken line may continue over them (left, below). But if the rests are long or extend over several measures, it is better to terminate the first *8ᵛᵃ* sign and begin a new one over the first note following the rests (right, below).

EXAMPLE 25 - 4

Clefs   The aspirant notator will need to decide whether he wishes to practice the delicate calligraphy necessary to reproduce certain of the printed clef-signs, or to employ consistently the standard simplified forms now generally acceptable. That for the treble-clef sign is drawn to conform to the general shape of the printed symbol but without the contrasting thick and thin shadings (as in Examples 25-2–4).

A simplified version of the bass-clef sign may be achieved merely by omitting the shading characteristic of the printed form. (Compare Example 24-6, for instance, with Examples 26-4, 26-6, and 26-7.)

Because the printed version of the **C**-clef sign is especially difficult to approximate, many simplified versions have been devised for manuscript writing. Of the several variants given below, the first is closest to the authentic printed sign, and is therefore preferred over the others.

recommended   acceptable   not recommended

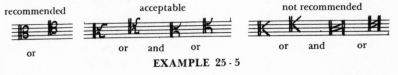

or   or   and   or   or   and   or

EXAMPLE 25 - 5

Notes   Note-heads in manuscript writing should be slightly oval in shape rather than perfectly round. Care must be taken that all note-heads are centered *on* lines or *in* spaces; one should never have to wonder in reading manuscript whether the note is on a line or in a space (as in the right-hand example below). This point cannot be too strongly stressed, as careless note-placement is probably "Public Enemy No. 1" in the world of music notation.

Stems must always join the note-heads, and should not be left "up in the air." Likewise, flags must touch the stems, and beams rest solidly on the ends of the stems. Moreover, stems should bisect all secondary beams, firmly touching the primary beam.

correct   incorrect

EXAMPLE 25 - 6

Stems may be drawn by hand if one's eye and hand are steady (chord stems should not wiggle nor slant). Otherwise, they should be made with the help of a ruler. Lengthy beams are likewise best drawn with a ruler rather than freehand; short beams are easily made without a ruler.

Rests   In writing 16th, 32nd, 64th, and 128th rests, care must be taken to space the hooks evenly, whatever the position of the rest-sign on the staff. The hooks should always be placed in *spaces,* and never on lines.

correct   incorrect

EXAMPLE 25 - 7

Dots   Augmentation dots should relate clearly to the notes they follow and should always be placed in the appropriate staff-space. What is more, they must be heavy enough so that they are immediately visible. Dots too hastily written can become literally lost on the page, with unfortunate results for performer and listener.

Accidentals   All of the accidental signs must be carefully centered *on* lines or *in* spaces. Easiest of the signs to draw is the flat, made somewhat like a printed small **b** except that the bottom is more slanted: **b** (letter); ♭ (flat).

A natural sign is most quickly made with two strokes: a capital **L** with the bottom slanted upward very slightly—∟—and the same figure inverted — ٦ —joined to the first one midway on its perpendicular line: ∟ + ٦ = ♮

The sharp is made in four brief strokes: two thin vertical lines—the one on the right set slightly higher; two thicker horizontal strokes, slanted upward and crossing both of the vertical lines: ‖ + ⁼ = ♯

A shorthand version of the double sharp is a simple **x**, but a more accurate version adds "extremities" to the points. These may be simple dashes at the four ends of the **x**: ✕ or ✖ .

Barlines   In music manuscript-writing, barlines should always be drawn with a ruler. A 12-inch ruler is adequate for 10-, 12-, or 14-staff paper; a 15-inch ruler is necessary for larger pages, particularly if the barlines are to extend through many staves, as in orchestra or band scores.

Plotting Lines and Systems   The wise copyist plots out in advance the length of each measure on a line (or system), using as a basis the measure with the most notes. Depending upon the page size, which in turn affects the size of the printed staves, an arbitrary length can be assigned a measure of four horizontally placed notes; of six, eight, or any chosen number. Assuming that a measure of four notes or their equivalent space (accidentals will take up the same space as notes) requires an inch and a half, a measure of six note-spaces would take up two and a quarter inches; of eight note-spaces, three inches; and so on. A certain amount of give and take has to be observed, so that the last measure on each line ends at the end of the line, and that all measures are more or less proportionate in length. It is far better to allow too much room than not to allow enough; crowded measures are not only irritating to the performer, but also unnecessary if one plots out the page carefully.

Vocal Texts   In copying vocal or choral music on transparent manuscript-paper (see page 426) the text may be either hand-written or typed, provided one's typewriter can accommodate the size of paper being used. For typing, the notator backs up the master sheet with black or orange carbon paper, face up, so that when typed the words appear on both sides of the transparency. This is essential for clear reproduction.

If the manuscript paper is too wide to fit in a typewriter, the vocal text must be hand-copied. Transparencies should never be folded; the creases will show up as dark smudges on the reproduced pages.

TOOLS

Paper, ink, pen-points, rulers, reproduction "transparencies"—these seem items almost too elementary in a text for adult musicians. But they are vital tools of the notator's craft, and can make all the difference between a dreary chore and a satisfying accomplishment.

In respect to the materials available to him, the composer-notator or arranger today is infinitely better off than the copyists of a century ago. Especially is this true in the matter of manuscript paper, both for everyday writing and for permanent reproduction. Formerly a notator had to draw all the staff lines on blank paper (usually of inferior quality). Now he has at his disposal an immense variety of manuscript papers of all sizes—from a 9-stave sheet used for marching band parts (5½ by 13¼ inches) to a 30-stave page for large scores (11 by 17 inches). His greatest blessing, however, is the invention of transparent (actually, translucent) manuscript paper. By writing all his final copies on this kind of paper (known in the trade as "transparencies" or "onion skins") the composer can have any number of copies duplicated—from one to one thousand, literally—and at a comparatively modest cost.

At the time of this writing, a page 8 by 11 inches in size costs roughly 10¢ to duplicate from a thin master-sheet. To have this same music recopied by hand would cost a minimum of $1.50. A large score-size page, 11 by 17 inches, now costs about 18¢ to reproduce from a transparency; to have it recopied would amount to well over $8.00 per page. However prices become inflated, the contrast in costs will remain. The point need not be labored: no composer "in the know" today ever makes final copies on anything but transparencies.

The newer thin master-sheets are printed with the staff lines on the reverse side. The copying is done on the facing side as usual, for the lines are entirely visible and distinct. The special advantage is that mistakes may be scratched out with a single-edged razor blade or an electric eraser (never a regular eraser) without disturbing the staff lines. Formerly, any such corrections removed the lines as well as the wrong notes. It then became necessary to ink in new lines over the scratched portion of the paper, with frequent blotting or blurring of the lines resulting.

If an error in copying should be too extensive for simple erasure, the part affected may be cut out of the master sheet by using a razor blade with a ruler guide. A correct section of transparent paper may then be inserted, using a special transparent scotch tape applied to the back of the original sheet. The insert must be cut slightly smaller than the space it is to cover; otherwise a dark, overlapping impression will show on the reproductions.

All types and sizes of transparent music-paper may be ordered from a number of firms specializing in music-reproduction services. Among these are: *Al Boss Music Reproduction* (Philadelphia); *Cameo Music Reproduction, Inc.* (Hollywood); *Circle Blue Print Co.* (New York City); *Les Davis Music Papers* (Morton Grove, Ill.); *Independent Music Publishers, Inc.* (New York City), and *National Blue Print Co.* (New York City). Brochures are usually available from each firm, listing styles of paper (number of staves per page; whether with braces and clefs or plain; page size) and citing the cost of each style per quire (24 sheets). Prices are usually listed for reproduction and for such extra services as spiral or saddle-stitch binding, covers, and lettering. In addition, several of these firms are equipped to store the composer's master transparencies in special fireproof vaults—a great boon to the urban composer short on storage space.

Almost any blueprint company—in the larger cities at least—can reproduce copies from transparencies; these are known as "vapo," "black and white," "diazo," or "ozalid" prints. Very few of these companies are equipped to do binding; a city directory or a classified telephone directory would list available book-binders.

As for pens—instead of having to cope with quills or scratchy metal nibs, the only problem of the contemporary notator is to choose one of many good pens. It is impossible to give any hard and fast recommendation, for pen choices are highly personal. Some composers prefer to use old-fashioned fountain pens (not ball-points) that help them control the line they desire; these are dipped into the ink rather than filled, as most manuscript inks are not suitable for fountain pens. Others like to use regular steel nibs fitted into an ordinary pen-holder, while certain other copyists swear by the specially-made music pens such as an Esterbrook with No. 9312 italic point or the various grades of Osmiroid point. One can only try each in turn and then decide which is the most comfortable to use and gives the most satisfactory results.

Whatever pen is used, all superfluous ink must be removed on the neck of the ink bottle after each dipping. Blots are fatal! Moreover, pens should be cleaned frequently for best results; let them soak for an hour or so in clean water, and then wipe them dry with a piece of tissue.

In the matter of ink, only a jet-black carbon ink is satisfactory. One should try various brands: those manufactured by music-reproducing firms as well as those from such venerable ink-specialists as Higgins, whose Eternal Black and Engrossing Inks have long been standard for music copying. Some professional copyists mix three parts Engrossing Ink to one part Eternal Black; each writer must do a certain amount of experimentation to determine what ink suits his own manuscript style. Whatever the formula, never shake the bottle to mix carbon inks; to do so causes bubbles to form in the ink. Instead, stir the ink amalgam gently with a clean object such as an ordinary pencil reserved for this purpose.

India ink *may* be used, but it tends to clog a pen quickly. Regular fountain-pen ink should *never* be used; it is pale and watery, and does not reproduce well. And—it goes without saying—one should never copy with ordinary pencil on transparencies; the effort will be entirely wasted, for pencil marks are nearly invisible in any duplicating process unless one uses a specially-made copying pencil.

As a final tool for copying, one should have a 12-inch and a 15-inch steel-edged ruler or plastic ruler-protractor on hand. The steel edge is especially important; unblotted lines cannot be drawn with an ink-covered pen-point against a wood-edged ruler. And speaking of blotting—an adequate supply of old-fashioned blotters should be on the copyist's desk. It is useful to have one on which to set the ink bottle, or to lay down the pen so that it does not drip ink onto the desk surface.

A further aid in copying is a sheet of fairly absorbent paper to place under one's hand while writing. This prevents blurring the ink of the manuscript with perspiration from the hand. A long-sleeved shirt also helps prevent soiling the manuscript paper.

Although it is not exactly a "tool," it is more than helpful to have a large piece of heavy (but smooth) cardboard on which to place the manuscript paper while copying. This cardboard (an over-size, heavy sheet of regular opaque music-paper will serve as well) should have a number of regularly spaced vertical lines drawn in ink from top to bottom a half-inch or an inch apart. These lines—visible through the thin master-sheets—are an immense aid in aligning notes on the various staves. Their help will be especially appreciated when one is copying a full orchestra score and has to line up a triplet group in the flutes with a similar group in the violas!

PROOFREADING

In the days—not too long ago—when all published music was hand-engraved, proofs of each page were sent by the publisher to the composer or arranger in the form of negatives, printed in white on a dark green or gray background. The corrections were made directly on the proof-sheets, usually in heavy black pencil. All corrections appeared *twice:* in the margin, where they were circled or boxed, and in the nearby measure where the specific correction was to be made—the two corrections joined by a line. This procedure ensured that the nature of the correction was clearly understood by the engraver, and enabled him to check off in the margin each correction as it was made.

Today, not all printed music is hand-engraved; because of the serious shortage of qualified engravers and current high labor costs, music is also being prepared for publication by several other methods. Much of it (such as the musical examples in this book) is done by autographing—a photographic process of reproducing hand copying by highly skilled professional copyists using very special tools. Still other full-scale serious works—symphonies, operas, string quartets, and so on—are issued these days as facsimiles of the composer's manuscript (see Examples 26-1 and 26-3, for instance). In this case the only possible corrections are those made by the composer himself on the original transparencies. After inspecting a trial copy the composer must make all his final corrections before photographing in quantity is done from the master sheets.

Proofs—except for engraved material—are now very often sent to the composer on a glossy white stock with the notes and other printed matter in black, just as they appear in the published form. But each page has stapled to it an overlay sheet of thin tissue-paper on which the corrections are made. They are handled in the same way as on the traditional negative proof-sheets: the corrections are made in the margin opposite the point of error in the music; they are ringed, and a line is drawn to the actual location of the error—visible through the tissue sheet—where the correction is again indicated.

In reading music proofs one should systematically follow certain procedures. Clef signs, key- and time-signatures are best checked independent of notes and other matter. The end of each system and the beginning of the next line should be scrutinized for missing tie-marks and phrase-slurs. All rests should be checked for proper position in the measure; the vertical alignment of all notes on two or more staves should be carefully examined; ancillary markings—dynamic signs, wedges, accents, staccato dots, accelerando and ritardando signs—all should be checked separately. Tempo indications (including metronome marks) call for individual attention, along with accidentals, flags, beams, and augmentation dots.

In proofreading vocal solos and choral music, the text should receive special attention; word spellings, punctuation, and syllable divisions merit careful comparison with the original manuscript. The vertical alignment of notes between voice parts and accompaniment must be carefully checked, especially when unequal note-groups are involved.

For any note or other symbol that must be taken out, the standard deletion sign is used: 𝒆 . The correction of a wrong note should be shown in the margin on a small staff, accompanied by a verbal warning, such as: *E, not D*. When a certain symbol is missing on the proof-page at several adjacent places (such as a sharp missing before two or three notes) a single correction is given in the margin with the indication: **2x**, **3x**, or whatever the number may be, with lines extending to the specific locations of the missing accidental. This practice should not be extended, however, to pages where the misprinted accidentals are widely scattered.

A composer may often be tempted to make compositional changes while proofreading: that is, to add to, subtract from, or otherwise alter the original manuscript. Any such changes should be clearly differentiated from the correction of engraver's errors. Most publishers allow a certain minimum amount of last-minute changes on the composer's part, but excessive alterations are costly, and ought to be unnecessary if the composer has carefully thought through his music and has painstakingly carried out the notation process.

COPYRIGHT

In the United States all music manuscripts are automatically protected by Common Law, but such protection ceases when the composition is made generally available by means of reproduction or sound recording. To insure continued protection of their work in this country, composers should apply to the Copyright Office, Library of Congress, Washington, D.C., for Form E (registration of unpublished musical compositions). When this form, properly filled out, is returned to the Register of Copyrights, together with a fee of $4.00, full U.S.A. copyright protection will be in force from the date of such registration. The present law stipulates that copyrights remain in effect for an initial period of 28 years plus a renewal period of 28 years. A proposed amendment now awaiting Congressional approval would change the period to the lifetime of the composer plus fifty years, thus insuring continued copyright protection for the benefit of his heirs or estate.

When a composition is to be commercially published, statutory copyright is secured by the publisher in the firm's name and not that of the composer. A notice to this effect appears on every copy of the work offered for sale or sent out on loan (see Examples 26-1, 26-2, and 26-16).

By means of copyright registration, the imaginative concepts that shaped the composer's music and the specialized skills that committed them to paper are fully protected by law.

Commissioned in Celebration of the 75th Season of the Boston Symphony Orchestra, Charles Munch, Music Director
Dedicated to the Memory of Serge and Natalie Koussevitzky

SYMPHONY NO. 6

Walter Piston
(1955)

Facsimile of the Composer's Manuscript

AMP-9567-125 Printed in U. S. A.

EXAMPLE 26 - 1. Walter Piston: from *Symphony No. 6* (1955)
© 1957 by Associated Music Publishers, Inc., New York, N.Y. By permission.

26

Preparation of Score and Parts

Even with all the elements of notation mas-tered and the problems of idiomatic notation under firm control, the composer-copyist will still have many special considerations in the preparation of his score and parts. Adaptations of the notational elements, all types of cuing, plotting of page-turns, rehearsal numbers— all these will be considered in this final chapter as they affect full scores, condensed scores, and instrumental and vocal parts.

INITIAL PAGES

The initial page of any score and of all individual parts should have the title of the music centered at the top of the page. Dedications are set in small italics (or hand-written with smaller letters) and centered over the full title (see Examples 26-1 and 26-17). The composer's or ar-ranger's name, or both, usually goes at the right, below the title, and flush with the right-hand margin of the music staves. When a text is used, the author's name goes at the left-hand side of the page, on the same level as the composer's name, and flush with the left-hand margin (see Example 17-3). Required permissions for the use of vocal texts are placed at the bottom left side of the first page, just beneath the lowest system. Copyright notices, when included, are always centered at the very bottom of the initial page (see Examples 26-1 and 26-2). Initial tempo indications, including metronome marks and any descriptive or qualifying directions, are placed just above the highest staff and flush with the time-signature (see Examples 26-1 and 26-2).

EXAMPLE 26·2. Gardner Read: From *Two Moods for Band* (1956) Individual parts display in addition to the information above the name of the voice or instrument, located at the left margin of the page (as in Example 26-17). On the succeeding pages, the name of the instrument or voice may be given in abbreviated form in the upper left-hand corner of each page, or centered on the page. The page number should always be centered, rather than put at the upper right or left. (see Example 26-16).

The first page of any score should present *all* the instruments and voices that will be required in the work, showing a staff for *each* instrument or voice, preceded by the full name. This should be done even if the music begins with only one or two instruments; the entire resources to be used should be indicated. For practices from the second page on, see the section immediately following.

NOTATIONAL ELEMENTS

Only one *system*—as demonstrated above—will appear on the initial page of most large-scale works. Thereafter, whenever few performers are involved, it is possible to divide the score page into two or more systems, each listing only those instruments or voices actually performing. The systems on the page do not have to agree with each other in this listing, so long as they are separated from each other by broad, slanting dashes placed at the left—and sometimes also at the right—of the page (see Example 26-3).

Braces and brackets in full score and in chamber-music works follow the rules detailed in Chapter 2 (see Examples 2-1–2-4).

Octave signs may be freely used in preparing the score, as space is often crowded and ledger lines can become illegible. In instrumental parts, however, *8ᵛᵃ* signs should be used according to individual preferences. Wind players in particular prefer to read ledger lines rather than *8ᵛᵃ*, and octave signs should be employed sparingly in parts for flute, clarinet, tuba, viola, and 'cello. Violinists, on the other hand, are quite accustomed to reading both *8ᵛᵃ* passages and ledger lines, though not *15ᵐᵃ*.

Notes in individual parts should always be of adequate size, but large and clear note-heads are imperative when players must read from a distance. For instruments such as trombone, tuba, 'cello, double bass, and most percussion, this precaution is of utmost importance.

Whole rests on score pages now follow the modern practices fully covered on page 108. Partial rests, of course, must in every case be written in. Even though it means "silent," the term *tacet*—frequently encountered in vocal and instrumental parts—is not a wise substitution for a lengthy rest within a movement. If the tuba were required to rest from measure 32 to 108, let us say, one should not notate in a single blank measure the term *tacet*, and then pick up measure numberings at

EXAMPLE 26-3. Walter Piston: From *Symphony No. 6* (1955)
© 1957 by Associated Music Publishers, Inc., New York, N.Y. By permission.

108 and go on with the part. During the intervening measures there may have been ritardandos, new tempo-marks, or innumerable meter-changes—none of which the tuba player can be expected to know

without specific indication. The term *tacet,* therefore, should be used *only* to indicate that a player rests throughout an *entire movement.* In printed music this would be indicated:

II. TACET

In manuscript parts this would have to be notated on a blank staff in the following way:

EXAMPLE 26 - 4

Time signatures—as often mentioned in previous chapters—now tend to abandon the outmoded convention of a separate signature on every staff in favor of oversize signatures on the combined staves of each major instrumental choir. All the formats illustrated in Example 26-5 appear in modern published and manuscript scores, and the choice between them may be left to the notator. As long as the signatures themselves are absolutely clear, and of sufficient size to be read easily by the conductor standing on the podium—any plan illustrated is acceptable. Naturally, the larger the meter-signs, the easier they are to comprehend immediately.

For full-scale choral works, a single signature may be centered between the four choral staves if desired. In the case of double chorus, or of extensive *divisi* requiring extra staves, two large signatures would be advisable. A separate meter-signature should be placed on or between any accompaniment staves. (See Example 26-6.)

Barlines in complete *score* follow the practices outlined in Chapter 11. In instrumental *parts* for a single instrument using one staff, or two instruments playing *a2,* they are not used at the left-hand margin. If double staves are required, however, a barline—with or without a brace or bracket—does join them at the left (see Example 26-18).

Notational procedures used in printed music cannot always be literally imitated in manuscript copying. In published material, for instance, the first staff of each individual movement of a work is often indented (as in Example 26-17). In sonata literature the solo wind, brass, or string part is sometimes printed on a slightly smaller staff and with smaller notes in the copy used by the piano or other keyboard instrument. Both practices are impractical in manuscript.

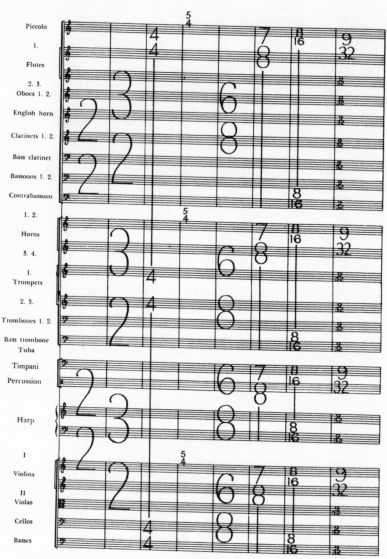

EXAMPLE 26 · 5

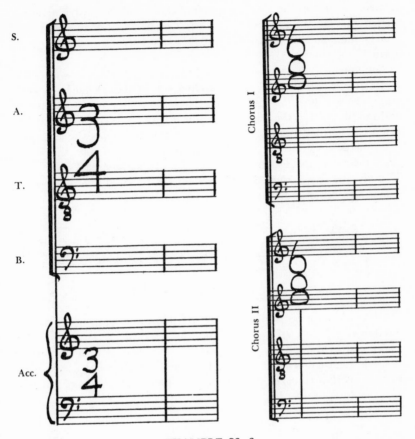

EXAMPLE 26 - 6

NEW ELEMENTS

Cues   There are two schools of thought regarding the necessity of cues in instrumental parts: the performers who are unhappy (to put it mildly) if their parts are not liberally strewn with cues; and those who are indifferent as to whether cues are given or not. In support of the second school, it may be said that most competent musicians need only minimum cuing, and that overabundant cues consume space on the page, making it cluttered and fussy.

Cues are, however, especially helpful *after lengthy rests*. A few measures before a performer is to resume after a long period of rest, it is customary to write into the part a prominent melodic or rhythmic element of the music, with an identification of the instrument or section playing it. The part of a weak-voiced instrument—or a secondary melodic strand of inconspicuous character—is of little use as a cue.

The notes of cues are written small, with accidentals, slurs, accents, and dynamic markings of corresponding size. If the cue-notes lie generally at the *top* of the staff, all the flags, stems, beams, slurs, accents, and the like go *up;* the player's (or singer's) rest is then put either beneath the bottom staff-line or under a ledger line below the staff (see Example 26-8). If, on the other hand, the cue-notes occupy the *lower* part of the staff, their stems, beams, flags, and ancillary marks go *down.* The player's rest is then placed beneath the top staff-line or below a ledger line, centered in the measure, above the staff.

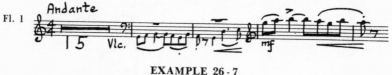

EXAMPLE 26 - 7

All cues should be *transposed* for transposing instruments. That is, if a horn in **F** has a **B♭**-clarinet cue, the notes of the cue should be transposed as though the horn were to play them. In the following example the cued clarinet part would sound a perfect fifth lower than written, as it is transposed in terms of **F**-horn transposition, and not as it would appear in the score.

EXAMPLE 26 - 8

Cross-cuing   Much school orchestra and elementary band music makes use of extensive cross-cues in score and parts; the notator writes in with small notes a melodic idea given originally to an instrument that in a small ensemble might be missing (or inadequate in technique). An oboe solo, for instance, will invariably be cross-cued, since good oboists are rare in small school or community orchestras—as are reliable bassoons, horns, violas, and 'cellos. The practice is to cue such parts for a more common instrument, one more easily played and generally available (such as clarinet, trumpet, or violin).

By cross-cuing important parts that might otherwise be missing or weak in performance, all essential elements of the composition will be present, even though the instrumental timbre or color will not be that originally conceived. Naturally, a cross-cue cannot be given to an instrument already occupied with an important element of the music. One has to arrange such cues so that the logical instrument for substitution is available when required. The following Table of Cross-Cuing shows the most logical choices of substitute instruments.

EXAMPLE 26 - 9. TABLE OF CROSS-CUING

Bassoon	cue in	Clarinet, muted Trombone, or Saxophone
'Cello	" "	Clarinet, Trombone, or Saxophone
English horn	" "	Muted Trumpet or muted Trombone
Oboe	" "	Muted Trumpet or Violin
Viola	" "	Clarinet, Trumpet, or Violin

Interchanging Instruments   In orchestral writing—band, too, in the more serious scores—woodwind instruments frequently interchange with family members. For example, the 2nd or 3rd flute will interchange with piccolo; the 2nd or 3rd oboe with English horn; the 2nd or 3rd clarinet with bass clarinet; and very infrequently a 3rd bassoon may interchange with contrabassoon. The directions for these changes must be given far enough in advance that the player has time to put down the one instrument, pick up the other, warm the mouthpiece, and get ready to play. This direction, then, should be given immediately following the last note played on the first instrument; one should not wait until just before the new instrument is to play, to direct the player to change from one to the other.

All cues—and these are a necessity when a player must switch instruments—should be notated in terms of the *alternate* instrument. If the 3rd oboe player is to change to English horn, going from a non-transposing instrument to a transposing one, the cue must be written in terms of English-horn transposition. The example below shows how the directions to change are given, and the proper method of cuing in the new instrument.

Ob. 3.

EXAMPLE 26 - 10

The Italian *muta* (above) means literally "change to." If the Italian term rather than the English is used, the name of the instrument should likewise be in the Italian form—as, in the above example, *Cor. Ing.* is the abbreviation for *Corno Inglese*. As we have pointed out before, score terminology should be consistent. "Pidgin English" is no more suitable in music notation than in other serious literature.

Page Turns   Page turns in instrumental parts can make or break a work. Having to stop playing to turn a page can quite literally break the continuity of the music; the fact that the copyist has not provided for logical and accessible page-turns can easily turn the performer against the music itself. True, to plan for proper page-turns often means sacrificing some space on the page. But it is poor economy to attempt to use every inch available, only to find that the player is expected to turn a page in the middle of a sixteenth-note run or arpeggio. By careful planning, one can arrange that the player has at least a measure or two of rest for turning the page.

If an instrument is to resume playing immediately after a page-turn, the abbreviation *V.S.* (*volti subito*, "turn quickly") is put at the bottom of the page just below the final measure or rest-symbol.

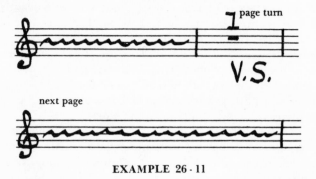

EXAMPLE 26 · 11

If there are further measures of rest at the top of the following page, it is not necessary to write *V.S.*; in fact, it can be misleading, for the player is then led to expect that he must begin playing again immediately (see Example 26-12).

Obviously, ideal page-turns are especially important for wind, brass, or percussion players; they are perhaps not so essential for the strings, as one player at a desk can always continue playing while his partner quickly flips over the page. But if *divisi* is involved and both players have different parts, one line will be momentarily sacrificed if the turn is not practical.

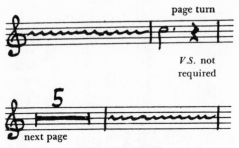

EXAMPLE 26 - 12

Rehearsal Numbers A consistent plan for indicating rehearsal numbers is a vital necessity in any music for two or more performers. One method employs either numerals or capital letters placed at strategic intervals throughout the score: following pronounced cadence-points; at changes of tempo, key, or meter; before prominent entrances by solo instruments or introduction of new material (as in lines 1. and 2. of Example 26-13). A second plan uses numerals as actual measure-indications, so that rehearsal number 11 occurs at measure 11; 26 indicates measure 26 (see part 3. of Example 26-13). A third method—in many ways the best—has the score and parts systematically numbered throughout, with a figure every five or ten measures (part 4. of Example 26-13 and Example 26-3).

Numbers are generally preferred over letters, as after 25 letters one must begin again with double letters (**AA**, **BB**, **CC**), which can become somewhat clumsy. If, however, letters are used, the letters **I** or **J** are usually omitted, the consecutive lettering going from **H** to **J** or from **I** to **K**. Arabic numerals are preferred to roman numerals, which are reserved for movement headings—I. for the first movement, II. for the second, and so on.

Either numerals or letters are usually *framed* by a circle or a square, though this is not imperative if they are prominent enough on the page. Manuscript scores and parts copied on opaque paper may have the numbers, letters, and boxes or circles drawn in red ink. This is not feasible, of course, on thin transparencies prepared for duplicating. With or without their framing boxes, the rehearsal numbers or letters go *above* the top staff of the system, and at the *immediate right* of the barline. They should *never* straddle the barline! In the example below, all the rehearsal indications are properly placed.

In the example on page 444, compare carefully the plan of part 4. with the format of parts 1., 2., and 3. The total number of measures shown is the same, but the division is different, owing to the arbitrary plan of marking every ten measures.

EXAMPLE 26 - 13

Also worthy of mention is the practice seen in many modern scores —chamber music as well as choral and orchestral works—of numbering *each measure* throughout the entire score. These numbers are placed just above, and at the right-hand side of, each barline.

EXAMPLE 26 · 14

Still another method of numbering score-measures is to put down the *cumulative number* of the first measure of each line or system only. This is placed above the left-hand side of the first measure, usually just above the clef sign.

Whatever method of indication is used, rehearsal numbers must take into account all changes of tempo, ritardandos or accelerandos, variable meters, or other alterations. Then, once the notator has decided which procedure is most effective for his purposes, he must employ it *consistently* throughout the entire work.

Condensed Scores   Condensed or "short" scores are a phenomenon of band and orchestra music written especially for schools or other amateur organizations. They do not exist in symphonic literature, or in works for other professional ensembles.

These condensed scores are published in two slightly different formats. The first—the so-called *"Piano-Conductor"* score—is a partial reduction of the music for piano, two (or four) hands; it is written on the conventional staves, with a single staff above (sometimes two) for material that cannot be included in the piano part. The supplementary staff or staves functions in the manner detailed on pages 30–32. The primary melody, secondary melody, harmonic accompaniment, bass line, and so on, are identified as to instrument, using the conventional abbreviations (see Example 26-15).

The other format for "short" scores goes by the name of *Condensed Score.* This is used almost exclusively for band music, and consists of a uniform three-staff reduction of the music. This form of score is not intended to be played on the piano; it is merely a reduced full score, with instrumentation labeled as in the *Piano-Conductor* score (see Example 26-16).

Both *Piano-Conductor* and *Condensed Score* formats are designed to assist the conductor who has not had much experience in reading from full score. From that standpoint they are practical; from the

EXAMPLE 26-15. Gardner Read: From *Gavotte* (1941)

Copyright 1943 by Carl Fischer, Inc., New York from "Music of Our Time"
(Karl D. Van Hoesen), 12 orchestral compositions by American contemporaries.

standpoint of indicating accurately the musical complexities of even
an elementary school band or orchestra composition, they are inadequate. If amateur conductors are ever to learn how to conduct, they
ought to do so from full scores rather than from condensed scores—
for the most obvious reasons.

EXAMPLE 26-16. Gardner Read: From *Two Moods for Band* (1956)

Individual Parts   Initial pages of instrumental parts are laid out as described early in this chapter, and as illustrated below:

EXAMPLE 26-17. Gardner Read: From *Prelude and Toccata* (1937)

Individual *orchestra parts* are usually copied on 12-line paper. Transparencies are strongly recommended for the originals of *all* parts, not just for the strings (where extra copies make transparencies the imperative choice). If a composer is fortunate enough to have his work played several times by different orchestras, he will find that the parts will rapidly become so marked up that they will have to be replaced. Writing all original parts on thin masters ensures that duplicate parts can be made at any time with a minimum of effort and expense.

Symphonic-band parts are copied on the same type of 12-line paper as orchestra parts. *Marching-band parts* are copied on 9-stave paper—the size to fit in the small music-holder attached to the instrument. *Choral parts* may be copied on special 12-line paper that encloses each four staves with a bracket but has no clef signs. The same paper serves for *string-quartet scores,* or any other chamber combination of four single-line instruments.

When all instrumental parts were copied on standard rag paper, separate parts were written for each individual player, with the exception of the strings, where one copy would serve two players sitting at one stand. This meant, for instance, that Fl. 1. had his individual part, Fl. 2. had his own, Fl. 3. or Picc. his own, and so on. With the advent of transparent manuscript-paper, it became advantageous to copy both Fl. 1. and 2. on the same page and, by duplicating the masters, provide each player with an identical dual part.

When copying two like instruments on the same page, however, double staves should be used whenever the parts are markedly different. For lengthy rests and for unison (*a2*) passages, a single staff can be employed. It is helpful to put the instrumental identification before each staff-line, or the abbreviation *a2* when the part is played in unison.

Only under optimum conditions should two parts be notated on a *single* staff. Generally speaking, optimum conditions occur only when the two instruments sharing the staff have simple rhythmic values, are

fairly well separated on the staff, and do not require an excess of markings—accents, slurs, dynamic markings, ritardando or accelerando indications, or other ancillary devices. The bottom staff of Example 26-18
illustrates these conditions.

EXAMPLE 26-18

Only *completely similar* instruments may be written on one part; it
is not feasible to try to combine Ob. 1. and English horn on a single
part, for example, even though two staves would be used throughout.
Instruments that could be combined on a single part, with double
staves where necessary, are:

Fl. 1. and 2.   Hn. 1. and 2. (sometimes 1. and 3.)
Ob. 1. and 2.   Hn. 3. and 4. (sometimes 2. and 4.)
Cl. 1. and 2.   Trpt. 1. and 2. (or 2. and 3.)
Bssn. 1. and 2.   Trbn. 1. and 2. (rarely, 2. and 3.)

The various clarinet-parts for band music must be copied *separately*,
as must the individual strings in orchestral works, for there may be
from four to eight players on each part. The same is true of cornets,
trumpets, and trombones in the band; each part (1., 2., and 3.) should
be copied individually rather than combined, as is usually done with
orchestral brasses.

The timpani part is *always* copied by itself; it never shares a part
with any other percussion instrument unless the timpanist himself is
required to play briefly on another instrument. In music that requires
only a modest use of the various percussion instruments, all the parts
except timpani may be written on a single sheet, using double or
triple staves if necessary. The part for each instrument should be

clearly labeled, and all entrances carefully anticipated. It is helpful
to the player if the name of a new instrument is boxed or circled just
before the entrance of the part.

In music that requires elaborate use of percussion voices, a full percussion "score" is not suitable as a *part* for each player; too many and
too constant page-turns would be involved. Under these circumstances
it is better to group not more than two or three instruments on a single
part; duplicate copies would be provided each player, of course. The
choice of groupings is somewhat arbitrary, but logically one could
combine bass drum, cymbals, and tam-tam on one part; snare and
tenor drums and triangle on another; and glockenspiel, xylophone,
and vibraphone on still another. If the mallet (pitched) instruments
are much used, they should share the same part rather than be mixed
with the instruments of indefinite pitch. If, on the other hand, an instrument such as xylophone were to be used but briefly (or if two mallet instruments, such as xylophone and glockenspiel, were to be played
simultaneously)—the pitched instrument would be notated on the
same part as one or two unpitched instruments. The example below
shows how a typical percussion-part might look.

EXAMPLE 26 - 19

When the transparencies have been completed, and before they are
sent out for duplication, all parts should be painstakingly checked for
errors. It is especially important that measure numbers be double-
checked, so that in lengthy rests for an instrument the correct number
of measures is given between rehearsal letters or numerals.

After duplicated parts have been returned from the blueprinter, the
notator is advised to underline, circle, or box with red pencil all re-
hearsal-numbers if they were not boxed on the transparencies. The red
pencil may also be profitably employed in underlining such directions
as *con sord.*, *sul tasto*, or *divisi*; then a final scrutiny for errors is again
advised. *Rehearsal time is too late for corrections*, as many a fledgling
composer has learned the hard way.

Postscript

CONTEMPORARY MUSICIANS ARE FACED WITH A SERI-
ous notational dilemma. On the one hand is an urgent need to expand
the existing symbols of music notation so as to indicate more precisely
and adequately—on manuscript paper and in printed scores—the complexities of modern musical thought. But on the other hand there is
a point of no return in notational invention—a point beyond which
the performer cannot or will not go.

The lay *listener* has long complained that much contemporary music
is unintelligible. Now the average *performer* joins the average listener
in the sensation that the music of the "far-left" experimenters is as
alien as Hindustani. The reason? Too frequently the obscurities of
avant-garde musical thinking are surpassed by the obscurities of its
notation—a closed book to all but a small inner circle of initiated professional musicians.

If notation—the written vehicle of musical expression—is to become so detached from all known frames of reference that it offers no
key to the composer's ideas, what useful purpose can it serve? What
musical communication can arise from such an enigma as this excerpt
from a score that gives no clue to the meaning of its format or to most
of its new symbols? (See Example 27-1.) That both symbols and format
have by now become familiar to those who play and study avant-garde
music does not alter the fact that no explanation for the non-specialist
is offered by the composer in his score.

Though we should never be so reactionary as to deny the value of
musical expression that does not *immediately* communicate to us, we
do adhere to the precept that music must eventually communicate
something—from the composer through the performer to the listener.

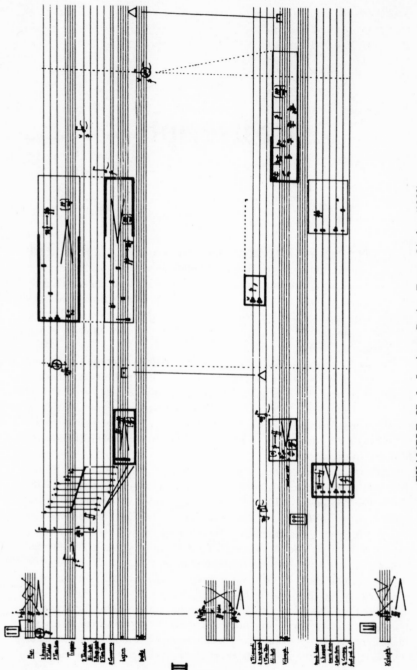

EXAMPLE 27·1. Luciano Berio: From *Circles* (1960)

We question, then, the validity of a notational alphabet that 99 out of 100 performers cannot interpret, thus excluding the great majority of potential listeners.

Even if we would not dictate to the composer what he must write or how he must write it, we do feel it only reasonable to insist that his notation be accessible to the average trained musician—not merely to the specialist in avant-garde performances. Scores prefaced by esoteric essays on temporal and spatial phenomena do not, unfortunately, significantly aid the performer in decoding new and confusing notational symbols. Before the philosophy of the new music can make sense, its format on the printed page must be clearly understood.

In all honesty, we must admit that many recent avant-garde scores *do* attempt to explain the new symbols used. Far too many, however, offer explanations that only end by being more obscure than the symbol itself. It is high time, therefore, to discredit the cult of unintelligibility in contemporary music notation.

If the composer says in effect to the performer: "I do not care whether you perform my music or not," we cannot argue the matter. But if he indicates: "I want you to perform and respond to this music," then his fundamental duty is to write his music so that it is accessible to interpretation. When the performer cannot approach the composer's meaning because of capriciously obscure notation, he may in effect say to the composer: "Why should I bother to puzzle out your music?"

The dedicated performer, of course, will always *try* to decipher the writer's intent. But should the composer precisely notate the impossible (such as Example 14-14) or obscurely notate the possible (Example 27-1), the resulting performance will be but an approximation of what he intends. And the creator who pretends that this agonized approximation is exactly what he was thinking of in the first place is guilty of unconscionable sham.

The first responsibility, then, is the composer's, not the performer's. In the introduction to this manual we stated that "to *master* the proper written language of his chosen profession is the minimum obligation of the aspiring musician to his art." To this we should now add: To *use* an accessible written language is the minimum obligation of those who profess that music is a communicative art.

BIBLIOGRAPHY

Apel, Willi—*The Notation of Polyphonic Music, 900–1600*, 5th Edition. Cambridge, Mass.: Mediaeval Academy of America, 1961

Bailey, Marshall—"Duodecuple Notation," *American Composers Alliance Bulletin*, Vol. X, No. 3. New York: 1962

Bartolozzi, Bruno—"Proposals for Changes in Musical Notation," *Journal of Music Theory*, Vol. V, No. 2. New Haven: 1961

Behrman, David—"What Indeterminate Notation Determines," *Perspectives of New Music*, Spring–Summer, 1965. Princeton: 1965

Boehm, Laszlo—*Modern Music Notation*. New York: G. Schirmer, Inc., 1961

Button, H. Elliot—*System in Musical Notation*. London: Novello and Co., 1920

Cardew, Cornelius—"Notation—Interpretation, Etc.," *Tempo*, No. 58. London: Boosey & Hawkes, Ltd., 1961

Carse, Adam—*The Orchestra in the XVIIIth Century*. Cambridge: W. Heffer & Sons, Ltd., 1940

Cazden, Norman—"Staff Notation as a Non-Musical Communications Guide," *Journal of Music Theory*, Vol. V, No. 2. New Haven: 1961

Cole, Hugo—"Some Modern Tendencies in Notation," *Music and Letters*, Vol. 33, p. 243. London: 1952

Copland, Aaron—"On the Notation of Rhythm," *Modern Music*, Vol. 21, No. 4. New York: The League of Composers, 1944

Cowell, Henry—*New Musical Resources*. New York: Alfred A. Knopf, Inc., 1930

———— "Our Inadequate Notation," *Modern Music*, Vol. 4, No. 3. New York: The League of Composers, 1927

Donato, Anthony—*Preparing Music Manuscript*. Englewood Cliffs, N. J.: Prentice-Hall, Inc., 1963

Fuller, Carol M.—"A Notation Based on E and G," *Journal of Research in Music Education*, Vol. XIV, No. 3. Washington, D. C.: 1966

Hindemith, Paul—*Elementary Training for Musicians*. New York: Associated Music Publishers, Inc., 1949

Johannis, Carl—*Notenschriftreform*. Stuttgart: 1961

Johnson, Harold—*How to Write Music Manuscript*. New York: Carl Fischer, Inc., 1946

454

Kagel, Mauricio—"Tone-clusters, Attacks, Transitions," *Die Reihe,* No. 5. London: Universal Edition, 1961
—— "Translation–Rotation," *Die Reihe,* No. 7. London: Universal Edition, 1960
Karkoschka, Erhard—*Das Schriftbild der neuen Musik.* Celle: Hermann Moeck Verlag, 1966
Kennan, Kent—*The Technique of Orchestration.* Englewood Cliffs, N. J.: Prentice-Hall, Inc., 1952
Osburn, Leslie A.—"Notation Should Be Metric and Representational," *Journal of Research in Music Education,* Vol. XIV, No. 2. Washington, D. C.: 1966
Otte, Hans—"Neue Notation und ihre Folgen," *Melos,* Vol. 28, No. 3. Darmstadt: 1961
Parrish, Carl—*The Notation of Medieval Music.* New York: Carl Fischer, Inc., 1946
Partch, Harry—*Genesis of a Music.* Madison: University of Wisconsin Press, 1949
Piston, Walter—*Orchestration.* London: Victor Gollancz Ltd., 1955

Read, Gardner—"Some Problems of Rhythmic Notation," *Journal of Music Theory,* Vol. 9, No. 1. New Haven: 1965
—— *Thesaurus of Orchestral Devices.* London and New York: Pitman Publishing Corp., 1953
Sachs, Curt—"Remarks on Old Notation," *Musical Quarterly,* Vol. 34, p. 365. New York: G. Schirmer, Inc., 1948
Salzedo, Carlos—*Modern Study of the Harp.* New York: G. Schirmer, Inc., 1921
Smith, W. J.—*A Dictionary of Musical Terms in 4 Languages.* London: Hutchinson & Co., Ltd., 1961
Stone, Kurt—"Problems and Methods of Notation," *Perspectives of New Music,* Vol. 1, No. 2. Princeton: Princeton University Press, 1963
—— "The Piano and the Avant-Garde," *The Piano Quarterly,* No. 52. New York: 1965.
Tappolet, Willy—*La Notation Musicale.* Paris: Neuchâtel, 1947
Williams, C. F. Abdy—*The Story of Notation.* New York: Charles Scribner's Sons, 1903
Winternitz, Emanuel—*Musical Autographs from Monteverdi to Hindemith.* Princeton: Princeton University Press, 1955
Wolf, Johannes—*Handbuch der Notationskunde.* Leipzig: Breitkopf & Härtel, 1919

INDEX OF
NOTATION SYMBOLS

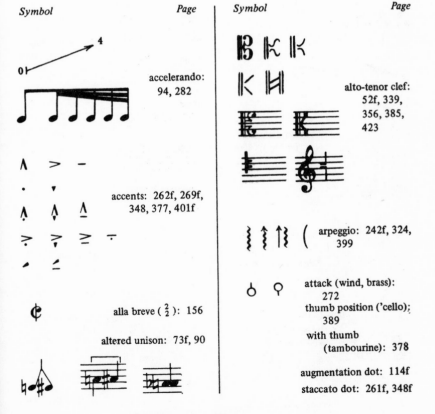

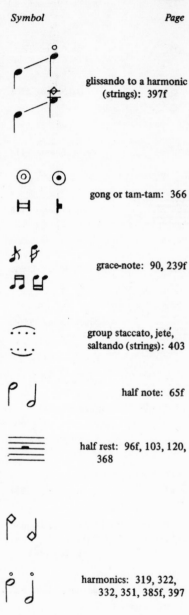

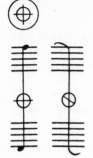

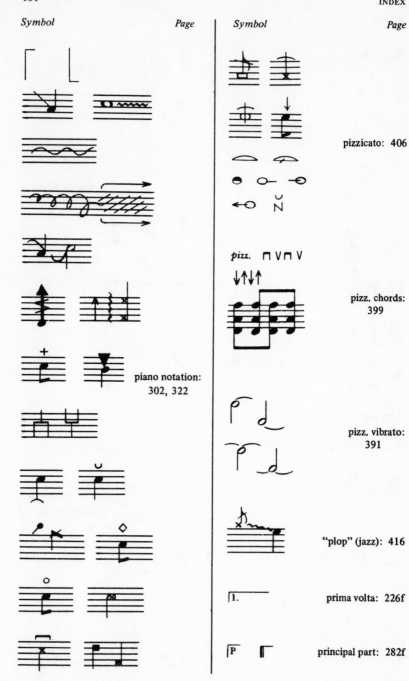

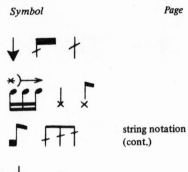
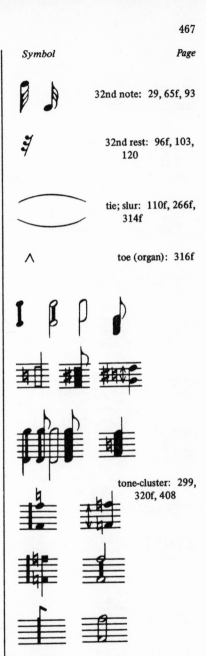

tone-cluster (cont.)

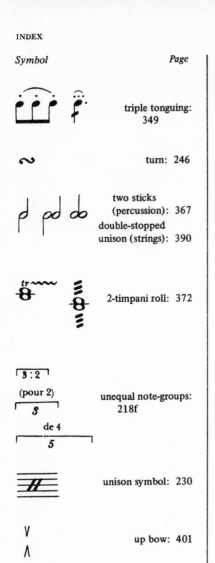

INDEX OF TABLES

GENERAL INDEX